Philosophy after Objectivity

Philosophy after Objectivity

Making Sense in Perspective

PAUL K. MOSER

New York Oxford
OXFORD UNIVERSITY PRESS

Oxford University Press

Oxford New York
Athens Auckland Bangkok Bogotá Buenos Aires Calcutta
Cape Town Chennai Dar es Salaam Delhi Florence Hong Kong Istanbul
Karachi Kuala Lumpur Madrid Melbourne Mexico City Mumbai
Nairobi Paris São Paulo Singapore Taipei Tokyo Toronto Warsaw

and associated companies in
Berlin Ibadan

First published in 1993 by Oxford University Press, Inc.
198 Madison Avenue, New York, New York 10016

First issued as an Oxford University Press paperback, 1999

Oxford is a registered trademark of Oxford University Press

Library of Congress Cataloging-in-Publication Data
Moser, Paul K., 1957–
Philosophy after objectivity : making sense in perspective /
Paul K. Moser.
p. cm. Includes bibliographical references and index.
ISBN 0-19-508109-9
ISBN 0-19-513094-4 (pbk.)
1. Objectivity. 2. Realism. 3. Relativity. 4. Perspective
(Philosophy) I. Title.
BD220.M67 1993 121—dc20 92-38864

9 8 7 6 5 4 3 2 1

Printed in the United States of America
on acid-free paper

For my mother and father

Preface

Philosophers, among other theorists, have long sought objective knowledge: roughly, knowledge of things whose existence does not depend on one's conceiving of them. Skeptics can effectively demand non-questionbegging evidence for claims to objective knowledge or truth, even if they typically despair of achieving such evidence. This book examines questions about objective knowledge in order to characterize the kinds of reasons available to philosophers and other theorists.

Philosophers, like other theorists, fall into two general categories: those who take skeptics seriously and those who do not. Philosophers who take skeptics seriously investigate the availability of non-questionbegging evidence for their claims, particularly their ontological claims about what actually exists. Philosophers who do not take skeptics seriously disregard their concern for non-questionbegging supporting evidence. It is not unusual for philosophers simply to ignore this concern for non-questionbegging evidence. Our ignoring skeptics will not, however, make them—or their concern for non-questionbegging evidence—go away. In contrast, our attending to skeptical concerns about evidence can yield important lessons about the status of our available evidence. This book identifies these lessons, and explores their implications for ontology, epistemology, the theory of meaning, the theory of practical rationality, and the philosophy of mind.

Questionbegging support for a claim fails to answer theorists whose questions are begged. If questionbegging support is acceptable in argument, we can support *any* position we prefer: We need only invoke our preferred position to support that position itself. This strategy would be maximally permissive and hence excessively permissive. It would tolerate an "anything goes" attitude that makes argument superfluous. Philosophers contending that we have objective knowledge, such as knowledge of a conceiver-independent world, inevitably prompt skeptical challenges regarding non-questionbegging support. A standard challenge concerns non-questionbegging support for the presumed reliability of various belief-forming processes and inference-patterns. Given such a challenge, one cannot, without begging a question at hand, merely presume the reliability of the belief-forming processes and inference-patterns under dispute. This book shows how skeptics can genuinely trouble nonskeptics on the matter of an absence of suitable non-questionbegging evidence for claims to objective knowledge or truth.

On the constructive side, this book proposes a reconciliation between skeptics and nonskeptics wherein the presumed support for philosophical claims does not clash with the demands set by skeptics. The relevant support, on this proposal, comes from variable conceptual, or semantic, commitments and purpose-relative instrumental considerations. This relativity to semantic and instrumental considerations does not entail the "anything goes" attitude to evaluative assessment fostered by substantive relativism. This book explains how we can reorient philosophical inquiry to accommodate lessons about reasons learned from skeptics, and to maintain, nonetheless, an explanatory role for philosophy. The book lays foundations for such a reorientation of philosophy by treating fundamental methodological issues in the areas noted above: ontology, epistemology, the theory of meaning, the theory of practical rationality, and the philosophy of mind. The task is large but worthwhile; for, it seems, in a land with no explanatory vision, philosophers (among other theorists) will perish. The discipline of philosophy, like any theoretical discipline, depends on explanatory aims. Accordingly, philosophers famous for shunning explanation in philosophy end up offering, contrary to their official positions, explanations of certain (perhaps only linguistic) phenomena. Even if we cannot disarm shrewd skeptics, we may continue with philosophy as an explanatory enterprise, acknowledging certain limitations on the support for our explanatory contributions.

This book explains how various perennial disputes in philosophy rest not on genuine disagreement, but on conceptual diversity: that is, talk about *different* matters. Acknowledgment of conceptual diversity, we shall see, can resolve a range of traditional debates in philosophy. The book also explains why philosophers need not anchor their views in the physicalism of the natural sciences. This lesson has important implications for the philosophy of mind, even though it runs afoul of a currently orthodox position in that area.

Philosophy, with or without optimism toward objective knowledge, benefits markedly from hard questions and criticisms. When such questions and criticisms come from others, one owes not just definite answers but sincere appreciation as well. Various sections of this book have received helpful comments from the following philosophers: Robert Audi, Lynne Rudder Baker, Kathy Emmett Bohstedt, Tom Carson, Suzanne Cunningham, Harry Gensler, John Heil, Al Mele, Dwayne Mulder, John Post, Shelley Stillwell, J. D. Trout, and Arnold vander Nat. I thank these philosophers for helpful questions and comments.

I presented earlier versions of parts of the book to various philosophical audiences: a 1989 American Philosophical Association Pacific Division Symposium on Epistemology; a 1990 American Philosophical Association Central Division Colloquium on the Philosophy of Mind; a 1992 American Philosophical Association Central Division Colloquium on Epistemology; a 1992 American Philosophical Association Eastern Division Symposium on Rationality and Morality; the 1990 and 1991 Conferences of the Illinois Philosophical Association; and philosophy colloquia at the following institutions: Loyola University of Chicago, Northern Illinois University, the State University of New York at Buffalo, Wayne State University, the University of Iowa, and the University of Wisconsin at Milwaukee. I thank these audiences for helpful discussions.

My graduate seminars at Loyola University of Chicago have been a source of valuable discussion. Dwayne Mulder and Bradley Owen stand out as helpful participants. I thank the members of my seminars for lively discussions on a number of topics relevant to this book. Loyola University of Chicago has provided a fine environment for work on this book, including a 1991 research leave of absence for completion of a penultimate version.

I am grateful to my family—Denise, Anna, and Laura—for tolerating my frequent absentmindedness at home, and for helping with this book in many ways. Remarkably, they consistently resist complaining about my philosophical obsessions. I thank my family for their patience, kindness, and encouragement. I also thank Angela Blackburn and the other members of the Oxford editorial staff who improved this book in many ways.

Some parts of this book have benefited from my recent publications. Some of chapter 1 draws on "A Dilemma for Internal Realism," *Philosophical Studies* 59 (1990), and "Realism and Agnosticism," *American Philosophical Quarterly* 29 (1992). Part of chapter 2 draws on "Justification in the Natural Sciences," *The British Journal for the Philosophy of Science* 42 (1991). Some of chapter 3 draws on "Malcolm on Wittgenstein on Rules," *Philosophy* 66 (1991), and "Analyticity and Epistemology," *Dialectica* 46 (1992). Part of chapter 5 makes use of some of "Physicalism and Intentional Attitudes," *Behavior and Philosophy* 18 (1990) and "Physicalism and Global Supervenience," *The Southern Journal of Philosophy* 30 (1992). In each case, I have revised the material in the original article.

Chicago, Illinois P.K.M.
Fall 1992

Contents

Philosophy after Objectivity

Let no one take you captive through hollow and deceptive philosophy.
Epistle to the Colossians 2:8

Introduction: Objectivity and Relativity in Philosophy

Philosophers of all stripes have theories to offer, for better or worse. Sometimes the only theory offered is that philosophers cannot—or at least should not—propose theories. Even skeptics, of one ilk or another, occasionally offer theories. Skepticism is, at least for various skeptics, an epistemological theory, with many different theoretical manifestations. Theories in philosophy, whether good or bad, aim to explain something, to answer certain explanation-seeking questions. Why is there something rather than nothing? Why is there what does exist, instead of something else? Why is there experience, including our experience as it now is? What is being? What is thinking? What is knowledge? What are we? And so on, virtually without end. Rare is the philosopher with no theory whatever to offer. Such would be a philosopher without a philosophy, an obvious candidate for impossibility. Equally rare is the philosopher whose proposed theory meets with anything like widespread acceptance. Why is this? Even that question calls for a theory.

Philosophers controvert not only theories about nonlinguistic things (for example, nonlinguistic events, objects, and their features) but also theories about theories and theorizing. The latter theories offer explanations of our own explanatory business. Such *meta*-explanation pervades philosophy, owing partly to a common suspicion that an unexplained explanatory strategy invites trouble. If unexamined presuppositions demand philosophical scrutiny, so too do unexplained explanatory strategies. The kind of philosophical scrutiny demanded is, however, itself a topic of controversy in philosophy. *Nothing* escapes controversy here, not even this trite claim itself. Controversy over proposed theories, of one explanatory level or another, is thus a hallmark of philosophy.

A familiar reaction from observers outside philosophy proper yields a simple injunction: Beware of philosophers bearing theories! The only problem with that injunction is its narrowness. Impartiality suggests another dictate: Beware of *anyone* bearing theories! Theories can, of course, serve our explanatory purposes, and can be favored accordingly. They can even be a necessary means to our explanatory goals, and can be endorsed on that basis. Is such purpose-relative support the only kind of ground available for a theory? Can a theory ever enjoy more objective, less variable support? Such questions motivate this book, and their answers will emerge in the following chapters. Different philosophers will, as expected, support different answers. This book's answers seek an argumentative edge, however, by facing some difficult questions about conditions for reasons, justifications, explanations, and evaluations: in particular, questions about the correctness and the justification of such conditions.

Explanations, within philosophy or without, have a common purpose. They aim to remove quandary, to make something understandable: in short, to make sense. Some explanations aim to make sense of *objective*, conceiving-independent things: things whose existence does not depend on one's conceiving of them. *Objective knowledge*, in the pertinent sense, is knowledge of such objective, conceiving-independent things. It is knowledge that entails objective truth—truth about objective, conceiving-independent things. Such knowledge is the quarry of many a philosopher, ancient and modern. It is the kind of knowledge questioned by typical skeptics, but endorsed by common nonskeptics. Philosophical disputes over objective knowledge go back to ancient Greece and still persist today. Perhaps they will never end, as the philosophical quest for objectivity dies hard, if ever.

Realists affirm the existence of conceiving-independent things. *Idealists* dissent, affirming the opposite. *Agnostics* withhold judgment, at least when pertinent evidence must be non-questionbegging relative to familiar agnostic questions about what is true or reliable. (Compare the analogous trio of familiar theological positions: theism, atheism, and theological agnosticism. I prefer the term 'agnostic' to 'skeptic', since 'agnostic' explicitly connotes one who withholds judgment on an epistemological matter.) Chapter 1, "Ontology, Evidence, and Philosophical Questions," argues in support of agnostics, with one proviso. It asks whether we have any non-questionbegging evidence for realism or for idealism, and it answers no.

Realism, put minimally, claims that there are conceiving-independent things: for example, conceiving-independent objects, events, or features thereof. Stated thus, realism does not make a claim about what is meaningful, what is true, or what we know. It is, in that minimal guise, nonsemantic, nonalethic, and nonepistemic in its claim. Whenever one affirms realism, however, we can ask what kind of reason or evidence, if any, supports the realism affirmed. Chapter 1 does ask this, and finds in favor of agnostics. This finding poses no threat to the *intelligibility* of realism. Chapter 1, on the contrary, raises doubts about any semantic shortcut to a rejection of realism. It finds no ground to conclude that realism or idealism is meaningless.

Evidence, characterized broadly, is a truth indicator of a proposition for a person. It indicates, perhaps fallibly and only probabilistically, for a person that something is actually the case. *Non*-questionbegging evidence favoring realism, for purposes of chapter 1, does not simply affirm a point at issue in the controversy between realists and agnostics. A typical questionbegging claim in favor of realism merely asserts a point that must be defended—for example, argued for—to play a cogent role in debates involving agnostics. Philosophers, among others, usually seek non-questionbegging supporting evidence for a simple reason: Questionbegging evidence fosters arbitrariness, in that it is easy to produce for *any* claim under dispute.

If questionbegging evidence is permissible in a dispute, all participants will enjoy support from permissible evidence for their claims: They need only support their disputed claims *with the disputed claims themselves*. Questionbegging evidence is thus dialectically, or argumentatively, useless, and it fails to advance inquiry regarding the questions begged. These considerations are compatible with the twofold platitude that what is questionbegging is relative to a context of pertinent questions, and every unsupported claim begs some question, even if not some question currently at issue. One question begged by every unsupported claim is whether that claim itself is true. Typically, however, we regard a claim as questionbegging only if it begs some question at issue.

A realist cannot cogently support realism now on the ground that many of us *see* some conceiving-independent objects. That ground is unstable, because questionbegging, against an agnostic's typical concerns. An agnostic questions whether what we call *seeing*—even when intersubjectively backed—is ever a reliable avenue to conceiving-independent reality. This questioning neither demands an infallible process nor insists on demonstrative, deductive justification. An agnostic typically asks whether any such "cognitive source" as perception, memory, introspection, testimony, or intersubjective experience ever serves reliably as an avenue to conceiving-independent reality. In asking this, an agnostic does not reject fallibilism or require certainty.

Some agnostic questioning focuses on the various justification-conditions favored by realists—for example, suitable coherence, maximal explanatory efficacy, or consistent predictive success. The key issue here is: What non-questionbegging evidence, if any, have we to affirm that the satisfaction of such a justification condition is ever a reliable avenue to conceiving-independent reality? Chapter 1 explains how this issue applies to the wide range of standards for justification used by realists. Realism nonetheless seems intelligible, and may even be true; its problem is thus not semantic.

The problem for realism is epistemic, or more specifically, *evidential*: Realism lacks support from non-questionbegging evidence. So far as a demand for non-questionbegging evidence goes, realism has nothing by way of defense against agnosticism. On this score, moreover, idealism fares no better against agnosticism. Agnosticism chases both realism and idealism into a losing battle over non-questionbegging evidence. Neither realists nor idealists, then, can take heart in the presence of agnosticism, when the concern is for non-questionbegging evidence. This lesson of chapter 1 recommends philosophy without presumed objectivity, at least when agnostic-resistant non-questionbegging evidence for claims to objectivity is sought. We may call this approach to philosophy *conditional ontological agnosticism*, for it is conditional on a demand for non-questionbegging evidence regarding ontological issues about conceiving-independent reality.

One might reply: Who cares? The answer is as easy as the question: Realists, at least, should care. They endorse realism, rather than ontological agnosticism, and agnostics will query the evidential support for their realism. By way of effective reply, realists must either deliver non-questionbegging evidence for their realism or make some concession to agnostics.

If realism lacks non-questionbegging evidential support, while the same is true of idealism, agnosticism emerges as a defensible alternative in any context where such support is valued. Indeed, in any such context, if we lack non-questionbegging evidence for realism and for idealism, agnosticism is our best option from an evidential point of view. When non-questionbegging evidence is at issue, agnosticism gives epistemically proper treatment to the evidence we have: evidence that decides in favor of neither realism nor idealism. This is a central lesson of chapter 1, a lesson that settles a major battle—if not the major battle—waged by philosophers since the inception of epistemology. With the settling of this battle, epistemology must seek a new direction, a direction away from losing battles with agnostics who demand non-questionbegging evidence for ontological claims.

If our ontological claims to what is objectively the case lack support from agnostic-resistant non-questionbegging epistemic reasons, what kind of support, if any, do they have? The remaining chapters develop an answer highlighting the role of variable semantic and purpose-relative constraints in inquiry, including philosophical inquiry itself. These constraints, according to chapters 2 through 5, figure in explanation, evaluation, justification, meaning, and understanding, at least as commonly understood. An important general lesson is that any theory disregarding variable semantic and purpose-relative constraints in inquiry will either seriously misconstrue or altogether neglect explanation, evaluation, justification, meaning, and understanding, at least as ordinarily understood. Such a theory will nonetheless have to face the troublesome question whether it itself needs support from variable semantic and purpose-relative considerations. (Chapter 5 shows how this question bears on certain versions of physicalism.)

Chapter 1 gives rise to questions about the status of the epistemological principles one might use to justify a controversial philosophical view, such as realism or idealism. In particular, in virtue of what are those principles themselves either correct or incorrect? Chapter 2, "Justification, Meta-Epistemology, and Meaning," raises and resolves this issue. It notes that failure to answer this question risks "meta-epistemic naivete" of a philosophically objectionable sort: that is, a superficial stance toward legitimate questions about the correctness of one's principles for justification. Chapter 2 notes also that circularity threatens if the needed answers come from the very principles at issue.

In place of the troubled options of naivete and circularity, chapter 2 recommends *semantic foundationalism*: One's explaining, evaluating, and arguing for epistemic justification (the sort of justification appropriate to propositional knowledge) and one's answers to questions about correct standards for such matters properly end in considerations about an operative *notion* for one regarding epistemic justification. A question whether a notion of justification can itself be justified requires a determinate notion of justifiedness. In the absence of such a notion, our offering an answer will be no better guided than archery without a target. Semantic foundationalism enables us to explain why this is so.

One's operative notion of epistemic justification consists of the constitutive standards one employs for the correct use of such terms as 'epistemic justification' and 'epistemic support'. (We may substitute any synonymous terms here, even terms from other languages.) Standards are thus constitutive for one when they are actually part of one's set of defining standards for correct use. Such standards, as chapter 2 explains, set indispensable conditions for one's justifying anything. An appeal to something, *X*, to provide justification presupposes a *notion* of justification relative to which *X* can and does provide justification in the pertinent sense. This holds for *any X*, including belief-forming processes, intuitions, inference-patterns, ordinary uses of language, universals, natural kinds, and such features of beliefs as coherence and explanatory or predictive efficacy. If we omit the presupposed notion, an attempted justification via *X* becomes obviously inconclusive. Semantic foundationalism builds squarely on this lesson.

Semantic foundationalism does not conflict with the conditional ontological agnosticism of chapter 1. It does not imply that we can deliver agnostic-resistant non-questionbegging evidence for realism or for idealism. The pertinent question now facing a realist is: What non-questionbegging evidence, if any, have we to affirm that the satisfaction of conditions definitive of what a realist means by 'justification' (or some synonymous term) is ever a genuinely reliable means to what is objectively the case? The argument of chapter 1 makes it doubtful that such evidence is actually available to us. We nonetheless can, and do, use constitutive standards for justification—including standards for so-called epistemic, or evidential, justification—that fail to allay concerns about non-questionbegging evidence. Such standards are not agnostic-resistant, but still figure crucially in our explaining, evaluating, and arguing for justification.

Our standards for justification serve certain purposes for us even though they leave conditional ontological agnosticism unscathed. We may thus bracket concerns about non-questionbegging evidence for ontological claims and acknowledge the relativity of our justificational standards to our variable semantic standards and theoretical purposes. We must also acknowledge that our claim to such relativity does not itself enjoy non-questionbegging evidence that is agnostic-resistant, nor can we effectively propose that all truth claims are merely purpose-relative. A redirecting of philosophy, and of inquiry in general, toward variable semantic standards and avowedly purpose-relative constraints must not at any level presume safety from an ontological agnostic's questions.

Our only recourse, if we are to allow a constructive, explanatory role for inquiry, is to change the subject and to understand justification accordingly. The changed subject must accommodate lessons learned from our inability to answer agnostic challenges regarding non-questionbegging support; it cannot responsibly ignore those lessons. Changing the subject, furthermore, does not entail that an agnostic's questions are inherently defective, nor does it entail that we cannot make claims about how things are. (See section 1.5 on claims concerning how things are, where the pertinent views of Hilary Putnam and Richard Rorty are found wanting.) Changing the subject entails rather that our avowed reasons and purposes in inquiry do not seek to answer an agnostic's typical questions.

Chapter 2 allows for conceptual, or semantic, relativism: Different people can, and sometimes do, have different operative constitutive standards for the correct use of such terms as 'justification' and 'warrant', at least at a level of specificity. In other words, different people can, and sometimes do, adopt different specific notions of justification and use those different notions in explaining, evaluating, and arguing for claims. This is relativism about the adoption and the use of specific notions in explanatory, evaluative, and argumentative contexts. It is not relativism about the understanding of notions or about what is true or false. Philosophers have not given due attention to the important distinction between relativism about the adoption and use of notions and relativism about the understanding of notions.

Conceptual relativism about the adoption and use of notions does not entail *substantive* relativism about justification: the view that whatever one takes to be justified is actually justified. It thus does not entail an "anything goes" attitude toward justification and evaluative assessment. 'Relativism' may be a dirty word in certain quarters, but becomes respectably clean with a few purifying distinctions. (Chapter 4 extends the treatment of conceptual relativism begun in chapter 2.)

Philosophers often talk of *the* notion of justification, truth, meaning, explanation, obligation, and so on. Given conceptual relativism, we may diagnose such talk as laboring under a myth: the "myth of the definite article" wherein a notion of *X suitable to one's conceptual purposes* is regarded as having the exclusive status of *the* notion of *X*. This myth has far-reaching consequences in philosophy, as it fosters the dogma that philosophers promoting different views on a topic—say, conditions for epistemic justification or moral rightness—disagree about some one thing: for example, the essential nature of epistemic justification or moral rightness. Given conceptual relativism, we must ask instead whether advocates of different views on a topic are actually operating with different notions, at least at a level of specificity. Even when proponents of different views on moral rightness share a general, unspecific notion of moral rightness, they often adopt and wield different notions of moral rightness at a level of specificity. They thus are not disagreeing, but are talking about different matters at a level of specificity. Similar considerations apply to other familiar notions often supposed to be points of disagreement among philosophers.

One might argue, then, that the "perennial" disagreements among philosophers only seem to be disagreements at a superficial level, and turn out upon examination to involve theorists speaking of different matters at a level of specificity. The conceptual relativism of chapters 2 through 4 lends credibility to this view. Whether this view deflates the significance of garden-variety philosophical "disagreements" rests on what that significance is, and that significance will get due attention in the following chapters. Perceived significance, in any case, is not necessarily actual significance.

One noteworthy issue, arising in chapter 2, is whether distinctively philosophical problems are purely conceptual rather than partly empirical. If they are partly empirical, their answers depend on empirical data (for example, empirical correlations) of some sort; if they are purely conceptual, their answers do not depend on empirical data. Purely conceptual problems depend for their solutions not on empirical investigation, but rather on adequately explicit formulations of the notions raising problems. Such formulations are arguably a matter of construction relative to one's conceptual purposes, not a matter of anything like empirical discovery. Here we have a basis for distinguishing purely conceptual problems in philosophy from empirical problems in the natural sciences. Chapter 2 suggests how we may distinguish the two.

One might reply that philosophers, even given conceptual relativism, typically disagree about how to analyze or otherwise formulate certain notions. This likely reply loses its threat once we individuate notions by the components one assigns to them. We then shall hold that different defining analyses entail different notions, while granting that people adopting and using different specific notions of *X* can still understand, adopt, and use common notions of *X* generally characterized. The latter point enables us to talk intelligibly of various specific notions of some one thing (generally characterized). Such specific notions function as different amplifications of a single general notion, a notion of *X* generally characterized. Even if you and I understand, adopt, and use a common unspecific notion of "moral rightness generally characterized" (say, as permissibility relative to a set of rules of a certain kind), we can still differ on the specific rules conferring rightness and consequently adopt and use different specific notions of rightness. Conceptual relativism, moreover, applies even to concepts of notions themselves: People can, and sometimes do, adopt and wield different specific concepts of, and specific constitutive identity-conditions for, notions. Conceptual relativism is, we shall see, no respecter of notions.

Some philosophers might appeal to "the correct" (analysis of the) notion of *X* to mitigate conceptual relativism. Chapters 2 and 4 show that notions of correctness and truth are as variable as notions of justification. We need, then, a determinate notion of correctness before we can assess claims to "the correct" notion of *X*. A dialectically effective or motivationally cogent appeal to "the correct" (analysis of a) notion of *X* must, we might argue, bear on the purposes for which one adopts and uses a notion of *X*. If what you call "the correct" notion of rightness has no bearing on the purposes for which I adopt and use a notion of rightness, I shall typically find an appeal to your "correct" notion altogether unconvincing and even irrelevant. Claims to "correctness" of notions or analyses typically owe their cogency to one's purposes in adopting and using notions or analyses, purposes that can vary over time and from person to person. Here we must be careful, however, because notions of cogency and dialectical effectiveness are not immune to the implications of conceptual relativism. (Chapter 4 elaborates on this theme in connection with so-called internalist and externalist notions of reasons for action.)

Chapter 2 highlights some lessons of semantic foundationalism via two epistemological extremes from the philosophy of science: the "scientific-community authoritarianism" of Thomas Kuhn and the "epistemological-standard authoritarianism" of Rudolf Carnap. Kuhn's view implies that the fundamental decisions, goals, and practices of a scientific community yield the ultimate standards for answering questions of scientific justification. Carnap's view, in contrast, finds our ultimate epistemological standards in certain a priori principles for knowledge and confirmation. Kuhn's social approach, when generalized to explain all justification, precludes our giving a noncircular epistemological assessment of our community's fundamental decisions, goals, and practices, for the latter determine our epistemological standards. Carnap's a priori approach raises a different problem: It gives no independent epistemological significance to the fundamental epistemological decisions, goals, and practices of a person or a group, and thus seems to allow for divorcing scientific justification, for example, from the fundamental cognitive goals of a scientific community.

Semantic foundationalism offers a diagnosis of the problems facing the epistemological views of Kuhn and Carnap. The problem facing Kuhn's view derives from a notion of justification relative to which a person's or a group's fundamental epistemological decisions, goals, and practices admit of noncircular epistemological assessment. (Kuhn's view does not allow for the kind of assessment enabled by such a notion.) The underlying notion may be sketchy and may even be filled out in various ways, but its presence drives the problem at hand.

The problem for Carnap's a priori approach stems from a notion of justification (however minimal) relative to which a person's or a group's fundamental epistemological decisions, goals, or practices have crucial epistemological significance. (Carnap's approach does not acknowledge the kind of epistemological significance credited by such a notion.) The underlying notion of justification credits the relevant decisions, goals, or practices as an ultimate basis of epistemological assessment. Semantic foundationalism acknowledges that epistemological problems of the sort noted are motivated by divergent epistemological notions. It recommends that we treat such problems by examining the relative merits and demerits of the various notions involved. Since the merits and demerits in question, on one familiar construal, will depend on one's purposes in adopting and employing a notion of justification, we again see the significance of purpose-relative considerations in inquiry. Given conceptual relativism, however, we cannot acknowledge a monopoly for purpose-relative considerations in inquiry, nor can we preclude alternative specific notions of "merit" or of "demerit."

Chapter 3, "Meaning, Interpretation, and Analyticity," gives an account of notions, meaning, and analyticity appropriate to semantic foundationalism and thereby reveals what lies at the basis of explaining, evaluating, and arguing for justification. It introduces a concept of *interpretively purposive* use of language to elucidate a notion of meaningful linguistic use agreeable with semantic foundationalism. Interpretively purposive use of language is purposive linguistic action of a distinctive sort. Such action requires that one use language with an end in view, to do something: for example, to assert that something is the case. One's meaningful linguistic use is, for present concerns, just one's using tokens that are meaningful for one. One's use of meaningful tokens may or may not be purposive, or intentional. What, however, makes certain tokens meaningful for a person?

Various specific notions of semantic meaning occupy the literature in philosophy of language, as conceptual relativism would lead us to expect. Philosophers therefore will not give just one answer to the question of what makes tokens meaningful for a person. Unqualified talk of "the" notion of meaning, in this connection, is at best misleading, even if philosophers can agree on some notion of *meaning generally characterized.* Agreement on a general notion of meaning does not preclude divergence in specific notions of meaning.

On our "everyday" notion of meaning, what one purports to do in using utterances or inscriptions (or any potentially meaningful tokens, for that matter) does not automatically determine what they mean for one; they may serve a purpose for one without meaning anything for one. I might utter complete nonsense to frighten or to fluster you. However purposive, this uttering would not automatically give meaning to what I uttered, at least on a common notion of meaning. Purposive utterings, on this notion, do not require the meaningfulness of what is thereby uttered, and a corresponding point holds for purposive use of inscriptions and other tokens. The meaningfulness of language does not derive just from purposive use, at least on our everyday notion of meaning. (My point here is explicitly conceptual, being relative to a certain notion of meaning.)

Chapter 3 introduces *semantic interpretationism*, according to which meaning depends on understanding, and understanding depends on a certain kind of interpretation of tokens: interpretation of tokens as indicating (that is, designating) or expressing something. Interpretive use of utterances or inscriptions, according to chapter 3, requires one's using utterances or inscriptions with an interpretation one gives them. One can interpret utterances or inscriptions to indicate or to express various things, if only to oneself. The range of what can be thus indicated or expressed is broad. It includes, among other things, questions whether something is the case, orders to do something, assertions that something is true, commitments to do something, declarations that something be the case, and exclamations about something.

In an interpretively purposive uttering of *X*, I intentionally use *X* to perform the act delimited by what I interpret *X* as doing: indicating or expressing a certain thing. In other words, I intentionally use *X* to perform the act I interpret *X* as accomplishing in virtue of what, on my interpretation, *X* indicates or expresses. An internal, conceptual connection holds between one's interpretation and the meaningful linguistic act one performs in interpretively purposive use of language. (Chapter 3 applies this point to cases where one uses an utterance, such as 'Fire!', to express more than one thing.)

I use 'Wake up!', for example, to command you to wake up now, this commanding action being delimited (for me) by what I interpret 'Wake up!' as doing now: expressing a command for you to wake up. In addition, I use 'There is a stout-bodied fly buzzing around my office' to assert that there is a stout-bodied fly buzzing around my office, where this act of asserting is delimited (for me) by what I interpret the sentence in question as doing now: expressing the assertion that there is a stout-bodied fly buzzing around my office. Finally, I use such demonstratives as 'this' and 'that' to designate things, these acts of designation being determined by what I interpret 'this' and 'that' as doing now: designating this and designating that.

If meaning encompasses designation, familiar use of demonstratives speaks against unqualified semantic holism implying that only in the context of a sentence does a word have meaning. We nonetheless may regard a broad range of individual words (for example, 'if', 'or') as having their meanings derivatively, in virtue of their contributions to larger tokens we interpret as indicating or expressing something. This presumed dependency is not surprising once we acknowledge that our primary purpose in using meaningful language is to indicate and to express things.

Interpretation gives semantical life to otherwise dead tokens. Indeed, meaning itself—even apart from purposive linguistic use—draws its life from interpretation. When I utter sheer nonsense to frighten you, I do not interpret the nonsense as indicating or expressing something; it is thus nonsense to me, even if it is meaningful to you owing to your interpretation of it.

Interpretation can be habitual, spontaneous, and implicit to consciousness; and it can occur at the speed of thought. My account of meaning is largely neutral on the conditions for an interpreter, and certainly does not require a dualistic Cartesian approach to selves. Semantic interpretationism does not require that there can be interpretation without tokens interpreted, nor does it require that we be able to interpret without reliance on language. Interpretation may arise, at least initially for a person, from uninterpreted habitual use of linguistic tokens. Semantic interpretationism is not, in any case, an account of the genesis of meaning; it is rather an account of what semantic meaning, as commonly understood, consists in.

Meaningful linguistic use is not essentially private when construed as interpretive use. When you recognize what my interpretive use of a token is, you understand what I mean by that token. Misunderstanding is possible, but certainly not necessary. Chapter 3, nonetheless, opposes the view that meaningful linguistic use is essentially social. It allows that I can use certain tokens meaningfully even when my social group—whatever that may be—does not. Meaning is sensitive to the interpretive uses of *individual* interpreters.

In interpreting tokens as indicating or expressing something, we give them conditions of success: that is, conditions of success in virtue of what they, on our interpretation, indicate or express. Questions are successful when answered; orders are successful when obeyed; assertions are successful when true; commitments are successful when kept; and so on. The relevant notion of success, like that of interpretive use, is thus multifaceted. Because the same is true of the notion of meaning suitable to semantic foundationalism, and our everyday notion of meaning, we have no problem here.

We have no overriding reason to judge a notion defective just in virtue of its being multifaceted: that is, its being irreducible to a highly specific, nondisjunctive set of individually necessary and jointly sufficient conditions. Whether a notion is defective for one depends on one's (variable) semantic standards regarding 'defective' (or some such term) and the purposes one has for that notion, not on an unconditional standard of unity or simplicity for notions. Our efficacious notions may simply not have the kind of unity or simplicity demanded by an unconditional standard. Shunning a common prejudice in philosophy, this antireductionist theme about notions emerges in chapter 3 (and recurs in chapter 4).

Linguistic use that is intelligible for you as indicating or expressing *X* is understandable, and thus interpretable, for you as indicating or expressing *X*, given what chapter 3 calls your "interpretive commitments." The ability indicated by the modal suffix 'able' in 'interpretable' need not be manifest in an episode or action. A token can thus be understandable for you even when you are not episodically interpreting it. Meaningfulness likewise can be episodic or nonepisodic.

Chapter 3's account of meaning is comprehensive in a way that does not tie meaningful linguistic use to *cognitive* linguistic use, that is, truth-valued use. It allows for meaningful use of terms (for example, 'Hi!', 'Ouch!', 'Darn!') whose meaningfulness does not depend on a role in truth-valued statements. *Noncognitive* interpretive use of terms yields noncognitively meaningful use. We may thus distinguish cognitively and noncognitively meaningful use in terms of two kinds of interpretive use: cognitive and noncognitive.

Chapter 3 uses semantic interpretationism to refine the semantic assumptions central to semantic foundationalism. A key result is a notion of analyticity that resists W. V. Quine's influential objections and enables a cogent treatment of some meta-epistemological issues that would otherwise raise problems. One such issue is: In virtue of what is a certain principle of justification—say, one that links justification with coherence or simplicity—*correct* (if only for a person at a time)? Chapter 3 explains how its approach to analyticity can handle such questions with ease and cogency.

We do not ordinarily think of notions as correct or incorrect in the way statements descriptive of household physical objects are. Notions of justification can nonetheless admit of evaluation, at least relative to a determinate notion of evaluation for notions. One such notion is instrumentalist, relying on considerations about a notion's being useful for certain conceptual purposes. We can evaluate a notion of justification, accordingly, from the standpoint of a theorist's *purposes* in adopting and using such a notion. If a certain notion of justification obviously serves those purposes better than does any other available notion, we can recommend that notion as reasonable, for the theorist in question, on purpose-relative grounds. Does such a recommendation necessarily presuppose a notion of justification, and thereby rest on circularity?

Whether circularity threatens depends on the notions at issue. We can imagine a case where satisfaction of my purposes for a notion of justification logically requires that a notion meet certain specific conditions, but where only one of the available candidates meets the required conditions. By hypothesis, the other candidates, relative to those required conditions, are nonstarters. In that case, one might recommend the single remaining notion on grounds of consistency, and circularity will not necessarily threaten if a consistency condition on justification is not at issue. Even here, however, a certain *notion* of instrumental reasonableness is clearly at work: a (perhaps minimal) notion of reasonableness as a function of superior purpose-satisfaction. Semantic foundationalism looms large even in the face of evaluative instrumentalism.

Reasons stemming from superior purpose-satisfaction need not be *epistemic*, or evidential, in any familiar sense. They need not concern either objective reliability of a belief-forming process or the objective truth of what is being endorsed on grounds of purpose satisfaction. Reasons indicating that a belief will satisfy certain purposes of a believer can be irrelevant to reasons indicating that the belief in question is objectively true. Instrumental reasons for *accepting* or *believing* that *P* need not be epistemic reasons indicating that *P* is true.

We might find reasons for accepting realism, for example, even while acknowledging that our reasons fail to indicate that realism is true. Reasons for accepting realism need not be reasons indicating that realism is true. We might learn that accepting realism serves certain of our purposes in theorizing better than does any alternative. Such a purpose-relative, instrumental reason need not involve considerations about the objective truth of realism. It rather involves considerations about achieving certain goals in theorizing, or in accepting certain claims. Such goals might include, for example, preservation of antecedently held beliefs and coherence with those antecedent beliefs. Achieving the latter conservative goals with one's beliefs does not entail that those beliefs yield reliable access—even fallible reliable access—to conceiving-independent reality; nor does a reason indicating that a belief satisfies those goals entail a reason indicating that the belief is objectively true, at least on some notions of a truth indicator. (I am illustrating a point now, not recommending the aforementioned conservative goals.)

Merely instrumental reasons for endorsing realism are not evidential reasons for what realism states. They are not evidence for the objective truth of realism. They rather are considerations in favor of a theorist's *endorsing* realism—considerations stemming from the (likely) satisfaction of certain purposes in theorizing. Because purposes in theorizing can vary, one theorist's instrumental reasons for endorsing a certain view do not necessarily transfer to another theorist. This suggests a kind of relativism about reasons: Reasons can vary from theorist to theorist owing to varying purposes. Here again an operative notion of instrumental reasons plays a crucial role.

Chapter 4, "Reasons, Truth, and Relativism," examines relativism about reasons and relativism about concepts of reasons and truth. It asks what sort of reason can recommend the adoption and use of one notion of truth, or one notion of reason, over another. *Purposive normative reasons*, according to chapter 4, are noteworthy in this connection. They are reasons indicative of purpose satisfaction. A purposive normative reason for adopting a certain specific notion of truth indicates that adoption of this notion of truth will satisfy one's purposes in adopting a specific notion of truth. Chapter 4 explains how purposive normative reasons can contribute to solving a "problem of normative relevance": the problem that nonmotivating, purpose-independent normative "reasons" and "requirements" seem too easy to come by. Purpose-independent "reasons" and "requirements" evidently can be introduced *ad arbitrium*.

Here we must consider a difference between internalism and externalism about reasons. Internalism implies that there is a prima facie reason for you to do *A* only if your motivational (and evidential) set recommends that you do *A*. Externalism, in contrast, implies that you can have a prima facie reason to do *A* even if your motivational set does not recommend that you do *A*. Some species of externalism tie reasons for action to the motivational set one would have if fully or adequately informed. An internalist will object that externalism does not guarantee motivationally cogent reasons, reasons able to compel or to constrain one's actions or attitudes. An externalist will be unmoved, being content with a notion of normative reasons that does not require actual motivational efficacy. Chapter 4 finds two different specific notions of a regulative reason at work here, even if internalists and externalists can agree on some general, unspecific notion of a regulative reason. Perhaps, then, internalists and externalists are actually talking about different matters, not disagreeing about some particular matter.

Chapter 4 treats the internalist-externalist debate with *conceptual instrumentalism*: the view that one's aims, or purposes, in adopting and using a notion of rationality, reasons, or obligations can cogently recommend, at least to oneself, an internalist or an externalist notion of rationality, reasons, or obligations. If, on the one hand, we now aim to evaluate attitudes and actions from one's actual evidential and motivational standpoint, we do well to use an internalist notion of rationality, reasons, or obligations. If, on the other hand, we now aim to evaluate attitudes and actions from a position independent of one's actual motivational standpoint, we need to use an externalist notion of rationality, reasons, or obligations. A single person, moreover, might use an externalist notion for certain purposes and an internalist notion for other purposes. We can generalize on such instrumentalism to formulate a general standard for deciding what notions to adopt and to use.

Chapter 4 offers conceptual instrumentalism as one straightforward way to answer questions about what notion of rationality, reasons, or obligations one should adopt and use. Such instrumentalism cannot, however, lay claim to a monopoly here. Given conceptual relativism regarding specific notions of obligation and corresponding uses of 'should', we must acknowledge various conceptual standpoints from which answers to normative and meta-normative questions can arise. We shall have to ask, nonetheless, whether a theorist's use of an externalist notion of rationality, reasons, or obligations itself draws support from one of the theorist's conceptual purposes: the aim to evaluate attitudes and actions from a position independent of one's actual motivational standpoint. Chapter 4 remarks on this issue in connection with conceptual instrumentalism.

One might propose that we can assess notions relative to something less variable than a person's aims: namely, relative to the reliability of a notion's portrayal of the real world. The rough idea is this: The real world is featured in certain objective, conceiving-independent ways (for example, many of its objects have "natural" boundaries), and our notions can be more or less accurate in how they "fit" the objective features of the real world. This proposal rests on realism to save us from the wages of conceptual relativism, and it might invoke *normative* realism (for example, moral and aesthetic realism) to accommodate the domain of normative concepts. In any case, the proposal helps itself to a kind of realism that must face the lesson of chapter 1. A central theme of this book is that we cannot cogently make use of such realism in the way proposed.

Among contemporary philosophers, realists are typically physicalists of one sort or another. Indeed, physicalism broadly conceived now enjoys the status of the dominant realist ontology. We thus do well to ask how physicalism, of one species or another, fares in the light of conditional ontological agnosticism and conceptual relativism. This issue provides a salient test of this book's main themes.

Chapter 5, "Physicalism, Action, and Explanation," contends that explanatory strategies—including physicalist explanatory strategies—are perspectival in the way justifications and reasons are. Their being perspectival consists in their being relative to certain variable semantic commitments, explanatory ends, or purposes, and explanatory standards for achieving those ends. Even physicalists must face the lessons of semantic foundationalism, conceptual relativism, and conceptual instrumentalism.

Chapter 5 assesses the prospects for a physicalist account of intentional attitudes and intentional actions. Such an account allows for a distinction between a naturalized *concept* of intentional attitudes and actions and a naturalized *ontology* for intentional attitudes and actions. Given variability of concepts, we should be wary of talk of naturalizing *the* concept of intentional attitudes or intentional actions. If philosophers wield a variety of such concepts, an assumption of just one such concept will be misplaced. Even if philosophers share a general notion of intentional action, some philosophers adopt and use different specific notions of intentional action. A similar point applies to notions of intentional attitudes. We cannot escape the lessons of conceptual relativism.

Chapter 5 raises doubts about naturalizing all psychological and action-theoretical notions in circulation. It also raises doubts about the availability of any physicalist ontology that can avoid the epistemological worries of chapter 1. It supports an instrumental, purpose-relative approach to the explanatory principles characteristic of physicalism, including nonreductive, reductive, and eliminativist versions of physicalism. This approach highlights the variable semantic and purpose-relative considerations constraining explanatory principles. Chapter 5 thus dulls the ontological edge—the presumption of objectivity—that accompanies various physicalist theories in philosophy. It puts the philosophical task of explanation—of making sense—in focused, purpose-relative perspective, where variable semantic standards play a definitive role. Chapter 5 uses the nonreductive physicalism of Donald Davidson to illustrate some of its main points, contending that Davidson's physicalism rests on some dubious ontological and methodological assumptions.

Philosophy after objectivity is philosophy directed away from losing battles against ontological agnosticism. It is, more specifically, philosophy compatible with the main lessons of chapters 1 through 5: lessons regarding, for example, conditional ontological agnosticism, semantic foundationalism, conceptual relativism, and conceptual instrumentalism. Philosophy after objectivity is, in the end, philosophy enough. Indeed, it evidently is the only philosophy we can actually have.

In the preface to the first edition of the *Critique of Pure Reason*, Kant strikes a congenial note about objectivity-seeking issues in philosophy: "Human reason has this peculiar fate that in one species of its knowledge it is burdened by questions which, as prescribed by the very nature of reason itself, it is not able to ignore, but which, as transcending all its powers, it is also not able to answer" (Kemp Smith translation). Such, in brief, is the fate of objectivity in philosophy: a fate wherein agnostic-resistant non-questionbegging evidence for objectivity is not to be had, even though objectivity-seeking questions themselves need not be unintelligible. Philosophy after objectivity owns up to this fate, and acknowledges variable semantic and purpose-relative features central to philosophical explanations, evaluations, and justifications.

Philosophy after objectivity is philosophy after realism and idealism, assuming agnostic-resistant non-questionbegging evidence for neither realism nor idealism. Such philosophy endorses making sense—explaining—*in perspective*, without presumptions of non-questionbegging evidence for claims to objectivity. Acknowledging no agnostic-resistant non-questionbegging evidence for matters ontological, philosophy after objectivity shifts focus to semantic and purpose-relative, instrumental constraints for explanations, evaluations, and justifications. As a result, the decisive roles of inquirers in inquiry, including philosophical inquiry, take center stage.

Philosophy after objectivity answers explanation-seeking and justification-seeking questions by avowedly perspectival, purpose-relative standards that depend on variable semantic commitments. It shuns, at every level, assumptions of agnostic-resistant non-questionbegging evidence for claims to objectivity. The distinctiveness of philosophy *after* objectivity lies in its presumed reasons, justifications, explanations, and evaluations, and in their presumed bearing on philosophical issues of objectivity. Disputes about objectivity (that is, conceiving-independent things), according to philosophy after objectivity, admit of no agnostic-resistant non-questionbegging answers. Kant, as noted, summed this up well; and, according to chapter 1, this is the human cognitive predicament. Philosophers may clamor for non-questionbegging evidence for their claims to objectivity, but, given this book's lessons, they should save their clamoring for something else.

Agnosticism runs deep in philosophy after objectivity, extending to all areas of philosophy: ontology, epistemology, philosophy of mind, theory of meaning, philosophy of science, and so on. Agnosticism does not, however, recommend a change in the language we ordinarily use. Linguistic revisionism gets no foothold in agnosticism, or in philosophy after objectivity. We can still use, for example, our familiar language of medium-sized physical objects and even of small- and large-sized physical objects. The vocabulary we ordinarily use attracts no fire from agnostics. Their concern is rather the sort of *support*, or *reasons*, we presume for our answers to explanation-seeking questions, particularly questions about objectivity.

Avowedly perspectival explanations and justifications avow relativity to an explanatory or justificational stance. Such a stance comprises an interpreted vocabulary, or conceptual apparatus, some explanatory or justificatory ends, and standards for achieving those ends. Avowedly stance-relative explanation or justification will not presume that its conceptual apparatus and operative standards enable agnostic-resistant non-questionbegging evidence for philosophical theses about conceiving-independent things. Philosophy after objectivity allows for—indeed, depends on—such stance-relative explanation and justification.

Avowed stance-relativity pervades philosophy after objectivity. Consistently, philosophy after objectivity acknowledges its own stance-relativity, without descending to an "anything goes" attitude toward normative assessment. In particular, it does not offer yet another ontological position, whether realist or idealist, needing defense against agnosticism. It endorses agnosticism about ontology, when the concern is for agnostic-resistant non-questionbegging evidence, and makes do with what we can have: perspectival explanations, evaluations, and justifications, in short, making sense *in perspective*. This book lays foundations for philosophy after objectivity, for making sense in perspective.

1

Ontology, Evidence, and Philosophical Questions

Ever since Plato and Aristotle, philosophers have pursued 'what is *X*?' questions. What is knowledge? What is meaning? What is being? What is causation? What is free will? What is justice? And so on. What, if anything, is the main point of such questions? This chapter examines the philosophical significance of 'what is *X*?' questions in the light of traditional philosophical essentialism. It examines two competing approaches to essences—realist and conceptualist approaches—and an influential Aristotelian approach to 'what is *X*?' questions.

One lesson will be that, contrary to various antirealists, we have no semantic shortcut to antirealism about essences or other conceiving-independent objects. Aristotelian ontological realism about essences and physical objects, we shall see, is arguably an intelligible position. This lesson does not, however, justify ontological realism about essences or physical objects, or otherwise lend it credibility.

Another lesson will be that ontological realism about conceiving-independent items faces a serious epistemological problem, a problem neutral on purely conceptual disputes over the exact conditions for knowledge and justification. On the basis of this epistemological problem, I shall support a (conditional) version of agnosticism about ontological realism in general, a version that gains credibility whenever agnostic-resistant non-questionbegging evidence for realism is sought. This agnosticism raises problems for both realism and idealism. My strategy is to give realism the best defense possible before raising problems from agnosticism. We begin with some essential background.

1.1 What the Greeks Wrought

Plato and Aristotle claim that wonder, or marvel, prompts people to philosophize (see *Theaetetus* 155d and *Metaphysics* 982b12). Wonder evidently produces philosophy, at least according to Plato and Aristotle, only when accompanied by a 'what is *X*?' question, or at least by a closely related question. This suggests that Plato and Aristotle do not regard wonder (*thauma*) as just a feeling of astonishment. Aristotle, in fact, illustrates his claim with an example of people wondering initially at "obvious difficulties" and then advancing to "greater matters": for example, matters about the genesis of the universe. Such wondering is no mere feeling of astonishment.

Aristotle adds that puzzled people who wonder consider themselves ignorant, and that philosophy aims to escape from ignorance. Aristotle's "greater matters," by his own illustration, consist of unanswered questions about various phenomena: for example, the moon, the sun, the stars. Aristotle thus apparently regards philosophy as beginning with wonder that includes, or at least prompts, questions of a certain sort, questions that typically take the form 'what is *X*?'.

Plato and Aristotle evidently construe philosophical 'what is *X*?' questions as *essence-seeking*. For instance, Plato's intractable question, 'what is knowledge?', in the *Theaetetus* (146e) aims to identify what knowledge *itself* is. It does not seek a list of the various sorts of knowledge. Similarly, his 'what is *X*?' questioning in the *Meno* (75a) asks for what is the same in, or common to, all *X*'s. It aims, in other words, for the essence (*ousia*) of *X* (*Meno* 72b; cf. *Euthyphro* 11a). Plato suggests that this aim involves identifying a definition (*logos*) of the essence of *X* (*Republic* 534b). Aristotle, too, characterizes philosophy in terms of knowledge of essence, which on his view reduces to knowledge of definition (*Metaphysics* 983a27f.).

Both Plato and Aristotle, then, understand philosophical 'what is *X*?' questions as essence-seeking; and both understand definition as the way to identify essence. They thus hold that philosophical 'what is *X*?' questions are definition-seeking as well as essence-seeking. The relevant definitions, according to Plato and Aristotle, are not stipulative; nor are they reports on conventional linguistic usage. They rather are *real* definitions: that is, essence-specifying definitions signifying the properties in virtue of which something is located in its proper genus or species. Aristotle (*Categories* 2b28–3a5) is especially clear on this understanding of real definition (as, incidentally, is Thomas Aquinas in *On Being and Essence*).

A troublesome circle emerges now. If we explain essence in terms of what is captured by real definition, and then explain real definition in terms of what captures essence, we have made no explanatory mileage. We have only gone around in a circle. "This useless circle," according to Richard Robinson, "is the best that can be extracted from Aristotle when we ask what is meant by 'essence', and it is strong evidence that there is no such thing as essence in his sense of the word."[1] Regardless of whether Aristotle himself escaped this circle, we should ask whether other proponents of philosophical 'what is *X*?' ques-

1. Robinson (1954, p. 154). Cf. Robinson (1953, pp. 51–62). Carl Hempel (1952, p. 658) has raised a similar criticism: "A 'real' definition, according to traditional logic, is . . . a statement of the 'essential nature' or the 'essential attributes' of some entity. The notion of essential nature, however, is so vague as to render this characterization useless for the purposes of rigorous inquiry." Cf. Pap (1958, pp. 269–275).

tions can escape. If this circle is inescapable, those proponents will lack an informative account of the sort of questions supposedly definitive of philosophical inquiry. In that case, their account of what philosophy itself is will be inadequate. We turn now to two prominent approaches to essences.

1.2 Realism versus Conceptualism

Let us stay, for illustration, with the main issue of Plato's *Theaetetus*: What is knowledge? This example of a 'what is *X*?' question will save our discussion from undue abstractness, and will enable us to see, in due course, the significance of 'what is *X*?' questions in general. We shall use the term 'essence-realist', or just 'realist', for any philosopher who, like Plato and Aristotle, holds that the correct answer to such a question as 'what is knowledge?' identifies certain "objectively" essential features: features whose being essential is *conceiving-independent* in that their being essential does not require one's conceiving of them as such. Such a realist denies that what is essential to something (for example, knowledge) depends for its being essential on conceivers taking, or conceptualizing, it as essential. Following Plato and Aristotle, an essence-realist regards the question 'what is knowledge?' as equivalent to this question: What is the conceiving-independent essence of knowledge, the essence of knowledge whose being that essence does not require its being conceived of as such?

Realists can use a distinction between strong and weak conceiving-independence. Something, *X*, is *strongly* conceiving-independent with respect to its having feature *F* if and only if *X*'s having *F* does not depend, logically or causally, on someone's conceiving of something. If, for example, the earth's magnetic field exists independently of anyone's conceiving of something, then the earth's magnetic field exists with strong conceiving-independence. Something, *X*, is *weakly* conceiving-independent with respect to its having feature *F* if and only if *X*'s having *F* does not depend, logically or causally, on someone's conceiving of *X*'s having *F*.

Everything strongly conceiving-independent is weakly conceiving-independent, but weak conceiving-independence does not logically require strong conceiving-independence. Even if one's conceiving of Socrates, for example, is weakly conceiving-independent (because it does not require one's conceiving of one's conceiving of Socrates), it is not strongly conceiving-independent. The same is true of one's believing or knowing, for instance, that Plato admired Socrates. Such psychological attitudes logically require conceiving, even if they do not logically require one's *conceiving of them* as psychological attitudes of the sorts they are. Realists typically hold that the essences of such psychological attitudes are weakly, but not strongly, conceiving-independent. Realists also typically use 'conceiving' in 'conceiving-independent' broadly, to signify any psychological attitude or activity: thinking, believing, intending, desiring, perceiving, and so on.

Talk of the conceiving-independence of certain things, we may assume (if only for the sake of argument), is sufficiently intelligible, if it amounts to talk of how certain things are apart from how conceivers take (those) things to be.[2] The parenthetical use of 'those' allows us to consider weak conceiving-independence in cases of psychological attitudes entailing conceiving. Essence-realists typically endorse strong conceiving-independence of essences, but propose weak conceiving-independence in cases of essences that logically cannot be strongly conceiving-independent.

Antirealists doubtful of the intelligibility of talk of conceiving-independence must acknowledge a distinction between the conceiving-dependence of a notion and the conceiving-dependence of what that notion designates or otherwise subsumes. Even if the pertinent notion, or the conceiving, of how things are conceiving-independently requires conceiving, perhaps the existence of *what* is thus conceptualized, or conceived of, is not similarly conceiving-dependent. In section 1.6, we shall consider an Aristotelian characterization of essentialism that seems intelligible enough. The assumption of its intelligibility seems, in any case, more plausible than any principle entailing its unintelligibility, at least given a common notion of intelligibility.

Weak conceiving-independence of essences does not require that every essence can exist while no conceiver exists. A realist might reject the latter requirement on the ground that there is an essence even of an actually existing conceiver, for example you. Realism is thus compatible with the view that some essences—for example, essences of conceivers—depend for their existence on the existence of a conceiver. A realist need not hold that your essence can exist even when you do not. The view that a conceiver's essence can exist even when a conceiver does not unduly limits realists to a non-Aristotelian view of the priority of essence to existence.

Invoking weak conceiving-independence, a realist need hold only that an essence does not depend for its being essential on any conceiver's taking it as essential. If the essence of knowledge is justified true opinion, as *Theaetetus* 202c suggests, a realist will hold that justified-true-opinion's being essential to knowledge does not depend on any conceiver's taking it as essential to knowledge. Essences, on this view, are thus not relative to the specific conceptual takings of conceivers, even if some essences require conceiving and conceivers.

The following quotation from Wittgenstein suggests a different view of essences, *essence-conceptualism*:

> . . . it is not the property of an object that is ever 'essential', but rather the mark of a concept. . . . [I]f you talk about *essence*—, you are merely noting a convention. But here one would like to retort: there is no greater difference than that between a proposition about the depth of the essence and one

2. Some support for this assumption can be found in Moser (1989, pp. 29–34; 1990a). Cf. Wolterstorff (1990, pp. 54–55). Section 1.5 returns to this assumption.

> about—a mere convention. But what if I reply: to the *depth* that we see in the essence there corresponds the *deep* need for the convention.[3]

Conceptualism states that essences depend for their being essences on a conceiver's taking them as essential, or as ontologically indispensable to the existence of a thing. It entails that something is an essence only if a conceiver takes it as such. (Wittgenstein himself recommended conceptualism as a conceptual, or "grammatical," thesis, not as an ontological thesis.)

Justified true opinion, for example, is essential to knowledge only if someone takes it as such. Apart from some such taking, knowledge has no essence. Conceptualism thus entails that something's being an essence always involves a conceiver's taking, or regarding, that thing as essential. It entails that an essence is always an essence only for—that is, relative to—some conceiver. No conceptual taking regarding essences, then no essences; this is the gist of conceptualism. The required taking need not, however, be a current episode present to awareness; it can be a currently unmanifest dispositional state implicit to consciousness. Conceptual taking thus can resemble implicit believing.[4]

Conceptualism suggests the familiar view that essential properties are relative to a description. Relative to the description 'this computer', for example, a certain functional, computational property is essential. Relative to another description (for example, 'this metal box'), however, that property is not essential. This familiar view is less explicit than conceptualism in one important way. Conceptualism identifies a conceiver's activity (namely, conceptual taking) as crucial to essences. (I here use 'activity' somewhat loosely, to include dispositional psychological attitudes.) The familiar view, in contrast, appeals to a description, without explicitly indicating any role for the activity of a conceiver. A realist might construe a description as an abstract item, such as a proposition. In that case, the active role of a conceiver can easily be obscured or minimized. Conceptualism, in contrast, explicitly gives a conceiver's activity a key role in essence-formation.

Conceptualism entails that the following two questions are equivalent:

- What is the essence of knowledge?
- What does some conceiver, or some group of conceivers, take as the essence of knowledge?

Realism, in contrast, entails that the first of these questions is strictly ontological (that is, about weakly or strongly conceiving-independent reality), and the second merely biographical. A realist endorses ontology without biography, essences without conceivers taking some things as essences. A conceptualist sees no cogent way to separate biography from ontology, no reasonable way

3. Wittgenstein (1978, Part I, sections 73–74, pp. 64–65). Cf. Wittgenstein (1953, sections 371, 373). For exposition of Wittgenstein's later views on essence, see Hacker (1986, pp. 193–206) and Baker and Hacker (1985, pp. 269–273).

4. On conditions for implicit belief, see Audi (1982), Lycan (1988, chap. 3), and Moser (1989, pp. 13–23).

to countenance essences apart from considerations of conceivers taking certain things as essential. A conceptualist regards essence-seeking 'what is *X*?' questions as making reference, if only implicitly, to a conceiver or a group of conceivers for whom something is essential. A realist denies that 'what is *X*?' questions are perspectival in that way.

Recall the circle threatening the essentialism of Plato and Aristotle. Conceptualism avoids this circle, because it does not use a notion of real definition to explain a notion of essence. A conceptualist uses instead a notion of conceptual taking, or conceptual convention, to elucidate a notion of essence. Realism will generate the threatening circle only if it entails that a notion of essence must be explained by a notion of real definition, which in turn must be explained by the aforementioned notion of essence. Realists need an account of essence that does not rely on such a notion of real definition. Realists also need an account that does not make essences depend on conceptual taking regarding what is essential. Otherwise, their realism will collapse into conceptualism. Is the needed account available? Have realists overlooked the crucial role of a conceiver's activity in essence-formation?

1.3 Essences and Conceptual Taking

When asking 'what is knowledge?', we need some understanding of what we are asking: specifically, what it is we are asking *about*—in this case, knowledge. We need something that determines the semantic significance of our question and thereby provides for a semantic difference between our question about knowledge and such an indeterminate question as: What is anything? We need something that delimits the semantic significance of our question *for us*, as we ourselves need to understand what we are asking.

Our understanding the question 'what is knowledge?' will not benefit from a wholly external means of delimiting this question, such as some independent means possessed solely by certain other people. Even if such a means provides genuine understanding for those other people, it provides no semantic benefit for us. We need our own means of semantic delimitation, our own semantically restricting considerations.

The main assumption here demands little and fits with any psychologically plausible approach to understanding. It is that your genuinely understanding a question or a claim, for instance, requires that you be familiar with certain considerations that delimit for you the semantic significance of what you understand.[5] In this sense, genuine understanding is *perspectival*. It depends on

5. This assumption is compatible with Christopher Peacocke's "Discrimination Principle" for intelligible content: "For each [intelligible] content a thinker may judge, there is an adequately individuating account of what makes it the case that he is judging that content rather than any other" (1988, p. 468). My assumption, however, requires that relevant delimiting, or individuating, considerations not be altogether unfamiliar to the person for whom a question or a claim is intelligible, or understandable.

person-relative considerations that distinguish what you understand from what you do not understand, including what is altogether semantically indeterminate from your psychological perspective. Your genuinely understanding a question goes beyond that question's being merely understandable in principle for you.

Genuine understanding is more akin to an actual ability than is mere understandability. Understanding, typically construed, is understanding for a person, and something about a person's psychological perspective makes the understanding that person's.[6] Let us refer to the latter feature of one's psychological perspective as what *delimits* understanding for one. It is what excludes a plethora of mere possibilities regarding understanding from what a person actually understands. Something, then, must delimit our understanding the question of what knowledge is, and whatever does this must be familiar to us. It cannot be something we do not recognize at all, because it must delimit understanding for us, from our psychological perspectives. What can delimit understanding in this way?

A prominent realist view implies that nondoxastic (that is, nonbelief) direct acquaintance, or intuition, can delimit for us what needs analysis or real definition. Acquaintance, on this view, links us nondiscursively with the weakly or strongly conceiving-independent essences our analyses aim to characterize discursively. Bertrand Russell characterizes acquaintance thus: "We shall say that we have *acquaintance* with anything of which we are directly aware, without the intermediary of any process of inference or any knowledge of truths" (1912, p. 46). Various realists from Plato to Russell have invoked nondiscursive direct awareness to relate us to essences subject to discursive analysis. Essences, on this view, are presented to us by nondiscursive direct awareness. (Note the passive voice.)

Our analyses, or real definitions, introduce conceptual formulations designed to capture, or to categorize accurately, essential features presented to us. Our intuitive grasp of the essence of knowledge, for example, can suitably delimit for us the question of what knowledge is, without thereby giving us either a discursive understanding or an analysis of knowledge. It can directly acquaint us with, and thereby constrain for us, what needs analysis. This realist theme has attracted many.

Russell countenanced direct acquaintance with universals, thereby motivating an account of how we initially access the universals we aim to analyze. Russell claims: "In addition to our acquaintance with particular existing things, we also have acquaintance with what we shall call *universals*, that is to say, general ideas, such as *whiteness*, *diversity*, *brotherhood*, and so on" (1912, pp. 51–52).[7] If the essence of knowledge is a universal, its relevance to the question of what knowledge is needs no special treatment from Russell-style

6. See Moser (1990d) and section 5.1 for some support for this point about meaning.

7. See also Russell (1912, chap. 10). See A. R. White (1981) and Sainsbury (1986) for expositions of Russell's doctrine of acquaintance. A realist might restrict acquaintance with universals to simple universals, but this would not affect the general point I shall make regarding Russell-style realism.

realism. Such realism implies that we have direct acquaintance with the universal *knowledge*, and that this suitably delimits, as a preliminary to analysis, the question of what knowledge is.

If knowledge is a natural kind similar to water, dog, and tree, a Russell-style realist will have to rely instead on a notion of direct acquaintance with natural kinds. Because such a realist has already admitted direct acquaintance with universals, similar access to natural kinds will not provide an altogether new phenomenon. If we allow the former, we probably should not balk at the latter, at least not owing to limitations on direct acquaintance.

Direct acquaintance with universals and natural kinds, one may object, will delimit for us a notion such as *knowledge* only if we have certain essence-delimiting intentions toward what is presented to us by direct acquaintance. Suppose that direct acquaintance is direct attention-attraction where one's attention is engaged, nondiscursively, by something presented in experience.[8] Suppose also that the universal or natural kind *knowledge* directly attracts your attention now, and in that way you are directly acquainted—or immediately presented—with knowledge. Nondiscursive content of such direct acquaintance (if there be such) does not set its own conceptual or classificatory boundaries for you, regarding what is essential to knowledge. Such content does not impose on you, or on anyone, one list of the essential properties and another of the inessential. It does not impose *any* such list. At most it engages your awareness nondiscursively. You decide, or somehow discern, what exactly is essential to what; and different people can typically discern differently, relative to different classificatory interests. Divergence in definition, for example, seems always to be a real option. Nondiscursive content, in any case, does not itself decide or discern what is essential.

Your genuinely understanding the question of what knowledge is requires your having some understanding of *what it is to be knowledge*. The latter understanding requires your recognizing certain features or considerations (for example, about justification, truth, or belief) as at least partly constituting what it is to be knowledge. Such recognizing will enable you to delimit, at least to some extent, what it is to be knowledge. It will thereby enable you to distinguish to some extent what it is to be knowledge from a plethora of possible alternatives—say, mere belief, false opinion, or wishful thinking. Such recognizing will thus prevent the question of what knowledge is from being altogether semantically indeterminate for you. This does not imply, however, that you need an analysis of the relevant concept of knowledge.

You will recognize certain features as at least partly constitutive of what it is to be knowledge only if you *take* those features as thus constitutive. This is part of what recognizing (of the relevant sort) involves. Apart from such taking, you will lack appropriate recognition of the constitutive relation of those features to what it is to be knowledge, or to the relevant concept of knowledge. Your taking certain features as at least partly constitutive of what it is to

8. For elaboration on this approach to direct acquaintance, see Moser (1989, chap. 2; 1985a, chap. 5).

be knowledge requires your conceptualizing, or classifying, those features as thus constitutive. Such taking entails your endorsing the constitutive relation of those features to what it is to be knowledge.

Your being merely presented with certain features, via direct acquaintance, does not require your taking those features as at least partly constituting what it is to be knowledge. Direct acquaintance, being nondiscursive, does not by itself entail any conceptual taking. This is one of the main assumptions of Russell's contrast between knowledge by acquaintance and knowledge by description. Direct acquaintance thus fails to yield the needed understanding of an essence-seeking 'what is *X*?' question.

Consider a succinct, generalized statement of my argument against an appeal to Russell-style realism to delimit essence-seeking questions:

1. Your minimally understanding the question of what *X* is requires that this question not be completely semantically indeterminate for you: that it not be altogether semantically indistinguishable for you from the plethora of alternative possible questions.
2. The question of what *X* is will not be completely semantically indeterminate for you only if you have some, perhaps minimal, understanding of what it is to be *X*—that is, of the relevant concept of *X*.
3. Your having some, perhaps minimal, understanding of the relevant concept of *X* requires that you take (that is, conceptualize) certain distinguishing features or considerations as at least partly constituting what it is to be *X*; otherwise, the relevant concept of *X* will be altogether semantically indeterminate for you.
4. Hence, your minimally understanding the question of what *X* is requires that you take certain distinguishing features or considerations as at least partly constituting what it is to be *X*.
5. Your being directly, nondiscursively acquainted with (an instance of) what is designated by, or subsumed under, the relevant concept of *X* is insufficient for your taking certain distinguishing features or considerations as at least partly constituting what it is to be *X*.
6. Hence, your being directly, nondiscursively acquainted with (an instance of) what is designated by, or subsumed under, the relevant concept of *X* is insufficient for your minimally understanding the question of what *X* is; specifically, it is insufficient to make the concept of *X* semantically determinate for you even to a minimal extent.

The needed understanding, given step 4, requires conceptual taking. Such taking is a form of intentional activity, given a rather broad construal of 'activity' allowing for dispositional psychological attitudes not always manifest.

Nothing in the argument requires that the needed conceptual taking be something of which a conceiver is conscious, or aware. Such taking could be a currently unmanifest dispositional state implicit to consciousness. It could also be provisional, tentative, or revisable conceptual activity. The argument, moreover, does not assume that one's minimally understanding a concept requires an analysis or a full explication of that concept. Its requirements on minimal understanding are moderate, yielding a minimal distinction between conceptual understanding and passive nondiscursive experience by direct acquaintance.

Step 5 speaks of *(an instance of) what is designated by, or subsumed under, the relevant concept of X*; for Russell-style realism appeals, for the needed delimitation, to direct acquaintance with the referent of a universal-designating term. If nothing is designated by, or subsumed under, the relevant concept of *X*, the question of what *X* is will be intractable for an appeal to direct acquaintance. In that case, one of the needed relata of the acquaintance relation will be missing.

An essence-realist, as suggested above, might hold that knowledge is a natural kind or, more generally, that the relevant 'what is *X*?' questions seek the essential properties of natural kinds. The argument 1 through 6 fits with a prominent contemporary view of reference to natural kinds. Saul Kripke and Hilary Putnam have introduced a notion of *fixing reference* to identify a sort of semantically relevant causal access to natural kinds that does not require a definition of natural-kind terms.[9] Their view of natural kinds entails a version of essentialism. It entails that once we have discovered what constitutes water, for example, we have discovered its essential properties. This is not, however, essence-realism in the tradition of Plato and Russell.

Kripke and Putnam hold that the essential properties of natural kinds depend, for their being essential, on referential intentions and practices. It is essential to water that it consist of H_2O, on their view; but this depends on our intention, or convention, that a liquid will count as water only if it has the same composition, or chemical structure, as (most of) our paradigm examples of water. The essence of water thus depends for its being essential on our referential intentions in using the word 'water'. When generalized, this point implies that conventional considerations will play an indispensable role in the understanding and the confirmation of claims about essences.

The Kripke-Putnam view of natural-kind terms agrees, then, with a main conclusion of the argument 1 through 6: namely, that a minimal understanding of essence-seeking 'what is *X*?' questions requires the taking of certain distinguishing features or considerations as at least partly constituting what it is to be *X*. On the Kripke-Putnam view, we take the natural-kind term 'water' to be applicable to a liquid only if that liquid has the same composition, or chemical structure, as certain familiar instances of water. We thus hold that water is essentially H_2O, after we learn that our familiar instances consist of H_2O. Apart from what we take as providing limits on the applicability of the term 'water', such talk of essential features loses its significance. Kripke and Putnam evi-

9. See Kripke (1980) and Putnam (1975). For critical assessments of the essentialism of Kripke and Putnam, see Mellor (1977), Nathan Salmon (1981), Coppock (1984), and Bealer (1987). Salmon (1981, Appendix II), Coppock, and Bealer have identified a key role for general a priori principles (or concepts) in the essentialism of Kripke and Putnam, a role that calls into question the assumption that empirical science by itself can establish essences. See Sidelle (1989) for elaboration on the latter topic.

dently admit as much. Their account thus seems compatible with the argument 1 through 6.

Conceptual taking figures crucially in an appeal to *same composition*. Determinate talk of *the same F* requires the availability of a standard relative to which sameness can, at least in principle, be said to obtain or not to obtain. Whence the needed standard? If talk of the same *F* is to be determinate for you, you must, if only implicitly, take something as providing the needed standard (for example, a measuring tape or a color wheel). This talk will not acquire semantic determinacy for you from the mere fact that some other people have a certain standard for sameness. You need something to delimit your own understanding of 'the same *F*', and this need will be met only by a standard you take as determining sameness.

We can produce a multitude of imaginable relations that *could* count as the same composition. One must, however, settle on a standard for sameness that determines which of those various relations counts for oneself as the same composition, if only at a particular time. Features of the external, conceiving-independent world do not identify themselves as having the same composition. They do not identify themselves as having anything in common, even if they have determinate, identifiable features that can attract our attention. We conceivers, for better or worse, have a monopoly on identifying. It thus is questionable whether an appeal to "the same composition" is really an appeal to a strongly conceiving-independent feature in the sense noted in section 1.2. It may actually be an appeal, at least implicitly and in part, to what someone takes as constituting sameness.

Have I confused semantics and ontology in a way misrepresentative of realism? Apparently I have assumed that because the *understanding* of essence-seeking questions (and terms for universals, natural kinds, and sameness relations) depends on conceivers and their conceptual activity, so too does the *existence* of essences (and universals, natural kinds, and sameness relations) themselves. A realist can concede that the language we understand, as well as our understanding itself, depends on us, but deny that this entails, or supports in any way, that the existence of *what our understood language stands for* depends on us. Semantic conditions for understanding language do not transfer automatically to the ontological conditions for what our language represents or designates. Ontology construed as what there is, one might argue, does not recapitulate semantics.

Step 4 of argument 1 through 6 concludes that your minimally understanding the question of what *X* is requires that you take certain distinguishing features or considerations as at least partly constituting what it is to be *X*. Call this *the conceptual-taking requirement* on minimal understanding. A Russell-style appeal to direct acquaintance with universals or natural kinds, I have noted, does not satisfy the conceptual-taking requirement. The lesson is that Russell-style realism does not yield an adequate account of our understanding philosophical 'what is *X*?' questions. I have not concluded, however, that the conceptual-taking requirement entails the falsity of essence-realism. I thus have not inferred an ontological moral from a semantic lesson. As far as my argument 1 through 6 goes, realism still lives. Can it survive?

1.4 Realism, Criteria, and Modes of Existence

Some antirealists, following Nelson Goodman and Richard Rorty, think that certain considerations about understanding raise doubts about realism.[10] Some preliminary clarifications will enable an assessment of that view.

Talk of being "essential to something" is typically understood as talk of what is "essential to *the existence* of something." Essential properties of *X*, according to the typical realist, are properties without which *X* cannot exist. These properties, according to most realists, go beyond the merely logical properties shared by all things (for example, self-identity) to include properties "special to the nature" of *X*.[11] Talk of properties essential to the existence of *X* is understandable, according to various realists, as talk of properties essential to the identity of *X* at a certain (span of) time.[12] Realists here seem to rely on a notion of the existence or the identity of *X as a thing*.

Realists typically aim to account for essences not only of what some call "substances," but also of such "things" as knowledge, meaning, understanding, and intentionality. The relevant notion of *thing* must therefore be broad, allowing for psychological states and abilities as things. Some philosophers, holding that identity statements in general require relativity to sortal terms,[13] claim that realists must rely on a notion of the identity of *X* as a certain *kind* of thing. We need not pursue questions about identity statements in general, but essence-realism does require us to consider identity statements of the sort underlying claims about essences.

Essence-realism entails that apart from conceptual-takings (about a thing), there is *the fact of a thing's identity*: a thing's "absolute identity." Many realists regard kinds of things as things, broadly speaking. These realists hold that apart from conceiving, there is *the fact of a thing's being of a certain kind*: an "absolute kind" of things.[14] Realism of this sort acknowledges conceiving-independent identities—"absolute identities"—and conceiving-independent kinds of things—"absolute kinds." Antirealism disowns absolute identities and kinds. It entails that conceivers, owing to their conceptual takings, are a source of the identity of things and kinds.

A dividing issue, then, is: What features or considerations are identity-constituting for things and kinds of things? This question is not epistemologi-

10. For the relevant suggestions from Goodman and Rorty, see Goodman (1978, pp. 3–4) and Rorty (1982, pp. xxvi, 14–15, 192). Cf. Putnam (1981, pp. 49–54, 60–64) and Dummett (1991, chap. 15).

11. For details on this condition, see McMichael (1986) and Plantinga (1970, pp. 357–358).

12. See Brody (1973) and Fumerton (1986).

13. See, on this view, Griffin (1977) and Noonan (1980).

14. For relevant discussion, see Butchvarov (1979, pp. 134–153) and Wolterstorff (1976).

cal, at least not explicitly. It does not ask how we know that certain features or considerations are identity-constituting. The question rather is ontological, asking what *is* identity-constituting for things and kinds of things.

Defining criteria, or standards, for what constitutes identity come in different forms, but share one feature: They are, barring criteria-Platonism, formulated by some conceiver or other. Certain Eskimo conceivers famously wield defining criteria for kinds of snow that are more discriminating than analogous criteria wielded by many Europeans (cf. Crystal 1987, p. 15). Both sets of criteria, however, have their origin in conceivers; at least this is a plausible non-Platonist view of defining standards. This is not antirealism about identity itself, about what (if anything) objectively constitutes identity. The conceiving-dependence of *defining criteria* of identity does not entail the conceiving-dependence of *what objectively constitutes identity* (if anything does). More generally, the conceiving-dependence of *concepts* (for example, concepts about identity or kinds) does not entail the conceiving-dependence of the existence of *what those concepts designate or otherwise subsume.* Even some realists have neglected this point, a point that harks back to the distinction between semantics and ontology.

Nicholas Wolterstorff remarks that "which phenomena are to be treated as identity-determining is entirely a matter of *our* decision," and then concludes as follows:

> Apart from our decision as to what shall count as *a* soandso, and what shall count as two presentations of *the same* soandso and what as two presentations of *different* soandsos, there simply is no such phenomenon as identity. In order to speak we must refer and predicate; and in order to do that, we must speak and think in terms of same and different soandsos. But that is to be seen as a condition of our speech rather than a reflection of reality. . . . Identity is indeed relative [to certain criteria] in the way indicated. (1987, pp. 259–260)

Such reasoning seems misleading for a realist's purposes. It neglects a distinction between (a) conditions for *our treating something as identity-constituting* and (b) conditions for *the existence of what we treat as identity-constituting.*

We do settle on what we treat as identity-constituting, just as we settle on what we treat as cat-constituting. This point concerns our constitutive criteria for what we call "identity" and "cat," that is, our *concepts* of identity and cat. Just as this point does not entail that the existence of what falls under our concept *cat* depends on our concepts or criteria, so too this point does not entail that the existence of what is identity-constituting, by our concept of identity, depends on our concepts or criteria. Conceiving-dependence of criteria for identity allows for conceiving-independence, even strong conceiving-independence, of the existence of what satisfies those criteria and what is, in that respect, objectively identity-constituting.

Realists can exploit a distinction between two modes of existence: existence *de re* and existence *de conceptu*. Existence *de re* is absolute: It does not depend on anyone's conceptual activity regarding what has such existence. Even the absolute existence of conceptual taking itself—if there be such—does not depend on anyone's conceptual activity about that conceptual taking. One might illustrate the absolute existence of what we call "planets," for instance, by noting that the things we now call "planets" had their existence prior to our formulating a concept of planets.

Existence *de conceptu* is relative existence: It is existence *as conceptualized* in a certain way. Such existence depends on the existence of a concept under which something has been subsumed. In accord with the broad construal of 'conceiving' in section 1.2, realists will typically construe '*de conceptu*' similarly broadly, to signify relativity to any psychological attitude or activity: thinking, believing, intending, desiring, perceiving, and so on. All relative existence is perspectival in that it depends on a psychological perspective. Absolute existence differs on this score: It does not depend on a psychological perspective regarding itself.

A distinction between absolute and relative existence need not multiply objects. It does not require quantification over relative existents (what some medievals called "intentional existents") in addition to absolute existents. The pertinent distinction fits with an adverbial approach resembling an adverbial construal of Kant's distinction between things-in-themselves and things-as-they-appear.[15] An adverbial approach appeals to different *modes* of existence that do not entail different objects having those modes. An object can have both absolute existence and relative existence.

Given my non-Kantian terminology, Kant evidently holds, in the *Critique of Pure Reason* (Bxxvi, A540 = B568), that every object having existence *de conceptu* has existence *de re*, or at least that we must think this way. A supporting consideration for Kant is that if we omit the existence *de re* of a thing, there will be nothing to have existence *de conceptu*. Existence *de re*, on Kant's view, is a necessary enabler, at least from the standpoint of how we must think, of existence *de conceptu*; hence the indispensability of the thing-in-itself. Realists will deny that every object having absolute existence must have relative existence too. What we now call "the planets," for instance, might not have been conceptualized by us; still, those objects would have existed *de re*, or absolutely. This is a familiar realist theme.

How, some antirealists ask, can we even talk coherently about absolute existence? In ascribing existence *de re* to something, are we not thereby conceptualizing that thing and making its existence *de conceptu*? We are indeed, but this poses no threat to realism. Whenever we ascribe any feature to a particular thing, we thereby conceptualize it; but this does not rob the thing of absolute existence. Conceptualized objects can have absolute existence, yet not as actually conceptualized. Absolute existence is existence at least weakly independent of conceptual taking, but objects having such existence can also be conceptualized. As conceptualized, an object does not have existence *de re*; it has only existence *de conceptu*. It does not follow, however, that such an

15. For adverbial construals of Kant's distinction, see Rescher (1974), Meerbote (1974), and Moser (1985b).

object lacks existence *de re*. It could still have existence *de re* as unconceptualized. An object's modes of existence depend on a perspective of conceptualization or the lack thereof. Once we separate these modes, we can see, according to realists, that talk of absolute existence is coherent.

The foregoing distinction between modes of existence can resolve certain conceptual disputes about realism, including essence-realism. Barring concept-Platonism, our concepts depend on us, and it even seems that we could have adopted and used different concepts: for example, a concept of whole number that excludes the evens and includes only the odds. We may now think of concepts as constitutive standards for (what it is to be) correct use of terms, for correctness in using terms. One's concept of existence, then, consists in one's constitutive standards for correctness in the use of 'existence' (or some synonymous term). (Chapters 2 and 3 return to the conditions for concepts and synonymy.)

Conceiver-dependence of concepts poses no problem for the realist thesis that what falls under our concepts has existence *de re*. The way that what falls under our concepts is categorized, described, or perceived by us does depend on us. This fits with a realist view of existence *de re*, for a simple reason: The fact that something has relative existence, from a particular conceptual perspective, does not preclude or make it doubtful that this thing, as unconceptualized, has absolute existence. Realism seems to benefit, then, from the distinction between modes of existence. This distinction enables realists to contrast conditions for one's conceiving of an object and conditions for the existence of an object that happens to be conceived of by someone.

1.5 Realism and How Things Are

Some antirealists, as suggested previously, fault the intelligibility of a realist's notion of how things are conceiving-independently (and thus of any notion of existence *de re*). Hilary Putnam's "internal realism" derives from Kant's view, in the *Critique of Pure Reason* (B310f.), that we lack not only knowledge, but even a positive intelligible *notion*, of reality in itself. Putnam endorses the Kantian view that truth construed as correspondence with how things are in themselves is "inaccessible to us and inconceivable by us" (1981, p. 64). The relevant notion of conceiving-independent reality, on Putnam's view, "makes no sense" (1987, p. 36).[16]

Richard Rorty likewise holds that the conceiving-independent world—the world of Kant's thing-in-itself and a realist's "intrinsic natures"—is a world "well lost." Rorty proposes that "'the world' is either the purely vacuous notion of the ineffable cause of sense and goal of intellect, or else a name for the objects that inquiry at the moment is leaving alone." He claims that the notion

16. Putnam is here speaking of Kant's notion of the thing-in-itself, but that notion can plausibly be taken as equivalent to a familiar notion of conceiving-independent reality. Cf. Putnam (1992, p. 433). See Moser (1990a) for an outline and criticism of Putnam's internal realism.

of the world in itself is "*completely* unspecified and unspecifiable."[17] Rorty thus endorses "the sterility of attempts to give sense to phrases like 'the way the world is'" (1989, p. 20).

The following semantic thesis summarizes the shared view of Putnam and Rorty:

> *ST.* Neither the notion of nor any claim about the way things are in themselves makes sense, or is actually intelligible.

Putnam's support for *ST* rests on this assumption: "What is wrong with the notion of objects existing 'independently' of conceptual schemes is that there are no standards for the use of even the logical notions apart from conceptual choices" (1987, pp. 35–36). This assumption seems not to support *ST* at all. A realist can grant that our *notion* of the way things are in themselves depends on our conceptual activity, including our conceptual choices. This concession does not entail that what our notion of the way things are in themselves designates, is about, or otherwise subsumes is similarly conceiving-dependent.

Consider, for example, certain geologists' and evolutionary biologists' notion of how the world was in the Cambrian Period (roughly 550 million years ago), prior to the origin of land life and sea vertebrates. Their notion is determined in part by considerations about trilobites, shelled sea-invertebrates, volcanic activity, and marine sedimentation. The conceiving-dependence of this notion does not entail that what this notion is about—trilobites, volcanoes, or whatever—is similarly conceiving-dependent. Acknowledgment of the conceiving-dependence of notions thus does not threaten the semantic viability of a notion of how things are in themselves.

Rorty supports *ST* as follows:

> Only if we have . . . some picture of the universe as either itself a person or as created by a person, can we make sense of the idea that the world has an "intrinsic nature." For the cash value of that phrase is just that some vocabularies are better representations of the world than others, as opposed to being better tools for dealing with the world for one or another purpose. (1989, p. 21; cf. p. 5, and Rorty 1991, p. 80)

This line of argument fails to convince. Rorty gives no support to his questionable claim that a notion of a determinate conceiving-independent world—a world with a conceiving-independent intrinsic nature—makes sense only if we take the relevant world to be either a person or the creation of a person.

Various realists since Aristotle have countenanced a world with a conceiving-independent intrinsic nature, but have not regarded that world as either a person or the creation of a person. Aristotle himself was such a realist. Without acknowledging a personal god, Aristotle held that form, or essence, is neither generated nor destroyed (*Metaphysics Z*, 1033a24–b20). The burden thus

17. Rorty (1982, pp. 14, 15). Cf. Rorty (1976, p. 327). See Moser (1993) for an exposition and assessment of Rorty's approach to debates over realism and idealism.

falls on Rorty to show that being a realist entails being an ontological personalist or a creationist. Rorty does nothing whatever to discharge that burden. Even if such truth-bearers as statements depend on persons, it is a separate issue whether what truth-bearers are about, or derive their truth or falsity from, is similarly person-dependent. Rorty's support for *ST* thus does not compel.

We must ask whether *ST* itself is a claim about the way things are in themselves: namely, a claim that the way things are in themselves, independently of our conceiving of anything as unintelligible, is such that neither the notion of nor any claim about the way things are in themselves makes sense. This would amount to the claim that the alleged unintelligibility is suitably real, and not just a matter of our regarding, or conceiving of, some notion as unintelligible. If *ST* is such a claim, then *ST* itself makes no sense, *given what it itself claims*. *ST* states that claims about the way things are in themselves make no sense. If *ST* is a claim about the way things are in themselves, and is included as a component of the theories of Putnam and Rorty, then their theories will, accordingly, rely on a claim that makes no sense by the very standards of their own theories.

If *ST* makes no claim about the way things are in themselves, we need to specify what it does make a claim about. Following suggestions from Putnam and Rorty, many antirealists think of truth as some sort of "warranted assertibility," however idealized.[18] They thus might propose that *ST* makes a claim only about what we are (ideally) warranted in asserting, not about the way things are in themselves. *ST* will then amount to the following epistemic thesis:

> *ET*. We are (ideally) warranted in asserting that neither the notion of nor any claim about the way things are in themselves makes sense.

Rorty gives no argument for *ET*; nor does he produce an account of meaning that entails *ET*. *ET*, moreover, is not self-evident, or obvious on its own. I, for one, do not consider myself as having the sort of warrant that *ET* ascribes; nor have I seen anyone else deliver such warrant. It is unclear, then, whom the use of 'we' in *ET* actually denotes.

A more serious matter concerns whether *ET* makes a claim about the way things are in themselves. If it does, it claims that the way things are in themselves, independently of our conceiving of anything as warranted, is such that we are warranted in asserting that neither the notion of nor any claim about the way things are in themselves makes sense. We are warranted, on this construal, in asserting that *ET* itself makes no sense, given what ET itself implies. It implies that we have warrant for asserting that any claim about the way things are in themselves makes no sense. (We may also use, on the present construal, the semantic thesis *ST* to infer that *ET* makes no sense.)

18. See Putnam (1983, pp. xvii, 84–85) and Rorty (1979, pp. 176, 385). Putnam understands truth in terms of idealized justification, on the ground that (a) ordinary justification, unlike truth, can be lost, and (b) ordinary justified beliefs can be false (1981, pp. 54–55; 1983, p. 85). Cf. Putnam (1990, pp. viii–ix, 114–115, 223).

What, then, does *ET* make a claim about? Putnam and Rorty might propose that *ET*, too, is epistemic, in the way we considered *ST* epistemic. We would then have an iterated epistemic thesis: We are *warranted in asserting* that we are *warranted in asserting* that neither the notion of nor any claim about the way things are in themselves makes sense. If we continue the foregoing line of questioning, and still seek refuge in iterated epistemic claims (to avoid commitment to unintelligible claims), we face a troublesome, potentially endless regress. The regress comes from ever-increasing iteration of the epistemic operator in *ET*. We have, however, no reason to think that we actually have the sort of complex iterated warrant required by such an endless regress. Neither Putnam nor Rorty gives us a reason to think that such a regress is unproblematic or even intelligible at a level of vast complexity. They show no awareness of the current problem.

We can put the problem as a simple dilemma: Either commitment to *ST* involves a statement unintelligible by the standard of *ST* itself, or it involves a statement containing an endless regress of levels of epistemic iteration. The latter alternative amounts to this problem: Commitment to *ST*, by way of avoiding unintelligibility by the standard of *ST*, involves a statement containing an endless regress of levels of iteration concerning what we are (ideally) warranted in asserting. Such a statement is troublesome for two reasons. First, it is not clear that we have, or even can have, the sort of complex iterative warrant it requires. It is unclear what such warrant would look like, and questionable whether we could even comprehend such warrant. Second, it is doubtful that we have standards for the use or assertibility of the complex iterative statement in question. It is thus doubtful that such a statement is intelligible on Putnam's own verificationist theory of understanding.[19] On either horn of the dilemma, then, serious difficulty threatens.

We should be wary of a view entailing that every notion of how things are conceiving-independently is unintelligible. If we find troublesome an endless regress of epistemic iteration, we must wonder whether commitment to *ST* presupposes the very notion it claims to be unintelligible. The foregoing dilemma recommends a *non*epistemic notion of how things are. It suggests that a statement concerning either the notion of how things are or what we are warranted in asserting presupposes, on pain of unintelligibility or infinite regress, a nonepistemic notion of how things are.

Antirealists must be cautious, then, of inferring any kind of "ontological relativity" on semantic grounds. Quine's ontological relativity amounts to this:

> It is meaningless to ask whether, in general, our terms 'rabbit', 'rabbit part', 'number', etc., really refer respectively to rabbits, rabbit parts, numbers, etc., rather than to some ingeniously permuted denotations. It is meaningless to ask this absolutely; we can meaningfully ask it only relative to some background language. . . . [I]t makes no sense to say what the objects of a

19. On Putnam's verificationist theory of understanding, see Putnam (1978, p. 129; 1983, pp. xiv–xv; 1988, pp. 114–116).

> theory are, beyond saying how to interpret or reinterpret that theory in another. (1969a, pp. 48, 50; cf. Quine 1981, p. 20)

Here a realist will invoke a distinction between *how the objects of a theory are* and *saying or asking how the objects of a theory are.* Saying and asking are, naturally enough, "relative to some background language," but it does not follow that the objects about which one says or asks something are similarly relative. Even if our understanding of the relevant objects is relative to a background language, it is a separate issue whether the objects understood are thus relative too. Linguistic relativity of the notions and statements of an ontology does not entail linguistic relativity of what those notions and statements are about. Antirealists often overlook this platitude. Realists can handle, then, the purportedly antirealist semantic theses of Putnam, Rorty, and Quine.

1.6 Aristotelian Essence-Realism

Recall the conceptual-taking requirement on understanding from section 1.3: Your minimally understanding the question 'what is *X*?' requires that you take certain distinguishing features or considerations as at least partly constituting what it is to be *X*. This requirement allows us to confront essence-realism with the following questions: Do our conceptual-takings regarding what is essential to the existence of things ever represent conceiving-independent reality, that is, how reality is apart from being conceived? Does our conceptual-taking regarding the essence of knowledge, for instance, represent weakly conceiving-independent reality? Does our taking knowledge as justified true belief (plus whatever else is needed to avoid the Gettier problem) identify, or correspond to, a feature of the weakly conceiving-independent world?

We must distinguish the following two questions:

> (a) Does something exist that we take to be knowledge consisting of justified true belief (plus a needed fourth condition); in short, does our term 'knowledge' denote something that actually exists?
>
> (b) Is it a weakly conceiving-independent fact that knowledge is essentially justified true belief (plus a needed fourth condition)?

Questions resembling (a) seldom take center stage in ontological debates between essence-realists and essence-conceptualists. Such questions are central, however, to debates between epistemological skeptics and nonskeptics. Questions resembling (b) typically focus disagreements between essence-realists and essence-conceptualists. Such questions ask whether something's being essential is conceiving-independent, and this issue does divide essence-realists and essence-conceptualists. (We shall see in section 1.7, however, that a typical realist does face a serious epistemological problem.)

Can an essence-realist find any support in a distinction between semantics and ontology, that is, between conditions for understanding and conditions for existence *de re*? What we mean by 'essence' depends on us, as all our understanding depends on us. Does the same dependency apply to the *existence* of what it is that our talk of essence signifies? Can there be such a thing as absolute existence, existence *de re*, for what such talk signifies? An essence-realist answers yes.

Essence-realism entails that something can have features whose being essential to that thing does not depend (weakly or strongly) on any conceptual taking. Because a feature's being essential to *X* is a matter of *X*'s having it necessarily (that is, *X* could not exist while lacking it), we may put an essence-realist's view in terms of necessity. Essence-realism entails that some things possess features necessarily, and their being possessed necessarily does not depend on any conceptual taking (regarding their being possessed necessarily). (We may still say that such features would satisfy, or fall under, certain concepts if those concepts existed.) Stated thus, essence-realism relies on a notion of *de re* necessity.

The most serious objections to essence-realism do not come from the pertinent notion of *de re* modality. Realists can easily eliminate expressions of *de re* modality in favor of equivalent expressions whose talk of modality is only *de dicto*.[20] We could say that an instance of knowledge has the property of justification essentially or necessarily if and only if this instance has justification and the proposition that this instance lacks justification is necessarily false. A worry about *de re* modality is not, then, the prime mover of antirealism.

Antirealists typically favor Quine's proposal that "necessity resides in the way in which we say things, and not in the things we talk about" (1966, p. 174). They understand this proposal as implying that apart from our conceptualizing, there is no necessity. This implication is the prime mover of antirealism about essences. Barring Platonism about definitions and conceptual relations, we would be hard put to contest this implication with respect to conceptual necessity: the sort of necessity familiar from explicit definitional truths (for example, 'all bachelors are unmarried men') and broadly logical or conceptual truths (for example, 'everything red is colored'). Conceptual necessities, non-Platonists will typically grant, owe their life to the way we wield our conceptual scheme; they depend on our conceptualizing for their existence. That is why we call them *conceptual* necessities.

Are all necessities conceptual, as antirealists seem to assume? What we mean by 'necessity' does depend on us and our conceiving; our understanding of necessity is thus conceiver- and conceiving-dependent. If a construal of 'necessity' makes ineliminable reference to our ways of conceptualizing as a source of necessity, then necessity of that sort is conceptual and conceiving-dependent. Essence-realists need a construal of 'necessity' that does not make ineliminable reference to our ways of conceptualizing as a source of necessity. They need a notion of *conceiving-independent* necessity. Is such a notion forthcoming?

Consider this broadly Aristotelian characterization: To say that feature *F* is necessary, or essential, to *X* as a ϕ kind of thing is to say that *X* constitutively

20. See Plantinga (1970, pp. 354–355; 1974, chap. 3) and Fumerton (1986).

owes its existence or identity *de re* as a ϕ kind of thing—its being what it is *de re* as a ϕ kind of thing—at least in part to F; that is, F is at least partly constitutive of what it is *de re* for X to be a ϕ kind of thing. Aristotle may have had such a notion of essence in mind, in the *Metaphysics*, when he used the distinctive expression "*to ti ēn einai*" ("the what it was to be"). A realist might try to capture what Aristotle had in mind by talking instead of something's "being what it is *de re*."[21]

To say, for instance, that justification is necessary, or essential, to an instance of knowledge is to say that this instance constitutively owes its existence or identity *de re*, as an instance of knowledge, in part to its having justification. Here we must observe the distinction between *our calling* something '*F*' and something's *being F*. Our calling something *knowledge*—that is, something's being knowledge *de conceptu*—depends on us and our conceptual activity. Something's being knowledge—its existence *de re* as knowledge—does not, according to essence-realism, depend on our taking something as knowledge.

The Aristotelian characterization of essence serves a realist's purpose because it does not appeal to ways of conceptualizing as a source of necessity. It appeals rather to something's constitutively owing its existence or identity *de re*, as a certain kind of thing, at least in part to a certain feature. Even if existence and identity *de conceptu* are relative to an intentional perspective, the same, according to realism, is not true of existence and identity *de re*. Given the relevant notions of existence and identity *de re*, an essence-realist evidently can avoid the conceptual circle noted in section 1.1. A realist can then get by without a troublesome notion of real definition that risks conceptual circularity.

The Aristotelian characterization allows for distinctions between familiar modes of necessity: for example, conceptual, ontological, and causal necessity. It accommodates these distinctions by acknowledging various modes of "owing existence": for example, conceptually owing existence *de conceptu*, and either causally or ontologically (that is, constitutively) owing existence *de re*. If something ontologically, or constitutively, owes its existence *de re* as a ϕ kind of thing to a feature, F, then F at least partly constitutes that thing's being ϕ *de re*. Such constitutive dependence does not necessarily involve considerations of causal origin. My mental functioning may be ontologically essential to me qua person, but it does not follow that this functioning is the causal origin of my existence as a person. The Aristotelian characterization thus has no special problem with distinctions between what is conceptually, ontologically, and causally necessary and essential.

Given the Aristotelian characterization, we may concede (at least for the sake of argument) that essence-realism does not face unavoidable conceptual problems regarding its intelligibility. Lacking a compelling semantic principle

21. For suggestions along this line, see Bealer (1982, pp. 208–209). For useful historical discussion of Aristotle's early (pre-*Metaphysics*) views on essentialism, see Nicholas White (1972). For an attempt to sketch a coherent story about Aristotle's doctrine of essence and primary substance in the *Metaphysics*, see Moser (1983a). See Kung (1977), Sorabji (1980, chap. 12), and Irwin (1988, chaps. 10–12) for wide-ranging discussions of Aristotle's essentialism.

to the contrary, we cannot plausibly deny that essence-realism is an intelligible position. The Aristotelian characterization identifies a proper essence—conceptual though it is—of essence-realism itself. It evidently provides a conceptually viable formulation of essence-realism.

Aristotelian essence-realism gives a straightforward answer to our opening question about the significance of philosophical 'what is *X*?' questions. Such questions can be either purely conceptual or ontological. If the question 'what is knowledge?' is purely conceptual, it amounts to this question: What do we or shall we call, mean by, or take to be, *knowledge*, given only our other purely conceptual commitments? Construed thus, 'what is *X*?' questions have no conceiving-independent ontological significance in themselves. They are wholly conceptual, being guided only by how we commit to classify or conceptualize. Such purely conceptual questions owe the correctness of their answers simply to conceptual coherence: that is, agreement with other purely conceptual commitments. (Sections 2.3 and 3.3 return to the topic of conceptual commitment.)

Construed ontologically, 'what is *X*?' questions show a different face. The question 'what is knowledge?' then amounts to this: To what features or conditions does what we call "knowledge" constitutively owe its existence or identity *de re*? Assuming that this question does not concern causal origin, a realist will regard it as seeking what is ontologically essential to the existence *de re* of knowledge. The correctness of an answer to such a question will depend not simply on conceptual coherence but also on the features of a certain segment of conceiving-independent reality. In this respect, such a question is ontological, and not simply conceptual. Plato and Aristotle, in asking 'what is *X*?' questions, were pursuing ontological, essence-seeking questions of that sort. They were not raising purely conceptual issues about how conceivers conceive.

An ontological approach to 'what is *X*?' questions is arguably intelligible once we separate purely semantic and conceptual issues from issues of existence *de re*. The former issues concern what notions conceivers use or are committed to using; the latter concern the features of conceiving-independent reality. Antirealists, as section 1.5 indicated, sometimes shun ontological 'what is *X*?' questions on semantic grounds by questioning the intelligibility of such questions, ontologically construed. Some antirealists will seek support for such an attitude in a strict verifiability criterion of meaning, but that only spells further trouble.[22]

A more moderate line of attack comes from the conceptual-taking requirement identified in section 1.3. The argument, in brief, is that since our understanding 'what is *X*?' questions requires our conceptual activity, such questions cannot be ontological in the relevant sense. The defect of such an argument should now be obvious. The fact that our understanding a question is conceiving-dependent does not entail that what that question seeks, or is about, is also conceiving-dependent. Conditions for understanding a question do not transfer automatically to conditions for what that question is about, construed as a con-

22. On the vicissitudes of verifiability criteria of meaning, see Hempel (1950, 1951), Putnam (1969), and Munitz (1981, chap. 6).

ceiving-independent item. We thus have no easy semantic shortcut to anti-realism. We may now concede this much to Aristotelian essence-realists, if only for the sake of argument.

What, then, is the point of Aristotelian 'what is *X*?' questions? The point is ontological (or metaphysical), aiming for truth about existence *de re*. As long as we aim to ask about such existence, we evidently cannot avoid philosophical 'what is *X*?' questions.

1.7 An Epistemological Problem

A concession regarding mere intelligibility will not placate essence-realists. Realists are not content with the view that realism is conceptually coherent, just as theists, for instance, are not content with the view that theism is intelligible. Essence-realists contend that realism is true, that there are things having essential properties (weakly or strongly) conceiving-independently. Their realism typically implies that some objects exist conceiving-independently and have their essential properties conceiving-independently. It also typically favors, as noted in section 1.2, a broad construal of 'conceiving' to encompass any psychological attitude or activity: thinking, believing, perceiving, and so on.

Realists can distinguish three theses: (a) there are conceiving-independent essences; (b) there are conceiving-independent objects; and (c) we know that (a) or (b). Essence-realists endorsing (a) typically accept (b) too, and claim to know that (a) and (b) are true. We may thus ask whether we know that (a) and (b) are true.

A. A General Agnostic Argument

Let us begin with an argument for *ontological agnosticism* concluding that we have no effective, non-questionbegging epistemic reason to affirm realism, about objects or essences, if we take seriously familiar skeptical questions about truth and reliability. (I use 'epistemic reason' to signify the kind of reason pertinent to propositional knowledge.) The argument does not support idealism about objects and essences. It supports *conditional ontological agnosticism*: if we demand support for our beliefs from agnostic-resistant non-questionbegging epistemic reasons, then we should withhold judgment on the truth of both ontological realism and ontological idealism about objects and essences.

Realists claiming knowledge of conceiving-independent facts, whether involving objects or essences, must face this argument for ontological agnosticism:

1. *Ontological* knowledge, by definition, is knowledge of conceiving-independent reality: for example, knowledge that a conceiving-independent fact obtains, such as a conceiving-independent fact entailing the existence of an essential property or a physical object.
2. Our *effectively* discerning (that is, discerning with non-questionbegging evidence) that anyone, including ourselves, has knowledge of conceiv-

ing-independent reality requires that we have effective access to conceiving-independent reality: that is, access whose use is not a source of questionbegging evidence regarding the pertinent questions concerning whether one actually has knowledge of conceiving-independent reality.

3. Access to anything by spatio-temporally finite conceivers, such as ourselves, depends on features or processes of conceivers—for example, perception, memory, introspection, testimony, intuition, common sense—that are subject to effectively unanswerable questions about whether they decisively influence or create what is accessed: in particular, questions about whether their input conveys something that exists independently of one's conceiving of it.
4. Hence, spatio-temporally finite conceivers, such as ourselves, cannot, or at least do not, have effective access to conceiving-independent reality.
5. Hence, we cannot effectively discern that we have ontological knowledge, even if we happen to have it.

If our believing is to be guided by effective, non-questionbegging epistemic reasons, then, given the argument 1 through 5, we should not endorse the realist view that we have knowledge of conceiving-independent facts entailing the existence of essences and physical objects. We should, in that sense, be *agnostic* about ontological knowledge of the sort proposed by realists. (A parallel argument applies to the weaker claim that we have objectively true beliefs regarding conceiving-independent facts. Because realists typically countenance ontological knowledge, however, we may continue with the argument 1 through 5.)

Premise 1 comes from what realists typically mean by 'ontological knowledge' or 'objective knowledge'. Its mention of "conceiving-independent" reality gets adequate clarification, for present purposes, from sections 1.2 and 1.4 through 1.6. The other premises are perhaps less transparent.

Premise 2 sets a requirement for effectively settling, in an epistemically relevant way, the question whether anyone has ontological knowledge. The requirement demands that a realist produce a means of access to conceiving-independent reality that does not involve begging pertinent questions about whether that means of access is indeed a reliable, or (typically or even sometimes) successful, avenue to conceiving-independent reality. Non-questionbegging support for realism, for current purposes, will not simply affirm a point at issue in the debate between realists and agnostics. (The following subsection will illustrate some points at issue here.) Typical questionbegging support for realism merely asserts a point needing defense to play a cogent role in exchanges with agnostics.

The requirement of premise 2 gains plausibility if our central question is whether we actually have knowledge of conceiving-independent reality, and we seek not to beg familiar questions from agnostics. Having ontological knowledge, by definition, entails having true belief about conceiving-independent reality. Agnostics will ask realists to provide an effective, non-questionbegging epistemic reason for thinking that we have such true belief. Lacking such a reason, we epistemically should withhold judgment on the claim to ontological knowledge, at least if our concern is an effective means of discernment.

It will do no epistemic good now to produce a noneffective, questionbegging epistemic reason in support of realism. Such a reason will provide no real challenge to, or even a defense against, distinctive agnostic questions about reliability of reasons. Such a reason will thus not advance the cause of realism, if part of the cause is a non-questionbegging philosophical defense. A non-questionbegging reason favoring realism, by definition, cannot simply presume the reliability of a cognitive process under dispute by agnostics about realism. Such a presumption would be questionbegging now.

The present disagreement about ontological knowledge rests on this question: Do we have any non-questionbegging epistemic reason to think that we actually have ontological knowledge? A cogent affirmative answer to this question cannot come from considerations that beg the question whether we have ontological knowledge, or whether certain cognitive processes are reliable as a means to ontological knowledge. Questions under dispute in a philosophical context cannot attract cogent answers from mere presumption of the correctness of a disputed answer. If we allow questionbegging in general, we can support *any* position we prefer: Simply beg the key question in any dispute regarding the preferred position. Given that strategy, argument becomes superfluous in the way circular argument is typically pointless. Questionbegging strategies promote an undesirable arbitrariness in philosophical debate. They are thus dialectically inconclusive relative to the questions under dispute.[23]

Premise 3 draws support from what it takes for us to have cognitively relevant access to anything. Such access involves our relying on cognitively relevant processes—such as perception, memory, or testimony—that fail to provide non-questionbegging evidence now in favor of their own reliability.[24] The underlying problem is that we cannot assume a position outside our cognitively relevant processes from which we can effectively discern their reliability, or success, regarding the accessing of conceiving-independent facts. This evidently is the inescapable human cognitive predicament. Realists claiming ontological knowledge have not explained how we can transcend this predicament; nor is there any straightforward way to help the cause of realism here.

Agnostics recommend withholding judgment on the issue whether our cognitively relevant processes ever relay conceiving-independent facts rather than generate their "input" on their own, even input that depends for its existence on our conceiving of it. The latter issue, owing to the human cognitive pre-

23. See Woods and Walton (1982) and Walton (1989, chap. 4; 1991, chaps. 2, 8) for details on the conditions for begging a question in a dialectical context. For doubts about any purely formal criterion of vicious circularity in argument, see Sorensen (1991). Walton (1991) and Sorensen illustrate that philosophers wield various notions of begging a question.

24. The relevant sort of circularity that threatens here has been discussed by Alston (1985; 1989a, chap. 12; 1989b). Alston claims that the threatening circularity "puts no limits whatever on the beliefs that can be justified, nor does it limit what can be known" (1989a, p. 349). Even so, that circularity precludes an effective, non-questionbegging reason for thinking we have ontological knowledge or ontologically reliable justification. This is the main concern of the argument under scrutiny.

dicament, is effectively unanswerable for us. This is the gist of premise 3. It bears on each of the realist's familiar epistemic bases: for example, reliability of cognitive processes, predictive theoretical success relative to our experience, and inference to the best explanation relative to our experience. The pressing question is: What non-questionbegging epistemic reason have we to think that (a) our cognitive processes such as memory or perception, (b) predictive theoretical success relative to experience, or (c) inference to the best explanation relative to experience ever provides accurate indications of a conceiving-independent world? I shall return to this issue presently, with special attention to (c).

The conclusion of argument 1 through 5 is not that we cannot have, do not have, or even do not know that we have, ontological knowledge. It rather is that we cannot effectively discern that we have such knowledge. (The parallel argument concludes that we cannot effectively discern that we have objectively true ontological belief.) The argument's conclusion, as stated, avoids currently irrelevant debate over the exact conditions for knowledge and epistemic justification.

Many epistemologists settle for an *internalist* justification-condition for knowledge that does not require effective discernment of objective truth. Some familiar internalist conditions for justification appeal to one or more of the following: internal coherence of one's beliefs, best available explanation of one's experiences, and agreement with "common sense." The argument 1 through 5 allows for internalist approaches to justification, so long as they do not claim to meet the demand for an effective reason in support of the truth of realism. The argument challenges only the view that we can have non-questionbegging epistemic reasons favoring a claim to ontological knowledge. *If* we demand that genuine ontological knowledge requires effective discernment of conceiving-independent truth, the argument 1 through 5 will challenge such knowledge. I shall avoid, however, currently irrelevant conceptual disputes about the exact conditions for knowledge and justification.[25]

The argument 1 through 5 does not rest on the familiar, but dubious, skeptical assumption that knowledge-relevant evidence for a proposition, *P*, must logically entail that *P*.[26] It also avoids the highly questionable assumption that to have knowledge-relevant evidence, one must know that one has such evidence. The latter assumption would amount to an implausible epistemic level-confusion. The argument does not rest on any special requirements for epistemic justification. It is compatible even with a fallibilist approach to justification allowing that all, or at least most, of one's justified beliefs are actually false. This is one of the argument's virtues: It avoids controversy over what exactly epistemic justification requires.

25. For indications of the extensiveness of these conceptual disputes, see Shope (1983), Moser (1989, 1990b), and Alston (1989a, chaps. 4, 7, 9).

26. This questionable assumption evidently underlies the defense of skepticism in Stroud (1984). For support for this claim, see Moser (1990c). Cf. Heil (1987).

The argument 1 through 5 relies on a notion of "effectively discerning" conceiving-independent truth. We cannot effectively rely on our eyesight to test the objective reliability of our own eyesight. The familiar Snellen test for visual acuity thus cannot effectively measure objectively reliable vision. I shall briefly develop this point to illustrate how effective discernment of conceiving-independent truth is typically unavailable.

The familiar Snellen chart tests the function of the fovea, the most sensitive part of the retina. Clinical use of this chart assumes that the component letters, 'E', 'F', 'P', 'T', and so on—which subtend an angle of five minutes of arc at the eye's nodal point—can be identified "appropriately" by the "normal eye." (Incidentally, many people can resolve letters subtending a smaller visual angle; accordingly, the letters on some Snellen charts are designed to subtend an angle of only four minutes.) Tests are typically given at a distance of six meters, or twenty feet. At this distance, the light rays from the chart's letters are roughly parallel, and human perceivers do not—or at least should not—need to strive to focus. If perceivers seated six meters from the chart read the line of letters subtending a visual angle of five minutes at six meters, we say that their vision is 6/6, or (in the foot-oriented U.S.) 20/20. The numerator of the fraction indicates the distance at which the test is given; the denominator denotes the distance at which the smallest letters read subtend a visual angle of five minutes.

We cannot plausibly hold that 6/6 vision, by the standard of the Snellen test, qualifies automatically as objectively reliable vision—vision conducive to objectively true visual beliefs. Testing for visual acuity relies on a standard of "normal vision" determined by reference to how the "typical human eye" actually operates in resolving the Snellen letters. The standard set by the subtending of a visual angle of five minutes arises from what is, liberally speaking, visually typical among the community of human visual perceivers. "Typical" human perceivers, loosely speaking, clearly see—without blurring, fuzziness, or duplication—three bars of an inverted 'E' when they are standing six meters from the Snellen chart. Such visual experience, according to the Snellen test, is the standard for "normal vision."

Vision normal by the Snellen standard does not automatically qualify as objectively reliable or truth-conducive in a way pertinent to agnosticism about realism. The Snellen standard for normal vision is based loosely on an assumed statistical average concerning human visual perceivers, not on considerations purporting to indicate objective reliability of vision. An agnostic will naturally question whether that statistical average is ever a reliable guide to conceiving-independent reality. It is doubtful that we have any non-questionbegging epistemic reason to hold that it is thus reliable. We cannot presume the reliability of our vision to deliver non-questionbegging epistemic reasons in favor of the reliability of our vision.

Standards for discerning correctness set by the Snellen test do not transfer automatically to serve as the desired standards for testing correctness regarding conceiving-independent matters. The Snellen test does rely on standards for discerning "correct" vision; and it may be tempting to assume that our cognitive processes, with respect to their relaying conceiving-independent matters, admit of noncircular testing for correctness. When, however, we inquire about the objective reliability of our cognitive processes, we lack a noncircular means of testing. We are then asking about a relation between our cognitive processes and an objective realm—a relation that does not admit of noncircular testing by reliance on the cognitive processes in question.

We cannot effectively rely on the deliverances of the sources of our evidence (for example, perception, memory, introspection, common sense, intuition, testimony) to test the reliability of those sources regarding their accessing conceiving-independent facts. Appeal to the deliverances of those sources would beg a key question now against an inquirer doubtful of the reliability of those deliverances and sources. The evidential sources in question need testing, with respect to their reliability, in order to provide non-questionbegging evidence for a realist's claim to ontological knowledge. A realist, we noted, typically claims to know conceiving-independent facts involving essences or objects. A doubtful inquirer will naturally demand an effective epistemic reason for the realist's claim. A questionbegging reason will settle nothing in this philosophical dispute.

The argument 1 through 5 for ontological agnosticism applies to a wide range of positions commonly called 'realism'. This range includes not only realism about Aristotelian essences but also each of the following species of realism: *weak* realism (that is, something objectively exists independently of conceiving); *commonsense* realism (that is, tokens of most current observable common sense and scientific physical types objectively exist independently of conceiving); and *scientific* realism (that is, tokens of most current unobservable scientific physical types objectively exist independently of conceiving).[27] Michael Devitt claims that weak realism is "so weak as to be uninteresting" (1984, p. 22; 1991b, p. 23–24). Even if it is, this is just so much coincidental biography. It does not excuse realists now from delivering non-questionbegging epistemic reasons in support of weak realism.

Realists cannot plausibly follow Devitt in appealing just to our current science to settle epistemological debates about realism. Realists must, to defend against agnostics, explain how our current science gives us the needed effective epistemic reason in favor of realism. It settles no philosophical questions simply to say, with Devitt, that "scepticism [regarding knowledge of conceiving-independent facts] is simply uninteresting: it throws the baby out with the bath water" (1984, p. 63; 1991b, p. 75). One pressing question is whether realists actually have a real baby—that is, effectively supportable ontological knowledge—to throw out. We cannot simply beg this question, if we wish to make genuine philosophical progress.

27. On such species of realism, see Devitt (1984, p. 22; 1991a, pp. 44–47; 1991b, p. 23). Even if, as Devitt notes, realism is nonepistemic and nonsemantic in what it claims, proponents must now provide non-questionbegging epistemic support for realism or, alternatively, make some concession to agnostics.

A likely realist reply appeals to considerations of best explanation of experience to support realism about physical objects. (We could formulate a parallel argument in support of essence-realism.) The argument runs, in outline, as follows:

1. We sometimes have determinate contents in our perceptual experiences: specifically, contents including apparent physical objects, that is, contents having objectlike features.
2. These contents are apparently involuntary, that is, (unlike the contents of voluntary imagination) apparently lacking creative input from us or from any other deceptive mechanism; at least, we have no indication in our experience of their being subjectively created.
3. Hence, the best explanation of these objectlike contents is that their occurrence comes not (at least not *just*) from within, but from corresponding external physical objects.
4. We are epistemically justified in believing what best explains the contents of our perceptual experiences.
5. Hence, we are epistemically justified in affirming the existence of external physical objects, at least those corresponding to some of our objectlike experiential contents.

As far as a defense of realism goes, this argument makes a long story very short.[28] It will serve, however, as an illustration of a likely line of reply from some realists. We may grant realists premise 4 if only for the sake of argument. Perhaps realists will regard that premise as supportable on the basis of their *notion* of epistemic justification. Even so, the argument attracts fire on other fronts.

Regarding premise 3, an agnostic can counter that just as we have no non-questionbegging indication in experience of an internal source for the objectlike contents, so also we have no non-questionbegging indication in experience of an external source. So far as experience itself goes, the issue is altogether undecided: We have a stalemate with effective evidence lacking on both sides of the issue. It seems, then, that the evidentially best explanation of objectlike experiential content will remain neutral on the question of an external source. At least, realists need to address the worry that experience itself indicates neither an internal nor an external source. Agnostics will take the apparent lack of such an indication to lend credibility to agnosticism. They will also question any assumption that if experiential contents have an internal source, there will be an experiential indication of this.

28. For a more detailed presentation of the case for realism based on explanatory considerations, see Moser (1989, chaps. 2–4) and Alan Goldman (1988, chaps. 9, 13). For other presentations of realism based on explanatory considerations, see Russell (1927a, chap. 20), Ayer (1973, chap. 5), Mackie (1976, chap. 2), Cornman (1980), Almeder (1992, chap. 4), and Carruthers (1992, chaps. 11, 12). For objections to the use of inference to the best explanation to support realism, see van Fraassen (1980, chap. 1; 1989, chaps. 6, 7); cf. Cartwright (1983, pp. 4–18) and Watkins (1984, pp. 58–67).

A related agnostic worry is this: As far as our (effectively) justifiable beliefs go, why must there be an explanation at all of our objectlike experiential contents, or at least an explanation that goes beyond neutrality on the issue of an external source for those contents? Why cannot our justifiable beliefs include a description of our objectlike contents, but remain neutral on their sources' being external or internal? Realists must explain why justification requires an explanation of the sort favorable to realism. Merely stipulative requirements on justification and explanation will not offer a challenge to, or even a defense against, agnostics. For any stipulative definition of 'justification' (say, a definition supporting premise 4), agnostics will request a non-questionbegging epistemic reason to hold that satisfaction of that definition is (sometimes) a reliable means to conceiving-independent matters.

Realists have a familiar reply now, a reply that appeals to a principle of rationality supposedly known a priori. The principle is: If we have experiential content including an apparent *X*, and we have no indication that this content comes simply from within or from some other source different from an *X*, then it is epistemically reasonable for us to affirm the existence of an independent, objective *X*. If this principle comes simply from definitional fiat, agnostics can allow realists this self-serving definition of 'epistemically reasonable'; for this definition of 'reasonable' lacks argumentative cogency against agnosticism. This definition comes with no effective challenge to, or defense against, agnostics.

Agnostics demand an effective epistemic reason in favor of realism, and mere definitional fiat fails to deliver. A realist's stipulative definition of reasonableness neglects agnostics' concerns represented by the argument formulated previously for ontological agnosticism. A stipulative definition will not itself deliver the needed non-questionbegging epistemic reason, given the open question whether that definition is a reliable means to conceiving-independent matters.

Enter the synthetic a priori. A realist turned rationalist will offer the foregoing principle of rationality as a substantive, nondefinitional truth known a priori. If this move is indeed available, we cannot quickly undercut the argument for realism from explanatory considerations. We can, however, plausibly shift a large, now self-imposed burden to the pertinent realists. They now owe us not only a defensible account of the synthetic a priori but also a non-questionbegging defense of the view that the disputed principle of rationality is actually a synthetic a priori truth. Agnostics can plausibly withhold judgment on the conclusion of the argument in question until that burden is discharged.

We cannot be very hopeful toward a realist's rationalist effort to sustain the synthetic a priori. As noted by Ayer and Waismann, it is unclear, if not simply mysterious, how propositions true or false in virtue of nondefinitional considerations can have epistemic warrant independent of any experiential considerations.[29] Some special kind of evidence or cognitive faculty will have

29. See Ayer (1946, chap. 4) and Waismann (1965, chap. 3). For further doubts about the synthetic a priori, see C. I. Lewis (1923), Schlick (1930), and Swinburne (1975). The later Wittgenstein's view of seemingly synthetic a priori propositions as conventional rules of grammar, or norms of representation, will obviously not support the cause of realism. On Wittgenstein's view, see Baker and Hacker (1985, pp. 338–347), Shanker (1987, pp. 274–288), and Baker (1988, pp. 256–267).

to provide such warrant. The fundamental problem is not simply that we lack reason to think that we have such evidence or such a faculty; it rather is that we lack specific constitutive conditions for our having such evidence or such a faculty. Even if there are such synthetic a priori truths as 'Nothing is both red and green all over at the same time', it will still be an open question whether principles of rationality qualify as synthetic a priori. In addition, agnostics will raise this pressing issue: What non-questionbegging epistemic reason have we to hold that one's preferred source of synthetic a priori knowledge is actually a reliable means to conceiving-independent matters? (This issue for the synthetic a priori recurs in the following subsection.)

We have reached the point where realists must be rationalists, committed to synthetic a priori truths about rationality, to challenge or even to defend against agnostics. Realists now seem to be in a troublesome corner. Agnostics have chased realists into that corner, but have not themselves been reasoned into any such corner. Realists have not yet delivered the needed non-questionbegging reason for their realism. This consideration bears favorably on the case for agnosticism.

Realists can question the following apparent assumption of the previous agnostic argument: If you have no effective evidence for or against realism, then you epistemically should withhold judgment on realism. Realists can offer this alternative: If you have no effective evidence for or against a proposition, you epistemically may affirm that proposition. Here we have a nonpragmatic analogue of William James's nonevidentialist principle of the "Will to Believe" (1896). The principle at hand apparently needs some qualification to exclude empirical propositions about which we lack available scientific evidence (for example, "the number of sizeable craters on Pluto is *X*"). Qualifications aside, realists can add that we are epistemically justified in accepting many propositions for which we lack effective evidence, including such apparently undeniable Cartesian propositions as "I am thinking" and "I am conscious."

We should avoid, as suggested earlier, irrelevant conceptual disputes over the exact conditions for epistemic justification. It would be preferable also to avoid questions about the exact significance of the previous, semantically slippery Cartesian propositions, especially familiar complex questions about the exact significance of 'I' in such propositions. Granting realists a liberal Jamesean concept of justification, we may reformulate the key agnostic assumption as follows:

> If you have no effective evidence for or against realism, then you epistemically should not presume that you can effectively challenge agnostics or even effectively defend your realism against agnostics on epistemic grounds.

This principle drives the previous agnostic argument and stays above the fray over purely conceptual matters about justification and knowledge.

Even if there are useful liberal notions of justification permitting endorsement of ontological realism, this consideration is irrelevant to the agnostic argument. The central issue is whether realists have any effective challenge to, or defense against, agnostics about realism. The liberal Jamesean line apparently concedes that, on the basis of pro-realist evidence, no effective defense against agnostics is actually forthcoming. So much the better, then, for agnosticism. (Recall that effective reasons must be non-questionbegging epistemic reasons.)

A realist's offense can continue, asking about the status of the premises in the previous agnostic argument. Must not agnostics assume knowledge of the objective truth of the relevant premises to deliver a forceful agnostic conclusion? Are agnostics thus forced to presume knowledge of ontological truths to challenge claims to such knowledge? Can agnostics avoid this threat of inconsistency? These rhetorical questions are too quick, as they overlook that agnostics, in the tradition of various Pyrrhonian skeptics (for example, Sextus Empiricus), can consistently argue via a *reductio* against realists.[30]

An agnostic's *reductio* strategy claims that on assumptions made by typical realists, we cannot have an effective challenge to, or defense against, agnosticism about realism. Given such a strategy, an agnostic need not countenance ontological knowledge to challenge such knowledge. An agnostic can consistently hold that, on typical realist (defining) criteria for justification, we are justified in endorsing the premises of the previous agnostic argument. This *reductio* strategy does not entail (or otherwise indicate) that the realist criteria in question are suitably effective, or non-questionbegging, as an avenue to ontological knowledge. An agnostic thus has plenty of room to escape the threatening inconsistency.

Agnostics can consistently shun endorsement of any form of ontological idealism entailing that the world is unfeatured or does not exist apart from our conceptual activity. Citing Berkeley as a proponent, Nicholas Rescher has characterized such idealism as idealism "of the traditional *ontological* type, holding that the material objects that all too evidently populate the physical world are only illusory and non-existent as such, but are mere 'works of the mind' (*entia rationis*)."[31] From an agnostic's standpoint of questions about reliability, ontological idealism is, like realism, just another presumptuous ontology. Idealism attributes to human conceivers a world-constituting role that, by any effective, non-questionbegging epistemological standard, is gratuitous—at least from the standpoint of typical agnostic questions about reliability of cognitively relevant processes.

Idealists committed to the following assumption will clearly face, from an agnostic's standpoint, a problem analogous to that troubling realists: It is (weakly) conceiving-independently the case that certain conceptual activity constitutes the world, including all material objects. An agnostic can subject

30. On *reductio* strategies in Pyrrhonian skepticism, see Striker (1980) and Annas and Barnes (1985, pp. 14, 45, 49–50, 60). Cf. Barnes (1990a, pp. 90–93).

31. See Rescher (1973a, pp. 1, 25, 192; 1991). Rescher's own *conceptual* idealism does not entail ontological idealism. Because ontological idealism is almost universally shunned by contemporary philosophers, and admits of a treatment analogous to an agnostic's treatment of realism, I shall treat it briefly.

that ontological assumption to questions paralleling agnostic questions facing realism, with a similar result about the absence of non-questionbegging supporting epistemic reasons. (The following subsection illustrates distinctively agnostic questions.)

Even aside from the assumption just noted, agnostic questions about reliability of cognitively relevant processes will bear on any cognitive faculty or source used by idealists to buttress their antirealism. The result is that idealists, like realists, will fail to deliver the non-questionbegging epistemic support demanded by agnostics. Ontological agnostics thus can avoid ontological idealism.

B. Refining the Agnostic Argument

The foregoing agnostic argument will benefit from specification of the agnostic questions begged by opponents of agnosticism. We begin with some stage-setting. Suppose that you are a realist claiming knowledge that external, conceiving-independent objects exist, and that you take such knowledge to entail that it is objectively the case that external objects exist. Suppose also that you fancy yourself as having a cogently sound argument for your claim to knowledge that external objects exist.

Your argument, let us suppose, takes this general form:

1. If one's belief that *P* has feature *F*, then one knows that *P*.
2. My belief that external objects exist has *F*.
3. Hence, I know that external objects exist.

Even critics of realism may grant premise 1, if only for the sake of argument. That premise may be just a straightforward implication of what a realist means by 'knows that *P*'.

Feature *F* can incorporate any of a number of familiar well-foundedness properties: either (a) suitable doxastic coherence; (b) maximal explanatory efficacy; (c) undefeated self-evidentness; (d) consistent predictive success; (e) uncontested communal acceptance; (f) causal sustenance by such a belief-forming process as perception, memory, introspection, intuition, or testimony; (g) adequate theoretical elegance in terms of such "virtuous" characteristics as simplicity and comprehensiveness; (h) survival value in the evolutionary scheme of things; or (i) some combination of (a) through (h). Such well-foundedness properties cannot, however, conceptually exhaust *F*; by hypothesis one's knowing that *P*, unlike those well-foundedness properties, entails its objectively being the case that *P*.

If knowledge involves more than objectively true belief, as it does on standard conceptions since Plato's *Theaetetus*, then *F* will be a complex property—involving the property of being objectively true plus some additional property. The additional property, on standard conceptions of knowledge, incorporates a well-foundedness feature of some sort (and sometimes a no-defeaters restriction on that feature to handle the Gettier problem). Let us call this *the well-*

foundedness component of F. A well-foundedness feature serves typically to distinguish knowledge from true belief due simply to such coincidental phenomena as lucky guesses. In this respect, such a feature may serve to make a belief "likely to be true" to some extent. An *internalist* well-foundedness feature is accessible—directly or indirectly—to the knower for whom it yields likelihood of truth; an *externalist* well-foundedness feature is not.

If, as standardly assumed, knowledge that *P* entails that it is objectively the case—or objectively true—that *P*, the relevant kind of likelihood of *truth* must entail likelihood of what is objectively true, or objectively the case. So, whether internalist or externalist, a well-foundedness feature must yield likelihood of what is objectively (or conceiving-independently) the case. It must, in other words, indicate with some degree of likelihood what is the case conceiving-independently. A well-foundedness component of *F* violating this requirement will fail to distinguish knowledge from true belief due simply to such coincidental phenomena as lucky guesses.

Premise 2 generates a problem motivating agnosticism. It affirms (1) that your belief that external objects exist is objectively true, and (if you hold that knowledge has a well-foundedness component) (2) that a well-foundedness feature indicates with some degree of likelihood that external objects exist. An agnostic can plausibly raise this question:

> *Q1*. What non-questionbegging epistemic reason, if any, have we to affirm that your belief that external objects exist is objectively true?

If you are a typical realist, committed to a well-foundedness component of knowledge, you will appeal to your preferred well-foundedness component of *F* to try to answer *Q1*. In particular, you will answer that the satisfaction of the conditions for that well-foundedness component provides the needed reason to affirm that your belief is true. This answer to *Q1* is not surprising, given the aforementioned assumption that a well-foundedness component yields likelihood of truth.

For any well-foundedness component a realist offers, an agnostic can raise this challenge:

> *Q2*. What non-questionbegging epistemic reason, if any, have we to affirm that the satisfaction of the conditions for that well-foundedness component of *F* is actually indicative, to any extent, of what is objectively the case?

Realists might reply that it is true in virtue of what they *mean* by 'indicative of what is objectively the case' that their preferred well-foundedness component is indicative of what is objectively the case. This move uses definitional fiat to try to rebuff agnostics, but actually fails to answer agnostics' main concern.

We can put the main concern more exactly:

> *Q3*. What non-questionbegging epistemic reason, if any, have we to affirm that the satisfaction of the conditions for a preferred well-foundedness

> component of *F*—including the satisfaction of conditions definitive of what a realist means by 'indicative of what is objectively the case'—is ever a genuinely reliable means of representational access to what is objectively the case?

Equivalently, what non-questionbegging epistemic reason, if any, have we to affirm that some claim satisfying the conditions for a preferred well-foundedness component (for example, the claim that external objects exist) is actually objectively true? We can grant realists their preferred definition of 'indicative of what is the case', but then follow up with *Q3*. An agnostic may begin with *Q1*, but will plausibly move to *Q3* once a realist appeals to a well-foundedness component of *F*. It would be a shallow agnostic indeed who failed to regard *Q3* as just as troublesome for realism as *Q1* is.

Clearly, your invoking your preferred well-foundedness component to defend realism against *Q3* would be questionbegging. The reliability of your preferred well-foundedness component is precisely what is under question now, and begging this question offers no cogent support for realism. Perhaps given your preferred well-foundedness component, that well-foundedness component is itself well-founded. This consideration, however, does nothing to answer *Q3*. *Q3* asks what non-questionbegging epistemic reason, if any, we have to regard your preferred well-foundedness component as ever being a reliable means to objective truth. In effect: *Apart from* appeal to (the reliability of) your preferred well-foundedness component, what reason have we to regard that component as ever being a reliable means to objective truth—for example, regarding your belief that external objects exist?

An agnostic's use of *Q3* allows for fallibilism about well-foundedness: the view that a well-founded belief can be false. Further, an agnostic's use of *Q3* does not assume that evidence on which a claim is well-founded must logically entail that claim. An agnostic's use of *Q3* is, moreover, neutral on purely conceptual disputes over the exact conditions for epistemic justification. These are some virtues of an agnostic's use of *Q3* to challenge realism.

Suppose that you are a realist wielding argument 1 through 3, along with the standard view that *F* has a well-foundedness component. You will then hold that your belief that external objects exist illustrates a case where a belief's meeting the conditions for your preferred well-foundedness component is an objectively true belief. You will then hold, given premise 2, that your belief that external objects exist is objectively true, and that your preferred well-foundedness component of *F* is satisfied by an objectively true belief in this case. You will, however, still owe agnostics a non-questionbegging epistemic reason for thinking that your preferred well-foundedness component of *F* is, in this case, a genuinely reliable means to objectively true belief.

A realist might seek to disarm agnostics by claiming that our concept of an external object is fully constituted, or wholly determined, by certain well-foundedness conditions involving one or more of the well-foundedness properties noted previously. The claim here is that certain conditions for well-founded ascription of our concept of an external object fully determine that concept. This claim entails a kind of verificationism about our notion of an external object and is not equivalent to the previous view that appealed to considerations of meaning regarding 'indication of what is objectively true'.

It seems, in reply, that our everyday notion of an external object logically outstrips various standard well-foundedness conditions for that notion. Our typical concept of an external object seemingly involves, for instance, the condition that any object falling under it does not perish whenever one looks away from it, but would exist even when unperceived. The condition that an external object would exist even when unperceived seems not to be logically entailed by various standard well-foundedness conditions for our typical notion of an external object. For example, maximally effective explanation of (the origin of) our common perceptual experiences does not logically require that there be objects that exist when unperceived.

Even if well-foundedness conditions fully determined our typical notion of an external object, it would still be an open question whether one's having our typical notion of an external object involves one's actually satisfying those well-foundedness conditions with one's belief that external objects exist. If those conditions entail the subjunctive condition just noted, an agnostic will plausibly demand a non-questionbegging epistemic reason to think it is ever actually satisfied; in that case, the now familiar worries motivating agnosticism will resurface. Realists, in any case, are not typically verificationists about their notion of an external object.

We may return, then, to an agnostic's main challenge, in *Q3*, for realists to deliver a non-questionbegging epistemic reason. Such a reason will not simply *presume* a realism-favoring answer to an agnostic's familiar questions about reliability. Some of these familiar questions concern the reliability, in any actual case, of our belief-forming processes—for example, perception, introspection, judgment, memory, testimony—that sometimes produce belief in the existence of external objects.

Some other familiar questions concern the reliability, in any actual case, of suitably coherent, explanatorily efficacious, or predictively successful belief regarding the existence of external objects. Each of the well-foundedness properties noted previously will attract such a question about reliability from an agnostic. An agnostic will thus be unmoved by observations concerning the simplicity and comprehensiveness offered by realism about external objects. The application of *Q3* will ask for a non-questionbegging epistemic reason to affirm that the simplicity and comprehensiveness offered by such realism are ever reliable means to objectively true belief. Further, any higher-order use of a well-foundedness component—to support a well-foundedness component—meets the same fate as first-order use; for *Q3* applies equally to any higher-order use. Lacking answers to an agnostic's questions, we cannot cogently infer that realism about external objects has been substantiated.

An agnostic is not guilty of this empty challenge: Give me a cogent argument, but do not use any premises. The challenge is rather: Give me a cogent, non-questionbegging epistemic reason to hold that your belief that external objects exist is a case where a belief satisfying your preferred well-foundedness component is an objectively true belief. The demand is not that realists forgo use of premises; it rather is just that realists forgo use of questionbegging premises: that is, premises that beg the questions about objective reliability motivating agnosticism. *Q1* through *Q3* illustrate some standard agnostic questions. A questionbegging argument from a realist will not even begin to approach cogency for an agnostic. Mere soundness of argument, then, is not at issue; cogent, non-questionbegging soundness is.

One familiar consideration—perhaps employed only for the sake of argument by agnostics—indicates that an agnostic wielding *Q3* will not be successfully answered by a realist. Cognitively relevant access to anything by us humans depends on such belief-forming processes as perception, introspection, judgment, memory, testimony, intuition, and common sense. Such processes are subject to question via *Q3*, and cannot themselves deliver non-questionbegging support for their own reliability. This consideration applies equally to any process or faculty (for example, rational intuition) assumed to deliver synthetic a priori knowledge. We evidently cannot, as noted before, assume a position independent of our own cognitively relevant processes to deliver a non-questionbegging indication of the reliability of those processes. We can now see how this human cognitive predicament motivates agnosticism.

A pragmatic defense of realism, in terms of a belief's overall utility, fares no better than the well-foundedness properties noted previously. A variation on *Q3* applies straightforwardly: What non-questionbegging epistemic reason, if any, have we to affirm that a belief's overall pragmatic utility is ever a genuinely reliable means of access to what is objectively the case? Clearly, it does no good here to note that it is pragmatically useful to regard pragmatic utility as a reliable means to objective truth.

An agnostic, once again, seeks non-questionbegging epistemic reasons. The pertinent issue concerns the (known) correctness of realism, not whether belief in realism is useful. Given the aforementioned human cognitive predicament, we can offer little hope for the needed non-questionbegging support on pragmatic grounds. Pragmatic support for realism is one thing; non-questionbegging epistemic support, another. An agnostic demands, but despairs of achieving, the latter. The burden of cogent argument is now squarely on the realist's shoulders, as the realist is committed to a positive ontological thesis.

Inability to deliver the needed non-questionbegging reason does nothing to undercut an agnostic's challenge. It rather undercuts claims to non-questionbegging epistemic support for realism in debates with agnostics. Is it, however, conceptually possible for one to produce the demanded non-questionbegging reasons for realism? This depends on what exactly is under question by an agnostic. A realist might aspire to an a priori proof that believers have a faculty that delivers objective truth in at least some cases. The aim of this proof might be to show that it is (more than pragmatically) self-defeating to deny realism.

Thoroughgoing cognitive-meaning and inference agnostics would officially be unmoved by *any* proof; for they question whether any truth-claim is genuinely meaningful and whether any inference is actually reliable. (One might, of course, be a thoroughgoing inference agnostic without being a thoroughgoing cognitive-meaning agnostic.) Such agnostics cannot—conceptually cannot—be given non-questionbegging evidence from any kind of argument; use of arguments will always beg certain questions raised by those agnostics. We simply cannot establish claims to the satisfaction of such thoroughgoing agnostics because they call into question what we must use to establish any claim: meaningful truth-claims and inference.

On pain of inconsistency, thoroughgoing agnostics must refrain from claims to meaningful truth-claims and to reliable inferences—at least apart from merely *reductio* strategies that contribute to their agnosticism. They can consistently offer neither a claim to the reliability of *reductio* inferences nor a claim to the meaningfulness of an agnostic truth-claim about which someone might be agnostic. Still, they can issue challenges, including challenges that one conceptually cannot meet. Even if these challenges (semantically or pragmatically) "presuppose" certain claims, agnostics need not make any unconditional commitment to the truth of what is thereby presupposed; they need not grant that presuppositions are objectively true or otherwise favorable to the cause of realism.[32] Agnostics can consistently proceed just "for the sake of challenge."

We might ask thoroughgoing cognitive-meaning agnostics whether their challenges are meaningful at all, even if not cognitively meaningful. Even if they remain uncommitted on this issue, their challenges could still bear on proponents of objective knowledge, insofar as those proponents understand their challenges. What agnostics happen to think about their own challenges does not necessarily determine the bearing of those challenges on others.

In issuing challenges, agnostics appear not to be simply making noise, but to be producing expressions meaningful in some way. From the standpoint of practice, they evidently proceed *as if* some expressions (namely, their challenges) are meaningful in some way. An alternative here is complete silence, but agnostics issuing challenges are not completely silent. These practical considerations do not, however, yield an epistemological challenge to agnosticism or an answer to an agnostic's challenges concerning non-questionbegging epistemic reasons. We cannot answer a challenge by faulting its carrier. At most we can say this: Because agnostics issuing challenges proceed as if some expressions are meaningful, they cannot consistently object to others proceeding likewise. (Chapter 2 returns to the role of meaning in epistemology.)

The conceptual impossibility of one's effectively meeting a thoroughgoing agnostic's challenge—say, about reliability of inference—does not entail or otherwise indicate that some inference is actually reliable. The fact that certain answers must beg questions against certain agnostics does not guarantee that those answers yield objective truth or are otherwise commendable. Conceivably, one's inferences are unreliable and one is conceptually unable to satisfy a thoroughgoing inference agnostic. Thoroughgoing inference agnostics, more-

32. On some relevant notions of presupposition, see Stalnaker (1972, 1974), Levinson (1983, chap. 4), and Soames (1989).

over, will find it arbitrary not to question the reliability of inferences once we raise questions about the reliability of beliefs and various belief-forming processes.

In challenging realism and idealism, this chapter has not recommended thoroughgoing agnosticism, or any unconditional agnosticism for that matter. It has, however, supported *conditional* ontological agnosticism: the view that if we seek agnostic-resistant non-questionbegging evidence for our ontological claims, we shall not succeed. I introduced the possibility of unsatisfiable thoroughgoing agnostics to motivate this important question: What is the significance of agnostic challenges for philosophical questions and claims? Let us turn to this issue.

1.8 Philosophy after Agnosticism

Ontological agnosticism about realism allows for the intelligibility of typical realist theses. What is intelligible for us can, we have seen, outstrip what is effectively answerable or testable by us. This chapter has shown that some major ontological questions can be intelligible but not effectively answerable—not answerable without begging some questions under dispute by ontological agnostics.

Ontological agnosticism does not aim to revise ordinary language by replacing its apparently realist assumptions. It seeks rather to curb the philosophical pretensions of realists and idealists aspiring to challenge or to defend against agnostics. We may retain ordinary language, but we are not entitled to assume that we have agnostic-resistant non-questionbegging epistemic evidence for claims about conceiving-independent facts.

Similarly, ontological agnostics must be cautious of philosophical pretense. They must resist the assumption that in all possible contexts of debate we shall have non-questionbegging evidence for thinking that we cannot have non-questionbegging evidence for claims entailing conceiving-independent facts. What is questionbegging is context-relative, that is, relative to the questions and assumptions actually at work in a context of debate. Ontological agnostics must also avoid, under all conditions, any assumption of non-questionbegging evidence for claims entailing conceiving-independent truths. They cannot consistently embrace such an assumption even for their own position. Instead, they must settle for contributing an instructive challenge about reasons—typically based on a *reductio* strategy—rather than an effective ontology.

Do ontological questions about realism and idealism merit our pursuit, even when they are effectively unanswerable? The answer apparently depends on the effects of that pursuit and the purposes we actually have (or at least evidently have). A process of pursuing effectively unanswerable questions can be fruitful in various ways, as the history of mathematics and cosmology illustrates at various points. In any case, one might pursue ontological questions via standards admittedly questionbegging against typical agnostics. One might, for example, be content to have one's ontological theses satisfy certain standards (for example, standards represented in ordinary language) that obviously fall short of agnostic-resistance. Unlike Richard Rorty (1982, pp. xxi-xliv), then, I shall not recommend that we dispense with the traditional ontological questions of philosophy, or that we replace philosophy as ontology with the comparing and contrasting of cultural traditions.

If we cannot have agnostic-resistant non-questionbegging epistemic reasons for realism or idealism, why should we care at all about such reasons? Why not simply change the subject to reasons of a different sort? We should care, on two counts, about the unavailability of agnostic-resistant non-questionbegging reasons for realism or idealism. First, some philosophers have suggested, against various skeptics, that they can support their realism or idealism with effective reasons.[33] Such philosophers must now counteract the main argument of this chapter. Second, we can benefit from an explanation of the kinds of reasons we can have for our claims within philosophy and without. Such an explanation will save us from gratuitous assumptions about the effectiveness of the reasons underlying our theories.

Whether we should change the subject to reasons other than agnostic-resistant non-questionbegging epistemic reasons will (given a certain notion of "should") depend on our purposes, including any purposes we have in discussing the nature of our reasons. So long as we are considering the antiskeptical philosophers just mentioned, we must attend to claims to agnostic-resistant non-questionbegging epistemic reasons. Suppose, however, that we accept the main lesson of this chapter and, as a result, decide not to wage losing battles against ontological agnostics. What then becomes of philosophy, after the acknowledged absence of agnostic-resistant reasons for ontological claims? The remainder of this book gives an answer.

Minimally, we should not regard our answers to philosophical 'what is *X*?' questions as supported by agnostic-resistant reasons that favor realism about essences or objects. This does not entail that our philosophical theses cannot be supported by reasons *at all*. Not all reasons are purportedly agnostic-resistant non-questionbegging epistemic reasons. The next chapter identifies a relevant kind of reason in connection with some problems of epistemology; it acknowledges a key role for semantic considerations in epistemology.

We shall see throughout subsequent chapters that philosophy can thrive—even as an explanatory discipline—under the influence of conditional ontological agnosticism. The goal will be to change the subject from agnostic-resistant reasons to a kind of support that is avowedly perspectival, relative to a theorist's

33. Notable attempts by realists to challenge skeptics include Moore (1939), Pollock (1967; 1986a, pp. 178–179), Lehrer (1974, chap. 10; 1990, chap. 9), Klein (1981), and Aune (1991). See also the works by the realists cited in note 28. None of these realists has effectively challenged the sort of ontological agnosticism presented in this chapter. I have critically discussed Moore's reply to skeptics in Moser (1994), and Pollock's reply in Moser (1988). See the Appendix for criticisms of appeals to interpretive charity to challenge skepticism.

(variable) semantic commitments and relevant purposes in theorizing. Changing the subject in that way entails that our avowed reasons and purposes in inquiry do not seek to answer an agnostic's typical questions. Whether our evidential support is *merely* perspectival, with respect to what it indicates, must remain as an ontological issue whose answer does not admit of agnostic-resistant support. The remainder of this book aims to lay foundations for a kind of philosophy directed away from losing battles against agnostics.

2

Justification, Meta-Epistemology, and Meaning

The conclusions in chapter 1 about non-questionbegging reasons for ontological truth-claims concern epistemic, or evidential, justification: the kind of justification appropriate to propositional knowledge. The conditional ontological agnosticism of chapter 1 gives rise to questions about the adequacy of the justificational standards, or principles, philosophers use to "justify" various philosophical views, including realism and idealism. Are those standards themselves adequate to achieve the epistemic ends for which they are formulated? If so, in virtue of what? This chapter pursues these questions. It identifies some epistemological dilemmas that require attention to meta-epistemology, or the epistemology of epistemology.

In particular, this chapter explains the importance to meta-epistemology of certain semantic considerations about epistemic justification. These semantic considerations, we shall see, identify some key constraints on explaining, evaluating, and arguing for justification, and on answers to questions about *correct* standards for such matters. They support *semantic foundationalism*: One's explaining, evaluating, and arguing for epistemic justification and one's answers to questions about correct standards for such matters properly end in considerations about an operative *notion* for one regarding epistemic justification. Semantic foundationalism, we shall see, fits with the conditional ontological agnosticism of chapter 1 and allows for an instructive kind of relativism about operative notions of justification.

2.1 Three Epistemological Projects

The theory of epistemically justified belief, according to the implicit assumptions of many epistemologists, has at least three main projects:

(a) the *semantic* project of specifying, in informative terms, what it means to say that something (for example, a proposition or a belief) is epistemically justified;

(b) the *explanatory* project of identifying informative explanatory conditions that state in nonepistemic terms when, or in virtue of what, a belief is justified; and
(c) the *evaluative* project of formulating standards for evaluating whether a particular belief is justified.

(Section 2.3 illustrates that another main epistemological project involves arguing for justification.) A proper understanding of how projects (a) through (c) relate to one another and of what constitutes the correctness of their solutions will help to solve some major problems in epistemology and in metaphilosophy. Talk of justification in this chapter will, unless otherwise noted, concern *epistemic* justification, the kind of justification appropriate to propositional knowledge.

The semantic project seeks to define the term 'epistemic justification' (or some synonymous term) by informative synonymous terms. This project, stated thus, is largely neutral on the controversial issue of what exactly constitutes synonymy. (The topic of synonymy itself must await sections 3.5 through 3.8, where Quine's qualms about meaning get due attention.) Some epistemologists construe the semantic project to require strictly defining conditions that are individually necessary and jointly sufficient for a belief's satisfying the schema 'Belief *B* is epistemically justified for person *S*'. Epistemologists divide, however, over the issue whether specification of a notion of epistemic justification requires an analysis or a strict definition via necessary and sufficient conditions. They also divide over the question whether we can adequately define 'epistemic justification' in nonepistemic terms. (On the latter question, see Moser 1989, pp. 38–44; 1990b.)

The explanatory project aims to identify informative explanatory conditions for justified belief. These explanatory conditions will ideally be in nonepistemic terms (at least according to some theorists) and will answer certain explanation-seeking questions about justified belief, questions that purportedly go beyond issues about the meaning of 'epistemic justification'. (We may now use 'explanation' loosely, to encompass answers to "understanding-seeking" what-questions, why-questions, and how-questions; chapter 5 examines conditions for explanation in general.) Explanatory conditions might include considerations about the sources of justified belief or about the extent of justified belief. Pertinent questions include: Are there any nonempirical sources of justified belief? If so, what are they, and how do they yield justification? Does justified belief extend to universal propositions? If so, how? (Some connections between explanation and definition will emerge later in this chapter; for now, we can leave the distinction rough.)

The evaluative project seeks criteria, or guidelines, for deciding whether a belief is justified. It aims to go beyond meaning and explanation, to a method for finding out what beliefs are justified: for evaluating whether certain beliefs actually have epistemic justification. Even if we have a definition of 'justification' and an explanation of the sources and the extent of justification, we may still lack effective standards for deciding what beliefs are actually justified. Our definitional and explanatory considerations about justification might be too general to serve effectively as guidelines for evaluating the presence of justification in particular cases. The evaluative project, according to some epistemologists, is not necessarily just the application of the results of the semantic or the explanatory project.[1]

Can we reduce the three projects to one? Verificationism about justification promotes such reduction by giving primacy to the evaluative project. It redefines the semantic and explanatory projects via the evaluative project. Such verificationism parallels more familiar verificationism about truth. The latter defines 'truth' by conditions for the *warranted assertibility* of a statement. Verificationism about justification likewise invokes conditions for warranted assertibility, but it does so to define 'justification'. Many proponents of verificationism about meaning in general would probably commit themselves to verificationism about the meaning of 'justification' in particular.[2]

Defining 'justification' in terms of the "warranted assertibility" of certain statements will not effectively accomplish the semantic project. The term 'warrant' is, for us, semantically too close to the term 'justification' to give an enlightening definition. In fact, this closeness risks circularity of definition. The evaluative project, in particular, makes ineliminable use of talk of justification and thus cannot settle the semantic project without definitional circularity. The semantic project is conceptually prior to the evaluative project. Justification verificationism is therefore an unhelpful approach to the semantic project. We cannot accomplish the semantic project simply by attending to the evaluative project.[3]

Justification verificationism fares no better with the explanatory project. If we explain what constitutes justification in terms of the conditions for the "warranted assertibility" of statements ascribing justification, we shall foster explanatory circularity resembling the circularity just shunned; for explaining what constitutes justification in terms of "warranted assertibility" conditions relies crucially on talk of *warrant*. The desired explanatory conditions must avoid such circularity to do effective explanatory work.

The explanatory project seeks, so far as is possible, an explanation in nonepistemic terms of what constitutes justification in general. The warranted assertibility conditions for statements ascribing justification do not characterize what constitutes the first-order justification ascribed by such statements. Those warranted assertibility conditions characterize higher-order justification: justification for ascribing justification to a statement. Such higher-order justi-

1. Some reliabilists, following Alvin Goldman (1979, pp. 1–2; 1980, pp. 28–29), treat the explanatory project as involving complex causal and historical considerations that preclude applicability for evaluation.

2. Proponents of verificationism about meaning are legion; they include Dummett (1978, pp. 17–18; 1991, pp. 317–321), Putnam (1983, p. xvi), Crispin Wright (1987, pp. 36–37), and Pollock (1974, pp. 17–18; 1986a, pp. 147–148). For relevant historical discussion, see Coffa (1991, Part II).

3. For more general problems facing recent verificationism about meaning, see Appiah (1986) and Moser (1988). For problems with earlier versions of verificationism, see Hempel (1950, 1951) and Munitz (1981, chap. 6).

fication applies to *epistemic* statements, statements that themselves ascribe justification. The conditions for such higher-order justification leave undetermined the justification for nonepistemic statements, such as ordinary empirical statements that do not ascribe justification.

The justification for *the statement that P is justified* does not entail justification for *P* itself; justified assertion can be false. This is an implication of any fallibilist approach to justification. It is unclear, then, how an appeal to assertibility conditions for justification-ascribing statements can adequately explain first-order justification. Because the explanatory project seeks an account of what constitutes justification in general, it pursues explanation of what constitutes *justification*, not just of what constitutes justified assertion that a statement is justified. The verificationism under scrutiny thus seems too limited to accomplish the explanatory project. We need an approach to the explanatory project that does not rest on talk of warrant or justification.

In sum, we cannot accomplish the semantic and explanatory projects simply by accomplishing the evaluative project. The evaluative project seeks standards for ascertaining whether a belief is justified. This project cannot settle the semantic project without threatening circularity, nor can it accomplish the explanatory project regarding justified nonepistemic, first-order statements. We thus should reject any view that redefines the semantic and explanatory projects by the evaluative project. The semantic project is conceptually prior to the evaluative project. What exactly does this mean, especially for the successful completion of the three projects? We turn now to a dilemma that highlights the urgency of this question.

2.2 An Epistemological Dilemma: Naivete or Circularity?

For any answer one gives to accomplish the evaluative project, we can raise this question: In virtue of what, if anything, is *that* answer adequate, at least for oneself, for discerning justified beliefs? In other words, in virtue of what, if anything, is that answer a *correct* solution to the evaluative project, at least for oneself? Perhaps one's solution is not adequate, or correct, at all. Even so, our question can take a modal form: In virtue of what can an answer be adequate, or correct? (For now, 'adequate' and 'correct' are interchangeable.)

Suppose that I formulate and accept a set of standards for evaluating whether a belief is justified. My evaluative epistemic standards will characteristically take this form:

> We may evaluate a (candidate) belief as epistemically justified if (and only if) that belief satisfies conditions *C*.

I might be a familiar empiricist whose evaluative standards invoke conditions regarding best available explanation of one's experiences; or I might be an equally familiar coherentist whose standards appeal to coherence of some sort among one's antecedent beliefs and candidates for belief.

Whatever my evaluative standards are, I shall face this question: In virtue of what, if anything, are my standards an adequate, or a correct, solution to the evaluative project, at least for myself? More specifically, what, if anything, constitutes the adequacy, or correctness, of my evaluative standards as principles for discerning justified beliefs, at least for myself?

Either I take the previous question seriously or I do not. If I do not, I shall disregard it as negligible, as not needing an answer. In that case, my acceptance of my standards for evaluating justification will be naive, or superficial, in at least one obvious respect. My acceptance will then be innocent of a cogent reply to a legitimate question about what, if anything, constitutes the adequacy, or correctness, of my epistemic standards. Call this *meta-epistemic naivete*. It is naivete about answering a question concerning the adequacy of one's epistemic standards. Such naivete allows for objectionable neglect of intelligible, legitimate questions about what, if anything, constitutes the correctness of one's epistemic standards.

Neglect here would indeed be objectionable, since affirmation that an epistemic standard, *E*, is a genuine solution to the evaluative project presupposes (for its being fully understood) affirmation that *E* is adequate, or correct, as a solution to that project. Even affirmation that *E* is an epistemically justifiable solution involves a notion of adequacy or correctness; it presupposes a claim to justifiable affirmation that *E* is an adequate, or correct, solution. A notion of correctness is presupposed because full understanding of a notion of a justifiable solution requires an answer to the following question in terms of correctness: Justifiable as what? The answer: As (probably) correct. We need, then, an account of what, if anything, constitutes adequacy, or correctness, of epistemic standards.

If I do take the previous question about adequacy seriously, I shall seek an answer to it. I shall then seek an account of what, if anything, constitutes the adequacy of my evaluative standards for discerning justified beliefs. If *E* is the set of my evaluative epistemic standards, I might appeal to a different set of evaluative epistemic standards, *E'*, to explain what constitutes the adequacy of *E*. This option will ultimately fail, however, for two reasons.

First, *E'* will face a direct analogue of the question facing *E*: In virtue of what, if anything, is *E'* adequate for discerning justified beliefs? Legitimate questions about what constitutes adequacy arise even at higher levels, indeed at every level. It does no good to invoke still another set of evaluative epistemic standards here. Such a pattern of reply will lead only to an endless regress of evaluative standards. One problem is that we finite humans do not have time to articulate an endless regress of standards when explaining adequacy of epistemic standards. The current reply thus fails as an account of our actually explaining adequacy. Another problem is that an endless answer to our question seems not to be a cogent answer. Such an answer seems too open-ended to offer a resolution of our question.[4]

4. I shall not pursue the exact reason for the latter point, as it would take us too far afield. For pertinent discussion on the analogous topic of endless regresses of justification, see Cornman (1980, pp. 135–138), Post (1987, pp. 87–91), and Moser (1985a, pp. 107–115; 1989, pp. 56–60).

The second reason for failure is more decisive. Standards for evaluating merely whether beliefs are justified—even beliefs about the justification of evaluative standards—do not themselves explain what constitutes the adequacy, or correctness, of an evaluative standard. Explanation of mere (evaluatable) justification is one thing; explanation of correctness, another. Verificationism about correctness seeks to collapse this distinction. For example, Michael Dummett's verificationism about meaning implies that we "must explain truth as attaching to a statement in some such way as that it does so when the statement either has or could have been verified" (1991, p. 318). Dummett's verificationism is doomed to failure here, because it construes verification in terms of an "acknowledged means of establishing a statement *as true*" (1991, p. 317; italics added). The relevant notion of verification thus presupposes a notion of truth; it does not define, or otherwise explain, that notion in terms of verification.

Typical talk of justification, like Dummett's talk of verification, presupposes talk of justification *as (likely to be) true*, or *as (probably) correct*. Such talk of justification thus does not enable us to sidestep questions about what constitutes correctness. We cannot effectively rely on a notion of correctness—even an implicit notion of correctness—to explain what constitutes correctness. Such a vacuous strategy would make our explanations uninformative and thus pointless. Conceptual circularity is, then, no promoter of effective explanation.

Consider another approach to our question about what constitutes adequacy of epistemic standards. Because, by hypothesis, I already accept a set of standards for discerning what is justified and what is not, I might invoke those very standards to explain what constitutes the adequacy of my standards for discerning justified beliefs. The general idea is this: If *E* is my evaluative standard for discerning justified beliefs, then if *E* meets its own requirements, it is an adequate, or correct, solution to the evaluative project, at least for me.

As noted previously, evaluative standards for discerning simply whether beliefs are justified—even beliefs about the justification of evaluative standards—do not themselves explain what constitutes the adequacy, or correctness, of an evaluative standard. What constitutes adequacy, or correctness, of a standard relative to the evaluative project is one thing; what constitutes mere justification of a standard is something else. Typical talk of justification of a standard presupposes a notion of correctness of a standard, at least insofar as full understanding of such talk requires a notion of likely, probable, or evident *correctness*. Answering questions about what constitutes correctness of standards by appeal to justification, confirmation, or verification of standards thus risks conceptual circularity.

Typical notions of justification, confirmation, and verification presuppose a notion of correctness in need of explanation. They presuppose a notion of correctness inasmuch as full understanding of them requires answers to these questions: Justification as what? Confirmation as what? Verification as what? The presupposed answers are all of one kind: *as (probably) correct*. The verificationism of Dummett and others overlooks such conceptual circularity.

Even if my evaluative standards for discerning justified beliefs might fall short of their own requirements, this question arises: What, if anything, constitutes the adequacy of those requirements for discerning justified beliefs in the first place, aside from what standards actually satisfy those requirements? If the only answer comes from an appeal to the very standards in question, an obvious circle threatens. Clearly, a cogent explanation cannot take this form: My standard E is adequate because my standard E is adequate. We could use that explanatorily useless form to "explain" the adequacy of whatever we like. The needed explanation, moreover, does not come from a claim that E meets its own evaluative standard for discerning justified belief. We have just seen that a mere evaluative standard, even when applied to an evaluative standard, does not explain what constitutes the adequacy, or correctness, of an evaluative standard. The verificationism that implies otherwise offers only conceptual circularity—a kind of circularity inimical to effective explanation.

Some philosophers have acknowledged the unavoidability of a circle in the justification of standards for justification or rationality. Nicholas Rescher acknowledges a circle as follows:

> The overall justification of rationality *must* be reflexive and self-referential. To provide a rationale of rationality is to show that rationality stands in appropriate alignment with the principles of rationality. From the angle of justification, rationality is a cyclic process that closes in on itself, not a linear process that ultimately rests on something outside itself. There is accordingly no basis for . . . any dissatisfaction or complaint regarding a 'circular' justification of rationality. We would not (should not) want it otherwise. (1988, p. 43; cf. Rescher 1985, pp. 139–142)

Rescher is not alone in acknowledging unavoidable circularity.

Richard Foley has acknowledged circularity as follows:

> We want to be able to defend or at least explain the reliability of our methods of inquiry, but the only way to do so is within our own system of inquiry. We seek to use our methods to show that these same methods are to be trusted. . . . This is no more than a generalization of the problem of the Cartesian circle, and it is a circle from which we can no more escape than could Descartes. (1990, pp. 75–76)

Ernest Sosa has likewise acknowledged an unavoidable circle straightforwardly:

> Suppose we reach a position to say that, at bottom, it is always factor F that makes a belief of our own justified, whatever the belief might be. . . . And suppose we are then challenged to explain what justifies us in holding that very belief. What can we possibly say in reply except that here again it is the presence of factor F? Will someone object that we beg the question and argue in a circle? The answer is, of course, that we do, but that, at this level of generality, it simply cannot be helped, and that regretting it is as bad as regretting that we cannot make a round cube (1987, pp. 714–715).[5]

5. Cf. Feigl (1950, pp. 118–119): "The emergence of circularity, here as well as elsewhere, is symptomatic of the fact that we have reached the limits of justification, that we are at least in the neighborhood of what are called 'ultimate presuppositions'." Feigl did not leave the matter here. He appealed to a notion of pragmatic "vindication" to supplement considerations of (epistemic) justi-

Acknowledgment of such circularity, however inevitable, lends no plausibility to the kind of conceptual and explanatory circularity shunned previously.

Clearly, if I hold that feature *F* is justification-conferring for every justified belief, I must hold—on pain of inconsistency—that *F* is justification-conferring even for my (supposedly) justified belief that *F* is justification-conferring for every justified belief. Excepting the latter justified belief would require qualification of the universal claim that every justified belief owes its justification to *F*. Given these considerations, then, we must acknowledge a kind of circularity in the justification of the belief that *F* is justification-conferring for every justified belief.

The previous question about adequacy seeks an answer free of conceptual circularity of the sort fostered by Dummett's verificationism. It does not, however, challenge the inevitable sort of circularity arising from a claim that some particular feature is justification-conferring for every claim. The question about adequacy pursues what constitutes the *correctness* of an epistemic standard; and it shuns the conceptual circularity of "answers" that use without explanation the very notion of correctness needing explanation. Shunning such circularity nonetheless allows for an epistemic standard justified by the very feature it acknowledges as justification-conferring.

Our question about adequacy for the evaluative project leads thus far to a bothersome dilemma: either naivete or circularity. Each of these horns is troublesome, if not fatally sharp, for effective philosophical explanation.

An analogous dilemma challenges the explanatory project. Suppose that I formulate and accept conditions that explain, in nonepistemic terms, what makes a belief justified. An explanatory standard for epistemically justified belief will characteristically take this form:

> A belief is epistemically justified if (and only if) it satisfies explanatory conditions *C*.

Perhaps I am a "process-reliabilist" whose conditions appeal to reliable, truth-conducive processes of belief-formation in the absence of defeat, processes such as reliable perception, memory, and introspection.[6]

Whatever my explanatory conditions are, this question will arise: In virtue of what, if anything, are my proposed conditions adequate, or correct, as a

---

fication, or "validation." (See also Feigl 1952; cf. Rescher 1977, chaps. 3, 5; 1979, pp. 100–114.) An appeal to pragmatic considerations can, as we shall see in chapter 4, have explanatory and justificatory value. On the account I shall develop, however, Feigl and Rescher, along with the others just cited, neglect certain semantic considerations crucial to giving justification. We shall see that even pragmatic justification and evaluation (that is, the giving thereof) depend on the semantic considerations identified in this chapter.

6. As this is only a rough illustration, we may overlook the difficult question, for reliabilists, of what actual or counterfactual situations must exemplify the truth-conduciveness of belief-forming processes that confer justification. On that question, see Pollock (1984), Feldman (1985), and Moser (1989, pp. 196–202). For attempts at an answer, see Goldman (1988), Sosa (1991, pp. 281–284), and Schmitt (1992, chap. 6).

solution to the explanatory project, at least for me? In other words, what, if anything, constitutes the correctness, at least for me, of my explanatory conditions as an answer to the explanation-seeking question of what constitutes epistemic justification? As before, our question can take a modal form for cases of false epistemic standards: The issue then is what *can* constitute correctness of one's standards.

We now return to a familiar theme. Either I take the previous question about adequacy seriously, or I do not. If I do not, I shall consider it negligible, as not needing an answer. In that case, my acceptance of my explanatory conditions for justification will be naive, or superficial. My acceptance will then lack a cogent reply to an intelligible, legitimate question about what, if anything, constitutes the adequacy of my explanatory conditions. This is a species of the objectionable meta-epistemic naivete mentioned before. If, alternatively, I do take the previous question seriously, I shall seek an answer. Because, by hypothesis, I already accept a set of explanatory conditions for justification, I might offer those conditions to explain what constitutes the adequacy of those conditions as a solution to the explanatory project. (I assume, as before, that an appeal to an infinite regress of epistemic standards fails.)

If I am a reliabilist whose explanatory conditions appeal to processes of reliable belief-formation, I might answer that my acceptance of these conditions enjoys reliable, truth-conducive formation in the absence of defeat. What would such an answer accomplish? It certainly could accomplish consistency. Indeed, thoroughgoing reliabilism about the explanatory project requires that we appeal to reliability to explain the justification of reliabilist standards. If all justified belief, on our view, comes from reliable belief-formation, then, on pain of inconsistency, we shall need to invoke reliable belief-formation to explain the justification of our belief that reliabilism is correct. The point here is general, and not peculiar to reliabilism. For any explanatory condition *C*, if we hold that *C* characterizes all cases of justification, we must hold that *C* characterizes even the justification of our acceptance of *C* as yielding a correct solution to the explanatory project.

Suppose, then, that we accept an explanatory epistemic standard *E* as an adequate, or correct, solution to the explanatory project. May we invoke *E* itself to explain what constitutes the adequacy of *E* as an answer to the explanatory project? A cogent explanation, I suggested previously, cannot take this explanatorily useless form: My standard *E* is adequate because my standard *E* is adequate. This makes no explanatory mileage at all. In addition, the desired explanation does not emerge from a claim that *E* satisfies its own explanatory standard for justification. A mere explanatory standard, *E′*, when satisfied by an explanatory standard, *E*, does not explain what constitutes the adequacy, or correctness, of *E* as an answer to the explanatory project, even when *E′* is identical with *E*. The satisfaction of *E′* by *E* explains at most what constitutes the justification of *E*.

Epistemic standards explaining only epistemic justification do not themselves explain what constitutes the correctness of an explanatory epistemic standard. What constitutes adequacy, or correctness, of an epistemic standard relative to the explanatory project is one thing; what constitutes mere justification of an explanatory standard is something else. This parallels a lesson we learned earlier, in connection with the evaluative project.

If, in accord with verificationism, we try to answer questions about what constitutes correctness of explanatory standards by appeal to the justification of those standards, we risk conceptual circularity. Talk of the justification of an explanatory standard typically presupposes a notion of correctness because such talk typically requires, for its being fully understood, a notion of the justification of a standard as (probably) correct. Use of an explanatory epistemic standard to answer our question about correctness will thus typically rely on a notion of correctness whose explanation is at issue. Explanation gains nothing from such conceptual circularity. This, too, parallels a lesson that emerged previously, in conjunction with the evaluative project.

We lack, then, an independent, noncircular explanation of what constitutes adequacy for answers to the explanatory project. Any proposed answer to the explanatory project must face this open question: In virtue of what, if anything, is that answer adequate to explain justification, or correct as a solution to the explanatory project? A person for whom this question is open will get no explanatory benefit from being told that a proposed answer to the explanatory project itself answers the question. Such a reply will naturally raise the same question again, if at a different level. In general, such a reply lacks explanatory cogency, since what explains mere justification of a solution to the explanatory project differs from what explains correctness of such a solution. We risk conceptual circularity, moreover, if we invoke typical verificationism (for example, that of Dummett) to collapse the former distinction.

The problem is not that for one merely to have a justifiable answer to the explanatory project, one must be able to explain why, or to show that, one's answer has justification. One's merely having justification for *P* does not require one's being able either to explain or to show justification for *P*. The problem, moreover, does not stem from the false assumption that for one merely to have justification for *P*, one must have justification for thinking that *P* is justified. The problem does not arise from such an epistemic level-confusion.[7] It comes rather from an epistemologist's explanatory predicament.

Epistemologists responsible to their official explanatory goals in epistemology will not be satisfied to give merely correct or even merely justifiable answers (by their standards) to such questions as: What is the correct solution to the explanatory project? What is the correct answer to the evaluative project? Epistemologists must seek the deepest, most informative explanation available of what accomplishes the explanatory and evaluative projects. This requires that epistemologists give the most cogent explanations available in reply to questions or challenges from others, including questions about what constitutes correctness of solutions to the explanatory and evaluative projects.

Cogent explanations exclude conceptual circularity and explanatory circularity. Circular "explanation" can arise for virtually anything—just explain *X* via *X*; and we can "explain" any notion in terms of itself. Cogency in explana-

7. For detailed discussion of level confusions, see Alston (1989a, chaps. 3, 6).

tion is clearly harder to achieve. Epistemologists thus must explain justification and standards of justification in the most cogent manner available, even if the first-order unreflective having of justification does not require the same. Questions about what constitutes correctness of epistemic standards should be near the top of an epistemologist's list of issues demanding cogent explanation. Such questions about correctness are not only intelligible and legitimate, but also readily available at every level of epistemological theorizing. They will not go away, even if one chooses to ignore them.

Let us then restate the two meta-epistemological questions under consideration:

> (i) What, if anything, constitutes the adequacy, or correctness (at least for myself), of my evaluative epistemic standards as an answer to the evaluative project regarding the discerning of justified beliefs?
> (ii) What, if anything, constitutes the adequacy, or correctness (at least for myself), of my explanatory epistemic standards as an answer to the explanation-seeking question of what constitutes justification?

The relativity indicated by the phrase 'at least for myself' is semantic, not just a matter of what one believes to be correct. The way in which it is semantic will emerge shortly.

If you hold that coherence with your antecedent beliefs sets the evaluative standard for discerning justified beliefs, the pertinent instance of question (i) for you will be: What, if anything, constitutes the correctness (at least for yourself) of your coherentist standard as an answer to the evaluative project? If you hold that origin in a reliable process of belief-formation enables an explanation of what constitutes justified belief in general, you will confront this instance of question (ii): What, if anything, constitutes the adequacy (at least for yourself) of your reliabilist explanatory standard as an answer to the explanatory project? These questions seek explanations more informative than a circular explanation via the very standards under question.

Questions (i) and (ii) are not equivalent to the following questions:

> (iii) What evaluative standards, if any, have I for evaluating the justification of my evaluative standards for discerning justified beliefs?
>
> (iv) What explanatory standards, if any, explain for me the justification of my explanatory standards for justification?

Coherentists about evaluative standards for justification will invoke coherentist standards to answer (iii); and reliabilists about explanatory standards for justification will cite reliability to answer (iv). Questions (iii) and (iv) are open to such circular answers.

Questions (i) and (ii) seek a means of explanation that goes beyond appeal to the evaluative and explanatory standards under question. Given a distinction, then, between questions (i) and (iii) and between questions (ii) and (iv), how can we resolve the troublesome dilemma of either naivete unfit for philosophy or circularity inadequate for explanatory cogency?

We may begin by asking whether any special analogous dilemma troubles the aforementioned semantic project: the project of specifying, in informative terms, what it means to say that something is epistemically justified. By 'special dilemma' I mean a dilemma peculiar to the semantic project. Suppose that I answer the semantic project by defining 'epistemic justification' via talk of what is "permissible" relative to a specific set of epistemic rules or, alternatively, via talk of what is "good" from the standpoint of acquiring true beliefs and avoiding false beliefs.[8] Would either such answer raise a distinctive dilemma for the semantic project, a special dilemma analogous to our previous dilemmas?

The following question might seem to raise an analogous dilemma: What does it mean to say that my definition of 'epistemic justification' is itself epistemically justified? This question does not automatically generate a dilemma of naivete or circularity. Without being naive, one might reject the question as resting on a false assumption that it makes sense to say that definitions of 'epistemic justification' are themselves epistemically justifiable. One might hold, without naivete, that definitions of 'epistemic justification' are preconditions for talking about epistemic justification but are not themselves candidates for such justification. One's reason might be that definitions are ultimately stipulative—even if not capriciously stipulative—and thus are neither true nor false independently of stipulation. (This does not imply that one cannot be epistemically justified in holding that one endorses a certain definition. The proposition that one endorses a certain definition is not the same as the definition itself.) Talk of epistemic justification, on this view, makes sense only relative to a conceptually prior notion of epistemic justification; and this prior notion is a conceptual precondition, but not a recipient, of epistemic justification. Such a view seems not to be "naive" in the way the initial response to our dilemmas was.[9]

One might, alternatively, allow for the epistemic justifiability of definitions of 'epistemic justification', but plead innocent to any objectionable circularity in answering the previous question. Suppose that we accept a definition of 'epistemic justification' as what is permissible relative to a specific set of epistemic rules. When asked what it means (at least for us) to say that our definition is epistemically justified, we can plausibly reply that our definition itself gives the answer: namely, our accepting the definition is permissible relative to a specific set of epistemic rules. This seems unobjectionable. If the question asks just for what we mean by 'our definition is epistemically justified', we have given the full, most informative answer. We cannot be plausibly accused of having given an answer that is circular or shallow.

Let us consider another question facing any answer to the semantic project, a question analogous to questions (i) and (ii):

8. The former definition, made prominent by Roderick Chisholm, has been endorsed by Pollock (1986a, pp. 7–8) and Alvin Goldman (1986, p. 59), among others; the latter, by Alston (1989a, chap. 4).

9. Such a view seems to be suggested, if only vaguely, at various places in Wittgenstein's *On Certainty* (1969, sections 608–620). The following two sections return to this view.

(v) What, if anything, constitutes the correctness (at least for myself) of my semantic standards for 'epistemic justification' as an answer to the semantic project regarding what it means to say that something is epistemically justified?

The semantic project, as noted, seeks what it means to say that something (for example, a proposition or a belief) is epistemically justified.

If semantic meaning is person-relative, as chapter 3 explains, the semantic project aims to specify, in informative (or noncircular) terms, what it means for one to say that something is epistemically justified. (For now we can proceed with a loose notion of *informative* meaning as noncircular meaning, and a loose notion of *definition* as whatever specifies meaning for one.) Adequacy of a definition of 'epistemic justification', as an answer to the semantic project for myself, thus amounts to a specification, in informative terms, of what I actually mean by 'epistemic justification'. The latter specification, being adequate, is just my actual informative definition of 'epistemic justification'.

My actual informative definition of 'epistemic justification', even if multifaceted and somewhat vague, is definitive of my adequate, or correct, solution to the semantic project. It is what determines the adequacy—the correctness—of my solution. If I do not have any definition of 'epistemic justification' (or some synonymous expression), I shall lack a correct solution to the semantic project. In that case, I shall lack a determinate notion of epistemic justification. (The definitions pertinent now need not be highly specific in the way typical analyses of notions of justification and knowledge are; on this score, we may contrast definitions and analyses.)

When a definition is adequate, or correct, as a solution to the semantic project, *it* is what explains the adequacy of the solution in question; it then amounts to what one means by 'epistemic justification' (or some synonymous expression). There is thus an internal connection between (a) what one informatively means by 'epistemic justification', (b) one's actual informative, noncircular definition of 'epistemic justification', and (c) one's correct solution to the semantic project. Correctness here is constituted by what one actually means. What one means by 'epistemic justification' does not, however, preclude one's understanding other notions of epistemic justification. (Section 2.4 returns to this theme.)

We might ask how one can know or justifiably believe what one's actual definitions are, but this is not the concern of question (v). Its concern is rather to ask what constitutes adequacy of a solution to the semantic project; and its answer comes directly from considerations about what one informatively means in saying that something is epistemically justified. Insofar as one informatively means anything in saying that something is epistemically justified, the semantic project will not generate for one the dilemma of naivete or circularity posed earlier. One will then have a constitutive standard for a correct answer to the semantic project: an answer stating what it is that one informatively means in saying that something is epistemically justified. The semantic project thus lends itself to a cogent answer to question (v).

Semantic considerations hold the key to avoiding the other manifestations of the dilemma of naivete or circularity, and to solving the evaluative and explanatory projects. More specifically, considerations about what one informatively means by '(adequate for) discerning justified beliefs' and by '(adequate for) explaining justification' enable explanatorily effective answers to questions (i) and (ii) for the evaluative and explanatory projects. What one means by '(adequate for) discerning, or evaluating, justified beliefs' can effectively explain what constitutes correctness, at least for oneself, for an answer to the evaluative project. Similarly, what one means by '(adequate for) explaining justification' can effectively explain what constitutes correctness, at least for oneself, for an answer to the explanatory project. In the same vein, what one means by '(adequate for) effectively explaining' can effectively explain what constitutes correctness, at least for oneself, for an answer to a project seeking effective explanation. (Chapter 3 focuses on pertinent conditions for semantic meaning.)

If we neglect the internal connection between what one informatively means by 'evaluating justification' and 'explaining justification' and one's correct solution to the evaluative and explanatory projects, we risk changing the topic from what is actually one's correct solution. We then risk introducing such other topics as what solution is *justified* and what solution is *someone else's* correct solution. We saw before how verificationist approaches to correctness change the topic to justification and thereby risk conceptual circularity. We need instead a semantic approach to correctness in terms of what one means; this approach can avoid the dilemma of naivete or circularity.

In adopting a semantic approach to correctness, we can avoid troublesome commitments to ontologically dubious truth-makers for semantic epistemic standards: for example, Platonic epistemological entities and equally questionable epistemological natural kinds.[10] We can thereby avoid familiar skeptical questions about the support needed for claims to the existence of such truth-makers. If we can avoid such questions without loss, we are wise to do so. We saw in section 1.7, moreover, that even agnostics issuing challenges proceed as if some expressions are semantically significant. Consistency requires that they permit us to proceed likewise. This point does not answer the agnostic challenges of chapter 1; it merely identifies some common ground.

Talk of *one's* correct solution to the semantic project is not automatically talk of the solution one believes to be correct. It rather is talk of what is correct relative to one's own understanding of what constitutes correctness: that is, relative to what one *means* in saying that something is correct. The relativity here is thus semantic, not simply doxastic. Understanding of what constitutes correctness can vary, as section 4.1 illustrates, even if one's own notion of

10. Cf. Alvin Goldman (1989, p. 143): "Whatever one thinks about justice or consciousness as possible natural kinds, it is dubious that knowledge or justificational status are [*sic*] natural kinds."

"a notion of correctness (generally characterized)" sets some limits on what in general is, for oneself, a notion of correctness. (Section 2.4 returns to the topic of such semantic limits.) In accepting, offering, or considering a solution to one of the epistemological projects, a theorist is presupposing a notion of correctness: a notion of a correct solution. This presupposed notion can, and sometimes does, vary among theorists, with respect to its specific requirements.

Restricting my account to my own specific understanding of correctness would obviously rob the account of comprehensiveness. My account would then exclude many theorists who now fall within its explanatory scope. The semantic relativity I acknowledge does not preclude notions of objective correctness: correctness that does not depend on one's believing that it obtains. Notions of correctness and meaningful claims to correctness do depend on someone's understanding of correctness; and such notions and claims are involved in one's accepting, offering, or considering a solution to an epistemological project. It does not follow, however, that the existence of what makes a claim correct—apart from its being described as a determinant of correctness—depends on one's own understanding of correctness. Even if a notion of correctness depends on someone's understanding, a relation of correctness (on some notions) can be independent of conceivers' beliefs that it obtains. My assumption of semantic relativity fits with this consideration. (Explanation of semantic relativity continues in section 2.4 and in chapters 3 and 4.)

Let us briefly take stock. The following questions confront the semantic, explanatory, and evaluative projects:

> (a') *Question for the semantic project*: What, if anything, constitutes the correctness (at least for myself) of my semantic standards for 'epistemic justification' as an answer to the question of what it means to say that something is epistemically justified?
>
> (b') *Question for the explanatory project*: What, if anything, constitutes the correctness (at least for myself) of my explanatory epistemic standards as an answer to the explanation-seeking question of what constitutes justification?
>
> (c') *Question for the evaluative project*: What, if anything, constitutes the correctness (at least for myself) of my evaluative epistemic standards as an answer to the question of what discerns justified beliefs?

Question (a') for the semantic project is, we have seen in outline, open to an explanatorily effective reply. Questions (b') and (c') face a couple of dilemmas amounting to this: Either be meta-epistemically naive or settle for a kind of circularity lacking explanatory cogency. One's epistemology, if caught on either horn of this dilemma, would be shallow and unsatisfactory from an explanatory point of view. We saw, in brief, that pertinent semantic considerations can save the explanatory and evaluative projects from their dilemmas, in a way analogous to their role in saving the semantic project.

The dilemmas for the explanatory and evaluative projects might recall, but should not be confused with, the notorious problem of the criterion reported by Sextus Empiricus.[11] Following Chisholm (1973), we can illustrate the problem with two general questions: (1) *what* are we epistemically justified in believing, and (2) *how*, or in virtue of what, are we epistemically justified in believing anything? Question (1) asks about the extent of our justified belief. Question (2) asks about the basis for our justified belief. The problem is that without an answer to the first question we apparently cannot answer the second, and without an answer to the second we apparently cannot answer the first. On this basis, some skeptics conclude that we should endorse skepticism about justified belief.

The lesson of the problem of the criterion, according to some philosophers, is that we should not try to justify our (evaluative or explanatory) standards for justification solely by what those standards countenance as justified. Such an effort will always confront circularity. The problem of the criterion prompts us to ask whether there is any other means of justifying epistemic standards. On one reading, the problem concerns where an epistemologist should begin theorizing: with epistemic standards or with particular cases of assumed justified belief? Or somewhere else? Circularity will arise if one aims to justify epistemic standards by particular cases of assumed justification, *and* one aims further to justify those particular cases by those standards.

The earlier dilemmas for the explanatory and evaluative projects are more basic than the problem of the criterion. They illustrate that the explanatory and evaluative projects generate troublesome questions logically prior to issues about justification: questions about what constitutes *correctness* of epistemic standards accomplishing those projects. Specifically, they generate questions (b') and (c'). Those questions raise specific challenges to any epistemologist seeking explanatory or evaluative epistemic standards.

The epistemologist's predicament here is really any theorist's predicament. Wherever explanatory claims occur, we can raise legitimate questions about what constitutes correctness of the operative explanatory standards. Epistemologists have given considerable attention to the justification of epistemic standards, but have given relatively little consideration to the more fundamental issue of what constitutes correctness of explanatory and evaluative standards. We need to correct this deficiency.

If semantic considerations are definitive of correctness in one's explaining, evaluating, and arguing for justification, they will figure prominently in one's explaining, evaluating, and arguing for justification. We now need to reveal the prominent role of semantic considerations in this connection.

2.3 Semantic Foundationalism

The following broad thesis acknowledges a central role for semantic considerations in matters epistemological:

11. On some of the history of that problem, see Rescher (1980a, chap. 1), Striker (1990), and Barnes (1990b, pp. 218–224).

> One's explaining, evaluating, and arguing for epistemic justification and one's answers to questions about correct standards for such matters properly end in considerations about an operative *notion* for one regarding epistemic justification.

Call this view *semantic foundationalism.* It incorporates and extends the earlier lessons about semantic considerations that free the three epistemological projects from a dilemma of naivete or circularity.

A. Notions and Conceptual Commitments

One's *notion* of epistemic justification comprises semantic standards constitutive of what it is to be one's correct use of such terms as 'epistemic justification', 'epistemic support', and 'epistemic warrant'. (We may add any synonymous term to the list, including any synonymous term from some other language.) Such semantic standards are crucial to the individuation of notions, as they determine what a notion is a notion *of*; they determine the constitutive conditions of satisfaction, or fulfillment, of a notion.

I shall generally talk of "standards for correct use" rather than "standards for what it is to be correct use," but the two locutions are equivalent for me. Both concern the *category* of correct use for one, not just particular cases of correctness in use. One's semantic standards determine the category of correct use for one: that is, relative to what one means by 'correctness in use' (or some synonymous phrase). The pertinent relativity is, then, semantic, not just a matter of mere belief about what is true.

Semantic standards contribute determinacy to what tokens mean for one. Linguistic meaning, as ordinarily understood, has some determinacy: It does not admit every conceivable interpretation or use of a token as correct. It excludes some interpretations or uses as incorrect; and the more specific interpretations or uses it excludes, the more determinate it is. Exclusion of interpretations or uses comes from standards constitutive of correct use. Such standards guarantee that not just *any* arbitrary interpretation or use of a token is correct for one. An interpretation or a use of a token is incorrect for one if it violates one's semantic standards for correct use of that token; a requirement of correctness is thus conformity to one's semantic standards. In the absence of determinacy as exclusion, meaning languishes, indeed expires.

The determinacy of linguistic meaning as exclusion need not come from "objective modal facts" or any such ontologically questionable basis. It can come simply from one's commitment to interpret or to use a token in certain ways to the exclusion of other ways. (Section 3.3B treats such interpretive commitment.) Conceptual necessity need have no basis deeper than one's adopted constitutive standards for correct use of terms; it can arise from the exclusions due to one's semantic standards.

Semantic standards are not equivalent to empirical generalizations, but are presupposed by such generalizations. The subject- and predicate-terms of an empirical generalization require determinacy from standards for correctness in interpretation if that generalization is to be intelligible and empirically confirmable (as correct). Experienced features by themselves do not yield standards constitutive of (the category of) correctness in interpretation for one. Denial of an empirical generalization involving a notion of knowledge, for example, does not entail either meaninglessness or a change of subject (owing to a different notion at work). Denial of a semantic standard, in contrast, does entail either meaninglessness or a change of subject (as section 3.3B explains). Semantic standards are, then, irreducible to empirical generalizations.

An internal connection obtains between what a notion is *of*, for one, and that for which the notion sets the condition "what it is to be that thing," for one. One's notion of justification, for instance, sets constitutive, or defining, conditions for what it is to be justification, at least for oneself, and thereby sets one's constitutive conditions for genuine justification, in the relevant sense. (Recall that the relativity here is semantic, not merely doxastic.) A notion of epistemic justification, we shall see, is not itself a candidate for being justified by considerations independent of fixing meaning, or of conceptual commitment. We shall also see that certain notions can themselves have a kind of purpose-based, instrumental support.

A notion of justification is *operative* for one in a particular situation when one is committed to that notion as specifying what constitutes justification (for one) in that situation. One's currently operative notion of justification need not be one's only understood notion of justification. I might understand various specific notions of justification while being committed to only one as specifying what actually constitutes justification (for me). I could recognize that the alternative specific notions are amplifications of a common notion of justification generally characterized; still, I would not regard all the alternative notions as specifying what actually constitutes justification (for me). I could, nonetheless, adopt a variety of specific notions of justification that specify different species of justification (for me): moral justification, legal justification, and so on.

Commitment to a notion of epistemic justification is just commitment to certain constitutive, semantic standards for one's correct use of such terms as 'epistemic justification', 'epistemic support', and 'epistemic warrant'. Call any such commitment an *operative conceptual commitment*. We can now accommodate such talk as: I understand what Jones means by 'justification', but that is not what *I* mean by 'justification'; or I understand Jones's specific notion of justification, but Jones's specific notion is different from my (operative) specific notion of justification. Such talk suggests that we should not confuse conditions for an operative notion and conditions for an understood notion. (This point has obvious importance in section 2.4 and chapter 4, in connection with conceptual relativism about reasons.)

Difference in conceptual commitments, like difference in analyses, entails a difference in specific notions at issue. People operating with different specific notions of *X* can still, however, understand and even intentionally use common notions of *X generally characterized*. We thus can talk intelligibly of various notions of some one thing (generally characterized).

Even if you and I understand and intentionally use a common unspecific notion of "epistemic justification generally characterized" (for example, as permissibility relative to a set of rules of a certain sort), we can still differ on the actual rules conferring justification and thus have different operative notions of justification at a level of specificity. Even so, I could understand your notion of justification and acknowledge it as your elaboration, different from mine, on our common notion of justification generally characterized. I could therefore regard your notion as a notion of justification even though it differed from my specific notion of justification. I could, then, understand your specific notion of justification, even if it differed from my operative notion of justification at a level of specificity.

The relevant talk of *meaning* and of constitutive conditions *set by* one's operative notion of justification involves whatever constitutes, or actually makes up, one's operative notion of justification. One's operative notion of justification is the logical basis for one's "conceptual truths" about justification, those truths being whatever logically follows from one's operative notion. They are "one's" conceptual truths just in virtue of following logically from one's operative notion. (We might introduce a stricter notion of conceptual truth requiring one's awareness of a logical connection between the truth and one's notion, but I shall not.)

An operative notion (or definition) of justification need not be a logical analysis of justification in terms of specific nondisjunctive conditions that are individually necessary and jointly sufficient for justification. What one means by 'justification' may be based on "exemplars": certain paradigm-cases of justification that do not yield a logical analysis in terms of specific nondisjunctive necessary (and sufficient) conditions for justification.[12] Notions (and definitions) need not conform to rigid standards for an "ideal" or a "clean" logical analysis. They rather can depend on various exemplars to yield a standard that offers some determinacy by exclusion (cf. Wittgenstein 1953, sections 71, 75, 87).

What is constitutive of the meaning of a statement or term for one does not reduce to mere talk of logically necessary and sufficient conditions. What is merely sufficient for the truth of *P* for one is not necessarily part of the meaning of *P* for one; so also for what is merely necessary for the truth of *P*. Similarly, what is logically necessary and sufficient for the truth of *P* can include components extraneous to the meaning of *P* for one. Suppose that *C1* and *C2* constitute the meaning of *P* for one. In that case, the following will be logically necessary and sufficient for the truth of *P* for one: (*C1* & *C2*) & [(*C1* & *C2*) v *R*]. The latter disjunction is, by hypothesis, not part of the meaning of *P* for one. Constituents of meaning for one are exhausted by the actual components of one's constitutive standards for correct use of terms. (Section 3.3 examines conditions for notions in more detail.)

One's operative notion of epistemic justification is neither correct nor incorrect for one apart from a determinate semantic standard for correctness of

12. On the role of exemplars in meaning, see Rosch (1978, 1983), Rosch and Mervis (1975), and Lakoff (1987, pp. 39–57; 1989).

a notion of justification. Even if epistemic justification is a universal or a natural kind, the correctness or incorrectness of a notion for one relative to that universal or natural kind requires a determinate semantic standard for correctness for one. Lacking such a standard, one will not have a determinate notion of correctness of a notion, and thus one will not understand anything specifying correctness of a notion. Correctness of a notion for one will then lack its needed foothold in what one understands. As for (possible) objective, conceiving-independent relations of correctness, our talking intelligibly about them, and justifiably affirming them, requires a determinate notion of correctness. Section 1.7 challenges optimism toward our being able to confirm such relations without debilitating circularity.

Issues of conceptual correctness can arise indirectly, relative either to the implications of an alternative notion of justification or to claims about the scope or application of an operative notion of justification. We can ask, for instance, whether it is correct that a particular operative notion of justification captures either the conditions for a certain common use of the term 'justification' or the conditions for my operative concept or your operative concept of justification. An operative notion of justification thus can raise questions of correctness indirectly, in virtue of accompanying claims about scope or application.

A notion of justification, like any determinate notion, rests on a semantic standard that has broadly normative significance. At a minimum, a semantic standard sets a constitutive normative condition for correct application of certain terms.[13] When a semantic standard is prescriptive (for example, 'Let justification be such and such!'), it will not itself be true or false in the way assertions can be. Normative semantic standards can, however, give semantic significance to definitional assertions about justification. They can offer semantic norms, or constitutive standards, for correct use of epistemic terms and locutions in definitional assertions. Such standards can thereby contribute semantic significance to a truth-valued definitional assertion: for example, 'Justification, by definition, is truth-conducive belief-formation in the absence of defeat.'

A definitional assertion could be made true for me by my adopting a certain semantic standard (for example, a certain definitional prescription): that is, adopting the standard as constitutive of correct use of a term (for me). Such a definitional truth could arise for a person from its stating only what is prescribed by that person's operative definitional prescriptions. Semantic standards need not appeal to prior synonymy relations, nor need they be unrevisable. They thus can escape worries from Quine (1951) about the epistemological significance of considerations of meaning. (We shall consider such worries in detail in sections 3.5 through 3.8.)

Philosophers uneasy with talk of notions might prefer to substitute talk of *constitutive standards*, or *norms*, for correct use of certain terms. This substitution might seem to remove without loss a questionable semantic component

13. We may now leave open the question whether the relevant terms might occur only in a language of thought, rather than in a socially shared natural language. Sections 3.2 and 5.1 consider the role of social factors in meaningful language-use.

from the account under development. It allows us to talk simply of constitutive standards for correct use of epistemic terms, without talk of "notions" of justification. This move is just stylistic or notational, however, because notions, on my account, are just constitutive standards for correct use of certain terms.

Talk of notions does enable us to answer the following sort of question with ease: Why do you use those constitutive standards for correct use as constraints on *epistemic justification*? Such a question apparently presumes a distinction between one's operative constitutive standards for correct use of such a term as 'epistemic justification' and one's operative notion of epistemic justification. If we regard the relevant operative semantic standards as *constitutive* of one's operative notion of justification, we foreclose any such question. Talk of operative notions of justification thus serves a definite purpose in answering certain potentially troublesome questions about constitutive standards for correct use of epistemic terms.

Suppose that I am pursuing the explanatory project of explaining what constitutes justification. I endorse, we may assume again, the reliabilist view that justification consists in the truth-conduciveness of belief-forming processes, such as perception, in the absence of defeat. Being uneasy with reliabilism, you raise this now familiar question for my approach to the explanatory project: In virtue of what, if anything, are my reliabilist explanatory standards correct as a solution to the explanatory project, at least for myself? In reply, I might note that my acceptance of my reliabilist explanatory standards is itself supported by a truth-conducive belief-forming process in the absence of defeat. Thoroughgoing reliabilism, as noted in section 2.2, requires this answer to a question about the justification of reliabilist standards. You, of course, will not be satisfied by such an answer because you have asked about constitutive conditions for the correctness of my standards, not their justification. You naturally want a more suitable answer. A true statement, of course, is not necessarily a correct answer to a question at hand.

The best answer available to typical "process-reliabilists" is that their specific semantic standards for 'correct explanation of epistemic justification' involve considerations about reliable processes of belief-formation in the absence of defeat. These standards involving reliable processes are not, for typical process-reliabilists, extrinsically related to what it is correctly to explain epistemic justification; they rather are internally, or conceptually, related in virtue of an operative specific notion of correctly explaining epistemic justification.

An indicator of the conceptual nature of the relation between reliability and explaining justification for typical process-reliabilists is that they exclude the possibility of a mistake in their assumption that epistemic justification is correctly explained by appeal to reliability of belief-forming processes. They simply are not genuinely open to the possibility of a counterexample to this fundamental assumption of their reliabilism, even if other tenets of their theory admit of falsifiability. The fundamental assumption in question is, then, a conceptual truth for typical process-reliabilists: It is actually part (or at least an implication) of their operative specific notion of epistemic justification that beliefs resulting from truth-conducive processes in the absence of defeat are epistemically justified.

If semantic considerations figure crucially in what it is to be justification for a person (where the relativity is semantic), they should have some representation in an informative explanation of what it is for a person to explain, evaluate, or argue for justification. Semantic foundationalism accommodates this lesson by acknowledging a crucial role for considerations about an operative notion for one regarding epistemic justification. Explaining, evaluating, and arguing for justification come to an end, according to semantic foundationalism, with an appeal to an operative notion regarding justification.[14] We need not pursue a detailed account of meaning and notions now, as semantic foundationalism remains neutral on most of the controversial issues about the exact conditions for fixing meaning and having a notion. (Chapter 3 elucidates the semantic foundations of semantic foundationalism with an account of meaning, conceptual commitment, and analyticity.)

B. Arguing for Justification

Semantic foundationalism entails that arguing deductively for justification for any statement—including any statement about justification—consists paradigmatically of giving an argument in accord with, or reducible to, the following schema:

1. By my conceptual commitment, justification (for either my explanatory or evaluative epistemic standards, for example) consists in conditions *C* (for example, truth-conducive belief-formation in the absence of defeat).
2. The statement that *P* (expressing, for example, my explanatory or evaluative epistemic standards) satisfies *C*.
3. Hence, the statement that *P* is justified (at least for me).

This is an argument schema for one's deductively arguing for justification for a statement: that is, one's arguing deductively that a statement is justified (at least for oneself), not just that it is true. When the instances of steps 1 and 2 are true, the argument 1 through 3 for the justification of *P* will be sound; otherwise, we shall have an unsound deductive argument for the justification of *P*.

Schema 1 through 3 does not specify conditions for one's merely having justification for a statement. Merely having justification for a statement, on a common understanding, does not require giving an argument at all. It requires only one's having undefeated evidence for the statement in question; it does not require even one's having a notion of justification. In arguing or merely

14. We shall see in the next subsection that semantic foundationalism applies to operative principles of inductive and deductive logic as well as to other justificatory standards. Semantic foundationalism thus fits with the suggestion of Feigl (1950, p. 118) that "we may say that the *rules* of logic in their totality [that are operative for us] *define what we mean by correct reasoning*."

claiming that someone has justification for a statement, however, a theorist must employ a notion of justification. So long as we engage in any project of epistemology, by making claims about justification and knowledge, we shall confront the lessons of semantic foundationalism.

Schema 1 through 3 illustrates a deductive argument for (a conclusion affirming) the justification of the statement that *P* (for oneself), not for the justification of step 3 of the schema. One may use such an argument to infer that step 3 is true, not that it is justified. In general, a deductive argument is for its conclusion, not for one's assumption about the epistemic status of its conclusion. Argument for the latter assumption about epistemic status typically requires further, if analogous, considerations. (We may now bracket thorny issues about self-referential claims, letting it suffice to note that their justification, too, depends on considerations about an operative notion of justification.)

A paradigmatic deductive argument for the justification of steps 1 through 3, and even of claims to one's endorsing steps 1 through 3, will itself rely on a premise about an operative notion of justification—in a way analogous to how steps 1 through 3 argue for the conclusion that the statement that *P* is justified. We must observe, nonetheless, a conceptual distinction between an argument for (the truth of) a certain conclusion and an argument for the justification of that conclusion.

The following argument for the *probable* justification of *P* depends straightforwardly on considerations about one's operative notion of justification:

> By my conceptual commitment, justification consists in conditions *C*; *P* probably satisfies *C*; hence, *P* is probably justified, at least for me.

Such an argument concludes with (a conclusion affirming) the probable justification of *P*, not the probable justification of its conclusion. The conclusion is not that the claim that *P* is probably justified is itself probably justified for me. A deductive argument for the latter claim could, however, parallel the previous argument. The analogous argument would invoke the probable satisfaction of the conditions of an operative notion by the statement that *P* is probably justified. The second premise would then be: The statement that *P* is probably justified probably satisfies *C*. Even so, considerations about an operative notion of justification would still play a decisive role, in the manner just indicated.

Consider another simple argument for probable justification: Anna is generally reliable as an epistemologist; she believes that *P* is justified; hence, *P* is probably justified. This argument presupposes, for its inferential success, a notion of probable justification wherein a belief's basis in a generally reliable source yields probable justification. If we omit that notion, the argument's conclusion will not be conclusively, or validly, forthcoming. This point allows that theorists can wield different notions of validity at a level of specificity, owing to different constitutive standards for what it is to be truth-preserving or probability-preserving.

The key component of the operative notion is statable thus: By my conceptual commitment, if a belief has a basis in a generally reliable source, then that belief is probably justified, at least for me. If we insert this component as an explicit premise, we can make the argument obviously conclusive. Because talk of "probable justification" presupposes talk of justification, we can now see that a notion of justification is operative here, if only implicitly. Notions of "probable justification" can add any of a variety of qualifications to notions of justification; and, in fact, various such notions populate epistemology.

A related argument runs as follows: Most of Anna's assertions are true; Anna affirms that *P*; hence, *P* is probably true. My diagnosis is predictably forthright: This argument presupposes, for its inferential success, a notion of probability wherein a statement's membership in a set of mostly true assertions yields probable correctness. If we omit that notion, the argument's conclusion will not be conclusively, or validly, forthcoming. Inferential success here depends on an operative notion of probability.

My diagnosis does not entail that irreducibly inductive argument is impossible or that all adequate arguments are really enthymemes presupposing their own inference-patterns as separate premises. One can argue thus: Most *A*'s are *B*'s; *X* is an *A*; probably, therefore, *X* is a *B*. In irreducibly inductive argument, 'probably therefore' means something different from what 'therefore' means in deductive argument. The ambiguity in what 'therefore', 'hence', or some other conclusion-indicator means, although seldom noted, constitutes the difference between deductive and inductive argument. In deductive and inductive arguments, operative notions of conclusion-indicator are crucial to—indeed, constitutive of—what constitutes *inferential* success, or validity. Inferential success depends on the connection between an argument's premises and conclusion, not on the actual truth of the premises and conclusion. Nothing in principle precludes notions of irreducibly inductive success in inference.

At least part of what many of us mean by 'probably therefore' is determined by paradigmatic inferences of certain kinds, where these kinds characteristically require hedge clauses to block contravening factors. The previous inductive schema, for example, cannot cogently deliver a probable conclusion that octogenarians will become centenarians on the basis of their having survived all their previous birthdays. (Russell was vividly, if not painfully, aware of this.) The kinds of inferences in question need not be statable purely formally, and they may even be paradigm-based: that is, based on paradigmatic instances of inference. Different people, moreover, can mean different things by 'probably therefore' at least at a level of specificity, even if they agree to some extent on its general use.

Deductive use of 'therefore' follows suit: At least part of what many of us mean by '(deductively) therefore' is determined by paradigmatic inferences of certain kinds, where these kinds suffer fewer hedge clauses than do their inductive counterparts. Our notion of deductive inference is, accordingly, more determinate than our notion of inductive inference, at least at any level of specificity. The relative imprecision in our notion of inductive inference, at any level of specificity, accounts for much of the difficulty most of us have in formulating exact rules of inductive inference. Paradigm-cases of inductive inference do yeomanly work in setting constraints for many of us, but fail to deliver the exactness characteristic of deductive inference.

We need not attribute the difference in precision to anything deeply metaphysical about deductive inference; nor should we elevate its comparative exactness to crystalline purity. The determinacy of our notions of inference arises from the specificity of our conceptual commitments constitutive of those notions, and we can introduce specificity as we see fit. We simply do not always see fit to do so, for one reason or another (cf. Wittgenstein 1953, section 87). Our notions of inference are, after all, our notions, to do with as we deem appropriate. Philosophers rarely sound this note, occupied as they are with supposedly objective conceptual phenomena.

Perhaps equivocal use of 'concept' is partly responsible here: concepts as objective properties, and concepts as psychological constructs. G. E. Moore, for instance, proposed—in what Russell (1959, p. 42) called "the first published account of the new philosophy"—that a "concept is not a mental fact, nor any part of a mental fact" (1899, p. 179). Moore's talk of conceiving-independent concepts is obviously not synonymous with my talk of concepts, or notions.

Given the role I acknowledge for the meaning of conclusion-indicators, we need not regard all inferentially successful arguments as enthymematic. In particular, we need not portray successful arguments as always suppressing premises that express their inference-patterns. This result is fortunate, since, as Lewis Carroll (1895) illustrates, adding inference-patterns as required premises only generates an endless regress of required new premises. Conditions set by the meaning of 'therefore' or some other conclusion-indicator for one do not require the addition of new premises to an argument. Use of a conclusion-indicator is already a crucial meaningful component in what an argument expresses; it is not something demanding additional components.

Conclusion-indicators themselves, then, can represent the operative notions needed to determine what it is to be successful inference, or validity, in an argument for one. This widely neglected consideration blocks Carroll's famous regress and identifies how semantic foundationalism can allow for irreducibly inductive argument. The meaning of a conclusion-indicator for one can set conditions of inferential success for one, even conditions of irreducibly inductive inferential success. As for the justification of inference-patterns, deductive argument for such justification can follow schema 1 through 3. Semantic foundationalism thus extends even to the foundations of logic.

Premise 1 of deductive schema 1 through 3 has its basis in a conceptual commitment regarding justification: that is, in an operative semantic standard for correct use of 'justification' (or some synonymous term). In arguing for the justification of a statement, one uses, at least implicitly, a semantic standard as the basis for one's appeal to what justification requires or consists in.

One can, in certain cases, be wrong in a belief about what oneself means or has meant by 'justification'. Beliefs regarding past psychological states, such as a belief about what I meant, can and evidently do sometimes go wrong.

Various beliefs about one's present psychological states can go wrong too, the apparent exceptions being such Cartesian *de se* beliefs as that I think and that I judge. My intentionally using constitutive standard *C* to give semantic significance, or meaning, to a token, *T*, requires my accepting *C*'s normative implications for correct use of *T*. Even if *C* has merely prescriptive implications that are themselves neither true nor false, I can be incorrect in my belief about whether I actually endorse *C*'s implications as binding on me. My belief might have resulted from haste or carelessness of some other sort.

Semantic foundationalism allows for cogent arguments for justification (by certain standards) that are unsound, misleading, or incorrect, owing to a false premise. Cogency does not entail correctness, or truth. The history of the natural sciences can illustrate this point in detail. At least, fallibilist approaches to cogency allow for cogency without truth. As for constitutive standards for (what it is to be) cogency for one, and justification of claims to cogency, semantic foundationalism serves in a way paralleling its treatment of justification.

When arguing deductively for justification, I rely on steps having the form of argument 1 through 3, but do not thereby endorse *my endorsing* those steps. The latter, second-order endorsement is a separate matter. The justification given to *P* in step 3, however unsound, comes from the steps 1 through 3 themselves, not from the autobiographical consideration that I accept those steps. My being mistaken in assuming that I endorse steps 1 through 3 will not, then, necessarily affect the cogency of the argument for the justification of *P*.

Perhaps, in accord with the cognitive-meaning agnosticism of section 1.7, you have general skeptical doubts about my knowing what I mean when I assert something. I have already conceded that one can have no non-questionbegging supporting evidence that is resistant to a cognitive-meaning agnostic. I might, however, find some satisfaction in returning your skeptical doubts: How do you know what your skeptical challenges or questions signify? More generally, we might ask what (if anything) thoroughgoing semantic skeptics mean by 'justification' and 'knowledge', and whether they enjoy such justification and knowledge relative to the meaning of their own skeptical queries. This ad hominem reply might give an unmitigated semantic skeptic pause for thought, but it cannot deliver the non-questionbegging evidence demanded by such a skeptic.[15]

Semantic foundationalism does not pretend to have a non-questionbegging defense against a thoroughgoing cognitive-meaning agnostic. It does not offer what conceptually cannot be offered: an answer to cognitive-meaning agnosticism that does not depend on meaningful assertions. Chapter 1 concedes that battles against shrewd agnostics cannot be won and recommends that we change the subject in light of the lessons about reasons arising from those losing battles. (This book explains how we can change the subject while incorporating lessons from agnostic challenges and sustaining philosophy as an explanatory discipline.)

15. This ad hominem reply has some affinity with a recurring theme of Wittgenstein's *On Certainty* (1969, sections 114, 126, 456). Cf. Haller (1988). See Moser (1990c) for an earlier attempt of mine to appeal to meaning to challenge thoroughgoing skepticism.

Semantic foundationalism recommends the use of arguments instantiating 1 through 3 to answer challenges to the justification of, among other things, one's answers to the explanatory and evaluative projects. Why? The answer is straightforward: What it is to be a justification, for one (where the relativity is semantic), depends on—indeed, is constituted by—one's operative notion of justification, and arguments instantiating 1 through 3 will conclusively ground justification in the notion that is one's semantic foundation. The pertinent semantic foundation defines what it means for one to say that something is justified, not what it means for one to say that we may regard something as justified. Schema 1 through 3 acknowledges the crucial role of an operative notion of justification, as a semantic foundation, in what justification is for one.

When the relevant semantic foundation captures what one actually means in saying that something is justified, it enables an argument for justification that is sound, or correct, relative to one's actual operative semantic standards. In that case, an argument exemplifying 1 through 3 will be above reproach with respect to giving sound justification—at least for the person in question. Merely cogent justification, as just observed, can follow suit, but without the soundness: Justification can be deficient from the standpoint of correctness. We must distinguish, in any case, the justification of the statement justified according to the conclusion of 1 through 3 (namely, *P*) and the justification of 3 itself. Lower-order justification can get by without higher-order justification, despite any bothersome temptation to level-confusions.

C. Evaluating and Explaining Justification

Schema 1 through 3 illustrates how arguing deductively for justification for any statement, including any statement that ascribes justification, can properly end in considerations about an operative notion regarding justification. What about the evaluating and explaining of justification?

Semantic foundationalism extends readily to arguments of the following forms:

> By my conceptual commitment, correct evaluation, or discernment, of epistemically justified belief consists in conditions *C*; evaluative epistemic standard *E* requires just *C*; hence, *E* is a correct evaluative epistemic standard, at least for me.
>
> By my conceptual commitment, correct explanation of epistemic justification consists in conditions *C*; explanatory epistemic standard *E* requires just *C*; hence, *E* is a correct explanatory epistemic standard, at least for me.

These deductive arguments deliver conclusions about what evaluative and explanatory epistemic standards are correct. They do so on the basis of considerations about one's operative notions of correctly evaluating and correctly explaining epistemic justification. Schema 1 through 3, in contrast, illustrates how we can argue deductively, and fully, for conclusions affirming the *justifi-*

cation of evaluative and explanatory standards. Arguing for correctness of epistemic standards is one thing; arguing for their justification, another.

Given a cogent argument for the correctness of certain evaluative and explanatory standards, one can plausibly use those standards to evaluate and to explain epistemic justification. Recall from section 2.2 that a typical evaluative epistemic standard takes this form: We may evaluate a (candidate) belief as epistemically justified if (and only if) that belief satisfies conditions *C*. A typical explanatory epistemic standard, in contrast, takes this form: A belief is epistemically justified if (and only if) it satisfies explanatory conditions *C*. Some such standards are indispensable to any judicious evaluation or explanation of epistemic justification.

Common talk of evaluating and explaining justification is equivocal, as is usual talk of "giving justification." It sometimes connotes "arguing fully for justification," and other times, something else. If evaluating justification and explaining justification were just arguing fully for justification, we need say no more, given the previous application of semantic foundationalism to such arguing, especially via schema 1 through 3. When something other than arguing fully for justification is at issue, semantic foundationalism applies in a somewhat different way.

Talk of evaluating justification can signify just one's implementing the aforementioned sort of evaluative epistemic standard. An evaluative coherentist, for example, might consistently apply this standard: We may evaluate a candidate for belief as epistemically justified if and only if that candidate coheres (in some specified way) with my set of antecedent coherent beliefs. In applying this standard, a coherentist infers that *we may evaluate* some belief-candidate as epistemically justified. In applying such an evaluative standard, and inferring that we may evaluate some belief-candidate as justified, one need not present an argument for the conclusion that this belief-candidate is justified. Moreover, even if one infers the latter conclusion, one may stop short of anchoring one's standard in considerations about an operative notion regarding justification. In this respect, evaluating justification can differ from the kind of full arguing for justification captured by schema 1 through 3.

We have just noted that the correctness of an evaluative standard for one rests on an operative notion for one regarding (correctly evaluating) justification, and that schema 1 through 3 identifies conditions for arguing fully for the justification of any such standard. These are two key areas where semantic foundationalism bears on evaluative standards.

More specific bearing of semantic foundationalism comes from considerations about the condition supposed to be sufficient for permissible evaluation of a belief-candidate as justified. Given the previous coherentist standard, one will rely on an operative notion constitutive of what it is for a belief-candidate to cohere with one's set of antecedent coherent beliefs. This notion will play a decisive role in determining what it is for the coherentist standard actually to be satisfied by a belief-candidate; and it will figure in a full argument, following schema 1 through 3, for the justification of the claim that the standard is satisfied. Once again, we must distinguish correctness from justification.

Analogous points apply to the notion of permissibility motivating the use of 'may' in an evaluative standard. However this notion is specified, it will play a decisive role in determining what it is for one to be permitted to evaluate a belief-candidate as justified. It will also be operative in the use of schema 1 through 3 to argue fully for the justification of the claim that one may evaluate a certain belief-candidate as justified.

Coherentists can offer an obvious specification of permissibility here, if they hold that justification consists in coherence of a belief-candidate with one's set of antecedent coherent beliefs. The permissibility of evaluation for them will then arise from their evaluative standard's identifying what constitutes justification for belief-candidates. The pertinent use of 'may' will then amount to 'may correctly'. In that case, one's evaluative standard will perhaps add little, if anything, to one's explanatory standard specifying what constitutes justification for one.

Similarly, if 'may' amounts to 'may justifiedly', one's evaluative standard will perhaps add little, if anything, to one's explanatory standard. It will then specify conditions for one's justifiedly evaluating a belief-candidate as justified. If justifiedly evaluating is justifiedly believing, one's explanatory standard, in virtue of providing conditions for justified belief, will typically supply conditions of the sort offered by one's evaluative standard, thus making one's evaluative standard superfluous.

Other uses of 'may' are available, since sets of rules determining permissibility come in a wide range of distinctive members. Their range is as wide as the set of standards conducive to expediency and efficiency. The independence of evaluative standards from explanatory standards depends on constitutive standards for correctly using 'may' that do not reduce to semantic standards for 'may correctly' or for 'may justifiedly', where the latter standards explain what constitutes justification for one. Different theorists can offer different standards for using 'may' in evaluative standards. They can even leave the conceptual connections between what is "permissibly evaluated as justification" and what is "actual justification" somewhat indeterminate. (By analogy, some talk of what is "probably true," in principles for inductive inference, is vaguely related to talk of what is "actually true.") We can see, in any case, that the lessons of semantic foundationalism bear on what it is to be permissible evaluation for one, and on claims to justification for permissible evaluations.

Explanatory standards illustrate the same kinds of lessons as evaluative standards. We can grant that explaining justification for a claim need not yield a full argument for the justification of that claim. We often talk of one's explaining justification in cases where one simply applies an explanatory standard stating a sufficient condition for justification: for example, if belief *B* satisfies explanatory condition *C*, then *B* is justified. In simply applying such a standard, one infers that *B* is justified, and one does argue to that minimal extent. One does not, however, offer considerations about an operative notion of justification to anchor one's explanatory standard. Schema 1 through 3, in contrast, offers considerations about an operative notion in its premise 1 and thus represents a more complete kind of "arguing for" justification.

Even if explanation need not be full argument, the correctness of an explanatory standard for one depends on—indeed, is constituted by—an operative notion for one regarding (explaining) justification. Schema 1 through 3, furthermore, identifies conditions for arguing fully for the justification of an explanatory standard. These are not the only areas where semantic foundationalism bears on explanatory standards. Another area concerns the condition supposed to be sufficient for justification: *B*'s satisfying explanatory condition *C*. In using an explanatory standard of the form in question, one will rely on an operative notion constitutive of what it is for *B* to satisfy explanatory condition *C*. This notion will determine what it is for one's explanatory standard actually to be satisfied by a belief. It will also figure in a full argument, following schema 1 through 3, for the justification of the claim that the standard is satisfied. Even if explanation is not full argument, then, the lessons of semantic foundationalism apply to explaining justification.

The lessons of semantic foundationalism, as we should expect, apply to semantic foundationalism itself. In particular, what one means by 'properly end' in the earlier summary statements of the view will play a definitive role in what it means for semantic foundationalism to be a correct view. In fact, if we understand 'properly end' to connote 'correctly end', we may treat semantic foundationalism as conceptually correct in virtue of semantic considerations regarding the explaining, evaluating, and arguing for justification and the correctness of corresponding epistemic standards for such matters.

Worries about circularity are misplaced now, as section 2.2 suggested in connection with the semantic project. Semantic foundationalism can be true in virtue of semantic considerations; and when asked what it means to say that semantic foundationalism is true, we can—indeed, must—appeal to the pertinent semantic considerations. After all, conceptual correctness is, by definition, correctness in virtue of meaning.

Going beyond mere correctness, schema 1 through 3 enables a full justification, even a sound justification, of semantic foundationalism for anyone with suitable conceptual commitments regarding justification. Consider an explanationist notion of justification (broadly in accord with Moser 1989, pp. 260–265) favoring an epistemological view that explains what needs to be explained better than any available competitor, while raising no decisive problems in doing so. We may regard explanation as the answering of pertinent why-, what-, and how-questions; and we may regard what needs to be explained as the (generally characterized) explaining, evaluating, and arguing for justification and the standards for correctness for such matters.

Betterness of explanation is a function of the problems raised and problems avoided by an explanation in comparison with competing explanations; but individual theorists can, and sometimes do, wield different standards for what exactly constitutes a *problem* for an explanation. An explanation that beats, or is as good as, any available competitor for one is a best explanation for one. An explanationist strategy for justification often takes this line: Let us consider the problem-questions (say, about justification) in *this* way, to see if we can answer the questions in a less problematic way than the available competitors; if we can, justification accrues accordingly. Even here, as semantic foundationalism suggests, an operative, explanationist *notion* of justification is crucial.

Semantic foundationalism owes its correctness, then, to semantic considerations, but can derive justification from explanatory considerations. Conceptual truths, holding in virtue of conceptual commitments, can have explanatory value; that is, truths arising just from what one means can contribute to the answering of explanation-seeking why-, what-, and how-questions. When conceptual truths do have explanatory value, they can accrue justificational value accordingly (at least relative to an explanationist notion of justification of the general sort characterized in Moser 1989). An explanationist approach to justification is especially suited to bear on what philosophers typically do: offer answers to explanation-seeking questions.

An explanationist argument for the justification of semantic foundationalism should show, then, that semantic foundationalism does not leave one open to any decisive problems concerning explaining, evaluating, and arguing for justification, or concerning standards of correctness for such matters. Problems arising from demands for agnostic-resistant non-questionbegging epistemic reasons are indecisive now; as noted in section 1.8, I aim to change the subject from agnostic-resistant epistemic reasons (while accommodating the lessons about reasons arising from agnostic challenges). I intend not to fight a losing battle against ontological agnostics. Any philosophical problem, then, is a fair means of challenge to semantic foundationalism, so long as it does not demand agnostic-resistant reasons of the sort discussed in section 1.7. (Section 2.4 takes up some likely objections to semantic foundationalism.)

Semantic foundationalism attributes correctness of epistemic standards to considerations about what one means by certain epistemic terms. It thus avoids the range of epistemological and ontological problems confronting objectivist construals of epistemic status as a natural kind or a Platonic universal. (Some of the relevant problem-questions emerged in section 1.7.) In acknowledging diversity of meaning, semantic foundationalism can easily accommodate the substantial variation among epistemologists in notions and standards of epistemic status. Even proponents of objective epistemic status rely on a particular *notion* of epistemic status in sanctioning certain objective considerations as constitutive of epistemic status.

One potential problem for semantic foundationalism is a threat of thoroughgoing relativism: relativism entailing an "anything goes" approach to correctness and justification. It might seem that schema 1 through 3 enables us to justify *anything* we like. This problem deserves, and gets, full attention later, in chapter 4. For now, let us simply note that the only relativism that actually threatens is conceptual: relativism concerning the notions or definitions used by people. Divergent uses of premise 1 in schema 1 through 3 will not entail the correctness of conflicting views about justification (in a specified sense); they rather will entail that some people *mean different things* by 'justification', at least at a level of specificity. Conceptual relativism does not entail that one's believing something automatically makes it true. Semantic foundationalism, then, does not entail thoroughgoing substantive relativism.

In sum, semantic foundationalism shows how perplexing questions about explaining, evaluating, and arguing for justification cease to perplex once considerations about conceptual commitments serve as a fundamental standard. Semantic standards, we have seen, can informatively answer questions about correctness and justification. We have no anchor more secure, no explanation more cogent. Semantic foundationalism saves us from a multitude of troublesome ontological and epistemological commitments regarding what makes epistemic standards correct. Some likely objections and general lessons now merit attention.

2.4 Objections and Metaphilosophical Lessons

A. Preanalytic Data, Ordinary Language, and Essences

Some philosophers approach epistemological notions in ways seemingly incompatible with semantic foundationalism. Three noteworthy alternatives imply that notions of justification can be either correct or justified in virtue of: (a) fitting our "preanalytic data" about justification, (b) describing our "ordinary use" of 'justification', or (c) capturing "the essence" of justification. Whether such approaches to notional correctness are ultimately acceptable will depend on one's semantic standards constitutive of what it is for a notion of justification to be correct. This, at least, is a lesson that arose earlier from semantic foundationalism. We shall see that those seemingly alternative approaches do not account for explaining, evaluating, and arguing for justification better than does semantic foundationalism. In fact, we shall see that they actually lend support to semantic foundationalism.

Consider first the appeal to "preanalytic epistemic data" as a basis for justifying a notion of justification. This approach has attracted many philosophers in the phenomenological tradition of Brentano and Husserl, and many philosophers in the commonsense tradition of Reid, Moore, and Chisholm.[16] The rough idea is that we have pretheoretical access, via "intuition" or "common sense," to certain considerations about justification, and these considerations can support one notion of justification over others. Two considerations raise problems for this approach if it aims to be an alternative to semantic foundationalism.

First, it is unclear what the epistemic status of the relevant preanalytic epistemic data is supposed to be. Such data, we often hear, are accessed by "intuitions" or by "common sense." We thus hear some epistemologists talk as follows: "Intuitively (or commonsensically), justification resides in a particular case like *this*, and does not reside in a case like *that*." A statement of this sort aims to guide our formulation of a notion of justification. A simple ques-

16. On Chisholm's "commonsensism," see Chisholm (1973, pp. 68–69; 1977, p. 121). For another recent endorsement of commonsensism, see Grossmann (1990, p. 14).

tion arises: Is such a statement self-justifying, with no need of independent epistemic support? If so, what notion of self-justification can sanction the deliverances of intuition or common sense, but exclude spontaneous judgments no better, epistemically, than mere prejudice or guesswork?

Literal talk of self-justification evidently admits unrestricted justification. If one statement can literally justify itself, solely in virtue of itself, then every statement can. Statements do not differ on their supporting themselves: For any statement *P*, *P* guarantees *P*. Such "support" is universal. A widely accepted adequacy condition on standards of justification is that they not allow for the justification of every proposition, that they not leave us with an "anything goes" approach to justification. Literal self-justification runs afoul of this condition. Some philosophers apparently use 'self-justification' in a nonliteral sense, but we need not pursue this interpretive matter here.

Intuitive judgments and commonsense judgments can, and sometimes do, result from special, even biased, linguistic training. Why then should we regard such judgments as *automatically* epistemically privileged? Perhaps we should not. Intuitive judgments and commonsense judgments certainly can be false, as but a little reflection clearly illustrates. Such judgments, furthermore, seem not always to be supported by best available evidence. Consider, for instance, how various judgments of "common sense" are at odds with our best available evidence from the natural sciences. It is unclear, then, why we should regard intuitive judgments or commonsense judgments as the basis of any of our standards for justification.

Perhaps, as Clifford Geertz suggests, we should not regard common sense as a reliable faculty or source for our judgments:

> Common sense is not a fortunate faculty, like perfect pitch; it is a special frame of mind, like piety or legalism. And like piety or legalism (or ethics or cosmology), it both differs from one place to the next and takes, nevertheless, a characteristic form. (Geertz 1983, p. 11; cf. Geertz's chapter 4, "Common Sense as a Cultural System")

We have, in any case, no straightforward answer to the question why we should deem the judgments of common sense or intuition epistemically privileged. We have, moreover, a firmer, more cogent basis for epistemic standards identified by semantic foundationalism, whether the standards be semantic, explanatory, or evaluative.

The second problem for appeals to intuitions or common sense is this: If we presuppose an operative notion of justification implying that a notion of justification is itself (to be) justified by conformity to intuition or common sense, we are doing in a specific way what semantic foundationalism says we do in general. We are relying on a certain operative *notion* of justification to anchor our justificational constraints and the justification thereby provided. Commonsense theorists ultimately rely on an operative notion of justification implying that common sense is a source of justification, perhaps even for notions of justification. Semantic foundationalism entails that theorists explaining, evaluating, and arguing for justification do just this: namely, depend on an operative notion regarding justification. A reliable sign of a conceptual commitment at work among commonsense theorists is that they are not genuinely open to potential counterexamples to their assumption that common sense is a source of justification. A directly analogous point bears on friends of intuitions.

Commonsense theorists might object to semantic foundationalism on the ground that their operative notion of justification is itself ultimately justified by common sense. This ground is stable, however, only if commonsense theorists can appeal to their operative notion of justification—a notion that determines for them what it is to be justified. Without appeal to this notion, commonsense theorists' case for justification via common sense will be decisively incomplete. This case requires that commonsense judgments be appropriately linked, via a notion of justification, to *justified* judgments. Commonsense theorists' operative notion of justification thus does essential work in their appeal to common sense as a source of justification. This fits with, indeed confirms, semantic foundationalism.

Analogous points apply to an attempt to use one's "reflective" or "considered" judgments to argue for the justification of conceptual theses or epistemic standards.[17] Appeal to such judgments to explain, evaluate, or argue for justification for statements presupposes considerations about an operative notion implying that such judgments have a certain epistemic significance. An operative notion of justification enables one to deem suitable "reflection" a source of justification, and to hold that reflective judgments yield justification. Apart from the operative notion, one lacks a decisive link between reflection and justification.

Consider next an appeal to our "ordinary use" of 'justification' as the basis for explaining and arguing for justification. Explaining and arguing for justification come to an end, on this view, with an appeal to how we ordinarily use the term 'justification'. If I am a reliabilist, for example, I can ultimately justify my position by appeal to this statement: We ordinarily use the term 'justification' in accord with reliabilist assumptions. (See Malcolm 1942 for an appeal to ordinary language for such epistemological purposes.)

An appeal to ordinary language-use raises problems on three counts. First, there is troublesome vagueness in the phrase 'our ordinary use'. What determines *ordinary* use? In particular, who exactly are the relevant language-users? It is doubtful that straightforward answers are forthcoming. Ordinariness of use, in any case, seems context-relative and subject to variation. Second, it is unclear why we should think that ordinary language-use favorable to reliabilism is sufficient to justify reliabilism. It seems quite conceivable, at least on various notions of justification in circulation, that ordinary language-use is unjustified under certain circumstances.

17. A recent example of such an attempt in epistemology comes from Alston (1989b, p. 14). For an appeal to "reflective considered judgments" in ethical justification, see Nielsen (1991, chaps. 9–11). Cf. Sosa (1991, chap. 15). For criticism of various epistemological uses of reflective equilibrium, see Stich (1990, chap. 4).

The third consideration recalls part of the previous reply to an appeal to intuitive or commonsense judgments. Ordinary-language philosophers might object to semantic foundationalism on the ground that their notion of justification is itself ultimately justified by ordinary language-use. This ground has stability, however, only if ordinary-language philosophers presuppose a notion of justification, a notion that makes conformity to ordinary language a source of epistemic justification. Lacking such a notion, ordinary-language philosophers will be unable to make their case, as they will lack the crucial connection between ordinary linguistic use and justification. Ordinary-language philosophers' operative notion of justification thus does essential work in their epistemology. This confirms the main lesson of semantic foundationalism.

Consider finally the view that our basis for explaining and arguing for justification is an appeal to "the essence" of justification. We might think of essences as Platonic universals accessible by direct acquaintance. Russell, as noted in section 1.3, once endorsed a doctrine of direct acquaintance with universals. One problem for any such approach arises from the difficulty of explaining our epistemological access to the essences in question. Do we have a special, reliable faculty for intuiting essences? It is not obvious, at least to some of us, that we do. Even if we do, we need an account of how exactly that faculty figures in explaining and arguing for justification. Proponents of Russell-style realism have not delivered the needed account.

Another problem is that in fully explaining or arguing for justification one must specify what it is that yields justification. Given an appeal to essences of justification here, one must specify what one means by 'essence of justification'. Even if direct acquaintance with the essence of justification suffices for one's merely having justification, it does not suffice for one's fully explaining or arguing for justification. The latter requires one's specifying what it is that yields justification for one; in the present case, this calls for specification of what one means by 'essence of justification'.

Since an explanatorily adequate definition of 'essence of justification' entails a definition of 'justification', the current approach seems to fit with semantic foundationalism. It presupposes an appeal to what one means by 'justification'. Platonism about essences may preclude relativism about correctness of definitions. The crucial work, however, in fully explaining and arguing for justification—even for a Platonist about essences of justification—comes from considerations about meaning, from an operative notion of justification. Without appeal to a notion of justification, Platonists will be hard put to relate the supposed essences to what provides justification. This point obviously fits with the main lesson of semantic foundationalism. Directly analogous considerations, furthermore, bear on any appeal to justification as a "natural kind" to anchor explaining or arguing for justification. Theorists must specify *what* kind they are talking about and then connect this kind, via a notion of justification, to what provides justification.

The question whether a notion or a definition of justification can itself be justified requires a clear notion of "justified." In the absence of such a notion, the question will be more puzzling than instructive; for we shall then lack conditions definitive of a correct answer to the question. Semantic foundationalism suggests as much.

One might construe justification for a notion in various ways: for example, as either (a) its being inferable from another notion, which may or may not be justifiable in some sense; (b) its being conducive to a relatively simple but comprehensive classificatory system; or (c) its conformity to a certain familiar standard, such as ordinary language-use. Whatever construal one prefers, one's ultimate appeal must be to a *notion* of justification that links the considerations invoked (for example, compliance with intuition, common sense, ordinary use, or an essence) with *justification* of the relevant sort. Even inductive arguments for justification, as we saw in section 2.3, rest on an operative notion regarding justification.

Appealing to anything *X* (for example, belief-forming processes, intuitions, inference-patterns, ordinary uses of language, universals, or natural kinds) to provide justification presupposes a notion of justification relative to which *X* can and does deliver justification. Omit the presupposed notion, and the claim to supply justification via *X* becomes inconclusive. This is one of the main lessons of semantic foundationalism. Whatever constraints we link to justification, *we* make the linkage relative to a presupposed notion of justification. This does not entail, however, that a notion must be temporally prior to arguing for justification. The relevant point concerns only logical, or conceptual, priority.

B. Notions and Philosophical Problems

Philosophers often decide on their philosophical notions and their conceptual systems relative to their own purposes, or ends, in theorizing.[18] Philosophers, and not denizens of an impersonal external world, are doing their conceiving relative to their purposes in theorizing. An external world seems not to set by itself the boundaries of our philosophical concepts for us. We evidently set the constraints we do in light of a wide range of differing purposes. The simple ordering of "features" in perceptual experience is only one among many possible ends that can constrain concept-formation. (Chapter 4 returns to this theme.)

Notions, as section 2.3 suggests, comprise semantic standards constitutive of the correct use of terms. Many contemporary epistemologists adopt and use notions of justification that share a core with the notions of justification assumed by various leading epistemologists from Plato to Kant to Russell. The core of these notions derives from an interest in what Plato, Kant, and Russell were regarding as the third condition for knowledge. This common core is rather thin in certain cases, including in some cases only sketchy standards involving vague conditions of "well-foundedness," "nonaccidental connectedness with the

18. Here I agree with C. I. Lewis (1926, 1929). Cf. Waismann (1939) and Carruthers (1987). Sections 4.2 and 5.3 explain the role of purposes, or ends, in rational theorizing.

truth condition," "likelihood of truth," and so on. This common core does, nonetheless, set some general constraints. It rules out, for instance, justification as obviously contradictory belief-formation and, more generally, justification as an "anything goes" policy of belief-formation.

I may hold that another person's semantic standards for 'justification' must share the core of my own acknowledged set of such standards to qualify as semantic standards regarding justification. What exactly constitutes the relevant core will be up to an individual theorist. My own set of semantic standards for 'justification', on this view, will not conflict with the core of any alternative set that I (properly) call "semantic standards regarding *epistemic justification*." My semantic standards are thus my anchor not only for arguing for justification but also for deciding on genuine concepts of justification. I decide what counts as a notion of justification from my conceptual perspective: in particular, from the perspective of my adopted conceptual core (necessary) for any concept of justification. My conceptual perspective *might* be shared by others, but we have no conclusive reason to think that it must be shared—even if it must be in principle understandable, or shareable, by others.[19]

An important methodological lesson emerges here. Semantic foundationalism suggests that the perennial nonempirical problems of epistemology—and of philosophy in general—perplex us endlessly and even seem insoluble, typically because those problems are formulated via insufficiently explicit or detailed semantic standards for their key terms. The epistemological problems in question include: Is knowledge justified true belief? Does empirical justification have foundations? Is epistemic justification a function of reliable belief-formation? Once the relevant semantic standards for such terms as 'knowledge' and 'justification' are given sufficient detail (and this we typically do with an eye to agreement with our antecedent semantic standards and semantically based adequacy conditions for resolving problems of interest), then the problems surrender. They vanish as a result of our expanded, more specific semantic foundations. One may still face problems concerning which epistemological notions actually best serve one's theoretical ends, but that is a practical problem, a problem of applying relevant standards.

When the needed semantic standards lack specificity, perennial philosophical controversy ensues, owing typically to varying implicit specifications of those standards by different philosophers. Such is the usual way of "conflict" in traditional epistemology and in philosophy generally. The conflict here is actually "conflict," because variation in implicit specifications of semantic standards entails that philosophers are really talking about different matters. The resolution of such "conflict," in typical cases, requires *explicit* formulation of the notions formulating the "conflict." It requires the making explicit of semantic foundations. This will open the door, the only door, to our resolving the problem under dispute—if only by showing that the participants to the

19. For evidence that Wittgenstein's influential views on privacy are no threat here, see Moser (1991, 1992) and Baker and Hacker (1985, pp. 173–179). Sections 3.2 and 5.1 return to the relevance of social factors in meaning.

"conflict" are really talking about different matters. (Chapter 4 returns to this theme.)

Some philosophers will worry about specifying, or amplifying, a vague semantic standard in the *right* way. Such a worry seeks constraints for the "correct" amplification of a notion. We may think of notions as semantic packages, of varying complexity, constituted by semantic standards for the correct use of terms. We may think, for example, of the traditional philosophical notion of knowledge, stemming from *Theaetetus* 202c, as a semantic package including concepts of justification, truth, belief, and the absence of defeaters. Semantic packaging, I have suggested, is done by conceivers, even *if* the extension of a concept is sometimes conceiver-independent.[20]

Much semantic information comes to us seemingly "prepackaged," via social inheritance. Some inherited concepts, however, need our special repackaging: for example, amplifying for our philosophical purposes. Some concepts are too vague or too sketchy to settle our philosophical concerns. We thus need to fill in or to refill the semantic standards accompanying such concepts. Given strict conditions for individuating concepts, this will entail the formulation of a different concept, but we may talk of different specifications of a concept *generally characterized*. It is misleading to think of the task of supplementing or revising semantic standards as analogous to empirical discovery in the natural sciences. A better model is that of *construction* relative to theoretical purposes and accepted adequacy conditions for meeting those purposes. Even here, however, a *notion* of adequate, or correct, construction will play a crucial role in explaining, evaluating, and justifying alteration of semantic standards.

Worries about correctness of conceptual amplification may stem from one's acceptance of certain adequacy conditions for solving philosophical problems relevant to the concept being amplified. We thus should beware of regarding our preferred constraints on such correctness as being categorically binding. A constraint on semantic packaging, or on conceptual amplification, is either internal or external to a semantic package under revision. If *internal*, a constraint comes solely from semantic entailment relations with antecedent components of the package, and thus from prior conceptual commitments underlying that package. Such a constraint will be semantically entailed by an antecedent component of the package under revision. If *external*, a constraint will not be semantically entailed by an antecedent component of the package.

Use of an internal constraint simply makes explicit what is already implicit in a semantic package. We might, for example, come to see that our concept of knowledge involves a notion of adequate evidence, upon coming to see that our concept of knowledge involves an internalist notion of perspectival, person-relative justification. This would be a moderate internal amplification. Use

20. Semantic foundationalism is logically compatible with, but does not entail, a sort of realism about the extension of concepts. For some discussion of such realism, see Anscombe (1976) and Hacker (1986, chap. 11). My own commitment to semantic foundationalism is, of course, coupled with the sort of conditional ontological agnosticism defended in section 1.7.

of an external constraint is potentially more revisionary. Such a constraint comes from an independent adequacy condition accepted by a person assessing conceptual amplification. Independent adequacy conditions for correct formulation of concepts can, and do, vary among philosophers. This partly explains why many substantive philosophical disagreements resist resolution.

Familiar examples of independent adequacy conditions include (a) what one "would say" under certain imagined conditions, (b) some independent pattern of language use, for example, ordinary language use, and (c) certain explanatory requirements for an adequate resolution of a problem, for example, simplicity and comprehensiveness. Such constraints typically are not internal to concepts under amplification. They rather are introduced by a theorist wielding a particular *notion* of "correctness" or "justification" as a standard for conceptual amplification. A theorist thus may judge certain semantic standards as correct or incorrect, on the basis of such constraints. Such a judgment will rest for its intelligibility, however, on certain other semantic standards for correctness or incorrectness: at least on a semantic standard for correct conceptual amplification. We again see a particular instance of a recurring lesson from semantic foundationalism.

C. Conceptual Relativism Introduced

Semantic foundationalism allows for a kind of semantic, or conceptual, relativism. Different philosophers can, and in some cases do, have different operative semantic standards for the use of the term 'justification', at least at a level of specificity. This consideration should be underwhelming; indeed, it is a platitude if anything is. If this is all one means in saying that philosophers can, and in some cases do, have different operative concepts of justification, we have nothing to dispute.

If operative concepts are individuated by one's pertinent operative semantic standards, we need to allow for substantial variability of operative concepts. The contrary view entails the epistemological myth of the definite article: the view that there must be, or at least is, such a thing as *the* concept of justification or knowledge. Even so, different people can, and in some cases do, share a notion of justification *generally characterized.* They can, moreover, typically understand alternative specific notions of justification, even if they do not understand them as specifying what justification actually consists in. One's own specific notion of justification defines what justification consists in (at least for oneself).

Conceptual relativism does not entail *substantive relativism*: the view that whatever one takes to be correct, right, or justified is actually correct, right, or justified. On some concepts of epistemic and moral justification, fundamental epistemic and moral requirements show no cultural or personal variability, but rather are universal in scope. The rejection of substantive relativism thus leaves conceptual, or semantic, relativism untouched. The conceptual relativism allowed by semantic foundationalism does not entail an "anything goes," or substantively relativistic, attitude toward epistemic assessment. (Chapter 4 returns to the implications of conceptual relativism.)

Conceptual relativism still might seem bothersome. It *apparently* implies that conceptual variability admits of no rational assessment. Suppose a student, Jones, comes to us for advice on how to regulate beliefs. Jones is torn between two notions of justification. One notion, from a thoroughgoing mystic, implies that Jones can justifiably believe whatever arises spontaneously, without interference from inference. A second notion, from a W. K. Clifford–style scientist, implies that Jones can justifiably believe only what enjoys evidence in accord with an experimental, scientific method. Jones, being torn, asks us what she should believe. Should she believe in accord with the mystic's notion or the scientist's notion?

We naturally reply by complicating Jones's options. We introduce some additional notions of justification in circulation. If in doubt, we advise, then complicate. Where, however, does this advice take Jones? She will certainly wonder which of the various notions her believing should (aim to) follow. Such wondering, nonetheless, is thus far seriously indeterminate, and can be seen to be so upon reflection.

We do not yet know the meaning—the semantic standards—of 'should' in the question of what Jones *should* believe. This question becomes manageably determinate only when the meaning of 'should' is made definite: only with the specification of semantic standards for 'should'. Such standards will link the relevant use of 'should' to determinate notions of *obligation*, *permissibility*, and *justification*—to determinate semantic requirements constituting relevant notions of obligation, permissibility, and justification. Once this specification—this linkage—obtains, we have the needed basis for understanding Jones's question and for seeking an answer. We then understand what notion of obligation is determining Jones's use of 'should'.

If, for example, Jones is after what she should prudentially believe (instead of what she epistemically or morally should believe, for example), we shall ask what notion of justification is conducive to prudential belief in the relevant sense—a sense that may itself need specification.[21] The only remaining problem is practical, a problem of applying pertinent standards. (Jones may, of course, be asking something indeterminate for herself; in that case, we shall not have a determinate question to answer.) This recourse to an operative notion, to what one means, obviously fits with semantic foundationalism. It ultimately resolves a typical normative philosophical question by semantic considerations.

Semantic foundationalism clearly bears on nonepistemic and epistemic species of justification. If one seeks to give an instrumental justification for something, this justification will rest on considerations about a notion of instrumental justification relative to which certain factors can and do provide such justification. Corresponding points hold for moral, aesthetic, and legal justification, for example. Semantic foundationalism thus ranges widely, over any domain of justification.

21. For elaboration on this point in connection with the semantics of obligation-talk, see Moser (1985, chap. 6). Chapter 4 returns to this topic.

Let us turn now to two influential epistemological extremes in the philosophy of science to highlight some additional lessons of semantic foundationalism.

2.5 Two Epistemological Extremes

At one end of the epistemological spectrum, we have *scientific-community authoritarianism* as advanced by Thomas Kuhn's (1970a) account of scientific justification. At the other end, we have *epistemological-standard authoritarianism* stating that the standards for scientific justification are epistemically independent of the actual decisions, goals, and practices of scientists. The latter view typically finds a basis for epistemological standards either in certain metaphysical principles—as in certain Aristotelian philosophies of science—or in certain principles of inductive or deductive logic—as in Carnap's (1950) confirmation theory. Between the two extremes we have a number of views acknowledging the epistemological significance both of actual scientific decisions, goals, and practices and of certain standards independent of such matters. My illustration gains clarity, however, at the extremes.

Scientific-community authoritarianism states that the decisions, goals, and practices of a scientific community provide the ultimate standards for settling epistemological issues. Kuhn endorses this view regarding paradigm choice as follows: "As in political revolutions, so in paradigm choice—there is no standard higher than the assent of the relevant community" (1970a, p. 94; cf. p. 170). He endorses such a view regarding scientific justification in general.

Kuhn holds that the best way to decide whether one scientific theory is more reasonable than another is as follows:

> Take a *group* of the ablest people with the most appropriate motivation; train them in some science and in the specialties relevant to the choice at hand; imbue them with the value system, the ideology, current in their discipline (and to a great extent in other scientific fields as well); and, finally, let them make the choice. (1970b, p. 237)

Kuhn's approach to scientific justification is thus essentially social. It explains the justification of scientific theories not by ahistorical epistemological standards, but by the preferences of a scientific community: that is, by its shared "values," likes, and dislikes.

Kuhn gives us no reason to think that the values in question have epistemological significance independently of the preferences of a scientific community. Kuhn evidently holds that a scientific community's preferences and practices, rather than independent scientific values, are epistemologically fundamental. This approach naturally promotes the importance of historical case studies in the philosophy of science. The way to explain scientific justification, on this approach, is to explain the actual preferences and practices of a scientific community.

Kuhn's approach contrasts sharply with Carnap's epistemological-standard authoritarianism. Carnap's account of scientific justification relies on an account of "logical probability." Carnap regards logical probability as similar to logical implication, as a matter of "partial implication" (1966, p. 32). Logical analysis, on his view, gives us our understanding of relations of logical probability. Carnap claims: "By a logical analysis of a stated hypothesis *h* and stated evidence *e*, we conclude that *h* is not logically implied but is, so to speak, partially implied by *e* to the degree of so-and-so much" (1966, p. 33).

Carnap holds that his concept of logical probability is especially important for meta-epistemic scientific statements: that is, statements about justification in the sciences. He explains:

> We say to a scientist, "You tell me that I can rely on this law in making a certain prediction. How well established [justified?] is the law? How trustworthy [justified?] is the prediction?" . . . I believe that, once inductive logic is sufficiently developed, he could reply, "This hypothesis is confirmed to degree .8 on the basis of the available evidence." A scientist who answers in this way is making a statement about a logical relation between the evidence and the hypothesis in question. . . . His statement that the value of this probability is .8 is, in this context, not a synthetic (empirical) statement, but an analytic one. It is analytic because no empirical investigation is demanded. (1966, p. 35)

Carnap claims that analytic statements of logical probability can be known a priori (1966, p. 36). On his view, questions regarding the acceptability of a theory relative to certain evidence are thus answerable apart from any examination of the preferences or practices of actual scientists. Indeed, such questions are answerable apart from any empirical investigation. Here we have one main point of contrast with Kuhn's scientific-community authoritarianism.

Another point of contrast comes from Carnap's account of the evidence relative to which theories can be logically probable. Scientific evidence, on Carnap's account, comes from "observations" that are either passive and nonexperimental or active and experimental (1966, pp. 6, 40). Scientific observations are of "single facts," and thus give observers access to what needs scientific explanation. The evidential status of observations, on Carnap's account, owes nothing to the preferences or values of a scientific community.

Carnap's observational standard for evidence and probabilistic standard for theory-support are not inferred from actual scientific beliefs and practices. Carnap does not examine the history of science as a basis for recommending his epistemological standards. Instead, he recommends his standards on a priori grounds, specifically on nonempirical grounds concerning what is required for empirical knowledge. Carnap begins his epistemology of natural science with a certain a priori notion of empirical knowledge, and then uses this notion to formulate standards concerning the justifiability of claims made by scientists, even claims to knowledge. These standards, rather than the decisions, goals, and practices of actual scientists, have epistemological authority for Carnap.

We have, then, two epistemological extremes: Kuhn's empirical approach that relies on an examination of actual scientific practices to formulate and to justify standards for scientific justification, and Carnap's a priori approach that relies on an a priori notion of empirical knowledge to formulate and to justify standards for scientific justification. Given only these extremes, we face what many philosophers will regard as a troublesome dilemma. Either (a) given Kuhn's empirical approach, we preclude noncircular epistemological assessment of certain scientific decisions, goals, and practices because the latter determine our epistemological standards, or (b) given Carnap's a priori approach, we need give no independent epistemological significance to the fundamental decisions, goals, and practices of a scientific community.

Option (a) apparently robs epistemology of its normative clout, at least with respect to the epistemological evaluation of certain scientific decisions, goals, and practices. If certain scientific decisions, goals, and practices are the ultimate basis for our epistemological standards, we shall have no independent epistemological basis from which we can critically assess those decisions, goals, and practices. If there were such an independent basis, the decisions, goals, and practices in question would not really be the ultimate basis of our standards.

It will not help to suggest that we can assess certain scientific decisions, goals, and practices on the basis of other scientific decisions, goals, and practices. This suggestion goes nowhere without an account of why the latter decisions, goals, and practices, rather than conflicting decisions, goals, and practices, have epistemological authority. Toulmin (1972) and Laudan (1977) have illustrated amply that the history of scientific views and practices is sufficiently diversified to make any unqualified epistemological appeal to distinctively *scientific* decisions, goals, and practices highly problematic.

Option (b) risks divorcing our epistemology of natural science from natural science itself. If our standards for scientific justification can justifiably come solely from an a priori notion of knowledge unconstrained by the goals and assumptions of prevailing scientific practice, we shall be hard put to explain why these standards are *scientifically* relevant. The problem is that purely a priori standards for scientific justification need have no epistemic basis whatever in what is theoretically appropriate for accomplishing the cognitive goals of prevailing scientific practice.

We can formulate a priori standards for scientific justification that either have no direct relevance to the cognitive goals of practicing scientists or imply that all past and present scientific goals and assumptions are not scientifically justifiable. So long as these a priori standards need not be constrained by the cognitive goals of practicing scientists, but need only come from one's preferred notion of empirical knowledge, we can have a wide-ranging plethora of such standards that relate at best coincidentally to the cognitive goals of practicing scientists. A priori standards for justification are not hard to come by, if they can come, as Carnap suggests, solely from one's preferred notion of empirical knowledge. It seems, however, that our standards for scientific justification must have some substantive epistemological connection to the cognitive goals of practicing scientists. Otherwise, these standards will fail to be *scientific* in any relevant sense. Carnap's a priori approach does nothing to guarantee such a substantive connection.

An adequate epistemology must offer an informative response to the dilemma at hand. Einstein (1949, p. 684) apparently had something like this dilemma in mind when he claimed that "epistemology without contact with science becomes an empty scheme [and] science without epistemology is . . . primitive and muddled." The dilemma here has obvious application outside philosophy of science, to epistemology generally. A general society-oriented empirical approach to epistemological standards relies on our community's prevailing fundamental epistemological decisions, goals, and practices to formulate and to justify standards for epistemic justification. In contrast, a general a priori approach shuns reliance on such community matters and relies instead on an a priori notion of empirical knowledge to formulate and to justify standards for epistemic justification. A society-oriented empirical approach precludes noncircular epistemological assessment of our community's fundamental epistemological decisions, goals, and practices. A general a priori approach gives no independent epistemological significance to the fundamental epistemological decisions, goals, and practices of our community. The dilemma for Kuhn and Carnap thus bears on epistemology in general.

Semantic foundationalism enables a forthright diagnosis of our dilemma. The previous objection to a society-oriented empirical approach to justification depends for cogency on a notion of epistemic justification—however minimal—relative to which our community's fundamental epistemological decisions, goals, and practices admit of noncircular epistemological assessment. Analogously, the previous objection to a general a priori approach to justification depends for cogency on a notion of justification relative to which our community's fundamental epistemological decisions, goals, and practices have indispensable epistemological significance. The indispensability of their significance, on the notion in question, entails that they are not susceptible to independent epistemological assessment. They are rather the ultimate basis of epistemological assessment. Recall Kuhn's claim that there is no standard higher than the views of the relevant community.

Either a notion of justification allows for independent, noncircular epistemological assessment of our community's fundamental epistemological decisions, goals, and practices, or it does not. A single notion of justification cannot, on pain of internal inconsistency, have it *both* ways. The dilemma at hand is thus fueled by opposing specific notions of justification. Semantic foundationalism recommends that we acknowledge this and entertain the relative merits and demerits of the alternative notions at work.

We can assess relative merits and demerits from various standpoints, with various notions of merit and demerit. This is old news now, but important nonetheless. Perhaps notions are not correct or incorrect in the way empirical statements about household physical objects are; still, notions do admit of evaluation, given various notions of evaluation. We can ask, for example, about the purposes of an epistemologist in adopting and wielding a notion of epistemic justification (generally or specifically characterized). In particular, we can ask whether a certain notion of justification serves those purposes better than does any alternative notion of justification available. Such purpose-relative, instrumentalist assessment might not merit the title 'epistemic' in some cases—especially if we reserve that title for considerations of knowledge and truth-conduciveness—but that is no debilitating concession.

When it comes to reasons for adopting and wielding one notion of epistemic justification rather than another, purpose-relative assessment is clearly a live option, even if one's purpose is to get "the truth," or to portray the world as it "really" is. In contrast, epistemic assessment concerning what is truth conducive or likely to be true may not always apply to one's actual aims in adopting and wielding a notion: One might not aim, in adopting and using a concept, to portray the world as it really is. This is, as suggested before, no problem for semantic foundationalism. Even when one gives a nonepistemic instrumental justification for use of a notion, one presupposes a *notion* of instrumental justification relative to which certain considerations deliver the relevant kind of instrumental justification. Semantic foundationalism obviously applies even here. (Sections 4.2 and 5.3 clarify the role of purpose-relative, instrumental reasons in rational theorizing and rational action.)

In appealing to semantic considerations, understood in terms of conceptual commitments, semantic foundationalism makes explicit the decisive role of a decision-making theorist in an epistemology. An epistemology is, after all, the product of a theorist. It therefore is natural that an epistemological argument or account end with considerations about what its author means by such terms as 'justification' and 'knowledge'.

We are not left with Carnap's a priori approach, as we can still acknowledge that scientific justification—at least so-called—is a function of actual prevailing scientific goals. We can still acknowledge that neglecting such goals in a notion of justification will leave us with something other than a notion of *scientific* justification. At least, we would then have to explain how our notion of justification is actually relevant to the prevailing fundamental goals and methodological assumptions of practicing scientists. Simply calling a notion 'scientific' will not do the job. Sameness in mere terminology, being compatible with polysemy, delivers neither a conceptual connection nor a philosophically adequate explanation. Semantic foundationalism seeks an epistemological basis in conceptual commitments that yield notions crucial to giving justification of any sort.

2.6 A General Epistemological Moral

We now have semantic foundationalism before us. We have seen its resolution of some dilemmas for epistemology, and its helpful bearing on a range of epistemological issues. Can we say anything more for it?

Here is something general: Either our substantive (explanatory and evaluative) views in epistemology are logically linked to our semantic views, or they are not. If they are, our semantic views can provide the justificational anchor identified by semantic foundationalism. If they are not logically linked, our substantive epistemology will become either empirical or synthetic a priori.

As section 1.7 notes, it is altogether unclear how any synthetic truths can be justified a priori: It is mysterious how statements true or false in virtue of nonsemantic considerations can have warrant independently of experiential considerations. Empirical considerations, moreover, cannot by themselves solve the perennial problems of epistemology. Empirical matters only raise more of the same problems. An appeal to empirical considerations presupposes the settling of certain conceptual issues in epistemology. One must, as section 2.4 suggests, appeal to an operative *notion* regarding justification that enables the relevant empirical considerations to do the desired epistemological work. The presupposed notion regarding justification produces the indispensable link between the relevant empirical considerations and the providing of *justification,* in the pertinent sense. This is exactly what semantic foundationalism leads us to expect.

Semantic foundationalism finds the basis of explaining and arguing for justification in semantic considerations, not in such metaphysical entities as universals, essences, or natural kinds. It is thus ontologically more scrupulous than most approaches to epistemological correctness. It may even satisfy various agnostics who recognize, in accord with section 1.7, that they themselves are stuck with the importance of semantic considerations, at least in practice.

Semantic foundationalism does not require that we have agnostic-resistant non-questionbegging epistemic reasons for claims about conceiving-independent facts; nor does it assume that an appeal to meaning can deliver reasons of the sort demanded by an agnostic. Agnostics can demand, for instance, non-questionbegging reasons for thinking that what we mean by '*P* is justified' is ever reliable as a means to conceiving-independent facts, or is ever satisfied by a claim that is objectively true. In conceding that we cannot meet agnostics' demands, semantic foundationalism fits with the conditional ontological agnosticism of chapter 1. It shifts focus from demands for agnostic-resistant reasons to perspectival semantic and instrumental considerations. In doing so, it accommodates lessons about the perspectival nature of reasons arising from agnostic challenges.

We now need an account of the semantic considerations essential to semantic foundationalism: an account of semantic standards and their bearing on semantic meaning. This account will lay semantic foundations for semantic foundationalism. Chapter 3 takes up this task.

3

Meaning, Interpretation, and Analyticity

Whatever else we are, you and I are language users. Witness my writing this chapter, and your reading it. Reflection on what you and I are doing thus indicates that we are language users. Even if we lack exact identity-conditions for languages and language users, we do not forgo talk of such phenomena. Evidently, then, meaningful talk allows for considerable vagueness.

What exactly makes talk meaningful? What, more specifically, distinguishes meaningfulness from meaninglessness in our use of language? This chapter answers such questions and examines some influential alternative answers. It develops an account of meaning that fits with the conditional ontological agnosticism of chapter 1, and illuminates the semantic foundationalism of chapter 2. The result is a notion of meaning, including an approach to analyticity, that serves the purposes of philosophy after objectivity.

3.1 Ways of Meaning

We use language in a wide variety of ways: to classify, describe, refer, prescribe, recommend, promise, explain, exclaim, predict, request, and so on. Not all of these uses are truth-valued. Sometimes we use language in noncognitive ways, ways that do not express a truth or a falsehood. We sometimes express commands, for example, without thereby making a true or false assertion. Similarly, we sometimes use language to express feelings (for example, 'Ugh!', 'Ouch!', 'Darn!') without thereby making an assertion. Our functioning as language users thus goes beyond our using language cognitively, in a truth-valued manner.

Some language users, you and I included, sometimes use philosophical language. We sometimes raise philosophical questions and make philosophical claims. What, however, is distinctive of philosophical language? When, in other words, is a claim or a question philosophical? Perhaps philosophical language is just language *used philosophically*. What is that? How should we decide, furthermore, what that is? By appeal to "ordinary use" of the term 'philosophical'? If so, what sort of use is "ordinary"? How, moreover, should we decide that? By appeal to ordinary use of the term 'ordinary'? An endless regress, if not useless circularity, threatens. We seem to be making no real progress.

What does it mean to "make progress" on a semantic, or conceptual, question? What constitutes the correctness or incorrectness of a conceptual view about, for example, when a claim or question is philosophical? If you ask me, "When is a claim philosophical?," I will fully understand your question only if I understand somewhat the term 'philosophical'. It is not clear, however, what "full" understanding is. It is even less clear that I have such understanding of your question. My understanding of your question, 'When is a claim philosophical?', does exceed my understanding of the question, 'When is a claim eurteslaf?' I have some relevant understanding of each of the terms of the former question, but not the latter. I have no idea of what 'eurteslaf' means; in fact, it is meaningless for me (even if I concocted the term by a simple algorithm).

What is it to have some relevant understanding of the term 'philosophical', or of *any* term for that matter, and can such understanding be correct or incorrect? Philosophers have used the term 'understanding' in significantly different ways. I shall not digress to assess all those ways. Instead, I shall present an account of meaning that enhances the views developed in chapters 1 and 2 and avoids the defect of some alternative accounts. I shall not presume, however, that there is one such thing as *the* concept of meaning or *the* concept of understanding. Presuming thus would be to flirt with the previously noted myth of the definite article.

A *purely conceptual* question regarding understanding is not an empirical, or otherwise nonsemantic, question about whatever it is that we call "understanding." A purely conceptual question about understanding does not go beyond a semantic question of what 'understanding', or some synonymous term, *means*. On a common conception, a term's meaning is always meaning for someone or for some group. This is clearly the case if meaning is a function of interpretation, or construal; for interpretation is always for someone or some group. We thus have a kind of relativity in purely conceptual questions.

A purely conceptual question regarding understanding is a question about what a certain term—in English 'understanding' or some synonymous term—means for someone or some group. The same is true of a purely conceptual question about meaning itself. In contrast, a nonsemantic question regarding understanding does not pursue what a terms means for someone or some group. Such a question, nonetheless, presupposes a certain concept, or notion, of understanding; this presupposed concept makes it a question regarding understanding, rather than regarding only something else. (I here use 'regarding' rather than 'about', because I am not concerned with purely causal or "*de re*" aboutness-relations.)

On a common approach to meaning, terms do not have meanings on their own, quite apart from how they are construed by language users. If meaning arises from interpretation (of a sort to be specified), this is no surprise. Linguistic meaning is a relational matter, depending on certain relations between terms, or sequences of terms, and language users. What precisely is this relational matter? A defensible answer will offer a cogent account of linguistic meaning.

3.2 Rules, Regularities, and Social Agreements

Not just *any* use of terms is sufficient for meaningful use. Some uses of language are meaningless, and obviously so. We do not have the word 'gibberish' for nothing. We thus need to qualify, as specifically as possible, the sort of linguistic use amounting to meaningful use. Let us assume, by definition, that one's meaningful linguistic use requires one's using language that is meaningful for one. We shall then avoid any confusion of one's point in using language and the meaningfulness of the language used.

A. Rule-Governed Use

Perhaps answers to conceptual questions require the formulation of the rules for a person's correctly using terms, where such formulation is to be done for those people for whom the relevant terms are meaningful. One might answer the conceptual question of what understanding is for me, for example, by giving my rules for the correct use of 'understanding' or some synonymous term. My own rules for correct linguistic use, on this view, determine what terms mean for me. Call this *the view of meaning by autobiographical rules.*

The view of meaning by autobiographical rules assumes that meaningful language-use is *rule-governed* language use. Your use of language is governed by a rule when, and only when, you follow a rule in using language. Your following a particular rule requires, among other things, your being familiar with that rule to some extent. Gordon Baker and Peter Hacker have endorsed such a view as follows:

> There is no such thing as our following rules without our being able to explain or justify our actions by reference to them. There can be no hidden rules awaiting discovery, which we cannot yet formulate, but which we tacitly know and follow. . . . There is no such thing as meaning independently of *rules* which determine how an expression is to be used. Nothing counts as a rule independently of being used (or stipulated) as a rule, as a standard of correctness. (1985, pp. 36–37; cf. p. 63)

Following a rule, on this view, requires more than coincidental agreement, or compliance, with a rule. It requires one's being able to formulate the relevant rule, and to explain or to justify one's linguistic action by reference to that rule. Following a rule thus requires familiarity with, but not ever-present awareness of, a rule as a standard of correctness. Meaningful use of language, on this view, depends on such rule-following. (Baker and Hacker deny that meaningful use must be socially shared; they contend that it need only be share*able* in principle.)

Semantic rules, as standardly characterized, are principles concerning types of linguistic use. They concern conditions under which certain types of linguistic use are (a) correct or incorrect; (b) required, permitted, or prohibited; or (c) otherwise proper or improper, acceptable or unacceptable. In this respect, semantic rules are *normative*. When your use of language is rule-governed, you are familiar with a normative principle concerning a type of linguistic use, a principle that bears on the correctness, permissibility, or acceptability of your use of language.[1]

The view of meaning by autobiographical rules must face a likely objection. A common notion of meaningful language use seems to allow for one's using language meaningfully while one is unfamiliar with rules for one's use of language. Consider, in particular, two-year-old children who use language meaningfully. They typically lack familiarity with rules for language use; at least, they seem not to be familiar with such rules *as rules*. In addition, they seem not to be familiar with any concept of a rule for language use. Such children, in any case, are typically unable to formulate rules for their use of language.

The quotation from Baker and Hacker evidently implies that there are no rules for the language use of the children in question, and that therefore their language use is not meaningful. On a common notion of meaning, however, those children can use language meaningfully while lacking familiarity with rules (as rules) for their language use. It is unclear that such children actually have familiarity with formulated rules for their language use, even if we can describe regularities in their use. Such children evidently are unable to explain or to justify their linguistic actions by reference to explicit rules for their language use. A similar point holds for many adult language-users.

Just as a person can have first-order knowledge without being familiar with the defining principles, or standards, for one's having knowledge, so also one evidently can use a term meaningfully without being familiar with general rules (as rules) that prescribe or describe one's linguistic use. This, anyway, is a consequence of a common notion of meaning. The contrary view makes meaningful linguistic use excessively intellectual, too conceptually sophisticated, from the standpoint of this common notion of meaning.

One can, of course, introduce a more demanding notion of meaning, but one should recognize that one is doing just that. One must then articulate the purposes thereby served, in order to motivate one's demanding notion. These purposes will go beyond the purposes for which we have the aforementioned common, less demanding notion of meaningful use. (I do not give common notions special ontological status or unconditional normative status; I simply note that they are used advantageously by many people, given certain conceptual purposes.)

1. See Alston (1974), Baker and Hacker (1984, chaps. 7–8), and Martin (1987, chap. 7) for overviews of various positions on the role of semantic rules in meaning.

The problem concerns whether, and if so how, the rules describing or prescribing certain regularities in use must be familiar, or otherwise cognitively available, to language users exhibiting those regularities. We who can formulate rules sometimes make mistakes in identifying the rules pertinent to our own linguistic behavior, owing, for example, to haste, carelessness, or poor memory. When we do make such mistakes, the rules we actually formulate do not automatically identify what determines the meaningfulness of terms for us. Meaningfulness for us is thus not automatically what our actually formulated rules say it is.

We need, then, either clarification or revision of the view of meaning by autobiographical rules. One might conclude that meaning is not, after all, a function of rules in the way that view says. If rules for use are crucial to meaningful use, they evidently are not crucial as something that must be familiar to, or cognitively possessed by, all the language users for whom the relevant use is meaningful. Are rules crucial to meaning in some other way?

B. Regularities and Social Agreements

If meaningful use of language is not rule-governed in the way just considered, it still might be *rule-instantiating*, or *rule-complying*. This suggests *the regularity view of meaning*, a view sometimes inspired by misleading behaviorist construals of Wittgenstein's remarks concerning meaning and custom.[2] The regularity view states that meaningful language-use is just language use with a certain kind of regularity: that is, use in accord with, but not necessarily explicitly governed by, certain regular patterns of use.

If a child, for example, uses a term consistently in agreement with a certain pattern, then the term's use is meaningful, because customary, for that child. Regularity of use is meaningful use, on this view, regardless of whether a language user exhibiting the regular use is familiar with the rules describing or prescribing that use. The regularity view is less demanding than the previous view, with respect to a language user's familiarity with rules for use. It does not require for meaningful use a familiarity with general principles concerning types of linguistic use. It requires, instead, only a certain regularity of use. Meaningful use, on the regularity view, is just customary use, use exhibiting regularity of a certain sort.

The regularity view finds support from the behaviorism about linguistic use advanced by John Watson (1924, chap. 10) and Bertrand Russell (1927b, chap. 4). (Section 3.6 illustrates that W. V. Quine's approach to meaning is a similar example of behaviorism.) Such behaviorism construes meaningful linguistic use as a certain sort of habitual use of language. The relevant habitual use conforms to a principle, or "law," of association of bodily processes, put by Russell (1927b, p. 36) as follows: "When the body of an animal or human

2. For a corrective to such behaviorist construals, see Hacker (1990, pp. 224–253) and Zemach (1989; 1992, chap. 2). Cf. Budd (1989, pp. 17–19, 122–124). Zemach shows that on Wittgenstein's most mature views, meaningfulness of linguistic expressions does not consist in "their being used in complex maneuvers like those of schools of fish" (1989, p. 416).

being has been exposed sufficiently often to two roughly simultaneous stimuli, the earlier of them alone tends to call out the response previously called out by the other."

Acknowledging Watson's influence, Russell explicitly connects meaning with habitual linguistic use:

> I think myself that "meaning" can only be understood if we treat language as bodily habit, which is learnt just as we learn football or bicycling. . . . A child learns to understand words exactly as he learns any other process of bodily association. . . . When the association has been established [for example, between the word 'bottle' and the bottle], parents say that the child "understands" the word 'bottle'. . . . (1927b, pp. 46, 51)

Russell applies this general behaviorist view of meaning to various instances of understanding, including understanding by ostensive definition: "Understanding a word in virtue of an ostensive definition is merely one kind of habit" (1940, p. 296). He holds that we can understand talk of meaningful use just in terms of habitual regularity in use, just in terms of a causal story about associated bodily processes.

The regularity view seems insufficiently demanding from the standpoint of a common notion of meaningful language-use. Every way of using language agrees with some pattern, perhaps only the pattern distinctive of that particular way of using language. More pertinently, every way of using language, even use of meaningless language, can readily occur with regularity—even habitual regularity resulting from causal relations between associated bodily processes. I could be disposed to produce meaningless utterances whenever reminded, for instance, of snarks or certain so-called postmodern writers. This habit of mine, however annoying, would not automatically make my habitual utterances meaningful, even though it would give them regularity. Patterns and habitual regularities in use are too easy to come by, as they can arise for *any* way of using language, however pointless or meaningless. They can rest on nothing more than capricious, pointless use from the perspective of what is actually being done in my linguistic actions.

Even though every way of using language, however regular and frequent, exhibits some pattern, not every way of using language is meaningful in virtue of the meaningfulness of the language used. There is, after all, meaningless use of language, that is, use of meaningless language. Consider your favorite gibberish: Such gibberish will not become meaningful for you just in virtue of your using it with habitual regularity. It would still be *meaningless* habitual use in virtue of the meaninglessness of what is thereby used. Habitual use, then, is not automatically meaningful use.

The regularity view needs a special, suitably restricted notion of regularity or pattern. A view about the patterns or regularities pertinent to meaningful use by, and for, certain people can effectively appeal to what is actually being done by those people in using language. Such a view will attend to the linguistic aims—the linguistic purposes—of the people employing terms meaningfully. The relevant patterns will thus play a role in the goal-directed, purposive linguistic *actions* of the language users in question. On this approach, we shall not neglect what constitutes meaningfulness for them. (Section 3.3 returns to this theme.)

The need for special constraints on semantically relevant patterns and regularities in use has led some philosophers to invoke a social constraint: in particular, a constraint from social agreement. Saul Kripke (1982, p. 97) has offered the following reading of Wittgenstein on meaning:

> There is no objective fact—that we all mean addition by '+', or even that a given individual does—that explains our agreement in particular cases. Rather our license to say of each other that we mean addition by '+' is part of a 'language game' that sustains itself only because of the brute fact that we generally agree. (Nothing about 'grasping concepts' guarantees that it will not break down tomorrow.)

Kripke's concern, we should note, is with "our license to say of each other" that we mean something. This is an epistemological concern, given a construal of 'license' as warrant.

Kripke illustrates the relevant approach to meaning via the possibility of a private language that only one person can understand, such as in the case of Robinson Crusoe:

> . . . *if* we think of Crusoe as following rules, we are taking him into our community and applying our criteria for rule following to him. The falsity of the private model need not mean that a *physically isolated* individual cannot be said to follow rules; rather that an individual, *considered in isolation*. . . , cannot be said to do so. . . . Our community can assert of any individual that he follows a rule if he passes the tests for rule following applied to any member of the community. (1982, p. 110)

Acceptable (or warranted) talk of meaningful use of language, on this approach, presupposes a background of social agreement in linguistic use. If the members of our linguistic community agree that Crusoe is following linguistic rules (by our criteria for rule following), we shall "feel justified" in regarding Crusoe's use of language as meaningful.

Norman Malcolm (1986, pp. 158–159) has proposed a somewhat different reading of Wittgenstein that gives a central role to social agreement in meaning:

> . . . in order for there to be rules, different people who have had approximately the same training must *agree* in their application of the rules to new cases. . . . [T]heir *meaning* [that is, the rules' meaning] is fixed by the customary agreement *in action* of those who have been given the ordinary explanations and examples.

Malcolm (1989, p. 21) regards social training as the necessary background of "agreement in acting," a background that allegedly provides the independent basis for "the necessary distinction" between correct and incorrect use of language. Kripke (1982, pp. 111–112), in contrast, puts the view in terms of socially determined "assertibility conditions" for ascriptions of meaningful linguistic use, conditions that yield a distinction between justified and unjustified ascriptions of meaningfulness. Kripke denies that Wittgenstein offers a theory of true, or correct, ascriptions of meaning.

Regardless of their disagreements, Kripke and Malcolm share the view that, according to Wittgenstein, some kind of *social agreement* concerning linguistic use provides the standard for our (correctly or justifiably) deeming linguistic use as meaningful or meaningless. In short, the regularities of use that we may (correctly or justifiably) deem meaningful are just those that agree with our socially shared regularities or standards of use.

We now face this question: Why should we think that "agreement in acting" with respect to the actions of a *group* of people can support a (correct or justifiable) distinction between meaningful and meaningless use of language, whereas "agreement in acting" with respect to various actions of an *individual* cannot? As Malcolm notes, Wittgenstein (1978, p. 353) is not here concerned primarily with agreement in beliefs or opinions. The concern is not, for example, that members of some society agree in their opinions about what constitutes correct or incorrect (or justified or unjustified) language-use.

An appeal just to social agreement in opinions faces the following worry analogous to a worry expressed by Wittgenstein himself (1953, section 258): Whatever is going to seem right or justified (for example, regarding meaningful linguistic use) to my linguistic community *is* right or justified, and that only means that we here cannot talk about being right or justified. Agreement in the opinions of a social group is not, so far as what is meaningful goes, relevantly different from agreement in the opinions of an individual. As Wittgenstein suggests, rightness of use, like correctness in general, does not depend on a show of hands (1953, section 241). The same holds for justification regarding use. (Kripke, 1982, pp. 111–112, shifts between talk of assertibility conditions and talk of a community's "feeling" entitled or justified, and thus confuses justification with what a community believes to be justified.)

Suppose that the members of a linguistic community, to constitute a single linguistic community, must display considerable agreement in their applications of rules to new cases. Such agreement in acting, according to the interpretations by Kripke and Malcolm, serves as the basis for (correctly or justifiably) distinguishing meaningful from meaningless use of language. The uses that concur with our social agreements in acting—for example, in applying certain linguistic rules—may (correctly or justifiably) be regarded by us as rule-governed and meaningful; the uses that do not concur, may not.

If the relevant agreement is just agreement in acting—in the application of rules to new cases—why cannot the actions of an *individual* display such agreement? If we can talk intelligibly of agreement in the actions of a social group, regarding applications of a linguistic rule, we evidently can also talk intelligibly of similar agreement in various actions of an individual. In both cases we are talking of agreement in actions, in applications of a rule. From the standpoint of meaning, the social case seems not to be relevantly different from the individual case. In both cases we are talking of features of actions: in particular, agreement in actions. Considerations of a singularity or plurality of agents thus seem insignificant. A plurality of agents would be relevant if we took meaningful use to depend on justifiable discernibility of meaningful use, and we restricted such discernibility to intersubjective confirmation. Such social verificationism evidently motivates some influential arguments against privacy in meaning (as Moser 1992 illustrates).

The uses to which Kripke and Malcolm put agreement in social actions can be served as well by agreement in an individual's actions. Social and individual actions do not differ with respect to their being able to be in agreement or disagreement, nor do they differ from the standpoint of providing only a finite sample of instances of rule-application. They do not differ as a finite basis for exemplifying or formulating standards for agreement in rule-following. Both kinds of action—social and individual—can serve as a basis for a concept of agreement in action, and for corresponding evaluative standards for such agreement.[3]

Kripke's and Malcolm's appeals to social agreement neglect what constitutes meaningful use from the perspective of the linguistic *actions* of an individual language-user. From the latter perspective, one's linguistic actions may have nothing whatever to do with considerations of social agreement. One's linguistic actions may concern only the linguistic goals, or purposes, one has in performing them. If we neglect the point of an individual language-user's actions, and give social agreement a decisive role in determining meaningful use, we risk commitment to a sort of linguistic action at a distance. Social agreement, whether in opinions or actions, may be altogether irrelevant to the actual linguistic actions whose meaningfulness is supposed to be explained.

Because social agreement plays no indispensable role in (correctly or justifiably ascribing) meaningful linguistic use as ordinarily understood, Kripke and Malcolm have not identified what is distinctive of such use. They have rather introduced special notions of meaning that acknowledge crucial roles for social considerations. We now need a characterization of meaning that does not award an ineliminable semantic role to social agreement, whether agreement in social actions or social opinions. Such a characterization promises to be more sensitive to our everyday notion of meaning.

3.3 Semantic Interpretationism

In section 3.2B we saw some inadequacies in attempts to explain meaningful linguistic use in terms of either habitual regularities or social agreements. In section 3.2A we saw that a requirement of explicit rule-governed use is too demanding intellectually, at least relative to a common notion of meaningful use. The latter requirement demands familiarity with general rules (as rules) concerning types of linguistic use. Perhaps if we replace the latter demand with a requirement concerning one's ends, or purposes, in linguistic use, we can avoid an excessive demand.

3. For further elaboration of such doubts about Malcolm's social approach to meaning, see Moser (1991) and Baker and Hacker (1990). Cf. Moser (1992).

A. Purposive Linguistic Use

Your using language that is meaningful for you can be intentional or unintentional, purposive or nonpurposive. When purposive, your use of meaningful language includes your being committed to, or settled upon, doing something with the language that is meaningful for you. When nonpurposive, your use of meaningful language does not involve your being thus committed; you then use language that is meaningful for you, but you are not then settled upon an end in using that language. Owing merely to a slip of the tongue, for example, I might utter language that is meaningful for me. My uttering would then be nonpurposive, but the language uttered would nonetheless be meaningful for me.

Let us consider purposive use of meaningful language, where one uses meaningful language with some purpose, in a goal-directed manner. Goal-directed language-use requires commitment to do something with language. It thus requires one's having an end, an end that is typically an intended outcome. Purposive linguistic use, then, requires goal-oriented behavior. It does not require, however, either one's self-consciously deciding on a manner of use or one's undergoing a prolonged thought process; nor does it require one's conceiving of one's having a purpose, or end. People lacking a notion of purposive use—young children, for example—can nonetheless engage in purposive use. We often use the phrases 'in order to' and 'for the sake of' to signify goal-directed behavior. We typically apply such language to young children and adults.

Whether we formulate a notion of purposive behavior to apply to the activity of complex robots, heat-seeking missiles, and the like will depend for instrumental justification on our purposes in adopting and wielding such a notion. If, for some reason, we aim to include only the behavior of sophisticated animals relevantly similar to ourselves, we might supply certain requirements concerning biological etiology.[4] In any case, this is a matter for decision relative to our purposes in adopting and wielding a specific notion of purposive behavior. It is not a matter of just introspection, observation, or experimentation.

One's habitual language-use may or may not be purposive and meaningful from the standpoint of what one is doing. If one's habitual use involves one's being committed to, or settled upon, a goal in using language, it will be purposive; otherwise, it may be merely reactive use. I shall not assume that our everyday notion of purposive language-use admits of reduction to nonteleological notions. We might *construct* a notion that admits of this, but that is not my aim now.

Purposive use of language calls for purposive explanation of language use. A purposive explanation of linguistic behavior will not account for linguistic acts simply in terms of their causal antecedents. That would be a merely causal explanation. A purposive explanation can include causal considerations, but

4. For biological restrictions on the notion of goal-directedness, see Hacker (1990, pp. 168–170, 251–253). Against such restrictions, see Dennett (1984, chap. 3; 1987, chap. 8; 1990).

will account for linguistic acts in terms of what a language user intends as consequences, accompaniments, or constituents of an action. It will give an ineliminable role to purposive considerations that require attention to considerations about what is intended as consequences, accompaniments, or constituents of action.

The general idea is this: A person, *S*, uses linguistic tokens *T* in order to do *A* if and only if *S* uses *T* in virtue of (a) her being committed to (try to) bring about *A* and (b) her treating use of *T* as (a potential way of) bringing about *A*. Purposive action can be unsuccessful, given this principle. The end for the sake of which one acts need not be achieved. Talk of "being committed" in (a) and talk of "treating" in (b) admit of variation in fine points of explication. Different theorists have offered different details of explication. Because my subsequent account of meaning is compatible with a range of such details, we need not digress to variable fine points.[5]

We can make do now with these principles: Whenever one is committed to bringing about *A*, one is thereby settled upon, or determined toward, bringing about *A* (or at least one is settled upon trying to bring about *A*); and whenever one treats use of *T* as (a way of) bringing about *A*, one thereby (at least implicitly) regards use of *T* as (a manner of) bringing about *A*. The relevant kind of commitment has some motivational force, as it incorporates one's having an intention to do something. Our everyday notion of purposive linguistic action includes a notion of such commitment.

B. Meaning and Interpretation

One's purposively using utterances or inscriptions to do something is neither necessary nor sufficient for the meaningfulness, for one, of utterances or inscriptions—at least on a common understanding of meaning. Tokens can be meaningful for one without being purposively used by one, and tokens purposively used by one need not be meaningful for one.

One's set of meaningful terms can exceed the set of terms one has actually used either to form a sentence, to refer to things, or to achieve some other, perhaps noncognitive, purpose. Before now, the term 'trona', for example, was meaningful for me, but I had not had occasion to use it, and thus had not actually used it purposively or nonpurposively. The meaningfulness of 'trona' for me has not suffered from the absence of an occasion for my using it to do something. (My present talk of "using" a term fits with our everyday notion of using language.)

The set of tokens one purposively uses to do something can exceed one's set of meaningful terms. I might shout 'eurteslaf', for instance, to startle you,

5. On some of the pertinent fine points, see Mele and Moser (1994). For details on purposive explanations in contrast with merely causal explanations, see Larry Wright (1972; 1976, chap. 2), Wesley Salmon (1990, pp. 111–116), and Weir (1984, chap. 11). See also Cohen (1951), Taylor (1964, chap. 1), and Alston (1986). On the central role of purposive explanations in psychology, see Boden (1972).

because I enjoy using gibberish to startle people. This purposive use of 'eurteslaf' would not make that token meaningful for me. That token is meaningless for me even if I use it to serve a definite purpose. One's purposive use of gibberish does not, then, automatically turn gibberish into meaningful language for one.

What does enable a token to be meaningful, to have meaning, for one even if one does not actually use it to do something? What, moreover, prevents purposive use of gibberish from being purposive use of meaningful language? The previous section indicated that some philosophers mean different things by 'meaning', at least at a level of specificity. (This is further support for the conceptual relativism introduced in section 2.4 and developed in chapter 4.) An account of meaning will ideally explain the basis of this diversity. What, however, do I mean by 'mean' in 'mean different things by "meaning"' (and, for that matter, in the fifth word of this question itself)? What, furthermore, should I mean here in the interest of an adequate approach to philosophical questions about what constitutes meaning? Relevant notions of "adequacy" here can and do vary among philosophers, as conceptual relativism leads us to expect. I am, however, after an account of meaning that elucidates semantic foundationalism and accommodates our everyday notion of meaning as far as possible. (I am, after all, writing for users of our everyday notion of meaning, and stipulation would not benefit my current purposes.)

Consider this approach to meaning: The meaningfulness (or, the "having meaning") of certain tokens for one consists in one's understanding those tokens: that is, one's nonextraneous *interpretation*, or *construal*, of those tokens as indicating (that is, designating) or expressing something, if only for oneself.[6] Given a familiar assumption about meaning, we need the modifier 'nonextraneous' to exclude from the meaning of a token, for one, things coincidentally (interpreted as being) indicated or expressed. We must explain this modifier in a way that allows for conventional contingent relations between tokens of a natural language and one's interpretation of those tokens.

My interpretation of 'beings at least minimally conscious' as designating actual conscious beings may involve the (acknowledged) actual designating of only things with functioning sizeable brains. Even so, "having a functioning sizeable brain" would not therefore be part of the meaning of 'beings at least minimally conscious' for me, even if I hold that whatever is actually designated by 'being at least minimally conscious' has a functioning sizeable brain. My notion of "beings at least minimally conscious," in accord with most philosophical notions of consciousness, allows for conscious beings without functioning sizeable brains, even if I deny that conscious beings without brains

6. Incidentally, the term 'construal' is absent from most English dictionaries. The second edition of *The Oxford English Dictionary* (1989) does include it, citing Paul Ziff (1960) as a source. The problem is that the definition offered, "an act of construing or interpreting," is inadequate to common philosophical and literary use. 'Construal' is ambiguous between an act and content of construing, in the way 'assertion' and 'interpretation' are ambiguous. On my use, all acts of construal are contentful, being construals as such-and-such.

actually exist. (A notion's allowing for *X* does not, of course, entail this notion's implying that *X* actually exists.) One's interpretation of a token as designating something can involve (interpreted) designation of features extraneous to what that token *means* for one.

Extraneous (interpreted) designations are joined by similarly extraneous (interpreted) expressions. Consider, for example, my interpretation of the sentence 'My shirt pocket contains a vial of nitroglycerin' as expressing, naturally enough, the assertion that my shirt pocket contains a vial of nitroglycerin. Suppose that whenever I interpret that sentence as expressing the latter assertion, I interpret that sentence as expressing also the warning that I be careful of the nitroglycerin in my shirt pocket. Even if the two interpretations in question are constantly conjoined for me (in the actual world and even in all possible situations where our causal laws obtain), it does not follow that the expressed warning is part of the meaning for me of 'My shirt pocket contains a vial of nitroglycerin'. (It could be part of that meaning for me, but that is another matter.) Expressions constantly conjoined for one, even in virtue of causal considerations, are not necessarily *semantically* related as co-determinants of a particular token's meaning for one; for they are not automatically co-determinants of the category of correct interpretation of that token for one. Causal accounts of meaning suggesting otherwise are simply introducing an extraordinary notion of meaning, a notion that divorces meaning from constituents of the category of correct interpretation for one.

Constant conjunctions of designations or expressions, then, will not automatically determine meaning for one. Some interpreted designations and expressions can be extraneously related for one to an interpreted token's meaning for one. An interpretation of a token, *T*, will be extraneous in what it indicates or expresses for one only relative to an operative base-interpretation of *T* for one: a presupposed nonextraneous interpretation of *T* for one that is not constituted, even in part, by the extraneous interpretation. Such a base-interpretation is at least partly constitutive of the category of correct interpretation of *T* for one; it is at least part of one's constitutive standard for correct interpretation of *T*. (Later in this section, I shall introduce a notion of *interpretive commitment* to specify one way to understand talk of an *operative* interpretation.)

An operative base-interpretation of *T* for one serves as a constitutive standard for *what it is to be* a correct interpretation of *T* for one: a standard constituting *correctness* in an interpretation of *T* for one. The relativity to a person here concerns understanding, or meaning, not mere belief about what is correct. In the absence of a constitutive standard for interpretive correctness for *T*, one will not genuinely understand *T*; for *T* will then have no determinate meaning for one, if meaning requires a standard constitutive of correctness (cf. section 1.3 on the conceptual-taking requirement on understanding).

Determinate linguistic meaning, as commonly understood, requires standards for correct interpretations of tokens. These standards fix the category of correctness for language users, with varying degrees of specificity. Consider the token 'eurteslaf'. We have no standard whatever constituting its correct interpretation; consequently, that token has no determinate meaning for us, and thus no meaning at all for us. Consider also the token 'meaningful token'. We do have a standard, however imprecise, for correct interpretation of that token; and our standard excludes 'eurteslaf' from the category of meaningful tokens and from the corresponding category of correct application of 'meaningful token'—the latter two categories being delimited for us by our semantic standard.

Standards constitutive of the category of correct interpretation for one yield determinate meaning via inclusion and exclusion. They include certain, perhaps imprecise, interpretations as correct, and exclude certain (potential) interpretations as incorrect, as mistaken. A token has no determinate meaning for you if *any* arbitrary interpretation of it is correct by your semantic standards for it. In that case, you will have no determinate standard for correct interpretation of that token; consequently, that token will have no determinate meaning for you. Our ordinary notion of meaning permits ambiguity and vagueness, of course, but not completely unlimited ambiguity and vagueness.

Altogether indeterminate meaning is no meaning at all, on our everyday notion of meaning. Such indeterminate "meaning" is altogether interpretively unbounded and undefined, and thus admits of no comprehension, no delimiting understanding or interpretation. Its unbridled indefiniteness excludes it from our category of what is genuinely meaningful, and assigns it to the semantic void, where correctness in interpretation has no status. Even if correct translation of one's utterances is not made determinate by all the "facts" of physics, as Quine (1960, p. 27; 1981, p. 23) contends, meaning must be made determinate by something; otherwise, it (that is, "meaning") will violate our semantic standards for correct interpretation of 'meaning'. In that case, "meaning" will not be genuine meaning for us, even if it satisfies an alternative notion of meaning.

Incorrectness relative to semantic standards can take two forms. *Absolute* incorrectness relative to my semantic standards for correct use of *T* arises when one uses *T* without *any* interpretation, in the way I use 'eurteslaf' to startle you. Absolute incorrectness in use entails meaningless use, interpretively indeterminate use. *Relative* incorrectness from the standpoint of my semantic standards arises when one interprets *T* in a way conflicting with those standards. If, for example, you interpret 'propositional knowledge' as designating a case of unjustified belief (say, lucky guesswork), you thereby give an interpretation incorrect by my standards constitutive of correct interpretation of 'propositional knowledge'. It is part of the category of correctness in interpretation of 'propositional knowledge' for me that this token designate justified belief; and that category determines what it is for an interpretation of 'propositional knowledge' to be mistaken for me.

Your interpretation of 'propositional knowledge' as designating unjustified belief is not empirically incorrect for me, but conceptually incorrect: incorrect relative just to my semantic standards for 'propositional knowledge'. What I mean by 'propositional knowledge' excludes that token's designating unjustified belief. It is thus conceptually necessarily false for me that an unjustified belief is knowledge. Such conceptual necessity is relative to semantic standards constituting a concept. It does not depend on, or require reference to, conceiving-independent "possible worlds" or other objective modal facts or situations. (For some details of a conceptualist approach to modality, see Moser and vander Nat 1988.)

Semantic standards for correctness, as section 2.3A suggests, are not reducible to empirical generalizations about correctness. Your denial of my semantic standards for 'propositional knowledge' entails that you are talking about something other than propositional knowledge in my sense. In particular, your interpretation of 'propositional knowledge' as designating unjustified belief introduces a notion different from my notion of propositional knowledge. You thereby change the subject from propositional knowledge in my sense to something else. Denial of an empirical generalization does not automatically change the subject in that way. You and I could still be talking about knowledge, in a single sense, even if I denied your empirical generalization that all and only normal people over the age of three years possess propositional knowledge.

Semantic standards play a crucial role in determining our categories of correctness and mistakenness even for empirical generalizations. An empirical generalization (such as the previous one about knowledge) can be mistaken; and a semantic standard for correct interpretation of 'mistaken' (or some synonymous term) gives determinacy to our talk of a mistaken empirical generalization. An analogous point holds for talk of a correct empirical generalization. Similarly, the subject- and predicate-terms of an empirical generalization owe their determinacy, their meaning, to semantic standards for their correct interpretation. Semantic determinacy for us requires semantic standards for correctness for us; and mere causal relations between tokens and physical events are insufficient for such standards.

One's semantic standards for a token constitute the meaning of that token for one. Those standards, as section 2.3A notes, need not be a full logical analysis in terms of specific nondisjunctive necessary and sufficient conditions. Wittgenstein uses one's concept of a game to illustrate this point:

> What does it mean to know what a game is? . . . Isn't my knowledge, my concept of a game, completely expressed in the explanations that I could give? That is, in my describing examples of various kinds of game; shewing how all sorts of other games can be constructed on the analogy of these; saying that I should scarcely include this or this among games; and so on. (1953, section 75; cf. sections 71, 87)

Semantic standards, accordingly, can include exemplars, or paradigm-cases, that do not yield a specific logical analysis.

Our ordinary notion of meaning, as section 2.3A illustrates, is not captured by mere talk of logical necessity and sufficiency. The so-called logically necessary truths of mathematics and logic, for example, are logically equivalent, but do not all share a single standard of interpretive correctness for us. We do, in fact, interpret '2 + 3 = 5' as expressing something different from '25 + 25 = 50', even if one is necessarily true if and only if the other is. A statement's logical implications, accordingly, are not automatically part of the meaning of that statement for one. If they were, all mathematical truths would mean the same thing for us. Meaning is determined by interpretation, not logical implication.

Talk of "assigning features" will help now. Suppose that I assign the feature of "designating beings at least minimally conscious" to a token, *T*, and this feature is now conceptually necessary and sufficient for correctness in an interpretation of *T* for me. (I grant that others might have different standards for correct interpretation of *T*, and that I, too, might have had a different standard.) Suppose also that I assign the feature of "designating beings with a functioning sizeable brain" to *T*, but that this feature is not part of what constitutes, or is definitive of, correctness in interpretation of *T* for me.

My pertinent semantic standard does not include the designation of functioning sizeable brains, even if it might have included this. Given that sematic standard as my operative base-interpretation of *T*, I may properly deny that "designating beings with a functioning sizeable brain" is part of the meaning of *T* for me. The interpreted designation of functioning sizeable brains is thus extraneous to the meaning of *T* for me, even if such designation constantly accompanies the designation determining the meaning of *T* for me: the designation of beings at least minimally conscious.

We may now introduce this definition: An interpretive designation or expression, *I*, for a token, *T*, is *extraneous* to an interpretation of *T* for one if and only if one has an operative base-interpretation, *I'*, of *T*, and *I'* sets constitutive conditions for correct interpretation of *T* that do not include *I*, while no other base-interpretation of *T* for one includes *I*. Base-interpretations for a token are set for one by what interpretations actually constitute for one the category of correctness in interpretation of that token. *I*, then, can be an extraneous interpretation for you even if it is constantly conjoined with *I'* for you.

One's set of operative base-interpretations for *T* consists of the interpretations constituting the meaning of *T* for one. We may thus say that *I* is at least part of the meaning of *T* for one if and only if *I* is an interpretation of *T* for one and is not extraneous to the interpretations constituting the meaning of *T* for one: that is, the interpretations setting constitutive, definitive conditions for correctness in interpretation of *T* for one. Extraneous interpretations of *T* for one, in contrast, do not constitute the category of correctness in interpretation of *T* for one.

What can be interpretively indicated or expressed includes a wide range of things: for example, assertions that something is true, orders to do something, questions whether something is the case, commitments to do something, exclamations about something, and declarations that something be the case. (On questions about taxonomy of linguistic acts, see Searle 1979, chap. 1; and Levinson, 1983, chap. 5.) Nonextraneous interpretation imparts semantic life to otherwise dead tokens, even when the life imparted does not rest on a token's role in truth-valued assertions or on any actual use of the token in linguistic action.

We need not, then, restrict meaningful tokens to truth-valued tokens or to tokens that play a role in truth-valued sentential contexts. Such tokens as 'Hi',

'Ouch', and 'Darn!' can be meaningful for one, even if they have no role in truth-valued assertions. The key determinant of meaning is not a role in a truth-valued assertion, but rather a nonextraneous interpretation of tokens as indicating or expressing something. Such interpretation yields *conditions of success* for the tokens interpreted. These conditions of success derive from what an indicator or expression ostensibly seeks to achieve, in virtue of one's interpretation constitutive of its meaning for one. Characteristically: Assertions ostensibly aim at truth, and thus are successful when and only when true; orders ostensibly aim at compliance, and so are successful when and only when obeyed; commitments ostensibly aim at one's keeping them, and hence are successful when and only when kept; questions ostensibly seek a correct answer, and therefore are successful when and only when correctly answered; declarations ostensibly aim to constitute a certain status for something, and thus are successful when and only when that status is constituted, and so on. Having such conditions of success does not require that those conditions actually be satisfied.

The relevant notion of success, like the notion of expressing something, is multifaceted, being irreducible to a highly specific, nondisjunctive set of individually necessary and jointly sufficient conditions. Contrary to an assumption of some philosophers, such multifaceted notions are not automatically objectionable; their acceptability for one will depend on the purposes one has in using such notions. The latter purposes, moreover, can vary considerably. Unconditional standards for conceptual adequacy, in any case, may have an aesthetic significance for some theorists that is not advantageous to the conceptual purposes of other theorists. We must be wary, then, of philosophers bearing unconditional standards for conceptual adequacy. A notion may be in order—may fulfill its purposes—even apart from satisfaction of such unconditional standards.

Such demonstratives as 'this' and 'that' owe their meaningfulness to interpretation. I interpret 'this' and 'that' nonextraneously as designating something, where the relevant "thing" is often contextually identifiable. (Given section 1.7, I shall not pursue the issue whether referents are sometimes conceiving-independent.) The meaning of 'this' for me consists, in any case, in an interpretation constitutive of correctness for me in the interpretation and use of 'this'. Such an interpretation determines what "thisness" is for me, relative to my understanding.

A corresponding point applies to any appeal to a "thing" picked out to fix the meaning of 'this'. A defining notion of thing will require an interpretation that determines what "thingness" is for one, relative to one's understanding. "Things" by themselves, as section 1.3 indicates, do not fix understanding, apart from a standard constitutive of what "thingness" is for one. The latter standard will give one (at least vague) "boundary-conditions" for being a thing. Meaning, even via designation, thus requires interpretive considerations that go beyond mere causal considerations regarding tokens and referents.

Designators will be successful when and only when they actually pick out the thing one's nonextraneous interpretation construes them as picking out.

(Some philosophers use a notion of success for designators that requires absence of "causal deviance" arising from indirectness in designation.) If we regard meaning as including designation, such meaningful demonstratives call into question unrestricted semantic holism stating that only in the context of a sentence does a word have meaning. If demonstratives (or names, for that matter) can designate, or pick out, something apart from their role in a sentence, unqualified semantic holism is false.

Some people construe such common nouns as 'horse' and 'unicorn' nonextraneously as indicating a *kind* or a *class* of things, where a kind or a class can be "defined" by a (projected) paradigmatic instance or a list of constituting features. (Conceptualists, opposing Platonism, need not reify kinds and classes, but may regard them as conceptual constructs issuing via generalization from particular, perhaps experienced, features.) These people can allow that 'horse' can also designate an actual horse; two levels of designation are possible. Such people may deny, in any case, that common nouns have meaning only in the context of a sentence; they might argue, additionally, that our ability to understand new sentences typically depends on our sentence-independent understanding of some of those new sentences' constituents. These considerations do not preclude, however, that other people construe common nouns in accord with semantic holism. Construal of terms admits of variation, as the conceptual relativism of section 2.4 (and chapter 4) suggests.

We can grant—regardless of our views on demonstratives, names, and common nouns—that many individual words (for example, 'and', 'if', 'or', 'but') owe their meaningfulness to minimally holistic considerations: to their salient contributions to various larger tokens we interpret nonextraneously as indicating or expressing something. We could still have notions of "and," "if," "or," and "but," owing to constitutive standards for correct use of the relevant terms, standards that invoke a certain role in a larger, sentential context. Since our main purposes in using meaningful language are to indicate and to express things, the derivative status of the meaningfulness of some terms is not surprising. It is doubtful, however, that the meaningfulness of all terms is thus derivative for all language users. Construals, or interpretations, seem not to be uniformly holistic, across all interpreters.

Sheer nonsense for one lacks not only conditions of success for one but also a salient role in tokens having such conditions. One's *aim* in using sheer nonsense may have conditions of success, but such conditions will not derive from a nonextraneous interpretation of the used nonsense-token as indicating or expressing something. One does not have a nonextraneous interpretation of sheer nonsense for oneself as indicating or expressing something; nor does one have an interpretation of certain tokens in which sheer nonsense plays a salient role. One's lacking such interpretations is what makes nonsense meaningless for one. This explains why 'eurteslaf', for instance, is meaningless for me and, I suspect, for you too.

I *could* interpret 'eurteslaf' nonextraneously as indicating or expressing something, but I do not; it suits no purpose of mine to interpret this token thus.

Even if I shout 'eurteslaf' to startle you, I do not thereby construe it nonextraneously as indicating or expressing something. I might interpret it nonextraneously as expressing that you should be startled, that you are startled, or whatever; but I do not. The token 'eurteslaf' thus remains meaningless for me, even if I can utter it purposively. (The views surveyed in section 3.2 overlook the crucial role of individual interpretation in meaning.)

We should acknowledge the evident contingency of what tokens are actually meaningful for an interpreter. Any token can acquire meaning for one from one's nonextraneous interpretation of it as indicating or expressing something. Meaningfulness of tokens thus does not require actual regularity in use of tokens. We may judge that a certain interpretation of a token is mistaken in that it diverges from *our* nonextraneous interpretation; but this kind of "mistake" does not threaten the meaningfulness of the divergent interpretation for the wayward interpreter.

An act of interpretation, or construal, can occur at the speed of thought, whatever speed that happens to be. It can also be habitual, spontaneous, and implicit to an interpreter's consciousness. One can, furthermore, interpret a token nonextraneously as indicating or expressing something even when one does not conceptualize oneself as interpreting that token. Interpretation can proceed without such higher-order conceptualization or interpretation.[7] A contrary view risks an endless regress of required interpretations of ever-increasing iteration.

Our everyday notion of meaning as nonextraneous interpretation is psychological, and not reducible to "the language" of physics, chemistry, and biology. If there are correlations between interpretation and certain events as described in the language of the natural sciences, that is an empirical matter extraneous to our everyday notion of meaning as interpretation. One's having that everyday notion does not require one's being familiar with correlations between interpretation and certain events characterized by physics, chemistry, or biology. Our common notion of meaning as interpretation serves its various purposes apart from reducibility to the language of the natural sciences. Reductive and eliminativist physicalist scruples lose their unconditional force, moreover, once we appreciate the lessons of chapters 1 and 5 about reasons and explanations.

Interpretation does not require social agreement, even if private meanings are typically their own reward. One's nonextraneous construal of tokens as indicating or expressing something does not logically require social agreement in opinions or actions; in fact, it does not logically require a community of any sort. Social inculcation of interpretive habits, however pervasive, under-

7. My approach to meaning is psychologically less demanding than that of Searle (1983, chap. 6; 1991). Searle assumes that "meaning . . . involves the intentional imposition of conditions of satisfaction onto conditions of satisfaction," and that in the case of meaningful utterance "part of the conditions of satisfaction are that the intention should result in the production of a certain utterance" (1991, p. 83). This requires that a person for whom some language is meaningful have a *notion* of intention. Our everyday notion of meaning seems to permit, however, that tokens can be meaningful even for children (and others) lacking a notion of intention.

writes no argument for a *logically* indispensable social component in interpretation and meaning.

Your being able to understand what I mean does require that some of my interpretations be shareable. My meaning something, however, does not logically require your being able to understand me. Meaning does not logically depend on availability of communication, even if it enables communication. (Arguments to the contrary often confuse conditions constitutive of one's meaning something and conditions constitutive of someone else's discerning that one means something.) Communication between us is a real possibility whenever you recognize what my interpretations are, and I recognize what yours are. Denial that meaning is essentially social allows, then, for socially shared meaning. We must beware, however, of the dubious view that meaning departing from our socially shared interpretations is no meaning at all.

Interpretation as construal of tokens does not entail what we usually regard as "use" of tokens. We ordinarily think of use of tokens as involving such linguistic *acts* as making an assertion or a promise, issuing a greeting, raising a question, or even such things as frightening someone with the mere noise of an utterance, or bringing about some other effect via utterance or inscription. Interpretation does not require any such actual use of tokens; it construes tokens without putting tokens to actual use in linguistic acts. Nonextraneous interpretation simply puts a construction—a rendering—on a token, thereby giving it meaning, at least for one interpreter. (This view readily applies even to the token 'meaning' itself: Even the meaningfulness of 'meaning' derives from nonextraneous interpretation.) Given a common reading of 'use' as 'linguistic act', then, my view of meaning as nonextraneous interpretation contrasts with a doctrine of meaning as use. We may call the view under development *semantic interpretationism.*

Semantic interpretationism implies that meaning derives from understanding, and that understanding derives from nonextraneous interpretation, or construal, regarding a token's indicating or expressing something. Tokens that are intelligible for you as indicating or expressing something, *X*, are understandable, because nonextraneously interpret*able*, for you as indicating or expressing *X*, given your conceptual commitments of the sort identified in section 2.3. A token's being nonextraneously interpretable for you as indicating or expressing *X* does not require that your ability to interpret that token be manifest in a current episode. A token can, then, be understandable, or intelligible, for you even when you are not engaged in an episode of interpreting it nonextraneously as indicating or expressing something. Similarly, the meaningfulness of a token for you does not require a current episode of interpretation.

Semantic interpretationism can accommodate three conditions that indicate familiar standards for our use of 'understanding', 'meaning', 'intelligibility', and related terms. First, all understanding is understanding *for* some individual or other, and understanding can vary from person to person. One person can understand some statements that another person does not. Second, if you understand a term to some extent, then it is to some extent intelligible and meaningful for you, and conversely. Third, understanding, intelligibility, and meaning can come with varying degrees of precision and vagueness, depending on how well-defined, how exactly interpreted, the relevant tokens are. Some interpretations, given what they exclude, are very exact; some are not.

Because interpretations need not be current episodes, or current acts, we need to introduce a notion of *dispositional interpretive commitments*. A nonextraneous interpretive commitment with respect to any token, *T*, of a certain type is just a commitment to interpret *T*, at least under certain conditions for one's own case, in a certain way—a way that is nonextraneous for one. (We might regard types themselves as our constructs, being defined relative to our purposes; on some of the issues facing a type-token distinction, see Moser 1984.) In particular, such commitment is commitment to construe *T*, at least for oneself under certain conditions, as indicating or expressing a certain (kind of) thing, where the construal is nonextraneous for one. One can still recognize that others may construe *T* differently, and that therefore one's interpretation of *others'* use of *T* may differ from one's construal of *T* for one's own case. I can recognize, for example, that 'knowledge', at a level of specificity, means something different for you from what it means for me.

We may understand talk of dispositional commitment functionally as follows: You are dispositionally committed, during a certain time span *D*, to interpret *T* in way *W* under certain conditions, at least for your own case, if and only if at the start of *D* you intend to interpret *T* in way *W* for your own case, and as a suitably direct result, during *D* you will interpret *T* in way *W* for your own case in any appropriate situation. Theorists may fill out talk of "appropriate situations" in different ways, depending on how behavioral their construal of 'commitment' seeks to be; and similar flexibility characterizes talk of a "suitably direct result." Our everyday notion of disposition, being somewhat vague, does not explicate such talk for us.

We can now allow for a distinction between a dispositional interpretive commitment and one's being *merely disposed* to have such a commitment, given the role just assigned to an initiating intention to interpret.[8] We can also allow for changes in interpretive commitments, owing to changes in intentions, and for interpretive commitments that are episodic, or actlike. An interpretive commitment may or may not be voluntary, and it may or may not be explicit to consciousness. Such a commitment can be socially learned and need not arise from extensive reflection.

A nonextraneous interpretive commitment toward *T* can relate one psychologically to a constitutive standard for correct use of *T* for one. One might have other nonextraneous interpretive commitments toward *T* and, as a result, have other constitutive standards for correct use of *T* for one. A constitutive standard for one's correct use of a token is not necessarily a unique such standard for one. One can acknowledge polysemy and homonymy in tokens, on the basis

8. For a distinction between dispositional belief and a mere disposition to believe, and for a notion of nondispositional belief involving assent, see Moser (1989, pp. 13–23). On the difficulties that arise for an account of belief once we omit an assent condition, see Lycan (1988, chap. 3).

of contextually sensitive constitutive standards for correct use. (On polysemy and homonymy, see Crystal 1987, p. 106.)

Suppose, for simplicity, that I have only one interpretive commitment toward *T* (for example, 'horse-shaped'), and that I am committed nonextraneously to interpret *T* as indicating a certain shape: say, Black Beauty–like shape. The occurrence of 'nonextraneously' here, despite some vagueness in 'Black Beauty–like', can enable a constitutive standard of correctness in use of *T* for me, since it can yield something definitive of correctness in use of *T* for me: namely, indication of Black Beauty–like shape. My using *T* to indicate something other than Black Beauty–like shape (say, Mickey Mouse–like shape) would, on one common understanding of correctness, be a mistake relative to my nonextraneous interpretive commitment. Such an interpretive commitment is equivalent to what section 2.3 calls a *conceptual* commitment. (When nonextraneous interpretive commitments concern a token's expressing something, we do not ordinarily regard them as conceptual commitments.) The determinacy of my interpretation requires that Black Beauty–like shape have some determinacy for me, but does not require that this determinacy be conceiving-independent in the sense of section 1.2. My understanding of 'Black Beauty–like shape', when we are talking in English about my interpretive commitment, will require constitutive standards for use of that term, but that is another matter now.

One's nonextraneous interpretive commitments regarding a token determine one's constitutive standards for correct use of that token. If I am now committed to interpret *T* in way *W* that is nonextraneous for me, then correct use of *T* for me now is defined, at least in part, by *W*. If, in particular, I am committed to interpret 'Stig, wake up!' nonextraneously as expressing a command that Stig wake up, then the correct use of 'Stig, wake up!' for me is defined, at least in part, in terms of its being a command that Stig wake up. There is thus an internal connection between one's nonextraneous interpretive commitments regarding a token and one's constitutive standards for correct use of that token.

I am, as it happens, committed to certain constitutive standards for correct use of 'philosophical', but not for 'eurteslaf'. The opposite *could* have been true; at least, it does not seem contradictory to suppose that the opposite is true. Still, the opposite is not actually true. The inscription 'eurteslaf' is thus not intelligible for me, whereas the term 'philosophical' is. One's nonextraneous interpretive commitments toward a token identify what it is for one to use that token correctly. Neglect of this internal connection will prevent one from treating the topic of what constitutes correctness in use *for an individual language-user*.

Semantic interpretationism allows that one can interpret tokens to express more than one thing. For example, utterance of 'A glass of water would be nice' can be just an assertion (that a glass of water would be nice) in one context and a request (for a glass of water) in another. In addition, utterance of 'Fire' can be both an assertion (that fire is present) and a warning, or even a command, for you to be cautious of fire. What 'Fire' means for you in a particular context will depend on your nonextraneous interpretation of what it indicates or expresses in that context; and your interpretation may or may not agree with that of someone else, even the person uttering 'Fire'.

One might object that 'Fire' in standard English does not mean 'Be cautious of fire!' even if some people sometimes interpret it to express such a command. Such an objection admits of a forthright reply. Utterance of 'Fire' does mean, in standard English, 'Be cautious of fire!' for some English language-users in special circumstances: at least in some circumstances where fire is evidently an immediate threat and a terse warning or command seems appropriate. The rather special character of these circumstances, and of the corresponding meaning of 'Fire', does not exclude a nonextraneous prescriptive rendering of 'Fire' from standard English. (A prescriptive rendering, nonetheless, might be extraneous at best for some English language-users; for them a prescriptive reading would not be definitive of the meaning of 'Fire'.)

On one common notion, "standard English" is conventionally determined insofar as nonextraneous customary interpretations by a number of English language-users fix what "standard English" meanings are. 'Construal', for example, had a standard English meaning among English-speaking philosophers, literary theorists, and lawyers before it recently started to appear in English dictionaries. We cannot, of course, plausibly restrict "standard English" meanings to what English dictionaries actually list. Dictionaries rarely, if ever, capture *all* the standard English of the moment. English, like any live natural language, develops apace.

"Mistakes" in interpretation, I have noted, require a standard for interpretive correctness relative to which an interpretation goes awry. Some philosophers, including Malcolm (1986, 1989), regard social conformity as providing such a standard, even the only such standard available or possible for us. Semantic interpretationism allows for appeal to social conformity as a standard for one kind of interpretive correctness: correctness as agreement of a nonextraneous interpretation of a token, in specified circumstances, with a certain group's nonextraneous interpretation in similar circumstances. It allows for another, person-relative kind of correctness too: correctness as conformity of an interpretation with one's extant nonextraneous interpretive commitments. Given an extant nonextraneous interpretive commitment to render tokens of a certain type only in a certain way, I err if I interpret such tokens otherwise. I could, then, make a mistake in interpreting 'Fire' as, for instance, a question whether fish fly if my extant nonextraneous interpretive commitments prohibit that interpretation.

Semantic interpretationism properly allows for considerable indefiniteness in some cases of meaning. One could interpret 'water', for instance, nonextraneously as indicating whatever most experts (say, chemists) regard as the chemical structure of a certain paradigmatic sample. Such an indefinite interpretation might even exhaust the meaning of 'water' for a person. The meaning of 'water' could then become more specific for one as one's nonextraneous interpretation grew with one's learning what most chemists regard as the chemical structure of the relevant sample. As nonextraneous interpretation for one becomes more specific, so too does meaning for one. Meaning, we might say, often has a fluidity of its own, over time.

C. Interpretively Purposive Use

Let us say that when one uses an utterance or inscription, *T*, in order to perform an act delimited by one's nonextraneous interpretation of *T*, one uses *T via* one's nonextraneous interpretation. Let us call one's intentionally using *T* via one's nonextraneous interpretation *interpretively purposive use* of *T*. In such use, one intentionally uses *T* to perform an act one interprets *T* as accomplishing in virtue of what, on one's nonextraneous interpretation, *T* indicates or expresses.

Interpretively purposive use sustains an internal connection between one's nonextraneous interpretation of *T* and the meaningful linguistic act one performs with *T*. Suppose, for example, that I use 'Stand up!' to command you to stand up now, where this act is delimited by what I nonextraneously interpret 'Stand up!' as doing now: expressing a command for you to stand up. In this case, my nonextraneous interpretation determines the sort of linguistic act I perform. More generally, in interpretively purposive linguistic action, one's goal in using a token is set by one's nonextraneous interpretation of that token. In that respect, interpretively purposive linguistic action is uniformly meaningful linguistic use.

Interpretively purposive use can sustain more than one purpose. When I utter 'It is pouring rain' in your presence, I may have various purposes. I may, for example, aim to describe the weather in my vicinity. At the same time, I may aim to advise you to stay in the house. The nonextraneous interpretations determining my linguistic goals, however complex, identify what kind of interpretively purposive use obtains.

Semantic interpretationism can accommodate a version of the following observation by Wittgenstein: "The concept of 'meaning' will serve to distinguish those linguistic formations that might be called capricious from those that are essential, inherent in the very purpose [*Zweckes*] of language" (1982, section 326; cf. section 385). Semantic interpretationism implies that linguistic formations are semantically capricious, and thus meaningless, for one when they lack an interpretation for one. It implies also that the very purpose of language is to sustain interpretations, and that one's sustaining interpretations can contribute to a wide variety of interpretively purposive linguistic actions: asserting, commanding, requesting, promising, exclaiming, declaring, and so on.

Semantic interpretationism allows us to deny, as did Wittgenstein (1974, p. 190), that language in general—including German, French, and so forth—is "defined for us as an arrangement fulfilling a definite purpose," such as the purpose of communication. The purpose of sustaining interpretations is not definite in the relevant sense; it encompasses, as just suggested, a wide variety of subsidiary purposes. We can also hold, as Wittgenstein suggested (1974, p. 70), that the purposes crucial to (interpretively purposive) meaningful use can be "expressed by a rule of language": that is, a constitutive standard for correct use (embodied in a nonextraneous interpretation) that identifies a particular kind of linguistic action. Semantic interpretationism agrees, as well, with

Wittgenstein's suggestion (1974, p. 69) that (interpretively purposive) meaningful use cannot be understood just in terms of purposes as effects of linguistic action. Interpretive purposes are not mere effects of language use.

In Part I of the *Philosophical Investigations*, Wittgenstein takes a dim view of the role of interpretation in meaning. He writes:

> "But how can a rule shew me what I have to do at *this* point? Whatever I do is, on some interpretation, in accord with the rule."—That is not what we ought to say, but rather: any interpretation still hangs in the air along with what it interprets, and cannot give it any support. Interpretations by themselves do not determine meaning. (1953, section 198; cf. section 201)

Wittgenstein's related worry is that "an ostensive definition can be variously interpreted in *every* case" (1953, section 28; cf. section 29).

Wittgenstein neglects a key point in Part I of the *Investigations*: Even if I *can* interpret a token variously in every case, I actually do not. I interpret some tokens nonextraneously as indicating or expressing certain things, and my nonextraneous interpretations can set constitutive standards for correct interpretation and use of those tokens for me. There is an internal connection between one's nonextraneous interpretations, what one means, and one's standards constitutive of correctness in interpretation and use.

Wittgenstein's most mature views on rule following and meaning accommodate my point here. In *Remarks on the Foundations of Mathematics*, Wittgenstein writes:

> "By this rule it goes like *this*": i.e., you *give* this rule an extension. But why can't I give it this extension today, that one tomorrow? Well, so I can. I might for example alternately give one of two interpretations. If I have once grasped a rule I am bound in what I do further. But of course that only means that I am bound in my *judgment* about what is in accord with the rule and what is not. (1978, pp. 328–329)

In similar disregard of any essential role for social considerations, Wittgenstein adds: "I give the rule an extension" (1978, p. 331). The emphasized words in the quotation above call attention to interpretive considerations. I *can* give a rule a nonstandard interpretation, but this would be doing exactly that: giving it a nonstandard interpretation. One's interpretive commitments determine what is standard and what is nonstandard for one.

It does not follow that you are always altogether free in what you regard as correct adding, for instance. Given your nonextraneous interpretive commitment that *this* way of proceeding is addition, you are thereby bound. You might, of course, change your nonextraneous commitment, introducing a new one; but you will thereby introduce a different understanding, a different concept. Such change is often up to you, as concepts result from human doings. As Wittgenstein notes: "I give the rule an extension." Who gives the extension? *I* do, not my society.

Kripke (1982, p. 13) reads Wittgenstein as exploiting a skeptical worry about what "establishes" that I meant plus rather than something else by '+'.

If Kripke's skeptic is the meaning agnostic of section 1.7, we need not tarry. I have conceded that we cannot win a battle over non-questionbegging reasons against a shrewd agnostic. If, however, Kripke's skeptic is less demanding, we can appeal to the internal connection noted previously. My interpretation of '+' as plus, rather than something else, settles that I did not actually mean something else—even though I *could* have meant something else. Wittgenstein's most mature views on meaning accommodate this consideration.

According to semantic interpretationism, we need not always use language just to communicate or to formulate truths. Contrary to Paul Grice (1957, p. 220), we should not think of meaningful use as always aiming "to produce some effect in an audience by means of the recognition of [the language user's] intention." Such a view implausibly restricts meaningful language-use to intended communication. It thus excludes other forms of meaningful use, such as meaningful use of exclamations in the absence of an intended audience. An interpretation delimiting interpretively purposive use will identify a language user's purposes from the first-person conceptual perspective of that language user's linguistic actions. This perspective reveals what constitutes meaningful use for the language user in question: that is, meaningful use from the standpoint of what a language user is *doing*. Such a perspective allows for meaningful use in the absence of an intended audience or some third-person observer.

We can distinguish one's *using* language meaningfully, in interpretively purposive use, from someone's *construing* one's use of language as meaningful. If someone uses language without interpretation, I might still construe that use of language as meaningful, relative to my own interpretation of that language. My simply construing a person's use of language as meaningful does not entail, however, that this person's language-use is actually meaningful just from the standpoint of this person's use of language. From the latter standpoint, the use may lack an accompanying interpretation; it may be no different, in that respect, from my use of the nonsense-token 'eurteslaf' to startle you. The scribbling of a two-year-old, for example, might admit of an interpretation by us without actually being meaningful use of language simply from the standpoint of the two-year-old. The scribbling might not be accompanied by the child's interpreting the marks as indicating or expressing something.

We may contrast, then, the meaningfulness of an inscription for a person and the meaningfulness of someone else's use of that inscription. You might use some tokens capriciously without interpretation, but produce, fortuitously, an inscription that is meaningful for me. That inscription's being meaningful for me does not entail that you have used that inscription meaningfully, from your interpretive standpoint. It entails rather that I am able, given my nonextraneous interpretive commitments, to interpret that inscription as indicating or expressing something. Semantic interpretationism respects the perspectival, person-relative character of meaning.

Interpretively purposive use of tokens is, under that description, *purposive* linguistic behavior. What we regard in general as purposive language-use will depend on our nonextraneous interpretation of 'purposive' or some synonymous term. Interpretation here can and does vary, but typically involves considerations of acting "for a reason," where the relevant reason is appropriately related (for example, conceptually or evidentially) to a certain more or less definite goal. A *conceptual* account of purposive behavior, unlike an empirical account, looks to constitutive standards for correct use of 'purposive behavior' (or some synonymous term), rather than to empirical considerations about what physical states accompany what we call 'purposive behavior'.

While invoking talk of purpose to clarify talk of meaning, in the way noted earlier, Wittgenstein (1982, section 336) reports that he cannot give a "general answer" to the question of what an explanation of a purpose looks like. Our constitutive standards for correct use of 'purposive behavior' need not, however, be reducible to our constitutive standards for talk of accompanying physical states. Even if some proponents of reductive physicalism take the opposite view for granted, we can plausibly demand supporting argument for such reductionism.[9]

Our everyday notion of meaningful use, I have suggested, does not depend on an account of the physiological states that typically accompany meaningful use. Most people wielding that notion lack information about such physiological states, at least information in the language of the natural sciences. One might introduce a notion of meaning that differs on that score, but in doing so, one would be proposing an alternative to our everyday notion of meaningful use. This alternative notion may serve some purposes of certain theorists, but it is doubtful that it serves the purposes of all theorists. (Chapter 5 returns to the topic of physicalism and explanatorily acceptable vocabulary.)

3.4 Correctness in Use

Standards for correctness in language use can function as either *constitutive* or *prescriptive* standards.[10] Constitutive standards do not prescribe, but rather describe or otherwise identify, conditions definitive of a certain manner of use. Constitutive standards for linguistic use can and do vary among language users. Prescriptive standards for language use are evaluative regulations for the use of tokens. Such standards require, permit, or prohibit linguistic behavior of certain sorts. They thus regulate, at least in principle, language use for a person or a group. Rules of English grammar, for example, are now functioning prescriptively for me, as evaluative guidelines for sentence and paragraph formation. These rules play a role in determining what sort of sentence and paragraph formation is permissible for me. Prescriptive standards, like constitutive standards, can and do vary among language users. Even among skilled English language users, differing prescriptive standards for use are often at work.

9. For arguments against prominent attempts to reduce purposive descriptions to nonpurposive descriptions, see Larry Wright (1968). For some problems facing reductionism about meaning, see Boghossian (1989, pp. 527–540) and Schiffer (1987). On Schiffer's own alternative to reductive physicalism, his "sentential dualism," see Moser (1990e).

10. A related distinction between rules has been suggested by Rawls (1955), in connection with ethical rules. Cf. Searle (1969, pp. 33–42).

The distinction between constitutive and prescriptive standards for use marks how certain standards function for a person. Constitutive standards identifying correct use of a term for me can also be used by me to prescribe or to prohibit certain uses of language. I could issue a directive, perhaps only to myself: Use term *T*, in order to conform to constitutive standards *C* for correctly using *T*! Or: Don't use *T*, in order to avoid conflict with those constitutive standards! One's constitutive standards need not be used prescriptively. They might function only to identify a correct use for a person, a certain manner of interpretively purposive use.

Nonextraneous interpretations central to meaningful language-use are constitutive, and not necessarily prescriptive. We can use language meaningfully without ever prescribing, permitting, or prohibiting language use. We can just engage in interpretively purposive use without employing any standards for use prescriptively, and even without being familiar with prescriptive standards for use.

Whenever we do engage in interpretively purposive use, standards that identify the relevant purpose are in principle specifiable, in terms of operative nonextraneous interpretations. Such standards can determine correctness for interpretively purposive use of language. They identify nonextraneous interpretive commitments relative to which it makes sense to talk of subsequent use of certain terms as correct or incorrect. Nonextraneous interpretive commitments regarding a token can change over time. Meaning and constitutive standards for correct use can change accordingly.

Constitutive standards for correct and incorrect use owe their status as correctness-determining for a person to that person's nonextraneous interpretive commitment to them. Apart from such commitment, they have no correctness-determining force for the person in question, where the pertinent relativity concerns meaning and not mere belief about what is correct. Such standards thus have a contingent functional status for a person relative to that person's contingent nonextraneous interpretive commitment.

If language users had no commitment to standards at all, then no standards for linguistic use would have correctness-determining significance for those language users. In that case, there would be no actually correct or incorrect use for those language users; correctness and incorrectness for one depend on a standard for one determining what they are. Remove all standards constitutive of correctness and incorrectness for one, and you thereby remove not only sensible talk of correctness and incorrectness for one, but also the actuality of anything falling under those standards for one: that is, anything being correct or incorrect for one by way of those standards.

As it happens, some of us are committed to standards for the correct and incorrect use of terms. These standards give some determinacy to our talk of correct and incorrect use. Consider, for example, the commitment some of us have made to various standards for correct use of terms set by a typical English dictionary. Owing to these adopted standards, our talk of correct and incorrect use of various English terms makes some sense. We might have adopted different standards, but that takes nothing away from the efficacy of our actual standards, the standards for correctness and incorrectness to which we are actually committed.

Our everyday notion of meaning allows for some variation in how one is related to constitutive standards for correct use, owing to some vagueness in our talk of a standard of correct use "for one." A very strong notion of "for one" requires commitment to a nonextraneous interpretation of *T* as a constitutive standard for correct use of *T*. This notion requires one's having a notion of a constitutive standard for correct use. Baker and Hacker (1985), as section 3.2A indicates, endorse a strong notion of "for one," requiring explicit familiarity with rules (as rules) for correct use.

A weaker notion requires a nonextraneous interpretive commitment toward *T*, but does not require one's conceiving of the pertinent nonextraneous interpretation *as* a constitutive standard for correct use. This notion allows for interpretations that function as constitutive standards for correct use without being regarded as such. A still weaker notion comes from a case where I simply give *T* a nonextraneous interpretation, perhaps on a number of occasions, but refrain from an interpretive commitment regarding future interpretation of *T*. This notion treats correctness "for one" as agreement with unsurpassed interpretive precedent, regardless of lack of interpretive commitment.

I shall not pretend that our everyday notion of meaning unequivocally favors one of the three aforementioned notions; nor do I have any pressing reason to recommend one over the others, without qualification. It does seem, however, that a strong notion of "for one" faces problems from our frequent talk of meaningful use of language by young children. Our everyday notion of meaning evidently does not rely on such a strong notion in all cases.

Can standards for use themselves be correct or incorrect? The answer depends on the interpretation we give to 'correct' here. Because prescriptive standards for use function prescriptively, and not as assertions, they do not owe their correctness simply to their describing certain facts of linguistic use. We thus cannot discover their correctness or incorrectness simply by describing certain facts of linguistic use. A person can be committed to certain prescriptive standards for use that are not satisfied by actual linguistic use, including that person's own use. In this respect, the prescriptive and the descriptive need not agree. Correct use, when defined relative to prescriptive standards, rests not on one's actual use, but rather on compliance with certain regulative standards for use. Recall the contrast between regulative standards (prescriptions) and actual regularity in use. This approach does not, however, have a monopoly on the understanding of correctness; nor does any other specific approach.

We might introduce a special notion of correctness relative to which standards for use can be correct. We should recognize, at the same time, that this notion would not have an evaluative life of its own, apart from our interpretations setting constitutive standards for it. Standards for correctness, like anything meaningful, depend for their intelligibility on interpretation. Some philosophers, as section 3.2 notes, wield a social constitutive standard for correctness, while others use different standards. Our everyday notion of meaning, I have suggested, does not require a social standard for all meaningful use. One might depart from our everyday notion, but that departure will call for answers to questions about a rationale for such departure.

My constitutive standards for correct and incorrect use of the term 'philosophical', for example, determine the correctness for me of an answer to our earlier question: What makes a claim philosophical? These standards are mine in virtue of my interpretive commitment regarding the term 'philosophical', that is, regarding standards for the correct and incorrect use of that term. Lacking such a commitment, I would lack the standards needed to distinguish in principle between correct and incorrect use of 'philosophical'.

My interpretive commitment regarding 'philosophical' has been influenced by a number of sources, including the writings of Plato, Aristotle, Descartes, Kant, Russell, and Wittgenstein, among others. I might have been influenced by different sources, such as the writings of Confucius, Gautama Buddha, and the Dalai Lama; but, to my knowledge, I have not been. My construal of 'philosophical' proceeds accordingly. Given my explanatory and other linguistic purposes, I have found no need to form a different interpretive commitment regarding 'philosophical'. This does not mean that my interpretive commitment is necessary or privileged in itself. It means rather that given my explanatory and other linguistic purposes, this commitment has served adequately.

My constitutive standards for correct use can change, owing to various influences on me. My explanatory purposes might change, or the sources influencing my view of philosophy might change. Still, so long as I have my present commitment, it will determine correctness and incorrectness for how I use the term 'philosophical', and will, upon suitable reflection, determine what I regard as the correct answer (for me) to the question of what 'philosophical' means. It is, then, largely an autobiographical matter to specify what I mean by 'philosophical'. (I shall save the autobiography for another occasion.)

We might have developed without standards for correct and incorrect use, as animals that do not employ standards for the correct and incorrect use of language. In fact, we might have developed to use virtually all the inscriptions and utterances we now use, while lacking standards for correct use. In that case, we would have exhibited "linguistic behavior," perhaps even purposive linguistic behavior, without possessing standards that determine the correctness and incorrectness of that behavior. Talk of correct or incorrect use of language would then be out of place, at least from our standpoint. We would have no standard to distinguish, even in principle, correct from incorrect use of language. Our use of language, under such conditions, would be *correctness-blind.* Meaning is not just use; use, unlike meaning, requires no standards for correctness.

I, for one, am not correctness-blind in my use of language, at least not in all such use; nor, I suspect, are you. We often talk of correct and incorrect use of language, and we typically have more or less specific standards to make such talk sensible. When confronted with language for which we lack suitable standards, we also lack understanding—at least full understanding. In such a case, we might formulate standards for correct use, and thereby give intelligibility to what was unintelligible. Apart from some such standards, however, talk of correct or incorrect use would be altogether out of place for us. Semantic interpretationism treats meaningful talk of correct use in the way it treats meaningful talk in general: as dependent on nonextraneous interpretation that can vary from person to person.

Two likely objections to semantic interpretationism merit comment. First, we cannot explain (uniformly) meaningful language-use in terms of interpretively purposive use, since interpretation and purposive use depend on meaningful language-use. Interpretation and purposive language-use are not prior to meaningful language-use.

The objection hides some important distinctions. Because notions of meaningful use, purposive use, and interpretation can, and do, vary among theorists, I shall not reply that *the* notion of interpretively purposive use is prior to *the* notion of meaningful use. I am not familiar with any such single thing as the notion of purposive use, the notion of interpretation, or the notion of meaningful use, even if we have somewhat flexible everyday notions of each.

The objection's talk of dependency and priority needs clarification. Semantic interpretationism does not require that there be interpretively purposive use without meaningful use of language. In particular, it does not require that interpretively purposive use be temporally prior to meaningful use. Language use might have begun as mere reactive or habitual behavior that eventually came to be interpreted, or construed, as exhibiting a kind of regularity, a kind of conformity to patterns.[11] Upon interpreting regularity from a first-person perspective, we might suppose, language users began to engage in interpretive use of language, interpreting tokens themselves nonextraneously as indicating or expressing something. The emergence of such interpretation, according to semantic interpretationism, *was* the emergence of meaningful language. The two are really one and the same. Similarly, the emergence of interpretively purposive use *was* the origin of uniformly purposive meaningful use.

A relevant issue of conceptual dependency is whether every notion of interpretively purposive use presupposes a notion of meaningful use. This issue resists any easy affirmative answer, given the diversity of notions of interpretation, purposive use, and meaningful use in circulation. (Notions of presupposition vary too.) Whether conceptual circularity really threatens will depend on what one's notion of meaningful use actually includes. Very few philosophers have acknowledged an obvious conceptual connection between meaningful language-use and nonextraneous interpretation of a token as indicating or expressing something. This suggests that the connection identified by semantic interpretationism is not obviously circular and may deserve emphasis. My concern, moreover, is to elucidate our everyday notion of meaning; consequently, it would be pointless to introduce considerations far removed from that notion.

11. For some suggestions on this theme, see Sellars (1954; 1979, chap. 4) and Baker and Hacker (1984, pp. 255–256).

It is not obvious, in any case, that our everyday talk of doing something with an understood purpose always involves a notion of meaningful language-use. We often talk of infants, for example, as doing things purposively (for example, crying for food, warmth, or mother) prior to acquisition of a natural language. We even say that the baby wants food, warmth, or mother, thus treating the baby as more than a reactor to stimuli. This suggests that the gist of semantic interpretationism will not strike all people as conceptually circular. Conceptual circularity, in any event, depends on the content of a concept being explained, and it is not obvious that we need a prior notion of meaningful use to understand my talk of interpretively purposive use.

Second, one might object that talk of interpretively purposive use is irredeemably metaphysical, and so adds only further mystery to the already mysterious topic of linguistic meaning. What we really need is an account of meaning solely in terms of our best physical sciences, where talk of interpretation and purpose has no firm place.

The objection, reminiscent of the views of W. V. Quine and various other eliminative materialists and positivists, is just a manifestation of scientific chauvinism. We have no reason whatever to presume that our notion of linguistic meaning must be, or even is, reducible to the vocabulary of the physical sciences. Our linguistic purposes need not, and indeed do not, uniformly conform to the purposes of the physical sciences. It thus would be gratuitous to constrain an account of linguistic meaning by the language of the physical sciences. Given our everyday purposes in language use, the physical sciences do not merit a monopoly either on meaningful language or on the vocabulary for characterizing meaningful use. The physical sciences, moreover, depend on interpretively purposive use of language in their various explanatory ventures. Science without interpretation of tokens is no science at all. (Section 5.3 returns to this general theme, with special attention to physicalism and psychological explanation.)

The account of meaningful use offered by semantic interpretationism is not metaphysical, if being "metaphysical" requires an assumption of non-question-begging support for ontological claims. I have not proposed a "metaphysics of meaning," as Frege did with his Platonism about thoughts and Russell did with his physicalist behaviorism about language in general. I rather have tried to clarify a familiar concept of meaningful use, a concept that serves the purposes of the semantic foundationalism of chapter 2 and fits with the conditional ontological agnosticism of chapter 1.

The familiar concept in question is not one of correctness-blind, merely behavioral use. By our familiar concept, the ornate pattern of raindrops on the shore of Lake Michigan does not constitute meaningful use of symbols, even if that pattern arises in a lawlike manner and can be construed by us as a striking portrait of Sir Winston Churchill. A notion of interpretively purposive use is inextricably bound up with our everyday notion of (uniformly) meaningful use of language. The two are connected concepts. By way of conceptual clarification, semantic interpretationism explains how they are connected.

3.5 Whither Analyticity?

Given semantic interpretationism, we can refine the foundations of semantic foundationalism, including its reliance on a notion of analyticity (or truth by conceptual commitment). Ever since Quine's "Two Dogmas of Empiricism" (1951), philosophers have generally regarded talk of analyticity as suspect at best, and mythical at worst. The remainder of this chapter will rescue analyticity from the throes of suspicion and myth, at least so far as Quine's arguments go. It will explain why all epistemologists—including friends of Quine's naturalized epistemology—must rely on a notion of analyticity to answer certain questions about the correctness of their epistemic standards. Epistemologists typically overlook this point, owing to inadequate consideration of what makes an epistemic standard correct.

According to an orthodox story, Quine's "Two Dogmas" shows that any suitable appeal to analyticity presupposes a notion of cognitive synonymy that is no more transparent than talk of analyticity itself. One class of analytic statements—so-called logically true statements—does not draw this objection from Quine. Such statements, represented by 'No unmarried man is married', remain true under all reinterpretations of their nonlogical components.

A second class of statements, represented by 'No bachelor is married', does invite the orthodox story. Some philosophers hold of this class that its members reduce to logical truths by substituting synonyms for synonyms: for example, 'unmarried man' for 'bachelor'. Other philosophers have talked instead of reducing the second class of analytic statements to the first *by definition*. They propose, for instance, that we define 'bachelor' as 'unmarried man'. Quine objects, on the ground that such talk of definition, like Carnap's talk of explication, typically rests on a notion of synonymy concerning the definiendum and certain antecedent familiar usage. Again, the relevant notion of synonymy needs clarification as much as does the notion of analyticity.

Quine has related problems with the view that synonymy consists in interchangeability of linguistic forms *salva veritate*. In a language free of such modal adverbs as 'necessarily', interchangeability *salva veritate* will not guarantee the relevant kind of synonymy. It will provide, for instance, only: 'All and only bachelors are unmarried men.' Proponents of synonymy want such a truth to depend just on considerations of meaning, not on coincidental factual matters. We might therefore introduce the adverb 'necessarily' to raise the foregoing statement above the level of contingent facts. Quine balks, however, on the ground that such use of 'necessarily' is intelligible only if the notion of analyticity is already understandable, and it is not. We thus return to the problem of analyticity.

Quine's further target is Carnap's effort to explain analyticity by the notion of a *semantical rule*. Carnap proposes that a statement is analytically true if and only if it is true according to a semantical rule. Quine faults the unexplained phrase 'semantical rule': "Semantical rules are distinguishable, apparently, only by the fact of appearing on a page under the heading 'Semantical Rules'; and this heading is itself then meaningless" (1951, p. 34). The general point, once again, is that we make no explanatory mileage by accounting for analyticity by a notion equally in need of clarification.

Quine anticipates, finally, an effort to understand analyticity via a verification theory of meaning. An analytic truth, on this view, is a statement confirmed "no matter what," or "come what may." Quine proposes epistemic holism instead, the view that particular statements are confirmed or disconfirmed not individually on the basis of experience, but only as a "field." Given such holism, according to Quine, any statement can be accepted come what may, so long as we revise, perhaps drastically, other parts of our field of accepted statements. Conversely, no statement is beyond revisability (cf. Quine 1991, pp. 268–270). Quine concludes that the present approach to analyticity rests on an unduly atomistic approach to confirmation and disconfirmation.

Are we left then with no viable approach to analyticity? Not quite, even by Quine's lights in "Two Dogmas" itself. As Quine notes:

> There does, however, remain still an extreme sort of definition which does not hark back to prior synonymies at all: namely, the explicitly conventional introduction of novel notations for purposes of sheer abbreviation. . . . Here we have a really transparent case of synonymy created by definition; would that all species of synonymy were as intelligible. For the rest, definition rests on synonymy rather than explaining it. (1951, p. 26)

Quine says no more about this sort of definition as a basis for analyticity. He does not pursue at all the possibility that a philosophically important notion of analyticity emerges from such definition. I shall return to this possibility in section 3.7, while presenting my own account of analyticity.

Since the time of "Two Dogmas," Quine has offered some learning-based construals of analyticity, while consistently denying the epistemological importance of these construals. In *Pursuit of Truth*, for example, Quine claims:

> We can appeal to how the native speaker learns a word: certainly he learns 'bachelor' substantially through the explanation 'unmarried man'. In *Roots of Reference* (1974, pp. 78-80) I suggested a rough account of analyticity along the same lines: a sentence is analytic if the native speaker learns to assent to it in learning one of its words. . . . The importance of analyticity for epistemology lapses, be it noted, in the light of holism. (1990a, p. 55)

Even if there is a useful everyday notion of analyticity that applies to the bachelor example and the basic laws of logic (*modus ponens*, for example), Quine claims that this notion is "epistemologically insignificant" (1991, pp. 270–271).

The relevance of holism to the epistemological importance of analyticity, Quine now contends, settles the philosophically significant issue about analyticity:

> . . . I now perceive that the philosophically important question about analyticity and the linguistic doctrine of logical truth is *not* how to explicate them; it is the question rather of their relevance to epistemology. The second dogma of empiricism, to the effect that each empirically meaningful sentence has an empirical content of its own, was cited in "Two Dogmas" merely as encouraging false confidence in the notion of analyticity; but now I would

> say further that the second dogma creates a need for analyticity as a key notion of epistemology, and that the need lapses when we heed Duhem and set the second dogma aside. (1986a, p. 207)

On Quine's semantic holism, we do not need analyticity to account for the meaningfulness of logical and mathematical truths, for example.

The meaningfulness of logical and mathematical truths derives, on Quine's view, from their figuring in the natural sciences for the implication of various observationally testable statements. Logical and mathematical truths thus do not need to be divorced from empirical content. Given semantic holism, they participate, if only indirectly, in the empirical content of various observational statements.

Similarly, we do not need analyticity to account for the necessity of logical and mathematical truths. According to Quine: "Holism accounts for it by freedom of selection and the maxim of minimum mutilation" (1990a, p. 56). Necessity becomes just a matter of our current unwillingness to dispense with certain statements at the center of our web of belief.

Quine's main thesis about analyticity is, then, twofold: First, "for all its a priori reasonableness, a boundary between analytic and synthetic statements simply has not been drawn" (1951, p. 37); and second, the epistemological need for analyticity lapses once we accept holism of a certain sort. I shall contest both parts of this thesis. Let us begin with the dispute between Quine and Carnap over analyticity. This will set the stage for my reply to Quine's complaint about analyticity.

3.6 Standards for Analyticity: Carnap versus Quine

Quine's general complaint against notions of analyticity is this:

> Wherever there has been a semblance of a general criterion [for analyticity], to my knowledge, there has been either some drastic failure such as tended to admit all or no sentences as analytic, or there has been a circularity of the kind noted [earlier], or there has been a dependence on terms like 'meaning', 'possible', 'conceivable', and the like, which are at least as mysterious (and in the same way) as what we want to define. (1963, pp. 403–404)

In reply to Quine's complaint, Carnap uses talk of "meaning postulates" (1952; 1963, p. 918) and "analyticity postulates" (1966, p. 261). Carnap proposes that a statement is analytic if and only if it is a logical consequence of meaning (analyticity) postulates that specify meaning relations holding among certain terms. Quine (1951, p. 33) objects that we do not gain real understanding by talking of meaning (or analyticity) postulates because we lack clear understanding of talk of meaning (and analyticity).

This much seems right: We do need a standard of some sort for clarifying talk of meaning and analyticity. Quine demands an empirical *behavioral* standard, on this ground: "There is nothing in linguistic meaning beyond what is to be gleaned from overt behavior in observable circumstances" (1990a, p. 38; cf. 1969a, pp. 26–29; 1991, p. 272).

Quine's ground needs qualification, at least from the standpoint of various nonbehaviorist conceptions of meaning. The latter conceptions allow that meaning can be a function of psychological processes, events, or abilities that need not all be identifiable in overt behavior. Psychological behavior, on these conceptions, can be covert yet nonetheless constitutive of meaning, at least in part. Quine gives no argument to discredit such conceptions; nor is it easy to imagine what such a cogent argument would look like. Quine needs, then, to qualify the kind of meaning he anchors in overt behavior.

Quine's requirement that meaning be "gleaned from overt behavior in observable circumstances" must be restricted to socially learned, public linguistic meaning, the kind of meaning that accompanies shared natural languages.[12] Given such a restriction, we can plausibly let Quine have his behavioral standard. Socially learned linguistic meaning does depend on public behavioral evidence. That is what makes such meaning social.

Carnap (1963, p. 920) has tried to meet Quine's demand for a public behavioral standard for analyticity. Consider a case of two linguists disagreeing over whether the following sentence is analytically true for you in your language: 'All ravens are black'. These linguists test their competing hypotheses by asking you whether you would withdraw your assertion of 'All ravens are black' if someone showed you a white raven. You could reply in either of two ways: (a) I would withdraw my assertion if presented with adequate evidence for the existence of a white raven; (b) I would not withdraw my assertion because I do not call white birds 'ravens'; given my use of the term 'raven', there cannot be white ravens. Carnap holds that response (b) supports the hypothesis that 'All ravens are black' is analytically true for you, whereas response (a) supports the hypothesis that it is not. Carnap concludes that ascriptions of analyticity can be tested by observation of public linguistic behavior (1963, p. 920).

We can put Carnap's point generally: Whenever one rejects all falsifiers of an assertion, by invoking only considerations about one's usage of that assertion's constituent terms, we may regard that assertion as analytically true for one. This conditional offers a behavioral standard for analyticity, but not an infallible standard. One might reject all falsifiers, when queried, simply because of an aim to deceive us about what is analytic, or simply because of confusion over what one's usage of the relevant terms actually is. A rejection of all falsifiers by appeal to usage, then, does not guarantee analyticity in any familiar sense. Quine, however, cannot plausibly demand an infallible standard for analyticity. Such a demand would limit us to a vocabulary that is impoverished by any standard, if not altogether empty. At least, we have no reason to think that our best natural science depends on infallible standards for the use of its vocabulary.

12. For apparent agreement with this, see Quine (1969a, p. 26; 1990a, pp. 37–38; 1990b) and Føllesdal (1990, pp. 103–104). See Hylton (1991) for a reading of Quine on meaning that supports my interpretation.

An improved standard for analyticity is:

> A sentence, *S*, is analytically true for a person, *X*, if and only if *X*, when motivated just by her actual usage of *S*'s constituent terms, would reject all (potential) falsifiers of *S*.

This formulation restricts the basis of *X*'s rejection of all falsifiers. The basis must be just *X*'s actual usage of *S*'s constituent terms, and not linguistic confusion or an aim to deceive.

As interpreters, we might, of course, have difficulty discerning what *X*'s actual usage of *S*'s terms is. This would complicate only our discerning analyticity, but would not affect what actually *is* analytic for *X*. The standard thus allows for a sentence's being analytic for a person while certain interpreters are unable to discern that it is analytic, owing perhaps to inadequate evidence about actual usage. This is a virtue, not a defect. In cases where interpreters have adequate evidence about actual usage, they can make reasonable empirical judgments about analyticity. The standard apparently does all the work we can reasonably expect, at least with respect to behavioral considerations.

The standard needs still more refinement. In particular, its talk of *actual usage* needs elaboration. Quine himself raises no objection to talk of linguistic usage. In fact, he appeals to the use of words as the field of study for the semanticist, and adds this: "The sentences and stimulatory situations in which I would now use the word ['desk'] might even be said to constitute the *meaning* of the word for me now, if we care to rehabilitate the dubious term 'meaning'" (1978, p. 1). On Quine's behavioral approach, sameness of meaning, or synonymy, is sameness of use; nothing more, nothing less. What, however, is *use*, and when are two uses *the same*? Answers to these questions will give needed refinements to the proposed standard for analyticity.

Quine has his own answer. Roughly, one word is synonymous with (or has the same use as) another for you if and only if the substitution of the one for the other in a sentence always yields cognitively equivalent sentences for you: that is, sentences with the same truth conditions for you (1978, pp. 2–3, 5). You will give matching verdicts of true or false, or no verdict in doubtful cases, to cognitively equivalent sentences for you.

Quine is especially optimistic about explaining cognitive equivalence of *occasion* sentences, sentences whose truth values change from occasion to occasion, such as 'Here is a desk'. Two occasion sentences are cognitively equivalent for you if and only if you are "disposed to give matching verdicts in matching stimulatory circumstances," that is, in circumstances where the same set of your sensory receptors is triggered (1978, pp. 4–5; cf. 1990a, pp. 40–42).

Talk of matching stimulatory circumstances underlies Quine's notion of "stimulus synonymy." The stimulus meaning of a sentence is the class of all stimulations that would prompt assent or dissent with respect to that sentence (1960, pp. 32–33). Stimulus synonymy is just sameness of stimulus meaning. Thus: "Sentences are stimulus-synonymous for the individual if they have the same stimulus meaning for him, and stimulus-synonymous for the community if stimulus-synonymous for each member" (1990a, p. 44).

Quine refrains from generalizing his account to provide a definition of 'cognitive equivalence' for sentences that are not occasion sentences: so-called *standing* sentences. He does offer a sufficient condition: Two standing sentences are cognitively equivalent if one can be transformed into the other by the replacement of words or phrases by cognitive synonyms. Quine denies, however, that this approach works between languages, at least in the absence of bilinguals. He thus denies that it bears on his thesis of the indeterminacy of translation: the thesis that "two conflicting manuals of translation can both do justice to all dispositions to behavior, and that, in such a case, there is no fact of the matter of which manual is right" (1981, p. 23).

The limitation here comes in part from our lacking a manageable notion of intersubjective likeness of stimulation. Because you and I do not share receptors, we do not share stimulations either. Quine thus seeks no semantic work from intersubjective likeness of stimulation (1990a, pp. 40–42).

Quine's account of use and sameness of use in behavioral and sensory terms seems too narrow; for it uniformly ties the synonymy of words and phrases to their interchangeability in sentences with truth conditions. Our typical uses of some words and phrases, as section 3.1 suggests, cannot be understood in terms of their roles in sentences with truth conditions. Consider, for example, certain words or phrases that express commands ('Please'), wishes ('Would that everyone did'), greetings ('Hello', 'Hi'), or exclamations ('Ouch!', 'Darn!', 'Ugh!'). Quine's account fails to explain the sense in which synonymy, or sameness of use, can characterize such words and phrases.

It would be implausible, because gratuitous, to hold that there cannot be a relation of sameness of use between, for example, such imperatival terms as 'Please' and 'Kindly be willing', and such exclamatory terms as 'Damn!' and 'Darn!'. The mere fact that certain terms lack a role in truth-valued sentences does not preclude that those terms stand in synonymy or sameness-of-use relations to other terms. Quine's account is unduly restrictive, then, as a general approach to sameness of use.

From another angle, Quine's account is too liberal. The heart of the account is this: Two words are synonymous for you if and only if your substituting one for the other in a sentence will always be accompanied by your being disposed to give matching verdicts of true or false, or no verdict in cases of doubt. Nothing in the account restricts the basis of the relevant disposition. You might be disposed to give matching verdicts in all test cases only because you aim to deceive others about the meanings of certain terms for you, or only because you are seriously confused about your own usage of certain terms. This problem emerged for Carnap's standard too. It led us, in the improved standard, to anchor relevant verbal behavior in actual linguistic usage. Quine, then, has not avoided the problem that led us to invoke actual linguistic usage in the first place. We thus need an alternative to Quine's approach to linguistic usage and synonymy.

Carnap, we have seen, proposed a behavioral standard for analyticity that needed some refinement. Carnap does not himself give us an account of linguistic usage, but he does invoke the notion of such usage in his explanation of analyticity. He claims that with respect to the construction of a semantical system, theorists are "free to choose their [meaning] postulates, guided not by their beliefs concerning facts of the world but by their intentions with respect to the meanings, i.e., the ways of use of the descriptive constants" (1952, p. 225). The analytic truths of a system, on Carnap's approach, result from "intentions" or "postulates" specifying "the ways of use" of terms.

Carnap (1963, p. 921) denies that his approach identifies analytic truths with truths that, in Quine's language (1951, p. 43), "hold come what may."[13] Carnap distinguishes two kinds of change in accepted statements: a change in the language one uses, and a change in a truth value ascribed to a statement whose truth value is not fixed just by the rules of one's language. Analytic statements, by definition, do not undergo changes of the second sort. In that respect, their truth values do not change. One can change one's language, however, by adopting different meaning postulates. In that respect, what is analytically true for a person can change. On Carnap's view, some truth values are fixed just by rules of language use; others are not. This is the gist of Carnap's account of analyticity.

We still have not reached adequate understanding of analyticity, even if we have identified some mistakes and made some progress. We now need to clarify the relevant notion of language usage.

3.7 Analyticity Regained

My refinement of the standard noted previously will have some affinity with Quine's own 1934 position on analyticity, namely: "Analytic judgments are consequences of definitions, conventions as to the uses of words" (1934, pp. 47–48; cf. 1991, p. 266). Quine came to have qualms about the relevant notion of definition, owing to its apparent reliance on a questionable concept of synonymy. In fact, by the time of "Truth by Convention" (1936), Quine had come to have serious doubts about his earlier approach to analyticity.

Contrary to the emphasis of "Two Dogmas," the relevant notion of *definition* need not lean on a questionable concept of synonymy with antecedent usage. This is suggested by Quine's own talk of definitions as *conventions* for the uses of words. Whereas Quine (1934) talked of "conventions" for the uses of words, Carnap (1952) talked of "intentions" with respect to the uses of words. Neither held that analyticity must be understood in terms of synonymy relations concerning antecedent usage. The qualms about definition in "Two Dogmas" are thus puzzling, at least from the standpoint of what Carnap and Quine himself had actually held about analyticity.

13. Quine's use of such a characterization was evidently prompted by C. I. Lewis's (1923) conception of the a priori. See Quine (1934, p. 48). Putnam (1976, p. 92) claims that "Quine *confused* analyticity and apriority because of positivist assumptions (assumptions he was attacking)."

Quine came to doubt the significance of the notion of convention, largely on the ground that (a) we seldom verbally formulate the needed conventions, and (b) the idea of implicitly accepted, behavioral conventions leaves much to be desired. Quine's worry is that "it is not clear wherein an adoption of the conventions, antecedently to their formulation, consists; such behavior is difficult to distinguish from that in which conventions are disregarded" (1936, pp. 98–99). This worry led Quine to doubt that an ascription of truth by convention adds anything to a "behavioristic statement" that a truth is firmly accepted.

Aside from what is behavioristic and what is not, we must recognize the *person-relativity* of analyticity, at least on a view like Carnap's. What is analytic, on Carnap's view, can vary from person to person, owing to the variability of intentions with respect to use. My intentions regarding use can make the truths of arithmetic, for example, analytic for me. Those truths need not be analytic, however, for someone lacking the relevant intentions about linguistic use. Quine does not give due recognition to such person-relativity of analyticity.

Why did Carnap and Quine talk of conventions and intentions regarding use, instead of just use itself, as the basis for analyticity? The answer seems clear: Conventions and intentions for use have corresponding *standards for use*, standards that delimit a certain pattern of use: a *usage*. (Consider, for example, English usage and the accompanying grammatical standards that delimit it.) Usage, as Ryle (1953) notes, is not just use. Whereas usage involves an established pattern or custom, mere use need not. Use of terms can occur in the absence of any established pattern or custom; usage cannot. Everyday talk of usage thus indicates an established pattern or custom; talk of use need not.

The difference comes from the standards that delimit, or define, an established pattern or custom in usage. Indeed, the pattern's or custom's being "established" requires standards relative to which something can be established. Such standards are constitutive of an established pattern or custom of linguistic usage. They can be used prescriptively also, to indicate how one should or may behave. We sometimes appeal to the rules of English grammar, for example, not only to describe how we (correctly) speak and write but also to prescribe that someone speak or write a certain way.

How does this bear on analyticity and synonymy? As section 3.6 notes, we cannot plausibly understand synonymy just in terms of *cognitive* equivalence. Sameness of use for some terms is not a matter of their roles in sentences having truth values. My proposal for a broader approach to synonymy is:

> Two tokens are synonymous for you at a time if and only if your nonextraneous interpretive commitments at that time regarding what those tokens indicate or express are the same. (See section 3.3B for details on interpretive commitments and nonextraneous interpretations.)

My nonextraneous interpretive commitment regarding 'bachelor', for example, differs not at all from my nonextraneous interpretive commitment regarding 'unmarried man'. I interpret both tokens nonextraneously as designating just the feature of being an adult spouseless male. This says nothing, however, about the interpretive commitments *other* people might have.

I may generally prefer shorter to longer tokens, and so use 'bachelor' rather than 'unmarried man' in most cases. This is irrelevant, however, to considerations of synonymy as ordinarily understood. We must distinguish purely physical and stylistic differences between terms from differences pertinent to synonymy. Talk of constitutive standards for correct use, when understood in terms of interpretive commitments, can disregard purely physical or stylistic differences; such talk will then concern interpretation of a token as designating something or expressing a certain speech act (for example, an assertion, a promise, or a command). Relevant stylistic differences for poetic contexts, for example, need not undermine synonymy.

Synonymy does not depend on a single, sentential context. It depends rather on sameness of nonextraneous interpretive commitments, commitments that can bear on our wide range of uses of language, including describing, referring, prescribing, promising, requesting, and exclaiming. These ways of using terms cannot all be explained by the roles of words in truth-valued sentences. Those varied ways of use do, however, have at least one thing in common: They each represent a way of using language that is central, at some time or other, to interpretively purposive use of language.

Whereas Carnap and Quine talked of intentions and conventions regarding use, I have talked instead of nonextraneous interpretive commitments. The initially improved standard for analyticity here, inspired by Carnap, involved talk of actual linguistic usage. This talk led to questions about use and sameness of use, and then to doubts about Quine's approach to the latter. Prompted by Quine's and Carnap's talk of conventions and intentions regarding use, we saw the importance of constitutive standards for established use, in connection with a distinction between use and usage. I invoked the notion of nonextraneous interpretive commitment from section 3.3 to capture the pertinent idea of constitutive standards for established use. This left us with a straightforward approach to synonymy.

What about analyticity? The following standard fits with my approach to synonymy:

> A sentence, *S*, is analytically true for a person, *X*, at time *t* if and only if at *t X*, when motivated just by her nonextraneous interpretive commitments regarding *S*'s constituent terms, will reject all (potential) falsifiers of *S*.

In short, analytic truths are true solely in virtue of nonextraneous interpretive commitments regarding their constituents. This holds even for truths of logic, where analyticity does not entail synonymy as standardly understood. Analytic truths are true just in virtue of conceptual commitments; they are thus *conceptually* necessarily true (in the manner noted by section 3.3B).

Insofar as we can identify interpretive commitments by verbal behavior in response to certain questions, we have here a broadly behavioral standard, albeit a fallible standard. Its talk of interpretive commitment is not altogether different from Quine's own talk of "assent," at least if Quine's talk of assent is to have its desired explanatory significance. Even Quine must grant that we interpreters of verbal behavior *interpret* certain uses of utterances or inscriptions as "assent" and certain other uses as "dissent." No account of meaning pertinent to ordinary translation can make do without a notion of interpretation. If, moreover, one genuinely "assents" to tokens, then one must have some understanding—some interpretation—of those tokens whereby assent rather than dissent arises. Denial of this requirement will leave one with a notion of "assent" wholly different from our everyday notion. Quine's official behavioral approach to assent seems to gain effectiveness from unofficial associations with interpretation-based assent.

My standard for analyticity does not rest on terms like 'meaning', 'possible', and 'conceivable'—terms Quine finds as mysterious as talk of analyticity. It avoids talk of analyticity (or meaning) postulates and thus escapes Quine's worry about Carnap's approach. Similarly, the standard does without unexplicated talk of synonymy relations with antecedent usage. (I do not pretend, however, that my standard accommodates Quine's assumption that meaning is altogether behavioral.) My presupposed notion of constitutive standards for correct use, moreover, is not different in kind from Quine's own widely applied notion of standards, or "criteria," regarding identity of entities. Does my approach to analyticity have any epistemological importance?

3.8 Analyticity in Epistemology

Quine now finds the important issue about analyticity to be its relevance to epistemology, and not how to explicate it (1986a, p. 207). It is impossible, however, to separate the two issues. The relevance of analyticity to epistemology depends on how we characterize analyticity. Given the characterization in section 3.7, we can avoid the obstacles Quine identifies as undercutting the relevance of analyticity to epistemology. That characterization, we shall see, has wider, epistemological value.

Any epistemology relies on epistemic standards that specify what conditions epistemic warrant consists in, or at least depends on. Such standards give determinacy, or intelligibility, to talk of epistemic warrant. Even Quine and like-minded proponents of naturalized epistemology wield epistemic standards. One of Quine's key epistemic standards is his "maxim of minimum mutilation" (1990a, pp. 15, 56). This standard of conservatism implies that it is "well" not to alter our antecedent theory more than necessary. Quine does hold that a standard of the maximization of simplicity can prevail over his standard of conservatism, but this will not affect the point to be made. For ease of illustration, let us consider only cases where the standards do not conflict.

The pressing question now is: In virtue of what is Quine's epistemic standard of conservatism true, or correct, at least for Quine himself? In virtue of what is it true—or actually the case, at least for Quine—that epistemically warranted theory-revision conforms to the maxim of minimum mutilation (when the standard of simplicity is not at risk)? What, in other words, makes Quine's epistemic standards correct rather than false, at least for Quine? Another way of putting the concern is: Why regard Quine's standard of conservatism as a standard of *epistemic warrant*? Such questions will highlight the importance of analyticity for epistemology.

The foregoing questions are not directly epistemic. They are not questions about what we know or justifiably believe, or even about how we could acquire good reasons to wield Quine's epistemic standards. Further, they are not questions seeking a mere causal explanation of why certain people use Quine's epistemic standards. They rather are alethic questions about what constitutes the correctness of Quine's epistemic standards, at least for Quine himself.

What answer might Quine give? We can reasonably demand an answer from Quine. The relevant questions are intelligible and cannot plausibly be ignored. In addition, claims to the justification of Quine's epistemic standards presuppose, for their being fully understood, a notion of *correctness* of epistemic standards; for such claims require a notion of justification as (probably) correct (cf. section 2.2).

We cannot answer the pertinent questions by simply saying that the standard of conservatism requires that warranted theory-revision be constrained by the standard of conservatism. It is quite uninformative to say now that given the standard of conservatism, the standard of conservatism is true. We want to know what makes it the case that warranted theory-revision is constrained by the standard of conservatism. Why, or in virtue of what, does that standard constrain *warranted* theory-revision, at least for Quine? The most plausible answer is that it is just part of Quine's nonextraneous interpretive commitment regarding 'epistemic warrant' that the standard of conservatism constrains epistemic warrant. Given this answer, we may say that it is analytically true for Quine, in the way section 3.7 notes, that the standard of conservatism constrains epistemic warrant.

Quine has spoken to the following question: What is it that makes one complete physical theory true and another false? His answer: "I can only answer, with unhelpful realism, that it is the nature of the world. Immanent truth, à la Tarski, is the only truth I recognize" (1972, p. 180). Even if we accept Tarski's disquotational approach to truth, this question persists: What makes it the case, at least for Quine, that the standard of conservatism constrains epistemic warrant? Talk of "the nature of the world" is unhelpful now because we want to know what it is about "the nature of the world" that makes it the case, at least for Quine, that the standard of conservatism constrains epistemic warrant. The most plausible answer invokes Quine's nonextraneous interpretive commitment regarding 'epistemic warrant' (and related terms).

Quine suggests that his epistemic standards of conservatism and simplicity find support in actual scientific practice. He claims that these standards "are maxims by which science strives for vindication in future predictions" (1990a, p. 15). One might propose, in addition, that the standard of conservatism is *true* in virtue of its role in actual scientific practice. We can grant this proposal now, if only for the sake of argument, and then ask: In virtue of what is it true—or the case—that actual scientific practice constrains epistemically warranted theory-revision? The most plausible answer is that it is just part of a typical "naturalized epistemologist's" nonextraneous interpretive commitment toward 'epistemic warrant' that actual scientific practice constrains epistemic warrant. It is analytically true for a typical "naturalized epistemologist" that actual scientific practice constrains epistemic warrant. Appeal to scientific practice thus does not free one from the importance of analyticity.

Barring analyticity, we would have much difficulty answering meta-epistemological questions of the sort just raised. This may explain why Quine, early and late, remains largely silent on such questions. These questions concern the correctness of epistemic standards, standards that define an epistemology for the most part. The key question, in general, is simply: In virtue of what is it true, or the case, that a preferred epistemic standard actually identifies a feature (for example, simplicity, minimum mutilation, coherence, conformity to actual science) that constrains epistemic warrant? My approach to analyticity supplies the basis for the most plausible answer to meta-epistemological questions of that sort. It fits nicely with the plausible view that answers to such questions must avoid circularity and endless regresses, and derive ultimately from nonextraneous interpretive commitments regarding alethic and evaluative vocabulary.

Appeals to holism take nothing away from the importance of analyticity. In fact, they help to illustrate the point at hand. Epistemic holists typically have an interpretive commitment that makes it the case, for them, that coherence constrains epistemic warrant. A meta-epistemological question of the sort just raised can reveal the pertinence of analyticity even for typical epistemic holists, Quine included. As my characterization of analyticity is not a characterization of justification or evidence, it is quite compatible with *epistemic* holism, the sort of holism Quine uses in "Two Dogmas" to challenge analyticity (1951, p. 41).

Regarding *semantic* holism—holism about semantic significance rather than evidence—Quine's commitment is explicitly qualified (1986b, p. 426; 1986c, p. 620), given his view that observation sentences do have their empirical content individually.[14] As Fodor (1987, pp. 64–67) has noted, moreover, Quine's Duhem-style epistemic holism does not logically entail semantic holism. Holism about warrant does not logically require holism about meaning. Considerations of holism, then, do not threaten my claims about analyticity.

Quine and other friends of naturalized epistemology might seek refuge in the extreme view that we can simply forgo talk of epistemic warrant and all other such evaluative talk. This would be a move of desperation, a move inconsistent with Quine's own linguistic practices. It would banish all evaluative talk from epistemology and other domains of discourse. Instead of evaluating views relative to epistemic standards or ideals, we could, on this move, only describe views in terms of how entrenched, or firmly held, they are.

Quine himself does not settle for mere descriptions of how firmly held various views are; nor does any other proponent of naturalized epistemology.

14. This point does not get due attention in Putnam (1986) or in Fodor and Lepore (1992), among various other discussions of Quine's holism.

For example, Quine is well known for his view that "the lack of a standard of identity for attributes and propositions can be viewed . . . as a case of defectiveness on the part of 'attribute' and 'proposition'" (1960, p. 244). Such talk of defectiveness is not the language of someone shunning evaluative, or normative, talk. In "Two Dogmas" and elsewhere, Quine explicitly uses his views of actual scientific theory-revision to set evaluative epistemic standards—standards involving holistic coherence, simplicity, and minimum mutilation. As Quine does have evaluative epistemic standards, he must face the meta-epistemological questions about correctness raised here. Such questions reveal the epistemological importance of analyticity.

One notable virtue of my approach to analyticity is that it allows for semantic, or conceptual, relativism—for a diversity of interpretive commitments and resulting specific notions. Your interpretive commitment toward 'epistemic warrant' can differ from mine, at least at a level of specificity. Analytic truths involving 'warrant' for you can thus differ from such truths for me. This is, on reflection, no surprise. Epistemologists can, and often do, wield differing epistemic concepts at a level of specificity, even without noticing that they do. Witness, for example, the difference between Quine's broadly naturalistic concept of knowledge (1969b) and Chisholm's deontological concept resulting from a deontological notion of justification (1989, p. 60). These concepts are not the same by any ordinary standard of conceptual sameness, even if Quine and Chisholm could agree on some vague notion of knowledge *generally characterized*. It would be surprising if all epistemologists shared a single specific concept of knowledge or epistemic warrant. Interpretive commitments in epistemology often arise from explanatory purposes, and epistemologists often have differing explanatory purposes and differing (semantically based) adequacy conditions for achieving their purposes.

Conceptual relativism, as chapter 4 notes, is not substantive relativism: It does not entail that mere belief automatically yields actual correctness or justification. It thus does not entail an "anything goes" attitude toward epistemic assessment. Conceptual relativism entails instead a recognition of the diversity of specific conceptual commitments in epistemology. By analogy, our recognizing that concepts of truth vary among philosophers does not commit us to the substantive relativistic view that whatever one believes to be true actually is true. (Chapter 4 returns to this theme about truth.) We thus cannot fault conceptual relativism by faulting substantive evaluative relativism.

Let us return, finally, to the affinity between my approach to analyticity and analyticity by stipulative definition, the sort of definition unblemished by Quine's "Two Dogmas." Interpretive commitments need not be, and often are not, *purely* stipulative; so also for stipulative definitions. Interpretive commitments can include stipulations relative to definite explanatory purposes and adequacy conditions for achieving those purposes. Given a constraining role for such purposes and (semantically based) adequacy conditions, interpretive commitments and definitions would not be purely stipulative.

We should observe an important distinction neglected by Quine, especially in "Two Dogmas": the distinction between *what is true* just in virtue of an interpretive commitment (or a certain policy of linguistic usage) and *what justifies* an interpretive commitment. This is the distinction between what an interpretive commitment involves or entails and what supports such a commitment. Confusion over this distinction apparently underlies Quine's failure to appreciate the epistemological importance of analyticity. A statement can be analytically true just in virtue of an interpretive commitment, even if that commitment is supported, or justified, only by certain alterable explanatory purposes a language user has. The alterability of the supporting purposes does nothing to discredit the analyticity arising from an interpretive commitment.

The category of the analytic, as characterized here, is not the epistemological category of the a priori; nor does it entail unrevisability. Interpretive commitments can and do change, often as a result of changing explanatory purposes. Change in a nonextraneous interpretive commitment is, in effect, a change of language. More to the point, the category of the analytic is alethic, characterizing a kind of truth resulting just from nonextraneous interpretive commitments. It is not an epistemological category connoting a special kind of evidence or warrant. In fact, the notion of analyticity characterized here does not depend at all on a notion of evidence or warrant. It is thus a nonepistemological notion. Still, the category of analyticity can and does have epistemological importance: It enables answers to meta-epistemological questions about the correctness of epistemic standards.

Insofar as the category of truth by stipulative definition is nonepistemological, it resembles my notion of analyticity. Talk of stipulative definition seems more voluntaristic than my talk of interpretive commitment. An interpretive commitment, as characterized in section 3.3, can arise in the manner of a habit or some other dispositional trait. It might be only highly indirectly voluntary, if voluntary at all. Some of the truths that are analytic for you may not have arisen from any voluntary activity on your part. An interpretive commitment *can* be voluntary in the way stipulative definitions are. The voluntary decisions of an epistemologist, for example, can give rise to interpretive commitments and analytic truths. Analyticity can arise, then, from epistemological decision-making, but is not the exclusive possession of such decision-making. Such scope is a virtue of my characterization of analyticity. It allows for analyticity resulting from theoretical decision-making as well as from involuntary conditioning.

In sum, I have characterized analyticity in a way that (a) is nonepistemic, (b) avoids Quine's objections and fits some of his general strictures, and (c) explains the epistemological importance of analyticity. I have also explained why even Quine should value the epistemological importance of analyticity, in connection with questions about the correctness of epistemic standards. In light of these considerations, we may plausibly consider analyticity as having been rescued from the throes of suspicion and myth, as set by "Two Dogmas of Empiricism." We may also regard the semantic considerations central to semantic foundationalism as beyond suspicion and myth.

Given semantic interpretationism, we can now turn to the topic of reasons, truth, and relativism with a defensible semantic foundation.

4

Reasons, Truth, and Relativism

Philosophers often pursue this issue: Where should we begin a philosophical effort to say what sorts of things actually exist or, more broadly, to say what in general is true rather than false? Part of this question's difficulty comes from unclarity in its use of 'should' and 'true'. We lack clear standards definitive of correct use of such terms, at least in many cases. If we specify the needed standards, we have done so from our conceptual standpoint—a standpoint that might not be shared by others. Our standards will seem, and perhaps even be, optional at best from certain other conceptual standpoints. Can there really be such other standpoints, and what exactly are they?

Would the availability of alternative conceptual standpoints entail that relativism is unavoidable in our philosophical efforts? If so, what sort of relativism must we acknowledge? In particular, how thoroughgoing is it? Such questions confront any account of reasons and truth. This chapter provides answers that extend the semantic foundationalism of chapter 2 while accommodating the conditional ontological agnosticism of chapter 1.

This chapter supports *conceptual relativism* implying that different people can, and sometimes do, adopt and use different specific notions of truth and different specific notions of reasons. In particular, this chapter finds two different notions of a regulative reason at work in current debates over internalism and externalism about reasons for action. The resulting lesson is that internalists and externalists about practical reasons are actually talking about different matters (at least at a level of specificity), not disagreeing about some particular matter.

In reply to conceptual relativism, this chapter introduces *conceptual instrumentalism*: the view that one's aims in adopting and using notions of rationality, reasons, and obligations can cogently recommend, at least to oneself, an internalist or an externalist notion of rationality, reasons, and obligations. We shall see that such instrumentalism does not, however, have a monopoly on the assessment of evaluative notions. Conceptual relativism, especially regarding talk of cogency and assessment, blocks any such monopoly.

4.1 Concepts of Truth

Philosophers often talk blithely of "the" concept of truth, as if there were just one notion of truth in circulation. This is a familiar instance of what I earlier called "the philosophical myth of the definite article." Such use of the definite article typically misleads. It hides the conceptual complexity and diversity in our uses of language.

Philosophers have formulated various specific concepts of truth, including coherence, correspondence, and pragmatic notions, among others. No one of these can plausibly be called "the" concept of truth, as if the others had not been formulated. These notions do, however, have some significant features in common. Each notion, for example, has been regarded by various philosophers as characterizing not only (a) a necessary condition for propositional knowledge—the so-called first, "truth condition" requiring a statement of "what is the case"—but also (b) what satisfies (at least a salient necessary condition for) the primary goal of epistemically rational inquiry. (On standard analyses, propositional knowledge requires truth, belief, justification, and perhaps something else to block Gettier-style counterexamples; many philosophers construe the first condition to entail that propositional knowledge is "factual," characterizing "what is the case.")

In espousing different concepts of truth, philosophers are not offering merely different criteria, or guidelines, for *testing* truth. Proponents of a coherence concept of truth hold that truth consists essentially in coherence, or is defined in terms of coherence. They do not hold that coherence is simply a test of truth. It is, of course, an empirical issue whether some philosophers have endorsed a coherence concept of truth.

Brand Blanshard (1939, p. 260) is quite clear on the distinction between a definition and a criterion of truth. He regards coherence as not only a test for truth but also what is "constitutive of truth." "In the end," according to Blanshard, "the only test of truth that is not misleading is the special nature or character that is itself constitutive of truth [namely, coherence]" (1939, p. 268).[1] Blanshard thus endorses a coherence notion of truth, that is, a coherence approach to what truth essentially consists in.

William James offers his pragmatic account of truth as capturing "the meaning" of truth. In a chapter of *Pragmatism* entitled "Pragmatism's Conception of Truth," James writes:

> True ideas are those that we can assimilate, validate, corroborate, and verify. . . . That is the practical difference it makes to us to have true ideas; that,

1. Blanshard adds: "In *The Nature of Thought*, . . . I did take my stand for coherence as supplying both the nature of truth and its criterion. . . . I still think of ultimate truth as an ideal that would consist in the apprehension of a coherent whole in which every component was consistent with and necessarily connected with every other" (1980, p. 590). Ralph Walker (1989, chaps. 3, 5) contends that Spinoza and Hegel endorsed pure coherence theories of the nature of truth—and not just coherence tests for truth.

> therefore, is *the meaning* of truth, for it is all that truth is known-as (1907, p. 97; italics added).[2]

James restates the same pragmatic conception of truth in the Preface to his 1909 collection, *The Meaning of Truth*, and adds that "when the pragmatists speak of truth, they *mean* exclusively something about the ideas [of existent objects], namely their workableness" (italics added).

Before James, C. S. Peirce had offered a different, consensus-oriented pragmatic approach to the meaning of 'truth'. In his 1878 essay, "How to Make Our Ideas Clear," Peirce claimed that "the opinion which is fated to be ultimately agreed to by all who investigate, is what we *mean* by the truth" (p. 38; italics added).[3] It seems clear, then, that Peirce and James at times regarded their pragmatism as offering a distinctive concept, or notion, of truth, not just a special means of testing truth.[4]

Given the aforementioned coherence and pragmatic notions of truth, we must acknowledge alternatives to correspondence concepts of truth familiar from such theorists as Russell, Moore, and the early Wittgenstein. We must acknowledge that some philosophers wield different specific notions of truth, and not just different criteria for discerning truth. Following sections 2.3 and 3.3, we may regard a notion, or a concept, of truth as a set of semantic standards constitutive of correctness in use of 'truth' (or some synonymous term). A notion of truth does not necessarily provide readily applicable guidelines for testing for truth. Some correspondence notions, for example, invoke complex objective correspondence-relations that do not yield ready practical guidelines for testing truth.[5]

One might recommend that we regard pragmatic and coherence accounts of truth as offering only criteria for testing truth. Such a recommendation is coherent in itself, but it neglects the views of various actual proponents of pragmatic and coherence accounts. These proponents, as illustrated previously, regard pragmatic or coherence accounts as capturing the concept, or the notion, of truth. We thus may proceed with the assumption that some philosophers wield different specific notions of truth.

Why do we say that the coherence, correspondence, and pragmatic notions are three specific notions of a single property—truth—and not just three notions of three different properties: coherence, correspondence, and pragmatic utility? This question concerns identity conditions for what a concept is a concept *of*.

2. James claims, in addition, that the "static relation of correspondence" is an "absolutely empty notion" (1907, p. 39). For some of James's other endorsements of a pragmatic conception of truth, see James (1907, pp. 37, 102, 104). See Moser (1983b) for an exposition of James's approach to truth.

3. Citing this statement from Peirce, Dewey (1938, p. 345) claims that "the best definition of *truth* from the logical standpoint which is known to me is that of Peirce."

4. I do not assume that Peirce held his aforementioned 1878 view of truth throughout his philosophical career. On Peirce's later views on truth, see Misak (1991, especially pp. 35–45).

5. For elaboration on the distinction between a notion of truth and a criterion of truth, see Rescher (1973b, pp. 12–22; 1980b) and Moser (1985a, pp. 6–8). See Moser (1989, pp. 23–35) for a minimal correspondence notion of truth.

One likely answer is that there is in fact some one property—truth—and the three notions in question are somehow about that one property. This answer may be correct; for such an answer to be sufficiently informative, however, we need to know more concerning the one property in question and the relevant "aboutness" relation. We need a characterization of this single property beyond the statement that there is such a property characterized by the three notions in question. In short, we need to know what exactly makes the property in question a single property, relative to which the notions in question are specific concepts of that one property.

A more informative answer appeals to our construing differing specific concepts of truth as contributing in alternative ways to the single general but salient aim of amplifying a single notion of truth generally characterized. Given a single notion of *truth generally characterized* (say, truth as what satisfies the first condition for knowledge requiring a statement of "what is the case"), we may regard typical coherence, correspondence, and pragmatic notions as offering alternative amplifications of that single notion of truth generally characterized. If, then, we countenance a single general notion of truth, we may construe this notion as standing for a single general property—truth in general—amplified by the alternative specific notions of truth: coherence, correspondence, and pragmatic notions, for example.

If concepts are constitutive standards for correct use of terms, then when two people adopt and use different such standards for a term, they adopt and use different concepts relative to their respective uses of that term. In particular, different constitutive standards for correct use of 'truth' yield different concepts of truth. We do, however, regard certain (perhaps very general) standards as providing a core for a certain concept. When that core is absent, we deny that a certain concept is present: namely, the (perhaps very general) concept constrained by the relevant core. We need not hold, then, that just any concept is a concept of truth. (See section 2.4B on the limits we set on concepts.)

Our concept of a data table differs from our concept of a kitchen table, but we do not regard these as differing concepts of the same thing or property. Why is this? The answer is clear: We do not regard our concepts of data table and kitchen table as alternative amplifications of a broader single notion of *table generally characterized*. The case of polysemy (if not homonymy) regarding 'table' in English thus differs from the case of three specific concepts of truth. In the latter case, we construe the three specific concepts as amplifications of a broader notion of truth (generally characterized). We thus typically regard those concepts as specific notions of a single property, truth.

Conceptual relativism about truth is the view that with respect to truth generally characterized (say, as something stating "what is the case," or something satisfying the primary goal of epistemically rational inquiry), different people can, do, or may adopt and use different specific concepts. We have three noteworthy species of conceptual relativism about truth:

(a) *Modal Conceptual Relativism about Truth*: It is *possible* for different people to adopt and to use different specific concepts of truth (for example, for correctly answering the question of what truth, generally characterized, consists in at a level of specificity, at least on their understanding).

(b) *Factual Conceptual Relativism about Truth*: Some different people *actually* adopt and use different specific concepts of truth.

(c) *Normative Conceptual Relativism about Truth*: It is normatively (for example, rationally) *permissible* for people to adopt and to use different specific concepts of truth.

Given different notions of what is "possible," "actual," and "normatively permissible," we shall have correspondingly different notions of modal, factual, and normative conceptual relativism. Conceptual relativism itself, like concepts of truth, can thus come in various forms with varying connotations. Such relativism need not be restricted to truth, but can apply to the presumed "property" corresponding to any general concept subject to amplification in varying ways. Conceptual relativism can therefore serve as a view about concepts in general.

We have no decisive reason to reject either modal, factual, or normative conceptual relativism about truth. Some philosophers do adopt and use different specific concepts of truth among themselves, by their own testimony. This conceptual variance does not entail any obvious inconsistency with the laws of logic or physics. Such variance thus seems physically as well as logically possible. Conceptual variance regarding truth also seems normatively permissible for us. We seem not to share commitment to any normative requirement or prescription that is violated by such variance.

Someone might endorse a requirement prohibiting our wielding any but one specific notion of truth. Even so, we evidently do not actually share any such endorsement; nor does any of our shared goals or principles obviously demand that we endorse the sort of requirement in question. Conceptual variance regarding truth seems not to leave us with normative inconsistency. One might reply that the normative requirements binding on us need not be endorsed by us or recommended by any of the goals or principles we have. In that case, however, one must explain what does make normative requirements binding on us. This is no small task, as section 4.5 indicates.

Neither modal, factual, nor normative conceptual relativism entails an "anything goes" attitude about truth. In particular, none of those three views entails the substantive relativist view that whatever you believe is automatically true. Those versions of relativism do not commit us to any specific conditions for a proposition's being true. They rather concern actual, possible, or permissible variance of specific *notions* of truth.

Some notions of truth—including familiar coherence, correspondence, and pragmatist notions—are incompatible with the substantive relativist view that whatever you believe is automatically true. In allowing for a correspondence notion of truth, for example, conceptual relativism does not entail that every notion of truth is a notion referring to a person or even to what a person believes. It thus does not commit us to the implausible view that every notion of truth is a notion of "truth for someone."[6] Conceptual relativism allows for a distinction between a proposition's *being true* and a proposition's *being believed to be true*, and for a person's believing-true a false proposition. Conceptual relativism about notions of truth, then, does not entail the substantive relativist view that whatever a person believes is true.

Conceptual relativism does not require a distinction between conceptual schemes and empirical content of the sort challenged by Donald Davidson (1974a). It does not entail that there are certain concepts of truth, alternative to ours, that we cannot understand or translate into our own language. Conceptual relativism, as defined here, concerns possible, actual, or permissible variance in the *adoption* and the *use*, rather than in the *understanding*, of certain specific concepts. Relativism concerning the adoption and use of certain concepts does not require relativism about the understanding of those concepts. It does not require commitment to the existence of alternative conceptual schemes that are not intertranslatable. (See section 3.3 on pertinent conditions for understanding and meaning.)

Correspondence theorists, for example, can typically understand the alternative specific notions of truth espoused by coherence theorists and pragmatists, and can typically even translate those alternative notions into their own language. Correspondence theorists, nonetheless, do not adopt or use either a coherence or a pragmatic notion of truth for their own purposes concerning truth. They use a different, correspondence notion; and they take their own notion to specify what truth actually consists in (at least for themselves).

Factual conceptual relativism about truth entails variance of specific semantic standards for 'truth' (or some synonymous term). Semantic standards for 'truth' specify what one means by the term 'truth' because they specify constitutive standards for correct use of 'truth' for one (where the relativity concerns adopted semantic standards, not mere belief about truth). What some people mean by 'truth' may be *exemplar based*, consisting of certain paradigmatic instances of truth that may not all satisfy any specific (nondisjunctive) necessary conditions for truth.[7] This is not necessarily a defect in what one means. If one's purposes relevant to the use of the term 'truth' do not demand anything more, this may not be a defect at all. Nothing requires in principle that everyone's standards for the meaningful use of 'truth' must amount to a nondisjunctive set of defining conditions (cf. Wittgenstein 1953, section 87.)

Variance of semantic standards for 'truth' might seem philosophically troublesome. Even if it is troublesome for certain philosophical views, we still should acknowledge such variance, and make do with it. A philosophically adequate account of meaning cannot plausibly disregard the meanings of terms

6. On the familiar relativist locution 'true for', see Swoyer (1982). We should not confuse *semantic* relativity involving one's adopted semantic standards for 'true' and relativity involving mere belief about what is true.

7. On the role of exemplars in meaning, see sections 2.3A and 3.3B. See also Rosch (1978, 1983), Rosch and Mervis (1975), and Lakoff (1987, pp. 39–57; 1989).

for us. We should acknowledge that no one specific semantic standard for 'truth' seems unconditionally mandatory for, or otherwise required of, every language-user. This consideration may be troublesome for those who neglect the question of why *their* preferred specific notion of truth has normative significance for at least some inquirers: for instance, why that preferred notion, rather than some other notion, characterizes what satisfies the primary goal of epistemically rational inquiry at least for some inquirers. Given factual conceptual relativism, we must face that question head on.

Our question now is: What, if anything, recommends one specific notion of truth over others, at least for some people, with regard to characterizing what satisfies the primary goal of epistemically rational inquiry? Does anything make one specific notion preferable to others, at least for some people? A negative answer seems to support an "anything goes" attitude toward specific concepts of truth.

Some theorists do regard a certain specific notion of truth as more appropriate than other notions, with respect to characterizing what satisfies the primary goal of epistemically rational inquiry. What sort of reason, if any, can support this? Suppose that I regard the primary goal of epistemically rational inquiry, at least for myself, as the goal of formulating beliefs that achieve maximal explanatory coherence for me in inquiry. The primary goal of epistemically rational inquiry for *you*, I could still grant, is the goal of formulating beliefs that achieve *your* epistemic explanatory aims in inquiry. If I regard truth as what satisfies the primary goal of epistemically rational inquiry for myself, I shall characterize truth accordingly as whatever beliefs achieve maximal explanatory coherence for me in inquiry. This is a straightforward version of coherentist pragmatism about truth, a version that would disturb many proponents of correspondence notions of truth. (I am simply illustrating a point now, not recommending that approach to truth.)

We cannot plausibly deny, given the previous quotations, that some philosophers understand truth in terms of pragmatic considerations. William James and his followers are paradigmatic examples. Some philosophers, however, propose that we should not understand truth in pragmatic terms, but rather should understand it in different terms: for example, in accord with a correspondence notion. If we take this proposal as an unconditional, categorical imperative, we shall be hard put to find a cogent rationale for it. We cannot make such a proposal cogent just by insisting that it identifies what we ought to do, unconditionally. One might insist on the latter for *any* deontological proposal one prefers. Obviously, not every such proposal will thereby become cogent.

If, alternatively, we take the antipragmatist proposal as expressing a hypothetical imperative, a rationale may be forthcoming. We could then recommend against pragmatic construals on certain conditional grounds. For example, *if* one wants to capture what such philosophers as Moore, Russell, and the early Wittgenstein regarded as truth, or *if* one wants a notion of truth that does not make truth depend always on purposes in inquiry, then one should avoid a pragmatic approach. Such an appeal to a hypothetical imperative does not, however, settle the likely question of why we should be compelled—rationally or otherwise normatively—to accept the antecedent of the relevant conditional. Pragmatists will typically reject any such antecedent that recommends a correspondence notion. They will appeal instead to considerations that favor a pragmatic notion of truth. Hypothetical imperatives can serve all comers.

Correspondence theorists might contend that only a correspondence approach to truth preserves a definitive link between truth and "reality," or "how things are." Perhaps this is so, if we construe 'definitive link' in terms of a correspondence definition; the key issue now, however, concerns how we are to construe 'truth' at a level of specificity. Blanshard (1939) and various other coherence theorists will grant that true statements state how things are, but add that the truth of such statements derives from their "cohering" with their objects. Similarly, James (1907, pp. 96, 102–103; 1909, pp. 117–118) and various other pragmatists will accept that true statements "agree with reality," but render such talk in pragmatic terms. Talk of "stating how things are," as an explication of talk of truth, is thus subject to various construals.[8]

Let us return, then, to the foregoing issue about the sort of imperative underlying a recommendation of one notion of truth over others. This issue actually concerns what sort of *reasons*, if any, we have for adopting and using one notion of truth (or one notion of what satisfies the primary goal of epistemically rational inquiry) over others. A straightforward sort of reason involves (likely) satisfaction of one's purposes, or ends, in adopting or using a concept of truth. One might understand talk of purposes here as talk of acknowledged actual purposes, to exclude cases where, for some reason or other, certain purposes are inaccessible to one.

We can now raise a troublesome issue about the relevant notion of reasons—an issue prompted by factual conceptual relativism about (notions of) reasons. The issue is: What sort of reasons, if any, have we for adopting and using one notion of reasons over another? More generally, what sort of reasons, if any, have we for adopting and using *any* notion over others, including the notion of reasons employed in this very question? The self-referential character of this question indicates that we need to decide what notion of reasons is relevant to this question itself.

We must now make a conceptual decision, a decision about what notion of reasons will concern us in connection with questions about relativism. In the absence of such a decision, our questions about relativism and reasons will be indeterminate and intractable. Some people can, and will, make decisions here that differ from ours. In that case, they will be concerned with notions, and resulting questions, different from ours. Conceptual relativism leads us to expect as much. We need to examine more closely the role of reasons in questions about relativism.

8. This point holds even for correspondence approaches to truth; on this matter, see Prior (1967) and Mackie (1973, chap. 1). Cf. Stich (1990, chap. 5).

4.2 Concepts of Reasons

Philosophical talk of reasons, like ordinary talk of reasons, varies significantly in meaning. We can introduce a *generic* notion of a reason to capture much of the varied talk of reasons:

> An item (for example, event, state, or claim) *X* is a reason for another item *Y* if and only if *X* is a ground, basis, means, or source of support for *Y*.

This generic notion allows for support relations of various sorts between a reason and what the reason supports: for example, causal/motivational, evidential, and normative support, among other sorts.

Causal/motivational support for a person's doing something yields motivational reasons for action. What counts as genuinely causal can, and does, vary among theorists. Suppose that I desire to illustrate a certain point, and believe that by producing a certain example, I shall illustrate the point. If, as a direct result of this belief-desire pair, I produce the example, then this belief-desire pair is a causal/motivational reason for my producing the example.

Evidential support for a claim provides an indicator—perhaps only a defeasible probabilistic indicator—that this claim is true, or that something (what this claim asserts) is actually the case. Evidential, or epistemic, reasons are thus truth indicators, where the relevant notion of truth is, as noted previously, subject to variation.[9] Many people would regard my remembering that I drank water for breakfast this morning as an evidential reason for my belief that I drank water for breakfast this morning.

Normative support for one's doing something delivers normative reasons for action. Normative reasons are indicators—perhaps defeasible and probabilistic—that one's doing something will achieve goodness of some sort: for example, moral, prudential, or legal goodness. The relevant notion of goodness admits of considerable variation among theorists. If moral goodness precludes undue suffering, then my recognizing that a child is going to be hit by a cyclist could give me a normative reason to move the child from the cyclist's path. Insofar as normative reasons indicate that something is the case, they are broadly evidential; not all evidential reasons, however, are normative reasons.

Causal, evidential, and normative reasons are familiar species of reasons, yet do not necessarily exhaust the category of support relations constitutive of reasons. The foregoing generic notion of a reason illustrates that our notion of a reason is not essentially evidential, or epistemic. Insofar as support relations can be altogether nonevidential (for example, purely motivational), so also reasons can be nonevidential. Given the generic notion of a reason, we shall

9. See Moser (1989, chaps. 2–4) for an attempt to characterize the notion of a defeasible truth indicator in detail.

reject any claim that X is a reason for Y but does not support Y in any way. The generic notion of a reason fits with the following schema for reasons of varying species: X is a ϕ reason (for example, an evidential reason) for Y if and only if X is an instance of ϕ support (for example, evidential support) for Y. This schema indicates that the species of a reason corresponds to the sort of support the reason provides. Causal reasons yield causal support; normative reasons deliver normative support; and so on.

Something might serve as more than one sort of support or reason. On a hedonist approach to value, for instance, some sensory experience might serve as both a motivational and a normative reason. Motivational normative and evidential reasons are not, however, merely motivational, or causal, reasons. As characterized thus far, normative reasons do not necessarily motivate the persons for whom they are reasons. One's having a normative reason to perform a certain action does not automatically preclude motivational inertia owing, for example, to weakness of will. We should distinguish, then, motivational from nonmotivational normative reasons, while recognizing that notions of motivation can vary.

We can now return to the question raised at the end of section 4.1: What species of reason (for example, an epistemic, motivational, or normative species) do we have in mind when we ask whether we have any reason for adopting and using one specific notion of truth (or one specific notion of what satisfies the primary goal of rational inquiry) over others? It is doubtful that we have an evidential reason in mind. If we did, we would be asking whether we have a truth indicator that supports one specific notion of truth over others. Such a question takes us nowhere in a controversy involving proponents of alternative specific notions of truth. Its talk of a truth indicator, if sufficiently determinate, presupposes a specific notion of truth, and thus operates with a specific notion of truth subject to question by proponents of alternative specific notions. If, moreover, the question's talk of a truth indicator is insufficiently precise regarding a specific notion of truth, the question will fail to enable us to select uniquely from the range of alternative notions of truth.

It is doubtful that our question stems from our having simply a motivational reason in mind. If we were concerned only with a motivational reason, we would be asking merely whether we have some motivation to adopt and to use one specific notion of truth rather than others. Philosophers typically are not occupied with just such an empirical question about causal/motivational bases for adopting and using a specific concept of truth. Philosophical concerns about relativism characteristically go beyond such a straightforwardly empirical issue about motivation.

Perhaps our question about notions of truth concerns normative reasons. If so, it amounts to an issue about indications of the goodness, in some sense, of adopting and using one specific notion of truth rather than others. In particular, have we any indication that our adopting and using a certain specific notion of truth are *better*, in some sense, than our adopting and using other specific notions of truth? Presumably, we do not have moral goodness in mind here, as long as we are not doing theoretical ethics; nor do we now have in mind aesthetic, economic, or legal goodness, for example.

What about goodness as purpose-satisfaction—more specifically, goodness as the satisfaction of our purposes, or ends, in wielding a specific notion of truth? Goodness as purpose-satisfaction is, let us say, *purposive goodness*. When the purposes are those in adopting and using a notion of truth, we may speak of purposive goodness with respect to a notion of truth. Similarly, we may speak of *purposive normative reasons* as the sort of normative reasons indicative of purposive goodness. Such reasons may be causal reasons, but are not merely causal reasons. (See section 3.3A on the contrast between purposive and merely causal considerations.)

Our question now begins to make manageable sense. It becomes: Have we any indication that our adopting and using one specific notion of truth are purposively better (that is, have more purposive goodness relative to the satisfaction of our purposes) than our adopting and using other available specific notions of truth? If we do not have this sort of question in mind, it is not clear what we actually have in mind. Let us proceed then with the latter question, as it makes manageable sense of the sort of normative reasons for concepts some of us have in mind: namely, purposive normative reasons.

Different people can have, and sometimes do have, different purposes in adopting and using specific concepts of truth—and other concepts too, for that matter. This is a platitude if anything is, but an important platitude now. Variance of purposes with respect to adopting and using concepts can result in variance of purposive normative reasons for adopting and using concepts.

If, for example, you are a pragmatist whose only purpose in adopting and using a specific concept of truth is to have a practical standard for doxastic decision-making, you will not have a purposive reason for adopting a correspondence notion. (I do not presume that one should be such a pragmatist shunning a difference between a concept and a criterion of truth; the example is merely an illustration.) Correspondence notions of truth are notoriously unhelpful as practical standards for belief-formation and belief-revision. They are too objective—too aloof from (subjective) evidential considerations—to function as practical guidelines for decision-making. If, in contrast, your only purpose in adopting a specific concept of truth is to have a standard that captures what Moore, Russell, and the early Wittgenstein meant by 'truth', you will have a purposive reason to adopt a correspondence notion. Such variance of purposive reasons seems undeniable and need not be regarded as philosophically troublesome.

The underlying purposes themselves, however variable, need not admit of purpose-independent, nonperspectival rational assessment—whatever that might be. We evidently have no such position of privileged exile from our concept- and purpose-bound perspectives of inquiry. This, as section 1.7 indicated, is the human cognitive predicament, a predicament that questions the availability of certain sorts of objectivity in inquiry. Objectivity of the latter sorts comes only at the expense of leaving ourselves—our perspective-bound selves—out of inquiry. This expense is not readily available to us, however much some philosophers would like to pay it.

Relative to shared purposes, some people share purposive normative reasons for adopting and using certain concepts. As a result, these people might wield a common specific concept of truth, for example. Other people may share different purposive reasons, relative to different shared purposes, and thus wield a different specific concept of truth. Such conceptual variance entails variation only at the level of what a *concept* comprises for a person. It entails neither an "anything goes" attitude toward evaluative assessment nor a disagreement over what action (or belief) is actually rational (or correct) for a person in a certain context.

I can recognize that relative to your purposes a certain specific concept of truth, *C1*, is purposively rational, and that relative to my different purposes a different specific concept of truth, *C2*, is purposively rational. In recognizing this, I understand—make sense of—your concept of truth, but do not thereby adopt or use it to characterize what satisfies the primary goal of epistemically rational inquiry for me. I have different purposes, and different purposive reasons, for wielding a specific concept of truth. I need not thereby regard you as irrational with respect to your specific notion of truth, as I can recognize that you have different purposes. I can acknowledge a notion of rationality wherein what is rational can vary with varying purposive normative reasons. In addition, I can acknowledge that in articulating our respective specific notions of truth, we are, in effect, talking about different matters, at least at a level of specificity.

One's adopted specific notion of truth will influence how one explicates one's talk of truth. This does not entail, however, that one's adopted specific notion of truth will determine that this notion itself is effective for accomplishing one's ends in using a notion of truth. One's pertinent ends may very well favor an alternative specific notion of truth, and one could come to recognize this—even without relinquishing one's adopted notion of truth. The ends embodied in inquiry, for one, can thus offer a rationale for adopting one specific notion of truth rather than another. Those ends can thereby play a key role in one's reasoned defense of a certain specific notion of truth. They can also anchor one's adopting a notion of truth that excludes an "anything goes" approach to correctness.

Whatever our preferences regarding concepts, we have no indisputable unconditional, categorical imperative dictating that you and I must adopt the same concepts or share the same purposes in adopting concepts. As for where and how our purposes originate, we neither have nor need a single easy story to tell. The stories here may be as diverse as the people having purposes. This, however, poses no threat to conceptual relativism.

The proposed connection between normative reasons and purposes can free us from a serious, if widely neglected, problem facing normative reasons. The problem is that nonmotivating normative reasons are evidently too easy to come by. Indications of goodness of various sorts (moral goodness in varying senses, aesthetic goodness in varying senses, prudential goodness in varying senses, and so on) yield a plethora of (potential) normative reasons and recommendations. Species of nonmotivating goodness arise for each of the numerous kinds of normative idealization we can imagine, in connection with ethics, aesthetics, prudence, and economics, for example. We need some way to factor out *relevant* normative considerations: that is, normative considerations pertinent to our actual decision making. Call this *the problem of normative relevance.*

Purposive normative reasons offer a solution to the problem of normative relevance. They factor out the normative considerations pertinent to one's (acknowledged) actual purposes, or ends—such as one's purposes in wielding a certain concept. They factor out such considerations in a person-relative manner; and such sensitivity to individual perspectives and purposes is a virtue, not a defect. (Sections 4.4 through 4.6 return to the problem of normative relevance.)

Conceptual relativism draws on the following considerations to highlight the perspectival character of rational inquiry:

(i) My semantic standards for the correct use of 'rational' specify what it means, at least for me, to say that something (for example, a belief or an action) is rational.

(ii) My semantic standards for the correct use of 'rational' are evidently not forced upon, or otherwise required of, all inquirers. Such standards evidently can, and sometimes do, vary among inquirers (for example, Kantians and Humeans regarding the rôle of motivation in reasons); and I can consistently acknowledge this variance.

(iii) My semantic standards nonetheless do play a crucial role in how I, at least, use 'rational' in evaluative contexts. Those standards determine correctness and incorrectness in my use of that term.

(iv) When different people do use different specific semantic standards for 'rational', they are really using different specific notions of rationality. In that respect, they are concerned with different species of rationality, at least from the standpoint of a broader, encompassing notion of rationality. They are not necessarily disagreeing about what is rational, but are rather, in a straightforward sense, "talking about different matters." When, in contrast, people use the same semantic standards for 'rational', they are not using different notions of rationality. They may still disagree, however, over whether their common notion applies, or is satisfied, in certain concrete or hypothetical cases.

In sum, the notion of a purposive normative reason enables us to make good sense of conceptual relativism about truth. This notion enables us to explain how people can have reasons for adopting and using different concepts of truth. Relative to our evaluative purposes, we might settle on calling certain semantic standards *the concept* of truth. Such a purpose-relative commitment settles what truth, by definition, is, at least relative to our evaluative purposes. Because others can do the same, except with different semantic standards, we cannot thereby block conceptual relativism.

4.3 The Fate of Relativism

'Relativism' is a dirty word in certain philosophical quarters. In these quarters, relativists are numbered among the corrupt, as if they were guilty of an intellectual crime. Why is this? Part of the problem is that many philosophers shun relativism *tout court*, without recognizing that relativism comes in importantly different forms.

Versions of substantive relativism that entail an "anything goes" approach to truth, reasons, rightness, and goodness do run afoul of the notions of truth, reasons, rightness, and goodness espoused by many of us. (I did not say "all of us.") We can consistently resist endorsing such versions of substantive relativism, so long as we espouse certain nonrelativist evaluative notions. Further, if our core for those nonrelativist notions excludes an "anything goes" approach, we can even say that substantive relativist notions of truth, reasons, rightness, and goodness are not really notions of truth, reasons, rightness, and goodness, at least given our notions. (See section 2.4B on limits for concepts.) Not all versions of relativism, in any case, entail an "anything goes" attitude toward evaluative matters.

Conceptual relativism of the sort outlined here does not leave us with an "anything goes" attitude. It does not entail that whatever one believes to be true, reasonable, right, or good is thereby true, reasonable, right, or good. It entails only that people can, do, or may use different specific concepts of truth, reasonableness, rightness, and goodness. Such a view regarding variability of concepts conflicts in no way with the obvious consideration that some evaluative concepts (for example, Kantian and utilitarian moral concepts) preclude an "anything goes" attitude toward evaluative matters.

Variance of concepts allows that people mean different things in using terms. It does not entail that, given any single notion (of truth, for example), anything goes. The semantic variance allowed by conceptual relativism does not entail that whatever one believes about a matter is thereby correct. One might introduce a notion of "correctness" that does entail the latter view. Such a notion would not, however, serve the purposes many of us have in using a notion of correctness; nor would it automatically qualify as a genuine notion of correctness relative to the core of our notion. We must look elsewhere, then, for a challenge to conceptual relativism.

Hilary Putnam (1983, pp. 237–238) has argued that "cultural relativism" is "inconsistent." Let us ask whether his argument bears on conceptual relativism. Putnam contends that you, the cultural relativist, cannot acknowledge the reality of others if you think the only understandable notion of truth for you is the notion of "truth as determined by the norms of your culture." Suppose that you understand every utterance, *P*, you make (including every utterance you use to interpret others) as meaning that it is true by the norms of your culture that *P*. In that case, according to Putnam, other cultures become logical constructions out of the norms of your own culture. If you add that from the point of view of other cultures the situation is exactly reversed, you end up with inconsistency. Putnam thus claims that "the transcendental claim of a *symmetrical* situation cannot be *understood* if the relativist doctrine is right" (1983, p. 238).

Relativists do face trouble if they claim that all meaningful claims depend on their own cultural norms, and then add that meaningful claims for certain other cultures do not depend on their own cultural norms. Conceptual relativism, as outlined here, clearly does not entail such inconsistency. It does not imply that all meaningful claims depend on the norms of a single culture, and hence does not suffer the defect of what Putnam calls "cultural relativism." Semantic standards, according to section 4.2, can vary substantially relative to individuals and cultures.

Putnam has objected to relativism on the following ground:

> Relativism, just as much as Realism, assumes that one can stand within one's language and outside it at the same time. In the case of Realism this is not an immediate contradiction, since the whole content of Realism lies in the claim that it makes sense to think of a God's-Eye View (or, better, of a "View from Nowhere"); but in the case of Relativism it constitutes a self-refutation. (1990, p. 23)

This objection, like the previous objection, is irrelevant to conceptual relativism. Nothing in conceptual relativism requires that one be able to "stand outside one's language."

Conceptual relativism does entail that different people can, do, or may use different specific concepts of truth, reasonableness, rightness, goodness, and so on. This amounts simply to the claim that different people can, do, or may use different specific semantic standards for certain terms. It does not imply, however, that one cannot understand the alternative semantic standards in question, or that such semantic standards cannot be translated into one's own language. Conceptual relativism does not require, then, that one be able to understand something that is not understandable in, or translatable into, one's own language. It therefore does not require that one be able to "stand outside" one's own language, in Putnam's sense.

Many of Putnam's objections to relativism aim at Richard Rorty's relativism. It is worth asking, therefore, whether conceptual relativism entails Rorty's own version of relativism.

Rorty has characterized relativism as follows:

> 'Relativism' is the traditional epithet applied to pragmatism by realists. Three different views are commonly referred to by this name. The first is the view that every belief is as good as every other. The second is the view that 'true' is an equivocal term, having as many meanings as there are procedures of justification. The third is the view that there is nothing to be said about either truth or rationality apart from descriptions of the familiar procedures of justification which a given society—*ours*—uses in one or another area of inquiry. The pragmatist holds the ethnocentric third view. But he does not hold the self-refuting first view, nor the eccentric second view. (1991, p. 23)

The main defect in Rorty's relativism is its ethnocentrism: its appeal to *our* society as providing the only relevant procedures of justification for an intelligible characterization of the notion of justification. What reason have we to give our society such primacy—such a monopoly—by way of conceptual significance? Rorty offers no such reason, and I can think of none whatever.

Rorty's semantic ethnocentrism suffers the narrow-mindedness of most species of ethnocentrism. We do typically wield concepts of justification that stem from practices in our own society. We cannot plausibly gainsay social influences on our most familiar notions of justification. Even so, we can understand notions of justification that correspond to different practices in different societies. Anthropological evidence for alternative justificatory practices and notions, even among English language-users, is not beyond our ken. We have, then, no basis for ruling out the possibility or even the actuality of such alternative notions, notions that we understand but do not ourselves adopt or use for our own evaluative purposes. Conceptual relativism, unlike Rorty's ethnocentric relativism, fits well with this observation. Conceptual relativism does not give any single society—not even our own—a monopoly on such significant notions as those of truth, justification, and reasons.

Another familiar objection states that relativists have no basis whatever for recommending their evaluative concepts or beliefs to anyone who does not already share them. The alleged problem is that relativists must recognize the relativity of their own concepts and beliefs, and thus cannot presume or recommend the universal relevance of those concepts and beliefs. This objection is partly right and partly wrong.

The correct part of the objection is that relativists cannot simply presume that their evaluative concepts and beliefs are recommendable, *unconditionally*, to everyone. This part is correct, since a relativist's purposes in wielding evaluative concepts can differ substantially from someone else's purposes in using such concepts. Inasmuch as conceptual recommendations are purpose-relative, variance of purposes can indeed limit the recommendability of evaluative concepts. This point may apply equally, however, to the relativist and the nonrelativist. The opponent of conceptual relativism enjoys no obvious special privilege here.

The incorrect part of the objection is that relativists have no basis whatever for recommending their evaluative concepts to others who do not already share them. As long as relativists have purposive normative reasons for certain evaluative concepts, and others share their purposes underlying those purposive reasons, they can reasonably recommend their concepts to those others. In addition, relativists can reasonably recommend some purposes, for instance, to people having certain purposes that would be served if they had further purposes. Relativists might thereby recommend a certain purpose for adopting and using a notion of truth, rationality, or whatever. Common purpose can provide not only common purposive reasons but also a stable basis for recommending common concepts.

A final objection runs as follows. "Factual conceptual relativism commits us to the view that there are various notions of truth in circulation. If someone says that the conceptual relativist is in error here, we then have to discuss concepts of truth, and not the key implication of factual conceptual relativism about varying notions of truth. This is absurd." This objection rests on misunderstanding.

Conceptual relativism does not entail that we now have to discuss concepts of truth rather than the key implication about varying notions of truth. Conceptual relativism entails only, in this connection, that the intelligibility and the cogency of the objection that the relativist is in "error" depend on a determinate notion of "error"—a notion that must be suitably specified when we intelligibly ask, or even wonder, whether the conceptual relativist is in "error" (in the sense to be specified). In short, we must determine the relevant notion of "error" in connection with consideration of the implication in question, in order to determine whether that implication is in "error," in the relevant sense. This seems anything but absurd. It is rather a platitude, depending on this principle: No suitably determinate concept, no intelligible query. It is, moreover, an empirical issue whether some philosophers actually employ different notions of truth. We have previously seen some evidence that favors a thesis of varying notions of truth.

In sum, the familiar reasons for rejecting relativism leave conceptual relativism unscathed. Conceptual relativism is more durable than the familiar versions of relativism typically shunned by philosophers.

Where, then, should we begin a philosophical effort to say what in general is true rather than false? We should begin with an understanding of what it means (at least for us) to say that something is true rather than false. Our decision on what meaning to give to 'true' can receive support from purposive normative reasons, reasons indicative of the purposes we have in adopting and wielding a notion of truth; and the purposes we have in adopting and using a notion of truth can rest on other purposes we have. Relying on such reasons, we shall attend to the purposes we aim to achieve in answering philosophical questions about what is true. Such purposes can, and sometimes do, vary among philosophers. As a result, we confront variation of philosophical concepts. We thus have the basis for conceptual relativism of the sort defended here. (See chapter 2 on conditions for justifying claims to truth.)

Attention to the role of purposes in philosophical inquiry does support conceptual relativism, but does not support an "anything goes" attitude toward evaluative matters. The role of purposes in inquiry, I have explained, can block the problem of normative relevance and can highlight the explanatory significance of purposive normative reasons. The resulting conceptual relativism avoids the defects of familiar versions of relativism and deepens our understanding of philosophical inquiry. At least one species of relativism, then, resists derision and merits serious philosophical consideration. We might still fancy ourselves, occasionally and forgetfully, as having finally latched onto "the" concept of truth or "the" concept of rationality. Conceptual relativism now bids us, however, to be ever wary of the myth of the definite article.

4.4 Practical Ideals and Practical Relevance

Let us return to the problem of normative relevance mentioned in section 4.2. In the *Critique of Pure Reason* (A569 = B597), Kant claims that "human reason contains not only ideas, but ideals also, which although they do not have, like the Platonic ideas, creative power, yet have *practical* power (as regulative principles), and form the basis of the possible perfection of certain *actions*." Whereas Kant talked of "perfection" of actions, we shall talk instead of "improvement" of actions, where improvement encompasses approaching, achieving, and maintaining a certain status.

Which of the numerous possible ideals should we use to give sense to our talk of "improving" actions, or at least to regulate our actions for the purpose of improving them? We obviously face a plethora of possible ideals for regulating actions: for example, ideals from deontologists and consequentialists of various and sundry stripes.

We, as rational agents, need some nonarbitrary way to select those ideals that will appropriately regulate, or guide, our actions, so as to improve our actions. The latter need corresponds to the problem of normative relevance mentioned previously. Because we are now concerned with actions, we may speak of *the problem of practical relevance*: the problem of identifying, in a judicious way, what norms are relevantly appropriate to the regulation of our conduct, for the purpose of improving our conduct. We need a solution that specifies the kind of reasons appropriate to action-guiding normative judgments. The solution to be developed will bear directly on the sense and the significance of such perplexing evaluative why-questions as: Why should we be moral? Why should we be rational?

Practical ideals are standards, or norms, for "the possible improvement of certain actions," to modify Kant's phrase. *Theoretical* ideals are, correspondingly, standards for the possible improvement of certain theories. Practical ideals are regulative principles for actions; theoretical ideals are regulative principles for theories. Because theorizing is an action, or at least a series of actions, an account of practical ideals will have direct implications for the regulation of theorizing as well as actions of other sorts.

Principles that regulate theorizing can regulate theories too, at least indirectly. Standards for theorizing can exclude theorizing that produces theories with certain features (inconsistency, ad hocness, and so on) and require theorizing that produces theories with certain other features (consistency, broad scope, and so on). We shall pursue the question of what makes certain practical ideals, rather than others, relevantly appropriate to practical decision-making aiming at the improvement of actions.

The "possible improvement of actions" is the possible improvement of actions *in certain respects*. Practical ideals specify the respects in which actions can be improved and thereby give some determinacy to talk of "improvement" of actions. Lacking such ideals, our talk of improvement of actions will be indeterminate. It will then be talk of improvement without specification of the respects in which our actions can be improved. Such talk is as indeterminate as talk, for example, of "permissible" conduct unaccompanied by any identification of the respects in which the conduct is permissible. Our practical ideals can give semantic determinacy, and thus meaningfulness, to our talk of improving actions.

Talk of improving actions must not beg any questions about controversial dependency relations between "the good" and "the right."[10] Such talk must not simply presuppose the distinctive consequentialist view that the rightness of an action is a function of its consequent goodness. Kant, of course, was not presupposing that view with his talk of perfecting actions. He was assuming that to the extent that our actions satisfy appropriate normative ideals for regulating our actions, those actions are better—closer to "perfection"—than they would be otherwise. The latter assumption raises no special problems for a deontological approach to the rightness of actions. It does not entail that the rightness of actions depends on the goodness of those actions' consequences. We must now construe talk of improving actions in a similarly noncontroversial manner. Such talk, for current purposes, signifies just the improvement of our actions in virtue of their compliance with appropriate norms for regulating our actions. It does not seek to collapse any distinction between obligatory and supererogatory action.

Talk of "regulating" actions, whether by norms or by something else, needs clarification. One thing can regulate something else either causally or normatively (or perhaps even causally and normatively). *Causal* regulation is a matter of one thing's (for example, a certain series of events) causally originating and/or sustaining something else (for example, another series of events). My thermostat's functioning, for instance, causally regulates the functioning of the furnace in my house. *Normative* regulation, in contrast, is a matter of one's being subject to certain norms that bear on one's attitudes, states, or actions. A norm's bearing on a certain attitude, state, or action is, in general, that norm's having some evaluative implication for that attitude, state, or action.

Norms can bear on one's attitudes, states, or actions in various ways. *Deontological* norms require, permit, or prohibit certain attitudes, states, or actions. They are typically expressed by such locutions as: 'It is obligatory that . . .'; 'You ought to (or should) . . .'; 'It is permissible that . . .'; 'You may . . .'; and 'You should not . . .'. *Nondeontological* norms neither require, permit, nor prohibit anything. They do, however, provide evaluative standards, such as standards for goodness, badness, praise, or blame.[11] Our standards for good cooking or praiseworthy artwork, for example, are evaluative, but do not necessarily take the form of requirements or prohibitions. We might hold that cooking is good in virtue of a certain set of culinary features, without thereby committing ourselves to a requirement that those features be realized. Standards for goodness or praise, then, need not rely on deontological norms.

Normative standards, whether deontological or nondeontological, figure in various domains: for example, ethics, economics, aesthetics, law, and litera-

10. For an influential nonconsequentialist approach to the distinction between the good and the right, see Ross (1930, pp. 3–6, 156; 1939, chap. 12, esp. pp. 306–310). For related distinctions in epistemology, see Alston (1989a, chap. 4) and Moser (1989, chap. 1).

11. My distinction here corresponds in certain respects to G. H. von Wright's distinction between *principles* (or "norms of action") and *ideals* (or "ideal rules"). See von Wright (1963, pp. 14-16). Ideals, according to von Wright, are not reducible to principles. Ideals can, however, determine concepts, for example, a concept of a good teacher or soldier.

ture. Within each of those domains, various people typically espouse conflicting norms, norms that cannot all be satisfied. In each of those domains, a judicious person will thus typically face the problem of practical relevance: the problem of identifying, in a judicious way, what norms are relevantly appropriate to the regulation of conduct in the domain in question, for the purpose of improving that conduct. This amounts to the problem of discerning what norms are appropriate regulative guidelines for improving conduct, at least in a certain domain.

For simplicity, let us restate the problem of practical relevance from a first-person perspective, as follows: What norms are appropriate for regulating my conduct, for the purpose of improving my conduct? The problem of practical relevance for a person is now the problem of answering the former question in a judicious way. A norm can be appropriate for regulating my conduct even if I fail to accept or to comply with that norm. Such failure of acceptance or compliance might arise from mere confusion, ignorance, or indifference on my part.[12] We thus cannot automatically assume that the norms appropriate, or adequate, for regulating my conduct are necessarily the norms I actually accept or obey.

We can make progress now by considering the relevant notion of "improving conduct." The adequacy of the norms we espouse for the purpose of improving our conduct depends on what the improving of conduct consists in. Such adequacy is, after all, appropriateness *for the purpose of improving conduct.*

If we lack conditions constitutive of the improving of conduct, we shall also lack a correct account of what norms are adequate for the improving of conduct. In that case, we shall have no basis for correctly identifying certain norms, rather than others, as being adequate for the improving of conduct. We shall then have no standard for what constitutes satisfaction of the relevant purpose, or end: the improving of conduct. Indeed, in that case our talk of improving conduct will be indeterminate. Such talk will become determinate only when certain factors make it talk of one (kind of) thing as opposed to others. (See section 2.3 for analogous points about a notion of epistemic justification.)

How should we clarify the relevant notion of improving conduct? This question is perplexing, mainly because its use of 'should' is far from clear. Whenever we use 'should' but fail to indicate the constitutive standards for correctness in that use, we foster vagueness, if not complete indeterminacy, in normative discourse. The semantic determinacy of 'should' depends on the indication of such constitutive standards for correct use. This point holds even if we acknowledge that use of 'should', at least in action-guiding evaluative judgments, has an ineliminable prescriptive, or imperatival, component.[13] In that case, the

12. There might also be a kind of doxastic incontinence or weakness of will that accounts for failure of acceptance or compliance. For an overview of relevant approaches to weakness of will, see Charlton (1988); cf. Watson (1977). On incontinence in belief as well as action, see Mele (1987, chaps. 3, 8).

13. On such prescriptivism, see Hare (1952, chap. 11; 1963, pp. 23, 67, 77–82).

determinacy of use of 'should', at least for us, will depend on an understanding of a certain notion of prescription. My point holds, as well, for a consequentialist approach to 'should' that understands obligation in terms of an evaluative end for which one should conduct oneself in a certain way. We shall need, in that case, a determinate notion of the pertinent evaluative end. (See section 3.3B on the role of constitutive standards for correctness in meaning.)

Must we presume that all normatively relevant imperatives are hypothetical, and none categorical? It seems not, but the final answer will depend on the actual proposed constitutive conditions for correct use of a categorical imperative. If such conditions are lacking, we shall have indeterminacy precluding intelligibility. Kant's own categorical imperative, however, was anchored in conditions for rationality that gave the needed determinacy. An imperative's being categorical, on Kant's view, does not require its being altogether without conditions; defining conditions, for example, are not thereby excluded. I shall not assume, then, that categorical imperatives are automatically unintelligible.

All imperatives characteristically have a certain relatively trivial purpose, at least in ordinary circumstances of sincerity: the purpose of having done or realized what they command to be done or realized. The latter purpose identifies a condition of success for an imperative, in the sense noted in section 3.3B. If I prescribe, 'Keep your promises!', the purpose of this prescription, at least in ordinary circumstances of sincerity, is to have you keep your promises. This consideration does not preclude secondary purposes for imperatives.

Purposes in using evaluative vocabulary and judgments can vary widely. In general, they might be either moral, legal, aesthetic, epistemic, or prudential. Within those general categories, the relevant purposes can vary still further. If they are moral purposes, for example, they might be, among other things, either utilitarian in some way or other, deontological in some way or other, or egoist in some way or other. A proponent of a categorical imperative—even a Kantian—can acknowledge definite purposes in wielding that imperative: for example, to realize a certain kind of improvement of conduct. Such a proponent cannot, however, regard the relevant imperative as applying to a person only if the person actually desires or prefers the fulfillment of the imperative. That would make the imperative straightforwardly hypothetical.

The intuitionism of H. A. Prichard and W. D. Ross entails that we cannot give explanatory reasons why we should act so as to fulfill our moral obligations. Their intuitionism entails, in particular, that we cannot explain why the keeping of our promises provides for moral rightness. Prichard (1912, pp. 8, 16) and Ross (1930, pp. 32–33, 121–122) claim that we must simply *intuit* the morally relevant connection between certain actions and rightness.

R. M. Hare, in contrast, endorses this view: "if we make a particular moral judgement, we can always be asked to support it by reasons; the reasons consist in the general principles under which the moral judgement is to be subsumed" (1952, p. 176). Hare claims, in particular, that "'ought'-judgements, strictly speaking, would be being misused if the demand for reasons or grounds were thought of as out of place" (1963, pp. 36–37). Assuming the "supervenient character" of evaluative language, Hare holds that the relevant "general principles" will identify certain nonevaluative features of the thing or conduct to which the evaluative judgment applies. Hare proposes that it is impossible for actions to differ only with respect to their rightness and that "this impossibility is a logical one, stemming from the way in which, *and the purposes for which*, we use [evaluative] words" (1952, p. 153; italics added). Hare identifies the primary purpose in using evaluative language as that of advising and instructing, of guiding action via prescriptions.

Hare's prescriptivist account of evaluative language is, by virtually any standard, explanatorily more appealing than the intuitionism of Prichard and Ross. Hare explains features of evaluative judgments in terms of the purposes we have in using the evaluative vocabulary constitutive of those judgments. Such an appeal to our purposes makes good sense of various features of our typical evaluative judgments, such as their supervenient character. It enables an explanation of evaluative judgments in terms of the agents wielding those judgments: more specifically, in terms of the purposes of such agents in using evaluative vocabulary.

The intuitionism of Prichard and Ross does not enable any explanation of evaluative judgments in terms of our evaluative purposes. It bars such explanation with the assumption that we can only intuit, rather than explain in terms of reasons, connections between such activity as promise-keeping and its moral rightness. If we value explanation over appeals to mere intuition in normative inquiry, we shall find little, if any, satisfaction in the intuitionism of Prichard and Ross.

A notable difficulty for intuitionism is the following *problem of arbitrariness*: Barring an unexplanatory dogmatism about rightness, intuitionism must be accompanied by an explanation of when intuitions are reliable rather than gratuitous. Otherwise, we face a plethora of seemingly arbitrary, often conflicting intuitions, none of which we can judiciously recommend as more reliable than the others. Intuitionists cannot rest content with either dogmatism or arbitrariness. That would be to shirk their explanatory responsibility as theorists. Even intuitionists, then, cannot avoid the burden of explanation in normative inquiry.

Hare's prescriptivism identifies an important component in an account evaluative judgments: the role of agents' purposes in using evaluative vocabulary. Let us turn now to the issue of how this component contributes to the aforementioned notion of "purposive reasons" and to a notion of "should" pertinent to the problem of practical relevance.

4.5 Purposive Reasons and a Multiplicity Problem

Evaluative purposes, I have suggested, can provide explanatory reasons for evaluative judgments. What, however, are evaluative purposes, and how exactly can they deliver such reasons? Answering these questions will contribute to a solution of the aforementioned problem of practical relevance.

A. Evaluative Purposes and Relativism

When intentionally using evaluative vocabulary, we use such vocabulary purposefully, in a goal-directed manner, with some end in view.[14] Our *ultimate* purposes in using evaluative vocabulary are our purposes in using such vocabulary that do not depend for their existence on any further purposes we have in using such vocabulary. In many cases, our ultimate purpose in using evaluative vocabulary is twofold: to guide and to assess action in a certain way.

Whatever our ultimate evaluative purposes happen to be, those purposes enable an explanation of why we use such vocabulary as we do, at least from our intentional point of view. Those purposes thus provide *explanatory purposive reasons* for our using evaluative vocabulary as we do: reasons for action, including linguistic action, that derive from our purposes and enable an explanation of our action from our own intentional standpoint.

Purposive reasons can serve as motivating, causal reasons for our use of evaluative vocabulary and can figure crucially in an explanation of that use from our own intentional perspective. Such an explanation can take this form: I purport to accomplish *X* (in using evaluative vocabulary); my using evaluative vocabulary in way *W* (for example, as certain consequentialists do) will accomplish *X*; so I use evaluative vocabulary in way *W*. Purposive explanation of this sort figures prominently in commonsense psychology and in everyday efforts at interpreting ourselves and others.[15]

The ultimate purposes we have in using evaluative vocabulary can explain, then, why we use the particular evaluative notions we do use in assessing and guiding action. At a level of specificity, various people can, and often do, use different specific evaluative notions in assessing and guiding action. In particular, various moral theorists often use different specific notions of "improving actions." Correspondingly, various theorists may have different specific ultimate ends in using evaluative vocabulary.

Moral theorists can often agree on a rather vague *general* notion of improving actions: say, the notion of improving conduct by bringing it into compliance with appropriate normative standards. Nonetheless, *specific* conceptual commitments about what constitutes "appropriate normative standards" can and do vary among theorists. Consequentialists and deontologists, for example, typically have significantly different specific conceptual commitments about what constitutes appropriate normative standards. Supporting evidence here arises from the consideration that typical consequentialists and deontologists are not genuinely open to potential counterexamples to their respective (defining) consequentialist and deontological theses.

We now need to acknowledge *evaluative conceptual relativism*: the view

14. For relevant discussion of the role of goals in intentional action, see Brand (1984, chap. 8), Alston (1986), Mele (1992, chap. 8), and Mele and Moser (1994). Cf. section 3.3A above.

15. On the relation between purposive explanation and explanation in the natural sciences, see Alvin Goldman (1970, chap. 5) and Davidson (1974b, 1987). Cf. section 3.3A. Section 5.3 returns to the topic of purposive explanation.

that at a level of specificity various people can, may, and often do adopt and wield different evaluative concepts. (This is a species of the conceptual relativism introduced in section 2.4c and defended in section 4.3.) Such relativism does not entail that various people understand different evaluative concepts; nor does it entail substantive evaluative relativism, the view that whatever one believes to be right, good, or praiseworthy is right, good, or praiseworthy. It allows that, given certain evaluative concepts, some evaluative beliefs can be mistaken. Evaluative conceptual relativism entails that various people can, may, and often do *espouse* and *use* different concepts for assessing and guiding actions. Evaluative concepts, generally characterized, are just constitutive standards for correct use of evaluative terms: such terms as 'right', 'wrong', 'good', 'bad', 'praiseworthy', and 'blameworthy'.

In virtue of a specific conceptual commitment regarding correct use of 'morally right action' (or some synonymous term), consequentialists typically regard the moral rightness of action as a function of consequent goodness. Owing to a different specific conceptual commitment, deontologists typically regard the moral rightness of action as logically independent of consequent goodness. It is proper to speak of "conceptual commitments" here, because the distinctive theses of consequentialism and deontologism are characteristically not empirical claims, at least not in any ordinary sense of 'empirical'. The best available explanation of their being nonempirical claims appeals to their being conceptual claims: that is, claims to specific conceptual truths. Given this explanation, we can avoid excess metaphysical baggage in accounting for the nonempirical character of many evaluative theses.[16]

Typical consequentialists and deontologists adopt and use different specific notions of moral rightness, even if they can agree on a rather vague general notion of such rightness.[17] Such a general notion would be amplified in different ways by their respective specific notions of rightness. This difference in specific notions does not preclude that a consequentialist and a deontologist can understand each other's specific notion of moral rightness, even if they disagree over which specific notion is preferable and what is actually conceptually true at a level of specificity. They thus can communicate with each other, because the pertinent relativity is not in understanding. The relativity comes rather from a difference in specific notions adopted and used to assess and to guide actions.

An alternative to evaluative conceptual relativism is evaluative conceptual *absolutism*: the view that various people do not use different specific evalua-

16. One might propose that W. V. Quine, in his influential challenge to analyticity, has shown the vacuousness, or at least the explanatory futility, of any notion of conceptual commitment. See section 3.8 for argument that any such proposal would be misleading, as even a holist of Quine's persuasion needs to rely on a notion of conceptual commitment to answer certain meta-epistemological questions.

17. This thesis fits with G. H. von Wright's observation of "the notorious obscurity, ambiguity, and vagueness of the adjective 'moral' as an attribute of words like 'action', 'duty', 'motive', 'norm', 'rightness', and 'value'." See von Wright (1989, p. 794). For further support for conceptual relativism, see Unger (1984) and Arrington (1989, chap. 6). On the variability of notions of *rational* action in the history of ethical theory, see Frankena (1983).

tive concepts to assess and to guide actions. That view is uncompelling. Even if typical consequentialists and deontologists can agree on a rather vague general notion of moral rightness, their conceptual commitments toward moral rightness diverge significantly at any level of specificity. Given (a) that typical consequentialists and deontologists have divergent commitments regarding the specific conditions constitutive of (what it is to be) moral rightness for them, and (b) that those commitments are nonempirical in virtue of being conceptual (and being closed to potential falsifiers, for the relevant theorists), we can reject evaluative conceptual absolutism. At a minimum, absolutists have some difficult explaining to do.

Evaluative conceptual relativism fits well with *pluralism* about ultimate evaluative ends. Evaluative conceptual absolutism, in contrast, fits with *monism* about ultimate evaluative ends. Pluralists typically acknowledge the actuality of divergent ultimate evaluative ends, at least at a level of specificity. Monists typically reject the actuality of such divergence.[18]

Pluralists have an easier time than monists explaining conceptual diversity among evaluative theorists. Consider, again, familiar deontologists in contrast with typical consequentialists. Deontologists characteristically aim ultimately to assess and to guide actions, at least regarding their moral rightness, in a certain distinctive way: a way independent of considerations of consequent goodness. That consideration can benefit an account of why certain theorists are deontologists rather than consequentialists: specifically, why they adopt a deontological rather than a consequentialist notion of moral rightness. Consequentialists, in contrast, typically aim ultimately to assess and to guide actions, with respect to moral rightness, in a different way, a way that depends on considerations of consequent goodness. As a result, they adopt a consequentialist rather than a deontological notion of moral rightness.

Typical deontologists and typical consequentialists operate, then, with different specific ultimate evaluative ends, at least with respect to the assessment and guidance of morally right action. Even if such theorists share some vague general evaluative end, they clearly part company at a level of specificity of evaluative ends. Pluralists, but not monists, can make considerable explanatory mileage from this consideration. Pluralists can appeal to divergence in evaluative ends to explain divergence in actual use of evaluative vocabulary and in the corresponding specific conceptual commitments motivating such divergent use. Pluralists can regard divergent evaluative ends as lending purposive support to the divergent specific notions of rightness used by deontologists and consequentialists. Those notions can get reason-based support relative to corresponding evaluative ends. On such matters, pluralists about evaluative ends have a notable explanatory advantage over monists.

18. For support for pluralism about evaluative *epistemic* ends, see Moser (1989, chap. 5), and Stich (1990, chaps. 4–6). For some support for pluralism about moral practices and ends, see Phillips and Mounce (1969) and Warnock (1971, chap. 1). Pluralism is compatible with common *very general* moral ends, such as merely "getting to believe and getting to act." On the latter ends, see Cooper (1981, chap. 12).

Ultimate evaluative ends can, then, provide purposive reasons for using evaluative vocabulary in a certain way. If your ultimate evaluative end is to assess and to guide action independently of considerations of consequent goodness, you can have a purposive reason for using evaluative vocabulary in the manner of familiar deontologists. If, however, you have a different ultimate evaluative end, your purposive reasons for using evaluative vocabulary can differ accordingly. Purposive reasons are thus agent-sensitive in a way suitable to pluralism about ultimate evaluative ends.

Ultimate evaluative ends can play a definite role in answering such troublesome questions as 'Should I be moral (in a specific sense)?' and 'Should I be rational (in a specific sense)?' Before proposing answers to such questions, we do well to inquire about the conditions constitutive of the meaning of the evaluative terms 'should', 'moral', and 'rational'. Different people can, and often do, construe such terms in different ways, at least at a level of specificity. This is a key lesson of evaluative conceptual relativism.

We cannot give an adequate, or correct, answer to a question whose semantic significance is inadequately determinate; for inadequate determinacy undermines a standard for correctness and thus correctness itself. A usually effective way to clarify the semantic significance of an evaluative question is to clarify the questioner's ultimate evaluative ends in using such terms as 'should', 'moral', and 'rational'. Clarification of those ends can help to identify what evaluative notions are operative for a questioner—perhaps even oneself. Short of determining the meaning of pertinent evaluative terms, questions whether one should be moral or rational will perplex only because of semantic inadequacy, indeterminacy in what they are actually asking.

For illustration, let us consider the question, 'Should I do only what is morally right?' We may now use Roderick Firth's (1952) "ideal-observer theory" to clarify the meaning of the relevant moral terms.[19] Firth's theory aims to account for the meanings of moral terms and judgments. A claim that an action is morally right, on Firth's theory, *means* that an ideal observer would feel moral approval for that action if she reflected on it. Firth holds that ideal observers will always agree in their morally relevant attitudes, and that they share the following essential features: (a) omniscience about all nonmoral facts; (b) an ability to imagine vividly any situation or experience; (c) impartiality, including dispassionateness, toward individual persons and things; (d) consistency; and (e) normality, with respect to being human, in all other respects. Given an understanding of what such features are, we can grant that Firth's theory gives some semantic determinacy to moral terms and judgments—at least enough determinacy for the illustrative purpose at hand.

We can now reformulate our question as: Should I perform only those actions that would attract a feeling of moral approval from an ideal observer? The semantic significance of this question now depends, obviously enough, on the meaning of 'should'. Given the meaning of 'should' in Firth's ideal-observer theory, we can recast our question as follows: Would an ideal observer, upon

19. For a recent effort to refine Firth's ideal-observer theory, see Carson (1984, chap. 2).

reflection, feel moral disapproval toward my performing actions other than those that would attract a feeling of moral approval from an ideal observer (such as herself or himself)? If, as Firth holds, ideal observers always agree and feel either approval or disapproval toward the actions upon which they reflect, the answer is obviously yes. Indeed, this affirmative answer, given Firth's theory, is a conceptual truth: It results from the meanings of the question's constituent terms. Firth's theory illustrates nicely that, given certain relatively determinate meanings for moral terms, such questions as 'Should I be moral?' admit of straightforward answers.

Two noteworthy problems confront a normative theory like Firth's. First, it seems quite misleading, or at least questionbegging, to propose a single, relatively specific set of conditions—for example, conditions involving (a) through (e)—as providing *the* meaning of such moral terms as 'right' and 'wrong'. At a level of specificity, meanings of evaluative terms are more variant than Firth presumes. It is doubtful that ethical egoists or cultural relativists, for example, construe evaluative terms in accord with Firth's ideal-observer theory. Egoists and cultural relativists typically have no need for conditions involving omniscience and unrestricted impartiality, for instance.

Evidently only a small number of philosophers mean by evaluative terms what Firth's ideal-observer theory says those terms mean. Most people use evaluative terms meaningfully, but have no familiarity whatever with some of the conditions set by Firth's theory. Firth's theory fails, then, to capture the meaning of evaluative terms for most people. The meaning of a term for a person is, after all, a function of what that person means, or understands, by that term. This, given the account of meaning in section 3.3, is a platitude. Firth's theory gives inadequate attention to the phenomena supporting evaluative conceptual relativism.

The second problem is that the question of whether we should be moral is, at least for some people, not trivial in the way Firth's theory implies. That question, for some people, asks something different from the trivial question noted above. We might think of the question as involving a "rational" 'should' of some sort, a sense of 'should' going beyond the meanings set by Firth's ideal-observer theory. We accomplish little, however, with just the following question: Should I, in order to be rational, be moral? Use of 'rational' is, at a level of specificity, subject to nearly as much semantic divergence as the use of 'should' and 'moral'. Once a sense of 'rational' is specified (for example, in accord with some Bayesian decision-theoretic account of rationality), one can always ask: Why should I (care to) be rational *in that sense of 'rational'*? If we can make sense of the latter question, we can see that an appeal just to a certain specific notion of rational obligation will not settle all relevant questions about whether we should be moral or rational.

B. Internalism

An internalist approach to the question, 'Why should I (care to) be rational in that sense of "rational"?', invokes the notion of purposive reason introduced previously. On this approach, the latter question is reason-seeking owing to its using a reason-sensitive notion of 'should'. Specifically, its use of 'should' concerns purposive reasons, reasons deriving from one's purposes, or ends, relevant to one's being rational in a certain sense of 'rational'.

If I have an acknowledged purpose that would obviously be satisfied by my complying with certain standards for being rational, and no reason from my motivational and cognitive set calls into question the former condition or otherwise counts against compliance, I would have an undefeated purposive reason to comply with those standards for being rational.[20] If, however, no (acknowledged) purpose of mine benefits from my complying with certain standards for being rational, I shall have no purposive reason to be rational in the sense of those standards. In such a case, it is false, according to internalism, that I should be "rational" in the sense proposed.

The relevant notion of a purposive reason can give manageable sense to the question why one should (care to) be rational in a certain way. Is this the only notion of a reason—the only construal of 'should'—that can make sense of that question? We have no reason to think it is, especially given conceptual relativism about the use of 'should'. Some theorists, in fact, will question the normative significance of the relevant notion of a purposive reason. One issue is whether purposive reasons are normatively relevant only if they are themselves normatively constrained in some way. The underlying worry is that purposes, or ends, do not themselves always comply with normative standards. When they do not, the corresponding purposive reasons will be unconstrained by normative standards. It might seem, therefore, that purposive reasons can have normative significance only if they are themselves supported by reasons that are constrained by certain normative standards.

How, then, are we to understand 'should' in such questions as 'Why should I (care to) be moral (in a specified sense)?' and 'Why should I (care to) be rational (in a specified sense)?' Some people raising such questions understand their use of 'should' as having some *motivational* significance for them, given their purposive and cognitive set consisting of relevant purposes and evidence. Such people, espousing internalism, will not be satisfied by answers that introduce normative requirements having no basis whatever in their current purposive and cognitive set. For such an internalist, our question becomes: What considerations, if any, in my current purposive and cognitive set recommend that I should (care to) be moral or rational in the specified sense? Let us call this *the internalist reading* of our questions, as it acknowledges a key role for a questioner's own purposive and cognitive perspective.

The internalist reading avoids a use of 'should' that is irrelevant from a questioner's purposive and cognitive standpoint. It construes the use of 'should' in our previous evaluative questions to concern a potential recommendation based on an agent's purposive and cognitive standpoint. If a categorical imperative excludes any conditioning of a recommendation by one's purposive

20. For a detailed account of the conditions for the defeat, or undermining, of reasons, see Pollock (1986b, 1987).

standpoint, the internalist reading obviously excludes any answer including a categorical imperative. Since one's having a purpose, or end, is typically motivational to some extent, the earlier talk of purposive reasons fits with the internalist reading. Our purposive reasons constitute an explanatorily important part of our motivational sets.

Let us call certain standards of rationality *motivationally cogent* for you if and only if those standards have the power, on the basis of your actual evidential and motivational set, to regulate—to compel or to constrain—attitudes or actions for you. Motivationally cogent standards of rationality depend on motivational reasons, reasons that have a basis in one's actual motivational perspective. Standards of rationality that lack corresponding motivational reasons for one thus lack cogency for one. Such standards are at best arbitrary from the standpoint of one's motivational reasons. The arbitrariness comes from the absence of a relevant difference between such standards and the infinity of other possible standards lacking motivational significance for one. Standards of rationality that rely just on preferences one simply would have under certain ideal conditions will thus be arbitrary at best for one—at least from the standpoint of one's motivational reasons.

Nonarbitrary standards of rationality, according to internalism, must accommodate the motivational nature of reasons for the regulation of attitudes and actions. Suppose that my standards of rationality entail that doing *A* is rational for you even though you have no reason whatever, in your evidential and motivational set, for doing *A*. The claim that doing *A* is rational for you will then be arbitrary at best from your evidential and motivational perspective. An approach to rationality entailing such an arbitrary claim will itself lack motivational cogency for you. Given internalism, reason-based regulation of attitudes and actions requires efficacious motivational reasons. Arbitrary standards of rationality fail to provide such efficacious reasons; they thus fail to supply reason-based regulation by internalist standards.

Nonarbitrary standards for the regulation of attitudes and actions cannot rest just on evidential reasons, reasons indicating that such-and-such is the case. Even if certain evidential standards indicate that you rationally should perform action *A*, you can plausibly ask: Why should I care about satisfying *those* evidential standards? This question will remain open if you have no reason whatever in your motivational set for doing *A*. As just suggested, the claim that doing *A* is rationally required for you will then be arbitrary at best from your motivational perspective; and an approach to rationality entailing this arbitrary claim will itself lack motivational cogency for you. Given internalism, nonarbitrary standards for rational regulation must be sensitive, then, to one's motivational set.

A likely internalist proposal, regarding rationally *required* preference, is: It is rationally required for *S* to prefer action, attitude, or circumstance *X* if *S*'s (acknowledged) evidential and motivational set cannot be satisfied without her preferring *X*. A corresponding internalist proposal regarding rationally *coherent* preference—or what some would call 'rationally permissible' preference—is: It is rationally coherent for *S* to prefer action, attitude, or circumstance *X* if

S's preferring *X* is compatible with the satisfaction of her (acknowledged) evidential and motivational set. A related internalist principle concerning rationally *optimal* preference follows suit: It is rationally optimal for *S* to prefer action, attitude, or circumstance *X* if *S*'s preferring *X* is (an integral part of) the best available avenue to the satisfaction of her (acknowledged) evidential and motivational set. A fourth internalist principle concerns rationally *satisfying* preferences: It is rationally satisfying for *S* to prefer action, attitude, or circumstance *X* if *S*'s preferring *X* is (an integral part of what is) sufficient for the satisfaction of her (acknowledged) evidential and motivational set.

Talk of the *satisfaction* of an evidential and motivational set admits of this explication: One's evidential and motivational set is satisfied by situation *X* if and only if the set's motivational components (for example, one's desires, preferences, and intentions) are fulfilled by *X*, and the set's evidential components (for example, one's evidentially supported beliefs) indicate that one has the former motivational components and that they are fulfilled by *X*. This explication identifies a definite role for evidential as well as motivational components in the satisfaction of one's evidential and motivational set. (Cases of conflicting, jointly unsatisfiable, motivational components require special treatment. An internalist might let an individual's own preferences about the relative significance of conflicting preferences determine priority.)

Some theorists will oppose the internalist reading of our questions on the ground that we need a use of 'should' that shows no automatic sensitivity to an agent's actual purposive and cognitive standpoint. Let us call these theorists *externalists* because they hold that considerations about one's actual motivational set can be external to considerations about one's obligations. Externalists worry that one's actual motivational set might need "correction," relative to what is a "proper" motivational set for one: for example, a motivational set one would have under suitably ideal conditions of information.[21]

Internalists will object that uses of 'should' showing no sensitivity to an agent's actual purposive and cognitive standpoint are too easy to come by. Simply formulate a nonmotivational normative requirement (perhaps involving suitably ideal conditions of information)—*whatever* requirement comes to mind—and then define 'should' in terms of that requirement. We can do this at will, *ad indefinitum*, across a range of idealized conditions. (What level of idealization is the "proper" level, and why?) For each of the stipulated nonmotivational requirements, we get a nonmotivational use of 'should'. This is *the problem of multiplicity* regarding normative requirements that underlies the aforementioned problem of practical relevance.

Barring considerations about sensitivity to an agent's purposive and cognitive standpoint, what can offer, from the agent's standpoint, a judicious means of recommending some of the nonmotivational requirements over the others, for purposes of regulating conduct? An appeal to intuition, I have suggested, will not take us very far, in the absence of answers to troublesome questions

21. For discussion of theories of rationality invoking conditions of suitably ideal information, see Moser and Carson (1992). See also Audi (1985, pp. 428–430) and Gibbard (1990, pp. 18–22).

about when intuitions are reliable and about cases of conflicting intuitions.[22] I know of no epistemology of evaluative intuition that can answer such questions in an explanatorily compelling manner.[23] An appeal to intuitions about actual linguistic use of evaluative terms is especially unhelpful now. At any level of specificity, uses of 'should' can and often do vary.

An appeal to social consensus about the use of 'should' is similarly troublesome. It is doubtful that we could find any significant social consensus about the use of 'should' in the question whether I should (care to) be moral or rational. Even if we could find such a consensus, the relevant use of 'should' might still lack sensitivity to an individual agent's purposive and cognitive standpoint. In that case, why-questions of the sort under consideration would persist, without answers sensitive to what they seek on an internalist construal. Internalists, then, would not be satisfied.

We can relate the problem of multiplicity to G. H. von Wright's distinction between two uses of 'ought'.[24] One use stems from a "norm-authority," such as the will of a commanding agent. The other use stems from certain ends, or purposes, in human action. The former, in von Wright's terminology, is a "deontic ought"; the latter, an ought of "practical necessity." A deontic ought, as von Wright notes, normally rests on an ought of practical necessity. A deontic ought, however, might not be constrained in any way by an ought of practical necessity. It might rest solely on an agent's command, on a prescription that has no basis in our purposive and cognitive set. A deontic ought of that sort is too easy come by; hence the problem of multiplicity. Such a deontic ought only invites further evaluative why-questions.

Suppose that we bar appeal to an agent's purposive and cognitive standpoint in interpreting evaluative why-questions. In that case, according to internalists, an agent will be hard put to select judiciously, for purposes of regulating conduct, from the plethora of nonmotivational normative requirements. One will then face difficulty from the problem of multiplicity, the problem that motivates the general problem of practical relevance.

4.6 Conceptual Instrumentalism

Why should we (care to) be rational in the sense specified by the internalist approach to rationality? An externalist might begin an objection with that question, owing to worries about improper motivational sets. An internalist might reply as follows: Because 'Why (care to) be rational?' questions seek reasons

22. On the problem of conflicting intuitions for intuitionists, see Hare (1989, pp. 104–106, 109–111). Intuitionists are, of course, well aware of this problem. See, for example, Ross (1939, pp. 17–18, 39–40). Cf. Sidgwick (1907, pp. 338–343). They still lack, however, a decisive solution.

23. For contrasting approaches to evaluative intuitions, see Mackie (1977, pp. 38–41) and Boyd (1988, pp. 206–208). Boyd recommends that we regard moral intuitions as a species of "trained judgment," and denies that they have a foundational role in normative inquiry. It is thus doubtful that Boyd would appeal to intuition to solve the problem of multiplicity facing noninternalist standards.

24. See von Wright (1983, pp. 74, 79, 153). Cf. von Wright (1963, pp. 9–11, 100–101).

in one's actual evidential and motivational set, and because one desires to achieve the satisfaction of one's evidential and motivational set, one *does* care about satisfying that set. One thus does care about satisfying the evidential and motivational set providing the motivational reasons that can answer 'Why (care to) be rational?' questions.

An externalist will object to the internalist approach on the ground that it neglects certain normatively important 'Why (care to) be rational?' questions. In particular, an externalist will contend that an internalist has failed to answer why one *should* care about satisfying one's evidential and motivational set. An externalist will deny that we can answer the latter question simply by claiming that one does care to satisfy one's evidential and motivational set. An externalist here uses 'should' in a way irreducible to what one actually cares about, because to the extent that what one actually desires rests on faulty beliefs, one's desires may be faulty as well.

We now do well to give a concise characterization of internalism and externalism about reasons for action. *Internalism*, put succinctly, states that there is a prima facie reason for you to (prefer to) do *A* if and only if your motivational (and evidential) set recommends, explicitly or by implication, that you (prefer to) do *A*. *Externalism*, in contrast, states that you can have a prima facie reason to (prefer to) do *A* even if your motivational set does not recommend that you (prefer to) do *A*. One familiar species of externalism, inspired by Firth (1952), ties reasons for actions to the motivational set one would have if fully informed.

Both internalists and externalists can render the question "Why (care to) be rational?" as "Why should I (care to) be rational?" The difference is that internalists, unlike externalists, hold that one's reasons and rational requirements must have a basis in one's actual motivational set. Internalists will treat externalist 'Why (care to) be rational?' questions as follows: "I do not care about so-called rationality of that externalist sort and, further, I am not guilty of any kind of error in not caring; so I do not see why I *should* care."

Consider externalist 'Why (care to) be rational?' questions that seek reasons not in one's actual evidential and motivational set, but rather in some ideal evidential and motivational set. Suppose that someone knowingly prefers reasons based in an ideal evidential and motivational set, and thus seeks such reasons in asking 'Why (care to) be rational?' questions. Would not such a person be concerned with 'Why (care to) be rational?' questions different from those underlying the internalist approach to rationality? No. The case at issue includes someone who "knowingly prefers reasons based in an ideal evidential and motivational set." That preference is part of the person's actual evidential and motivational set. It thus provides a motivational reason of the sort underlying the internalist approach to rationality. We do not have here, then, a problem for the internalist approach. The externalist needs a different formulation of the objection at hand.

An externalist, as noted, does not demand that requirements of rationality have a basis in the motivational set of the person for whom they are rational requirements. An externalist might claim, for example, that I am rationally required to help my poor neighbors even if nothing in my motivational set inclines me to do so. An externalist could hold that it is irrational for me not to help my poor neighbors, and that I should care about helping them, regardless of my actual inclinations; for, by hypothesis, given suitably ideal information, I would be inclined to help them. An internalist must face such an externalist approach to what we should care about.

An internalist will counter that the main problem with externalism about rationality surfaced previously. According to internalism, an externalist requirement of rationality will be arbitrary, if not simply dogmatic, from the standpoint of agents lacking a supporting reason in their motivational (and evidential) sets. Externalism, in short, does not guarantee motivationally cogent reasons. An internalist will thus charge that externalism itself lacks motivational cogency as an approach to rationality.

Internalism's motivational approach to rationality does guarantee motivationally cogent reasons. It thus avoids the dogmatism and motivational irrelevance threatening alternative accounts of rationality. So long as we shun arbitrariness and dogmatism in standards of rationality, according to internalists, we shall have good reason to endorse an internalist approach to rationality. Externalists will, however, be unmoved. Externalism rests on a notion of a regulative normative reason that does not require actual motivational efficacy.

We are now faced with two different specific concepts of a regulative reason for attitudes and actions. An internalist concept assumes a necessary connection between a regulative normative reason and a motivational reason. An externalist concept disclaims any such connection. We can highlight the difference by asking whether ultimate consistent desires can be mistaken from a rational point of view. Externalists think so, but internalists disagree.

One familiar externalist concept anchors regulative normative reasons in certain moral or axiological facts, rather than in an agent's motivational tendencies. An externalist might hold that such facts determine normative reasons and rational requirements even for a person disinclined to conform to those reasons and requirements. Put broadly, the key issue is this: Is something, *X*, rationally preferable for you because you prefer *X* (or at least prefer something requiring *X*)? Or, alternatively, does the rationality of your preferring *X* depend on the rational preferability of *X* (where the latter is independent of your actual preferences). Internalists answer 'yes' to the former question and 'no' to the latter; externalists give opposite answers. Insofar as internalists and externalists use their respective answers to constitute their respective specific concepts of rationality, they are working with different specific notions of rationality and of regulative reasons. Even if internalists and externalists can agree on some very general, rather vague concept of rationality, their concepts of rationality diverge at a level of specificity. This divergence illustrates evaluative conceptual relativism about notions of rationality.

How, then, are we to decide on an internalist or an externalist concept of rationality? Some philosophers will appeal to our "intuitive," pretheoretic judgments to decide the matter; some others will look for an answer in our "ordinary use" of the terms 'rational' and 'reason'. It is doubtful, however, that either intuitive judgments or ordinary use will settle the matter without variation. Intuitive judgments about rationality and reasons vary significantly among philosophers. Philosophical disputes about rationality illustrate this, if they illustrate anything. Similarly, common use of the terms 'rational' and 'reason' offers no unmixed standard for recommending either internalism or externalism. Common use seems sometimes to favor internalism, and sometimes, externalism. What is common, in any case, need not be universal or unchanging.

Versions of moral realism bearing on rational action typically entail externalism about reasons for action. We should not assume, however, that versions of moral realism are automatically impervious to 'Why (care to) be rational/moral?' questions. Suppose, for the sake of argument, that moral realism is true, and that it entails that *X* is good. Suppose also that I could bring about *X* without bringing about anything bad. I am, as it happens, averse to bringing about *X*. Given moral realism, my aversion to bringing about *X* involves a mistake on my part. Why, however, should I care about avoiding such a mistake?

A moral realist might reply that I should care owing to the truth of moral realism. I could then reply that 'should'—like 'reason'—admits of an internalist as well as an externalist construal, and that I care only about internalist requirements, requirements having a basis in my actual motivational set. This reply illustrates 'Why (care to) be rational/moral?' questions that bear on the requirements of moral realism. A moral realist might insist on the "correctness" of the externalist requirements of moral realism, but even so, internalist 'Why (care to) be rational/moral?' questions challenge the universal applicability of those requirements. Even moral realists must, then, speak to 'Why (care to) be rational/moral?' questions.

Let us consider, in conclusion, *conceptual instrumentalism*: the view that our aims in adopting and wielding the vocabulary of rationality and reasons can cogently recommend an internalist or an externalist concept of rationality and reasons. If we aim to evaluate attitudes and actions from the actual evidential and motivational perspective of an agent, we do well to employ an internalist concept of rationality and reasons. If, however, we aim to evaluate attitudes and actions from a standpoint independent of an agent's actual motivational perspective, we need to use an externalist concept of rationality.

Conceptual instrumentalism bears at most on which concept of rationality we should adopt and use for our evaluative purposes, not on which concepts we understand. Externalists can understand an internalist concept of rationality, even if they prefer not to adopt or to use that concept for their evaluative purposes. We should also acknowledge that a single theorist might use an externalist concept of rationality for certain evaluative purposes, and an internalist concept for other purposes.

The semantic foundationalism of chapter 2 fits with conceptual instrumentalism. Semantic foundationalism acknowledges a crucial role for a notion of justification or cogency in one's arguing for justification or cogency. Conceptual instrumentalism, accordingly, depends on a notion of cogency or justification implying that the suitability of a concept for one's purposes can, and sometimes does, yield cogency or justification for that concept for one. Even if one's purposes can determine what is cogent or justified for one, our affirming this presupposes a relevant notion of cogency or justification that links instrumental considerations with cogency or justification. (See section 2.3 for the details of semantic foundationalism.)

Conceptual instrumentalism directs us to consider the purposive reasons that underlie a typical evaluative conceptual viewpoint. It advises us not to overlook the role of possibly optional evaluative purposes in the adoption and use of different evaluative notions. In short, we do well, in our explanatory efforts, not to take one's purposes out of an account of the evaluative notions one adopts and uses.

Conceptual instrumentalism does not put an end to 'Why (care to) be rational?' questions. It rather explains why certain 'Why (care to) be rational?' questions cease to be bothersome for internalists or externalists. The explanation appeals to the sort of standpoint from which one aims to evaluate attitudes and actions. Internalists and externalists, as suggested, favor significantly different standpoints for rational evaluation. Indeed, internalists and externalists work with different notions of rationality at a level of specificity. In effect, they are thus talking about different matters at a level of specificity.

Both an internalist and an externalist offer a standpoint from which to evaluate attitudes and actions, but they remain altogether unmoved by each other's 'Why (care to) be rational?' questions that seek to identify explanatory shortcomings and theoretical mistakes. The latter consideration supports the hypothesis that different specific notions of rationality are at work between internalists and externalists. In general, one's conceptual commitments are identifiable in terms of the points at which one refuses to acknowledge the possibility of mistake—that is, the points at which there are one's conceptual truths.

Neither semantic nor pragmatic considerations can favor the applicability of a single specific concept of rationality to all conceivable agents. Further, we cannot cogently argue that a particular concept of rationality must undergird everything that qualifies as a *moral* system. One might argue thus on semantic grounds, claiming that it is part of "the concept of morality" that morality requires rationality of a certain sort—or, in a certain sense of 'rationality', for example, impartiality or "impartial reason." This claim appeals straightforwardly to *the* concept of morality, and thus invites a 'Why (care to) be rational/moral?' question analogous to that under scrutiny.

Given a claim that morality requires us to be rational in a certain sense of 'rational', one can plausibly ask why we should care to be moral in *that* sense of 'morality'. Indeed, one might counter as follows: If that is what you mean by 'morality', I care not at all to be moral, in your sense. Here we confront direct analogues, concerning morality, of the previously points concerning internalism, externalism, and conceptual relativism about rationality. The 'Why care?' questions that trouble appeals to rationality have close cousins that are equally troublesome for appeals to reason-based morality.

One might, of course, just stipulate that anyone neglecting certain preferred standards is not really concerned with rationality or morality. Such stipulation does not offer a judicious treatment of typical 'Why care?' questions. An effort to offer reasons by mere stipulation will typically seem merely dogmatic, or at least pointless, from a questioner's standpoint. Mere stipulation cannot, in any case, prevent others from effectively using 'rational' with different specific semantic standards. We thus do well to speak of *our* (potentially optional) normative ideals, instead of "the" ideal of rationality or morality. We can even imagine cases where one's purposive and cognitive set requires neither the exclusion of inconsistent belief under all conditions nor the preference for advice issuing from "full information" or "impartial reason."[25] In such cases, opposing requirements would be subject to 'Why care?' questions that prompt noncompliance and perhaps suggest a charge of mere dogmatism as well.

Conceptual instrumentalism offers one straightforward way to answer questions about which notion of rationality (or of morality) a person should adopt and use. It does not, however, have a monopoly in that field; in fact, that field admits of no monopoly whatever. Given conceptual relativism involving 'should', we must countenance various conceptual standpoints from which answers to normative questions can be given. Instrumental considerations can save us from an "anything goes" attitude to evaluative assessment, but they do not exhaust the field of conceptual options. Such are the wages of conceptual relativism, for better or worse. Some philosophers may clamor for a position less variable, but they are well advised now to save their clamoring for something actually defensible. (Directly analogous points apply to debates involving internalism and externalism about epistemic justification.)

Can an internalist make any dialectical mileage from the observation that externalists aim, or purport, to evaluate actions from a nonmotivational standpoint? This observation will leave externalists unruffled. They can reply that their aim to evaluate actions in a certain manner plays no crucial role in the adequacy of their externalist evaluative notions for normative assessment. Here they can invoke a correspondingly externalist notion of adequacy. We cannot force shrewd externalists, on pain of inconsistency, to be internalists or conceptual instrumentalists. One could, nonetheless, observe the variable conceptual commitment underlying externalism, and note that this commitment does not serve one's own evaluative ends.

In sum, 'Why (care to) be rational/moral?' questions have led us to conceptual relativism, which in turn prompted conceptual instrumentalism as one way to avoid an "anything goes" attitude to normative assessment. Whatever the ultimate fate of such instrumentalism, 'Why (care to) be rational/moral?' questions wreak havoc for nonrelativist approaches to rationality and reason-based morality. Whether realist or nonrealist, those nonrelativist approaches must now explain how we can handle such troublesome questions.

We have seen, then, that conceptual relativism runs deep in matters evaluative, bearing on truth, reasons, and moral obligation. Such relativism speaks in favor of this book's central thesis: Philosophy negligent of the relativity of inquiry to semantic and purposive considerations resembles the unexamined presupposition, being unworthy of acceptance. Let us turn now to physicalism for purposes of testing this book's main theses.

25. On the admissibility of inconsistency of a certain sort, see Wigner (1960) and Rescher (1988, pp. 73–83).

5

Physicalism, Action, and Explanation

Naturalism, construed broadly, states that whatever exists is part of the natural order of things. One common understanding of the natural order implies that whatever is natural is explainable, at least in principle, by the natural sciences. For reasons of methodological unity, many philosophers and psychologists seek to accommodate such naturalism in their explanatory projects.

Naturalized theory of knowledge, for example, now has a life of its own, flourishing in various quarters with different manifestations. One manifestation explains knowledge and justified belief in terms only of such natural phenomena as physical objects, events, states, and processes, and their physical and causal interrelations. This is *ontologically* naturalized epistemology; it receives support from Quine (1969b) and many others. *Natural* epistemic phenomena, on this approach, do not include any mental or normative phenomena that resist, in principle, explanation in terms only of causally interrelated physical objects, events, states, and processes.

Some epistemologists hold that our ordinary, pretheoretical *concepts* (or, notions or definitions) of knowledge and justification are irreducibly normative. This view of epistemological concepts, I have illustrated elsewhere (1989, 1990b), is a matter of philosophical controversy. Such controversy has not, however, hindered efforts to naturalize epistemology. Some proponents of naturalized epistemology aim not for a mere description of our ordinary concepts, but rather for a kind of "explication" that, in the words of Rudolf Carnap, "consists in transforming a given more or less inexact concept into an exact one or, rather, in replacing the first by the second" (1950, p. 3).[1] Aiming for such explication, proponents of naturalized explanations and concepts often introduce conceptual substitutes for various ordinary epistemological and psychological notions needing clarification.

Ontologically naturalized epistemology does not preclude irreducibly normative concepts of knowledge and justification. It is one thing to provide a naturalistic *ontology* for the constituents of knowledge and justification; it is quite another to hold that our *concepts* (or, notions or definitions) of knowl-

1. For a similar approach to explication, see Quine (1960, pp. 257–262).

edge and justification lack irreducibly normative components. Our concepts of knowledge and justification can include components that are not represented by corresponding items in our ontology for the constituents of knowledge and justification.

By analogy, one's concept of ethical goodness can have an ineliminable prescriptive component involving commendation, even if one's ethical ontology implies that all actual instances of goodness are explainable just in terms of sensory pleasure states. Similarly, one's concept of a person might rest on a notion of a (potentially) responsible being, even if one's ontology entails that all constituents of persons are explainable just in terms of our best natural sciences. One's concept of something will exceed one's ontology for that thing in any case where one's concept includes acknowledged *projections* of one's own attitudes: that is, components arising just from one's own evaluations and commitments and not from attitude-independent situations.[2]

In general, a naturalized ontology for something, *X*, does not require a naturalized concept of *X*. A concept of *X*, consisting of constitutive standards for the correct use of certain terms, can include components that lack corresponding items among the constituents of the instances of *X*. A naturalized ontology for psychological phenomena thus does not entail eliminative physicalism, the view that we should eliminate mentalistic and normative vocabulary from our explanatory projects. A naturalized ontology is compatible with reductive physicalism that reduces, but does not eliminate, mentalistic and normative vocabulary. If, as some theorists hold, such an ontology allows for nonphysical properties of physical things, it is also compatible with nonreductive physicalism implying that the mental and the normative nonreductively supervene on, or are determined by, physical phenomena.

We might call nonreductive physicalism "impure ontological naturalism," given its property dualism; and we might call eliminative and reductive physicalism "pure ontological naturalism," given their physicalistic monism regarding properties and things. Ontological naturalists need not, in any case, eliminate psychological and normative vocabulary from their explanations.

Chapter 2 introduced conceptual relativism concerning notions of justification. It questioned the appropriateness of familiar talk of *the* notion of justification. Similarly, chapter 4 favored evaluative conceptual relativism over evaluative conceptual absolutism. Suppose, accordingly, that specific epistemological notions, including specific notions of justification and knowledge, can and do vary among various theorists. Talk of naturalizing *the* notion of knowledge or justification will then be misplaced. We shall then have various notions to consider for naturalization. Some of these notions might include irreducible normative components, for example, a notion of permissibility rela-

2. For discussion of the relevant kind of projecting in connection with philosophical debates about realism, see Blackburn (1980; 1984, chap. 6). David Hume, in his *Enquiry concerning the Principles of Morals*, Appendix I, identified the kind of projecting at issue as follows: "gilding or staining all natural objects with the colours borrowed from internal sentiment."

tive to certain epistemic rules.[3] At least we have no way to preclude this in principle. Some notions of justification and knowledge may be naturalistic, but we should not infer that the notion or all notions of justification and knowledge are naturalistic.

What would it mean to naturalize psychology, including action theory? Does such a project offer any real hope for success? What, moreover, is the significance of these issues for psychological explanation? This chapter answers these questions. It assesses the prospect for a physicalist account of intentional attitudes and intentional actions. Physicalism will end up with troubles on various fronts. In accord with chapter 4, we shall see the importance of variable semantic and instrumental, purposive considerations to explanatory strategies, including those guided by physicalism. Physicalism is now the dominant realist ontology, but loses its bid for a monopoly on psychological explanation when confronted with conceptual relativism and conditional ontological agnosticism. Such is the main thesis of this chapter.

5.1 Is Physicalism Coherent?

Philosophers and psychologists have long aimed to explain semantic meaning and linguistic representation in terms of intentionality. In contemporary philosophy this aim motivates Grice's program (1989) of intention-based semantics. In psychology this aim received support from Brentano (1924), and still plays a considerable role in psychological explanation. Intentionality, as standardly portrayed, is constitutive of psychological behavior that stands in an "aboutness" or "directedness" relation to certain meaningful content: for example, to certain properties, relations, or states of affairs. Similarly, intentional psychological states—such as beliefs, desires, fears, and hopes—are about, or directed toward, certain meaningful content. We believe or fear *that* such-and-such is the case, where the that-clause represents the intentional, or propositional, content of the belief or fear. Intentional states are individuated by their intentional content, at least in much psychological explanation.

In order to maintain the supposed physicalism of the natural sciences, many philosophers and psychologists have tried to account for intentional psychological states in terms of physical facts free of intentional components. These physicalists have tried to specify nonintentional and nonsemantic sufficient conditions for the existence of intentional states, such as belief-states and desire-states. Such conditions would yield a reduction of (talk of) facts about intentional states to (talk of) physical facts. Let us consider whether this project is coherent and plausible.

Lynne Baker (1987) has argued that physicalist psychology of any reduc-

3. Such notions of epistemic permissibility, as chapter 2 suggested, are popular in contemporary epistemology. See, for example, BonJour (1985, p. 8), Alvin Goldman (1986, pp. 25, 59), Pollock (1986a, pp. 124–125), Lycan (1988, p. 128), and Chisholm (1989, pp. 59–60).

tive sort cannot accommodate the needed notion of intentional content. Baker's argument merits attention, as it exemplifies an influential form of argument deriving from Hilary Putnam's (1975) and Tyler Burge's (1986a, 1986b, 1990) anti-individualist, social accounts of meaning.[4] I shall show that physicalism has the resources to escape Baker's argument unscathed. We shall see that physicalism can take advantage of a widely neglected lesson about the possible person-relativity of truth conditions for beliefs. My argument offers a defense of the coherence of physicalism against Baker's objection.

A. An Argument Against Physicalism

A full account of intentional content must specify how such content figures in the determination of truth conditions for beliefs. It must also identify how such content figures in the explanation of behavior.

Baker assumes that a physicalist account of content requires that molecularly identical individuals have the same psychological description. She assumes the following about physicalism:

> (C) Molecular duplicates necessarily make the same contribution to their psychological states: For some level of description in the vocabulary of the physicalist psychology, if a person, *S*, is in a state of that description, and if *S'* is a molecule-for-molecule duplicate of *S*, then *S'* is in a state of that same description. (cf. Baker 1987, p. 86)

This assumption, according to various physicalists, gains some plausibility via a notion of *narrow intentional content.*

A notion of narrow content characterizes intentional content nonrelationally and individualistically: that is, independently of features of a believer's actual external environment, including social environment and external causal history.[5] A specification of your belief-states' narrow content will not make essential reference to the intentional content of other believers. It will be individualistic in that it makes essential reference only to constituent features of you.

A physicalist explanation of behavior can appeal to narrow, individualistic content in such cases as the following: when two people have different external physical environments but similar beliefs; when two people have different beliefs but similar external environments; and when a person has a novel belief,

4. Burge himself (1986b, p. 15) has remarked on the implications of his nonindividualistic approach to meaning for physicalist identity theories. For a critical assessment of the influential arguments of Putnam and Burge on meaning, see Crane (1991). Cf. Wallace and Mason (1990).

5. For a detailed account of narrow content, see Loar (1987, 1988). For critical discussion, see Stalnaker (1990). Stalnaker grants (p. 145) that "something like Loar's conception of narrow content will help to describe and to explain the ways in which our uses of content to characterize the states of mind of ourselves and others are context dependent." We should not assume, in any case, that an account of narrow account must be equivalent to that of Fodor (1987).

say, about a unique personal experience, that is not shared—or even understood—by anyone else in her society. I shall regard a belief's narrow content simply as what a belief means for the individual holding that belief, relative just to the semantic standards of that believer. (See section 3.3 on semantic standards.) I shall also acknowledge a conceptual distinction between what beliefs an individual believer actually *holds* and what beliefs someone or some group *attributes* to that believer.

An account of how psychological states affect behavior must answer this question: *Under what description* does an object of an intentional state figure in explanatory generalizations about the relations between intentional states and their objects and between intentional states and actions? Fodor has answered this question as follows:

> What ["the rational psychologist"] wants is *whatever description the organism has in mind* when it thinks about the object of thought, construing 'thinks about' fully opaquely. So, for a theory of psychological states narrowly construed, we want such descriptions of Venus as, e.g., 'the Morning Star', 'the Evening Star', 'Venus', etc., for it's these sorts of descriptions which we presumably entertain when we think that the Morning Star is *F*. In particular, it's our relation to these sorts of descriptions that determines what psychological type we're in insofar as the goal in taxonomizing psychological states is explaining how they affect behavior. (1980, p. 251)

In short, a notion of narrow content allows for a sort of psychological explanation that is individualistic, or agent-relative.

A notion of narrow content enables psychological explanation to be sensitive to the significance of an individual's internal, subjective psychological perspective. It allows such explanation to abstract from an agent's actual external environment, including social environment and external causal history. This seems crucial for accurate psychological explanation, at least in some cases. Behavior need not be motivated—at least not solely—by completely correct information about the external environment; nor need it be motivated—at least not solely—by socially shared information. Consider, for example, cases where one is motivated by beliefs that either are false in virtue of nonreferring terms or are altogether idiosyncratic.

Psychological explanation of actual human behavior sometimes must, to be accurate to actual motives, attend to individual psychological perspectives. This gives some motivation for a notion of narrow intentional content. Psychological explanation cannot always rely just on causal considerations from social or external environmental factors. In some cases, such considerations do not tell the full causal story about individual behavior, at least not from the individual's own motivational and intentional perspective.

Physicalists promoting narrow content typically accept two theses:

> (S) A belief's narrow content and overall physical context are sufficient to determine truth conditions for that belief.

(P) If S has a belief with narrow content C, and S' is a molecular duplicate of S, then S' has a belief with narrow content C.

(P) is implied by the earlier principle (C). It guarantees that molecular duplicates will have the same narrow belief-content. (S) preserves a central role for narrow content in determining truth conditions for belief. It also acknowledges a role for other factors here, in particular, factors in one's external physical environment. (S) and (P) underlie various physicalist accounts of intentional attitudes.

Baker contends that no physicalist account of intentional content that satisfies (S) will satisfy (P). She considers molecular duplicates with the same physical histories and contexts to illustrate a case where their beliefs can differ in truth conditions. In such a case, given (S), the molecular duplicates will have beliefs differing in narrow content, and thus (P) will be falsified. By contrast, if (P) is satisfied in such a case, then the beliefs of the duplicates will have the same narrow content, but (S) will be falsified. I shall present a streamlined version of Baker's case.

Consider two teen-aged girls attending an embassy party in a foreign land. Call them Ann and Ilsa. Their societies developed independently, but are so similar in environmental conditions that the girls are molecular duplicates. Ann's country speaks American English, and Ilsa's country speaks a language—Venglish—that differs from American English in only one respect: In Ilsa's country 'vodka' designates gin, not vodka. (Expert translators have determined that 'vodka' in Venglish should be translated as 'gin' in English. In all other cases translation from Venglish to English is homophonic.) Ann and Ilsa look at a tray of clear drinks in shot glasses and utter, in English and Venglish, respectively, 'Vodka tastes good'. Ann thereby indicates that vodka tastes good, whereas Ilsa indicates that gin tastes good. They thus say different things, even though their verbal output is homophonic.

The girls acquired their beliefs in similar physical environments. Ann's beliefs about vodka and Ilsa's beliefs about gin originated in training sessions where Ann and Ilsa were shown indistinguishable lifelike paintings of a shot glass filled with clear liquid. The girls' respective teachers, we can suppose, used homophonic utterances while pointing to the paintings. This enables us to suppose that the girls are similar in all pertinent physical, nonintentional respects. They acquired their beliefs in similar physical contexts. These similar physical contexts enabled similar internal physical states for the girls. The girls, then, are molecular duplicates in similar physical contexts.

The girls' respective utterances of 'Vodka tastes good', according to Baker, have *different* truth-conditions. The statement that vodka tastes good does not share truth conditions with the statement that gin tastes good. Given (S), then, and the assumption that the girls have similar physical contexts, their beliefs differ in narrow content. (P) implies that the girls' beliefs do not differ in narrow content because the girls are molecular duplicates. (S) and (P) thus cannot both be satisfied in such a case. On Baker's reading, the foregoing example "suggests that (S) and (P) are not jointly satisfiable because they impose different identity conditions on narrow content; . . . the suggestion is that the intentional and semantic, in principle, may be irreducible to the nonintentional and the nonsemantic" (1987, p. 90). Is this really the lesson?

B. Individual and Socially Shared Truth-Conditions

Baker's argument runs as follows: (1) The girls' respective utterances of 'Vodka tastes good' have different truth-conditions. (2) The girls have similar physical contexts. (3) Principle (S) thus implies that if the girls' beliefs had similar narrow content, those beliefs would have similar truth-conditions. (4) So, given (S), the girls' beliefs do not have similar narrow content. (5) Under these conditions, where the girls are molecular duplicates, (P) will be falsified. This argument represents the gist of Baker's case against physicalism. I shall show that it rests on a highly questionable inference. (One might question assumption (2) in virtue of differing relational features, but I shall let this go for now.)

Differences between the truth conditions of Ann's and Ilsa's utterances for their respective communities do not entail differences between the truth conditions of those utterances for Ann and Ilsa themselves (or for the corresponding *beliefs* held by Ann and Ilsa). The truth conditions of utterances for a linguistic community, as well as the beliefs attributed by a community, are a function of that community's linguistic practices and distinctions. Those practices and distinctions need not be altogether familiar to a particular language-user within that community. The truth conditions of an utterance for an individual language-user need not match the community-prevalent truth conditions for that utterance.

The relevant utterances of Ann and Ilsa will have different truth-conditions *if*, following Baker, we allow those truth conditions to be determined by the general communities that speak English and Venglish. Suppose, however, that those truth conditions for Ann and Ilsa are determined, not by the communities that speak English and Venglish, but rather by nonsocial considerations pertinent to Ann and Ilsa. Individual interpretive commitments, as described in section 3.3B, will serve here. On the latter view, the difference between truth conditions of certain utterances for typical English and Venglish speakers will not require a difference between those truth conditions for Ann and Ilsa themselves (or between the corresponding beliefs held by Ann and Ilsa).

Baker's argument thus rests on a highly questionable inference: an inference from a difference between *socially determined* truth-conditions for utterances of 'Vodka tastes good' to a difference between *individual* truth-conditions for Ann and Ilsa themselves. (One might put the point in different terms, regarding a distinction between truth conditions for social utterances and truth conditions for individual *beliefs*.) A physicalist can appeal to a notion of individual truth-conditions in connection with (S), and thereby block an argument that (P) is falsified in the case of the two girls.

We have no reason to think that the truth conditions of the relevant utterances for Ann and Ilsa must be socially determined. Baker has provided no such reason. Wittgenstein's influential remarks against private language likewise do not provide such reason. They concern mere shareability in principle of language. They thus do not support a requirement of the presence of an actual social context.[6]

We can now identify an important point: When we are talking about truth conditions for a semantic item, we must specify the people for whom they are truth conditions. Even if many people in my linguistic community have conditions *C* as the truth conditions for an utterance *U*, *C* need not provide the truth conditions for *U* for me too. I could very well lack certain information that everybody else has. This could explain why the truth conditions for *U* differ for me and the rest of my linguistic community. Baker gives no reason to reject this crucial point, a point that leads to the demise of her argument.

We have no reason to think, then, that the beliefs of Ann and Ilsa differ in truth conditions *for the girls themselves*. On the contrary, their beliefs seem to have the same truth-conditions, if those conditions are determined, not by other speakers of English and Venglish, but by nonsocial considerations pertinent to Ann and Ilsa themselves. (See section 3.3B for relevant nonsocial considerations arising from interpretive commitments.) A claim to similarity of individual truth-conditions or of narrow belief-content receives support from the fact that the girls apparently lack sufficient information to distinguish the (that is, our) notion of vodka from the (that is, our) notion of gin. (Let us now construe a *notion* as a certain set of standards constitutive of correctness-of-application of a predicate for a person, perhaps a predicate only in a language of thought.)

We can assume that the girls have the same verbal and other behavioral dispositions toward vodka and gin. The relevant dispositional considerations will not enable their distinguishing the (that is, our) notion of vodka from the (that is, our) notion of gin. Nothing in Ilsa's notion of gin distinguishes her notion from Ann's notion of vodka. Similarly, nothing in Ann's notion of vodka distinguishes her notion from Ilsa's notion of gin. What it takes to have gin, from Ilsa's nonsocial psychological standpoint, does not differ at all from what it takes to have vodka, from Ann's nonsocial psychological standpoint. We have no basis for a presumed difference in individual truth-conditions or in narrow content for the girls' beliefs. What Ann believes, then, does not differ from what Ilsa believes, even if two different societies would attribute different beliefs to them.

Baker anticipates the view that Ann and Ilsa have the same belief in terms of narrow content, and replies as follows:

> As the story was told, if either of the girls has the belief ascribed to her, the other has the belief ascribed to her. . . . [A]ny principle that denied both beliefs would seem to be too strong; it would seem to make the following a necessary condition of *S*'s believing that *F* is *G*: for any kind of thing that is *H* and not *F*, there are circumstances in which *S*, without acquiring new information, can distinguish things that are *F* from things that are *H*. . . .

6. On this widely misunderstood matter, see Baker and Hacker (1985, pp. 171–179; 1990), where relevant unpublished-manuscript evidence is presented. See also Moser (1991).

> Clearly no such principle governs belief. If it did, most of us would lack the belief that gold pieces are costly (since most of us are unable to distinguish gold from "fool's gold" without acquisition of new information). (1987, p. 97)

This reply misses the mark. The physicalist need not invoke the questionable necessary condition Baker challenges.

The pertinent requirement for the physicalist is not that we must be able to distinguish actual gold from actual fool's gold. It is rather that we must be able to distinguish the set of satisfaction (or correctness-of-application) conditions for the predicate 'is gold' from the set of satisfaction conditions for the predicate 'is fool's gold'. The latter requirement allows that we may be sufficiently unskilled in *applying* our information to fail in sorting actual gold from actual fool's gold. Baker's reply thus goes awry.

The requirement useful to the physicalist is just this:

> *S*'s notion *N* differs from *X*'s notion *N′* only if *S*'s set of satisfaction conditions constituting *N* differs from *X*'s set of satisfaction conditions constituting *N′*.

If Ann's satisfaction conditions for the predicate 'is vodka' do not differ from Ilsa's satisfaction conditions for that same predicate, Ann and Ilsa have the same notion of vodka. Conceivably, Ann and Ilsa can have a notion of vodka that differs from that of the skilled bartender. Perhaps their notion is somewhat more inclusive, being equivalent to the bartender's disjunctive notion of *vodka or gin*. As described above, their notion *is* more inclusive. That is no real problem, however, so long as we are not testing bartending skills. The important point is that the physicalist need not invoke Baker's implausible principle to claim that Ann and Ilsa believe the same thing.

The assumption that a difference between external social uses of language yields a difference between the girls' beliefs—in particular, between the individual truth-conditions of those beliefs—seems questionbegging against physicalism. The physicalism under dispute entails, as a straightforward component, that no difference between the narrow contents or the individual truth-conditions of the girls' beliefs arises just from differences in external social uses of language.

We might put the point in terms of causal powers: Social relational differences between the girls that do not affect their psychological causal or motivational states do not affect the narrow contents or individual truth-conditions of their beliefs.[7] Social contextual differences will yield a relevant causal differ-

7. On this theme, see Fodor (1987, chap. 2). I see no reason to share Fodor's suggestion that individual, or narrow, truth-conditions are inexpressible. I do hold, however, that in some cases explanation from one's first-person intentional perspective need not agree with social explanation determined by considerations about truth conditions for one's fellow language-users. In particular, psychologically relevant *individual* truth-conditions for a belief need not agree with, or be determined by, *socially shared* truth-conditions for that belief's utterance. Individualism need not, however, favor the inexpressible or the antisocial. It opposes only a monopoly from social explanation

ence between the girls, according to the physicalist, only if a neural difference results between the girls. In that case, however, physicalism is not threatened. The denial of such a view seems to leave us with a highly mysterious view of psychological causation.[8]

Baker can avoid the questionable inference in her argument only by wielding a questionbegging assumption against the physicalism under dispute. A key issue for my purposes has been: In virtue of what can we truly say that what it takes to have gin from Ilsa's nonsocial psychological standpoint differs from what it takes to have vodka from Ann's nonsocial psychological standpoint? If Baker cannot give a plausible answer here, she will lack a plausible basis to support an alleged difference in the individual truth-conditions or the narrow contents of the girls' beliefs. We cannot plausibly appeal to external social uses of language in the girls' respective communities. This would beg a key question against physicalism: the question whether narrow, individual truth-conditions are always socially determined.

Baker might seek a difference in truth conditions for the girls' beliefs by appealing to a notion of "wide" truth-conditions for beliefs. This strategy goes nowhere. Apparently the needed wideness of truth conditions for beliefs, for purposes of Baker's example, comes from external social uses of language. Such an appeal to socially determined truth-conditions is questionbegging now against the physicalist.

A physicalist can plausibly distinguish, at least conceptually, (a) truth conditions of a belief or utterance for an individual believer and (b) truth conditions of that belief or utterance for a certain community of language users. Even if the truth conditions of the girls' beliefs differ for the girls' linguistic communities, the truth conditions of the girls' beliefs for the girls themselves could be the same. I have suggested that they are the same for the physicalism at issue. A proponent of physicalism can construe (S) accordingly.

A key lesson in my defense of physicalism is that truth conditions can be person-relative and person-variable, and should not be understood as necessarily socially determined. The truth conditions of a belief, *B*, for a person, *S*, are determined by *B*'s truth conditions *for S*, and not necessarily by truth conditions endorsed by most of the language users in *S*'s community. *S* need not share the truth conditions for *B* espoused by most members in her community. At least we have no reason to think otherwise. Until we do, there is, as far as Baker's argument goes, no reason to think that a physicalist account of intentional attitudes is incoherent.

A distinction between truth conditions for an individual and truth conditions for a community supports an important lesson about psychological explanation.

8. Cf. Davidson (1990a, pp. 310–311): "There are those who are pleased to hold that the meanings of words are magically independent of the speaker's intentions; for example, that they depend on how the majority, or the best-informed, or the best-born, of the community in which the speaker lives speaks. . . . This doctrine entails that a speaker may be perfectly intelligible to his hearers, may be interpreted exactly as he intends to be interpreted, and yet may not know what he means by what he says. I think this view . . . reveals nothing of serious philosophical interest about the nature of truth or meaning."

We should not confuse psychological explanation, in terms of beliefs and desires motivating an individual's behavior, with sociological explanation. We should be wary of forcing psychological explanation of an individual's behavior into constraints set by social factors. An individual's beliefs need not share the truth conditions of utterances for a community, even the individual's own community. An appeal to a community's intentional perspective to explain an individual's behavior can be quite misleading. Psychological explanation needs to be sensitive to individual agents, specifically to the intentional perspective of individual agents. This means that psychological explanation, in order to provide accurate explanation, needs a distinction between truth conditions for an individual and truth conditions for a community.

C. Physicalism and Reduction

Acknowledgment of the mere coherence of reductive physicalism will not placate the physicalist. Reductive physicalism entails that every intentional state is identical with something physical. It requires the truth of bridge principles reducing intentional-attitude truths to physicalist truths: paradigmatically, the truths of physics and related natural sciences. It requires nonintentional physicalist conditions that are sufficient for intentional-attitude truths.

Physicalists endorsing *type identity* identify each particular *type* of intentional state (for example, belief states) with some particular type of physical state. Proponents of *token identity* hold that each *token*, or instance, of an intentional state is identical with some particular instance of a physical state. Token-identity theorists need not support identities between particular types of intentional states and particular types of physical states. It is misleading to talk of reducing intentional states or properties to physical states or properties. Reductive bridge principles linking physics to psychology, for example, do not reduce states or properties themselves, as if states or properties of an agent were themselves being altered by compression. The reduction concerns vocabulary or statements: in particular, bridge principles reducing (interpreted) psychological vocabulary or statements to physical vocabulary or statements.

Reduction of vocabulary and statements can enable reduction of theories: for example, the reduction of thermodynamics to statistical mechanics and the kinetic theory of matter. Reduction can come from either definition or law. Reductive physicalists need not, however, be eliminative physicalists. They need not deny that there are truths in the language of psychology. Reductive physicalists can acknowledge such truths while holding that they are somehow reducible to physical truths. (Section 5.3 returns to eliminative physicalism.)

Ernest Nagel has criticized talk of reducing properties of one domain to properties of another:

> The conception is misleading because it suggests that the question of whether one [domain] is reducible to another is to be settled by inspecting the "properties" or alleged "natures" of things rather than by investigating the logical consequences of certain explicitly formulated *theories* (that is, systems of statements). . . . [W]hether a given set of "properties" or "behavioral traits"

> of macroscopic objects can be explained by, or reduced to, the "properties" or "behavioral traits" of atoms and molecules is a function of whatever theory is adopted for specifying the "natures" of these elements. (1961, pp. 364–365)

Reduction is not absolute, but theory-relative. It depends on a theory enabling the explanation of one domain by another, whether by definition or by law.

If the support for the explanatory reducing theory comes ultimately from variable semantic and instrumental considerations, the support for the reduction will ultimately be similarly variably semantic and instrumental. Given the conditional agnostic argument of section 1.7, the theory in question will lack support for conceiving-independent truths that is non-questionbegging against ontological agnosticism. The needed support, according to the semantic foundationalism of section 2.3, will come from variable conceptual commitments; and some conceptual commitments, according to the conceptual instrumentalism of section 4.6, can get support instrumentally, from variable considerations about (theoretical) purpose-satisfaction. The variability in such support blunts the ontological edge—the presumption of objectivity—that accompanies many physicalist theories in philosophy. (Section 5.3 returns to this matter.)

Aside from epistemological considerations, many philosophers fault reductive physicalism for failing to accommodate all the psychological truths that need accommodating by their lights. A common objection is that some mental phenomena (for example, the "achiness" of pains) are not nothing but physical phenomena. The objection is that some truths concerning psychological properties are not in fact reducible to physical truths. Such a claim to irreducibility is, however, as theory-dependent as typical physicalist claims to reducibility; for it depends on variable conceptual commitments that preclude reducibility of certain vocabulary and statements to certain other vocabulary and statements. Claims to irreducibility thus lack a sharp ontological edge, an edge that can cut through the agnostic argument of section 1.7. Many philosophers inclined to physicalism have, however, been moved by claims to irreducibility. The result is nonreductive physicalism of various sorts.

5.2 Nonreductive Physicalism and Supervenience

Typical contemporary physicalism, like the seventeenth-century materialism of Hobbes and Gassendi, rejects substance dualism, the dualism between matter and mind as two sorts of substance. Unlike much traditional materialism, contemporary physicalism typically does not entail that there exist only atoms and the void. Contemporary nonreductive physicalism, while shunning Cartesian dualism, countenances two sorts of properties: psychological and physical properties. Nonreductive physicalism can thus acknowledge psychological properties of thinking, believing, and sensing, for example, while disowning mental substances. In this respect, such physicalism is ontologically hospitable without admitting all comers.

Various species of nonreductive physicalism now compete for the best account of mind-body relations. Nonreductive supervenience-relations give life to nonreductive physicalism, making such physicalism popular in certain quarters. Such supervenience relations, by design, prevent psychological properties from being altogether undetermined by physical conditions. They maintain a kind of priority for the physical without sacrificing the reality of the psychological. I shall argue that one influential approach to nonreductive physicalism, depending on certain "global" supervenience relations, faces a serious epistemological problem. This problem has not received due attention from proponents of global supervenience.

A. Global Supervenience

Renewed interest in nonreductive physicalism originates, for the most part, with Donald Davidson's following remarks:

> Although the position I describe denies there are psychophysical laws, it is consistent with the view that mental characteristics are in some sense dependent, or supervenient, on physical characteristics. Such supervenience might be taken to mean that there cannot be two events alike in all physical respects but differing in some mental respect, or that an object cannot alter in some mental respect without altering in some physical respect. Dependence or supervenience of this kind does not entail reducibility through law or definition. (1970, p. 215)

Davidson recommends a brand of physicalism where psychological phenomena somehow supervene on physical phenomena, but where no definitional or nomological reduction holds between the psychological and the physical.

Nonreductive physicalists share Davidson's rejection of definitional and nomological reduction of the psychological to the physical. They divide in a number of ways, however, over the preferred supervenience-relation between psychological and physical phenomena.[9] We need note, for current purposes, only one general point of division. Proponents of nonglobal supervenience invoke property-to-property relations, involving the psychological and the physical, between individuals in just one possible world, such as the actual world. Proponents of *global* supervenience, in contrast, talk globally of various possible worlds to identify connections between psychological and physical phenomena. They thus compare phenomena from different possible worlds, to achieve a nonreductive connection between the psychological and the physical.[10]

Universal global supervenience concerns not just physically possible worlds that are suitably similar to the actual world in some sense, but *any* physically possible worlds with the same physical conditions. (We can proceed with an understanding of a "physically possible world" as any possible world having

9. For detailed taxonomy of supervenience relations, see Kim (1984; 1990a; 1990b, pp. 50–52).

10. Proponents of global supervenience include, with irrelevant variations: Hellman and Thompson (1975), Horgan (1982), David Lewis (1983), Post (1987, 1991), and Papineau (1990).

only laws compatible with the physical laws (known to obtain) in our world.) Appeals to such universal supervenience are popular among nonreductive physicalists, in part because they avoid complications from specifying a kind of "suitable similarity" beyond physical possibility and sameness of physical conditions.[11]

A straightforward, representative principle of universal global supervenience comes from John Post:

> *GS*. Given any two physically possible worlds *W1* and *W2*, if the same physical conditions obtain in both, the same nonphysical conditions obtain in both. (1991, p. 118; cf. Post 1987, p. 185)

To avoid reductionism, Post recommends *GS* on the ground that it accommodates cases where something's nonphysical properties are not determined even by that thing's own physical properties and relations.

Post imagines a case where you come to believe that Saturn's rings contain a certain ammonia molecule called "Ammon." Suppose that this belief of yours is true, even though no causal connection holds between your belief and Ammon. If the truth of your belief is a nonphysical property, then one of your belief's nonphysical properties is determined in part by Ammon's physical properties. A duplicate of your belief, the same even regarding causal and physical relations, would be false in a case where Saturn's rings lack Ammon. So, Post infers, there could be two physically possible worlds, *W1* and *W2*, where your belief that Saturn's rings contain Ammon has the same physical properties and relations, but where it is true in *W1* and false in *W2*. The lesson gathered by some nonreductionists is that a supervenience principle must allow that the nonphysical properties of something can be determined by factors having no specific physical relation to that thing.[12] Hence we have global supervenience principles like *GS*.

We can imagine someone saying that *GS* is conceptually, or analytically, true: true just in virtue of meanings or of how we use the relevant terms 'physically possible world' and 'nonphysical condition', for example. Given certain definitions of those terms, it would be very hard, if not pointless, to dispute *GS*. Nonreductive physicalists, however, do not typically take *GS*, or a like supervenience principle, to owe its truth just to definition, analyticity, or any such merely semantic factor. Many nonreductive physicalists, Post included (1991, pp. 19–23), share Quine's familiar qualms about analyticity, and so would shun any claim to the analyticity of *GS*. Post thus claims of his principle for global supervenience that it "need not be a logically necessary truth but can be contingent (and probably is)" (1987, p. 187).

A troublesome question arises now: If *GS* is not to be recommended as

11. On some of the relevant complications, see David Lewis (1986, pp. 20–27).

12. I shall not pursue the question of what exactly Post and others mean by 'no specific physical relation'. Evidently the relational property of a belief's being held while Ammon exists in the rings of Saturn does not count; otherwise, the two worlds in question would be characterized by different specific relational physical properties.

analytically true, in virtue of what sort of epistemic support can it be recommended at all? What in that case recommends it as a component of an epistemically warranted theory of psychological phenomena? These questions, we shall see, are much more threatening than they seem at first.

B. A Problem for Universal Global Supervenience

Let us begin with a case illustrating that the negation of *GS* is imaginable, or conceptually coherent. We shall then ask whether the negation of *GS* is physically possible, or consistent with the (known) laws of physics. Consider two physically possible worlds *W1* and *W2* where the same physical conditions obtain, but where the following holds: Although the proximate nonphysical effects of the physical conditions in *W1* and *W2* are the same, sameness lapses for the nonphysical effects of the former proximate nonphysical effects. Call the relevant proximate nonphysical effects *first-level psychological phenomena*, and their nonphysical effects *secondary psychological phenomena.*

The physical facts in *W1* and *W2*, we may suppose, are the same and determine (causally, or in whatever sense the proponent of *GS* prefers) the same first-level psychological phenomena. Owing to differing laws of psychological causation in *W1* and *W2*, however, the same first-level psychological phenomena in *W1* and *W2* do not determine the same secondary psychological phenomena. More specifically, in just one of many easy scenarios, psychological events of assenting generate dispositional, or habit-like, belief-states and intention-states in *W1* but not in *W2*.[13] By hypothesis, *W2* does not share *W1*'s laws of psychological causation, notably with respect to assenting. All this seems imaginable enough, with only mild exercise of imagination.

Call the imagined situation *psychologically uniform* at the first level, but *psychologically divergent* at a secondary level. *GS* precludes such divergence in the case of *W1* and *W2*, where the same physical conditions obtain. On what ground can it do this? More concretely, because the denial of *GS* is, as just illustrated, conceptually coherent, what sort of ground have we for thinking it true at all, let alone conceptually true?

GS clearly is less restricted than the following generalization: In any two comprehensive physically possible situations that are suitably similar to the actual world, and include the same physical conditions, the same nonphysical conditions obtain in both. The latter restricted conditional is perhaps innocent enough for most people with mild physicalist inclinations. Even that conditional, however, needs supporting evidence. Talk of "suitable similarity" is, of course, vague, but can be clarified in various ways without leading to the universal generalization of *GS*.[14] As for *GS* itself, it happily avoids vague talk of suitable similarity, but is seriously troubled on other, epistemological fronts.

13. On the dispositional character of belief states and their relation to assenting, see Moser (1989, pp. 13–23).

14. On some suggestions for the needed clarification, see David Lewis (1986, chap. 1). I do not intend to defend the restricted conditional; I shall use it only as part of a foil against *GS*.

GS owes its main epistemological troubles to its unqualified reference to *any* two physically possible worlds with the same physical conditions. The troublesome issues, put succinctly, are: What sort of evidence, empirical or a priori, enables us to generalize, as in *GS*, to *any* two such worlds? Further, what sort of inference pattern can secure such a universal generalization as *GS* on the basis of the evidence in question? Until we have answers, *GS* has no place in a warranted account of psychological phenomena.

I have not shown that my imagined case of psychological divergence at a secondary level is a case of *actual* physical and nonphysical conditions. This point concedes nothing, however, to *GS*. To falsify *GS*, the foregoing example need only provide two physically possible worlds with psychological divergence under the same physical conditions; for *GS* embraces any two physically possible worlds with the same physical conditions.

The pressing questions for proponents of *GS* are: Why are not the imagined *W1* and *W2*, in the case of psychological divergence, physically possible after all? What reason have we to think that some physical law is violated in the case of *W1* and *W2*, given that the same physical conditions obtain in both? These questions now need an answer, for the sake of *GS*. We are, however, without a ready answer, as will become clear. Until proponents of *GS* deliver an answer, we should, at a minimum, pull back on *GS*'s unqualified reference to any two physically possible worlds with the same physical conditions.

The aforementioned case of psychological divergence surely appears to be one of physically possible worlds with the same physical conditions. It seems, moreover, not to violate any known physical law. In the absence of contrary evidence, then, we may proceed with the assumption of its being physically possible.

One might object that my example requires the violation of a principle of the conservation of momentum; for the example gives psychological features a nonredundant role in causal laws. Such an objection will work, however, only given the additional assumption that the physical world is closed, at least so far as we know, to nonphysical causation. This further assumption is anything but obvious. Any view of physical laws that requires this assumption seems epistemically gratuitous at best. Proponents of such an assumption owe us supporting evidence that seems not to be forthcoming. Because much remains unexplained about our thoughts, desires, and actions, as Ernest Sosa notes, "it would be a mere physicalist pretension to claim knowledge of all forces affecting human thought and action, and to suppose that full explanation awaits only the filling of details" (1988, p. 39).[15]

The additional assumption in question seems not to be fitting for the sort of antireductionism that motivates global supervenience principles in the first

15. For further elaboration on this point, see Crane and Mellor (1990, pp. 198–200). Crane and Mellor raise some serious difficulties for reductive physicalism too. They give inadequate attention, however, to Donald Davidson's influential version of nonreductive physicalism, which receives attention later in this chapter.

place. Such antireductionism, as noted before, recommends property dualism: a dualism of physical and psychological properties. It should, correspondingly, acknowledge the real possibility of *nomological* dualism: a dualism of physical and psychological laws.

My main point is epistemic: Nothing we know about the physical world entails that this world is actually closed to nonphysical, psychological causation. Moreover, even if all actual physical events (and even all physical events in physically possible worlds, with the same physical conditions, that are suitably close to the actual world) have their causal powers solely in virtue of their physical features (as Papineau 1990 suggests), we still have no reason to generalize here to physical events in all physically possible worlds with the same physical conditions. In particular, we still cannot get to the generality of *GS*.

An antireductionist might try to deliver epistemic warrant for *GS* by appealing to observed correlations or relations of dependence between certain physical and psychological phenomena. This would amount to an appeal to psychophysical laws of some sort, at least on the plausible assumption that the relevant correlations and dependencies are lawlike. If they are not lawlike, it is quite unclear how they will support a generalization like *GS*. Proponents of *GS* have not, in any case, delivered the needed observed correlations and dependencies. Further, as Kim notes (1989b, p. 42), "where there are psychophysical laws, there is always the threat, or promise, of psychophysical reduction," the last thing wanted by the proponent of nonreductive physicalism. Such physicalism is, as already noted, inconsistent with nomological as well as definitional reduction. There thus seems to be little room for confidence here for the proponent of *GS*.

It will not help to invoke a principle entailing that causal determination must be transitive in such a way that secondary effects must be determined by the relevant physical conditions, determined so as to preclude divergence in the secondary effects. Such a move would be questionbegging now: It would presume the very sort of determination principle at issue. What we now need from proponents of *GS* is a compelling reason to think that causal determination is transitive in the way suggested, across all physically possible worlds with the same physical conditions. The case of divergence does rely on causal determination, but this does not mean that it assumes transitivity in the aforementioned sense.

The case of divergence questions transitivity by considering an alteration in the laws of psychological causation in the two situations *W1* and *W2*, an alteration where the same first-level psychological phenomena in *W1* and *W2* do not causally determine the same secondary psychological phenomena (even though *W1* and *W2* have the same physical conditions). An appeal to such alteration seems fair game, in the absence of a known physical law that precludes it. Proponents of *GS* must now deliver reasons for thinking that there is such a law, a law that extends to all physically possible worlds with the same physical conditions. Lacking reasons for thinking that there is such a law, we should pull back on the generality of *GS*. (Note that my argument does not require that the proponent of *GS* deliver a *particular* physical law that is violated.)

Another likely objection is that I have unjustifiably left proponents of *GS* with the burden of showing that the situation of my *W1* and *W2* is physically impossible. Is not the burden rather on me, the proponent of the criticism, to show that the situation is indeed physically possible? More generally, can we refute a principle of supervenience just by imagining a merely conceivable case where it fails, and then challenging its proponents to identify evidence indicating that a physical law has been violated? Does not such a strategy automatically doom all principles of supervenience? It seems not, even though that strategy does not accurately summarize my actual argument against *GS*.

A principle of supervenience, I have already noted, need not concern all physically possible worlds with the same physical conditions. It does seem, in any case, that the burden is now on proponents of *GS* to show that the case of *W1* and *W2* is not physically possible. We apparently have no violation of physical law in the case of those worlds. Given the assumptions of my case with respect to sameness of physical conditions, however, *GS* implies that there is such a violation. Proponents of *GS* thus must substantiate the assumption of the violation of a physical law. They must produce reason to think that some physical law is violated in that case.

My argument does not construe *GS* to imply that the same nonphysical conditions obtain in any two physically possible worlds. The argument rather focuses on a case where the same physical conditions obtain in two physically possible worlds, but where the nonphysical conditions diverge. Assuming sameness of physical conditions here, along with divergence of nonphysical conditions, we must deny physical possibility if we aim to preserve *GS*.

What, if anything, entitles us to deny the physical possibility of the imagined situations featuring psychological divergence? This is the key question now, the question whose answer seems not readily available. It would be questionbegging to say simply that there must also be physical divergence somewhere between the two situations, or that there cannot be psychological divergence. Evidently, we thus need, at the least, to restrict *GS* to physically possible worlds, with the same physical conditions, that are "suitably similar" to the actual world. I do not pretend, however, to have an account of suitable similarity that gives a compelling alternative to *GS*. My aim is rather to show that *GS* suffers from its own epistemological problems.

It will do no good to recommend *GS* now on the ground that it is initially plausible and contributes to a maximally coherent account of the physical world, or on the ground that it plays a key role in an empirically adequate interlevel theory. We need a defensible answer to my objection before *GS* can be recommended as plausible and conducive to a maximally coherent explanatory account. The objection requires proponents of *GS* to identify the relative merits of *GS* over a more restricted empirical generalization.

In fact, the case of psychological divergence recommends a less generalized supervenience principle, one that begins with talk, not of any two physically possible worlds with the same physical conditions, but of physically possible worlds, with the same physical conditions, that are suitably similar to the actual world. No empirically established interlevel theory seems to preclude the aforementioned case of psychological divergence. At least, we cannot plausibly rely on *GS* now to rule out that case; for *GS* is the principle currently at issue. The epistemological adequacy of any interlevel theory including *GS* is now under dispute. The case of divergence recommends that certain principles less general than *GS* will fare better by way of confirmation. (Even those less general principles will, however, face serious epistemological problems of their own. See sections 1.7 and 5.3B on such problems.)

We can imagine a further relevant case of divergence in connection with the activation-synthesis (AS) model of dreaming. The AS model implies that dream qualia are determined by certain brain processes involving the "REM-on" group of neurons. The evidence for this model comes from certain observed correlations in experimental situations. Post (1991, pp. 132–137) reads the AS model as illustrating the global determination-relation of *GS*: Given any two physically possible worlds, if certain brain processes and other physical conditions are the same in both, then so are the dream qualia, even in terms of their proximate effects. It seems doubtful, however, not only that the AS model illustrates such a general principle but also that the principle in question is epistemically defensible.

The AS model seems perfectly compatible with a determination principle much less general than *GS*, a principle that settles for talk of physically possible worlds, with the same physical conditions, that are suitably close to the actual world. The particular principle in question, moreover, faces a case of divergence analogous to the previous case. Let us keep the brain processes the same across a pair of physically possible situations *W1* and *W2*. Let us keep all the laws of physics and any other physical conditions the same too.

Why, or in virtue of what, would we have physical impossibility, or the violation of a law of physics, if the following were so? In situation *W1*, owing to laws of mental causation *L1*, the relevant dream qualia *Q*, determined by the subvenient physical conditions *C*, bring about throbbing pain. In *W2*, owing to different laws of mental causation *L2*, the same dream qualia *Q*, determined by the same subvenient physical conditions *C*, bring about, not throbbing pain, but unadulterated exhilaration. Keeping the physical conditions the same, then, what reason have we to think that a physical law would be violated? I do not claim that such a case of divergence is actual, or even suitably close to the actual world. I claim only that we have no reason to regard it as physically impossible and that it seemingly fits some physically possible worlds with the same physical conditions.

We can now venture a diagnosis of the problem facing *GS*. The culprit seems to be the attempt to anchor property dualism in physicalism, across *all* physically possible worlds with the same physical conditions. Our known physical laws seem not to exclude all divergence of laws of psychological causation at a secondary level in physically possible cases with the same physical conditions. Given a dualism of physical and psychological properties, and given the possibility of secondary-level psychological laws, our known physical laws do not preserve, across all physically possible worlds with the same physical conditions, the sort of uniformity between the physical and the psychological recommended by *GS*. Property dualism thus resists such taming by our known physical laws. More directly, our known physical laws seem quite consistent with the negation of *GS*.

Lay the blame where you will: on the shortcomings of known physical laws or on the strangeness of possible psychological laws. Trouble remains for *GS* in either case. Secondary psychological properties are untamed by known physical laws, at least in some physically possible worlds including the same physical conditions. Witness the previous cases of psychological divergence.

The key issue is whether the proponent of *GS* can justifiably generalize to any two physically possible situations with the same physical conditions. One might try to get such a generalization by appeal to the transitivity of determination. I have already noted that such a move begs the main question raised by cases of divergence. Such cases raise the issue of why, or in virtue of what evidence, we should acknowledge the relevant sort of transitivity to the psychological domain, in all physically possible worlds with the same physical conditions. We thus cannot challenge cases of divergence by a general appeal to transitivity of determination. The empirical evidence for the AS model takes us at best to all relevant actual experimental situations and counterfactual situations suitably close to those actual situations. We stretch the evidence too far if we move to all physically possible situations with the same physical conditions. A good indication of such overstretching comes from the fact that proponents of *GS* have nothing specific as a challenge to the aforementioned cases of divergence.

The proponent of *GS* might claim that in all physically possible worlds with the same physical conditions and physical laws, the same laws of psychological causation will always obtain. In effect, this claim proposes that laws of psychological causation supervene on relevant physical conditions, including physical laws. Such a proposal is perhaps natural for the physicalist, but it seems not to resolve the real problem at hand. We have no reason whatever to think that in all physically possible worlds with the same physical conditions and physical laws, the same laws of psychological causation always obtain. It seems quite plausible to suppose, after all, that the aforementioned cases of psychological divergence at a secondary level involve physically possible worlds. The anticipated proposal is thus questionbegging.

The previous cases of psychological divergence do not rest on a questionable inference from the mere conceptual possibility of a certain physical possibility to its actual physical possibility. The key contention is rather that, contrary to proponents of *GS*, we have no evidence whatever to support the assumption that the aforementioned cases of divergence do not involve physically possible worlds. Those cases of psychological divergence are, of course, conceptually possible. That, however, is not the relevant point now. The problem for proponents of *GS* is that we have reason to hold, and no reason to deny, that those cases involve physically possible worlds.

GS thus still needs a means of confirmation in light of cases of divergence. It is now doubtful that the needed confirmation is actually forthcoming for *GS*, even if less general principles of determination fare better in the face of physically possible divergence. Given cases of divergence, we might introduce a principle of supervenience that requires sameness of laws of psychological as well as physical causation. We shall then have departed significantly, however, from the sort of supervenience favored by proponents of *GS*.

Property dualism is, then, relatively unruly stuff. It will not always line up with the same physical conditions, in the way required by *GS*, even in physically possible worlds. Should we banish the unruly, or make room for it by retreating from *GS*? The answer will depend on what our theoretical purposes actually are. I cannot pretend to know what they are for all concerned. My contention rather has been that *GS* faces a serious, but widely neglected, epistemological problem. Proponents of *GS* now owe us a way out of that problem. My concern has been not to show that certain laws of psychological causation obtain, but rather to raise doubt about a widely held principle of supervenience.

Nonreductive physicalism, as noted previously, stems from a notion of supervenience proposed by Donald Davidson. Davidson himself has promoted a version of physicalism called *anomalous monism*. An examination of such physicalism in connection with intentional action will reveal some additional epistemological problems for physicalism.

5.3 Physicalism and Action Theory

Psychologists and philosophers often seek to explain individual and social human behavior of various normal and abnormal sorts. One might construe human behavior as mere bodily movement, but this construal would fall short of what psychologists and philosophers typically regard as behavior needing explanation. Psychologists and philosophers often seek explanations that identify the *reasons* or the *purposes* for certain (kinds of) human behavior. In doing so, psychologists and philosophers regard certain forms of behavior as *actions* that are intentional, or purposive, in some respect.

Intentional, or purposive, actions are not mere bodily movements; they incorporate a kind of goal-directedness identified in familiar psychological explanations of behavior in terms of beliefs, desires, and intentions. These explanations specify, among other things, the aim, intention, or meaning of certain behavior. They are thus often called *intentional explanations*. Action theory aims to account for behavior that is intentional in some respect.

If we allow for intentional explanations of human behavior in terms of reasons and goals, our principles of psychological theorizing will be markedly different from the explanatory principles allowed by eliminative physicalism. One key difference is that psychological theorizing will have available psychological notions (for example, those of belief, desire, and intention) that are unavailable to eliminative physicalism. This will entail a fundamental difference in psychological taxonomy—the system of categories for the description and explanation of human behavior. We shall see the explanatory importance of this and other differences in due course.

Ontologically, the naturalizing of action theory is the explaining of intentional action, including reason-based action, in terms only of such natural phenomena as physical objects, events, states, and processes, and their physical and causal interrelations. Intentional action, on such a purely naturalistic ontology, does not consist of any phenomena that resist explanation in terms only of causally interrelated physical objects, events, states, and processes. Naturalized action theory is, in this pure sense, *ontologically* naturalistic. It shuns ontological commitment to phenomena that cannot be explained in terms only of physical phenomena. (Let us not prejudge now the exact conditions for explanation; section 5.3B considers some key conditions on explanation.) Ontological naturalism is, as noted earlier, compatible with *conceptual* non-naturalism, with the use of concepts whose content goes beyond appeal to physical phenomena. We could hold, for example, that every actual object, event, state, and process is physical, but that our epistemological, ethical, or action-theoretical concepts of those physical phenomena include normative or mentalistic considerations.

Actions, for example, might be altogether physical, even if we conceive of them in a way involving normative or mentalistic considerations. Myles Brand (1984, p. 169) evidently suggests conceptual naturalism of some sort, in claiming that "action theory is naturalized by bringing its conceptual basis closer to that of scientific psychological theories." He also speaks of his goal of showing that the "area" of action theory is "continuous" with scientific theory (1984, p. 255). He suggests, in addition, that we can naturalize action theory by giving empirical claims about action epistemological primacy over conceptual claims (p. 199). It is clear, nonetheless, that Brand's characterization of naturalized action theory does allow for "conceptual elements" derivative of mentalistic psychology (p. 236). Brand is not explicit, however, on the previous distinction between ontological and conceptual naturalism. We shall see the importance of attending to that distinction.

We now have two key questions: Can a defensible action theory be ontologically naturalistic? Can it, moreover, be conceptually naturalistic? An affirmative answer to the former question does not automatically answer the latter question. A commitment both to a naturalistic concept of action and to a non-naturalistic ontology for action, however, would seem bizarre indeed. If non-naturalism is not required by our concept of action, why introduce it in our ontology for action? Such an ontology would outstrip our concept of action in a way that seems explanatorily gratuitous.

We might be tempted by a corresponding worry when a non-naturalistic concept of action goes with a naturalistic ontology for action. Why not prune the concept of its non-naturalistic components if the accepted ontology makes do without such components? Perhaps one should, given a preference to let semantics follow ontology. Semantics, however, does not necessarily follow ontology. As it happens, some people have, by their own testimony at least, non-naturalistic concepts of action. For such people, it is an evident fact of the matter that their concepts of action include normative or mentalistic components, regardless of their preferred ontology. Whether they should alter their concept to follow ontology depends on the preferability of the autonomy of semantics relative to ontology. A preference on that matter may plausibly go either way, depending, as we shall see, on one's theoretical aims.

A. Two Modes of Explanation

The potential divide between conditions for an ontology and conditions for a concept suggests a corresponding divide between two kinds of explanation. An ontological explanation of something, in terms of its causally relevant constituents, might be altogether naturalistic, whereas another kind of explanation of the same thing might depart from naturalism.

Donald Davidson has contrasted two modes of explanation for action:

> Two ideas are built into the concept of acting on a reason. . . : the idea of cause and the idea of rationality. . . . One way rationality is built in is transparent: the cause must be a belief and a desire in the light of which the action is reasonable. . . . The advantage of this mode of explanation is clear: we can explain behaviour without having to know too much about how it was caused. And the cost is appropriate: we cannot turn this mode of explanation into something more like science. (1974b, p. 233; cf. 1970, p. 225)

Davidson's proposal is just this: All events are physical, and susceptible (at least in principle) to scientific explanation via strict laws; but events *described as actions* are not susceptible to such scientific explanation. The latter limitation comes not from ontological considerations about the events themselves, but rather from conceptual considerations about how we describe or think of those physical events in action-theoretical terms.

An example will help. Suppose that in a moderate act of "righteous indignation" I send my young daughter to her room for repeatedly mistreating her younger sister. I confidently believe that such mistreating of one's sister is wrong, and firmly desire and intend to prevent it. I confidently believe, in addition, that sending my daughter to her room with a moderate display of righteous anger will reduce the probability of her mistreating her sister in the future.

In accounting for my behavior, an intentional explanation will make straightforward use of claims about my relevant beliefs and desires. It will specify, in particular, my intention to prevent my daughter from mistreating her sister. Such intentional explanation, in terms of beliefs, desires, and intentions, is a common form of psychological explanation. It allows, in the present case, for a plausible distinction between the kind of anger that actually motivates my behavior—"righteous anger"—and various other kinds of anger, for example, vindictive and impulsive anger.

A neurophysiological explanation of my behavior in terms of strict laws would make no claims about my beliefs, desires, and intentions. It rather would account for my behavior in terms of my neuronal or synaptic functioning relative to strict laws and antecedent relevant physical conditions. Such neurophysiological explanation would subsume my behavior under strict laws, and would not describe that behavior in mentalistic terms. It thus contrasts with ordinary intentional explanation.[16]

We have two modes of explanation here, even if the actual events underlying, and described differently by, the two explanations are the same. The way we describe the events in question—as mental or as neurophysiological—will constrain not only the sorts of explanation to which the events are susceptible (for example, intentional or strictly scientific explanation), but also the conceptual relations those events sustain to other events. Mental events, for example, will be conceptually related to certain other mental events, but not to neurophysiological events, at least on ordinary construals of mental events.

Davidson accounts for the explanatory divide as follows: "events are mental [for example, intentional or rational] only as described," and "the explanations of mental events in which we are typically interested relate them to other mental events and conditions," which do not constitute a closed system and thus fail of prediction and explanation by strict laws (1970, pp. 215, 225).[17] In contrast, our scientific theory of physical events, according to Davidson (1970, 1974b), does promise a closed comprehensive system that offers unique descriptions of physical events subsumable under deterministic laws. (A closed explanatory system, on Davidson's understanding, must be free of *ceteris paribus* clauses.[18])

On Davidson's extensional notion of event, all mental events are identical with physical events; hence the *monism* in Davidson's "anomalous monism." To recall the previous example: My righteous anger toward my daughter is identical with physical events, but an explanation of my anger in terms of beliefs, desires, and intentions—unlike a neurophysiological explanation—does not enjoy strict laws free of *ceteris paribus* clauses. Davidson denies further that there are strict psychophysical laws linking mental events with physical events; hence the *anomalous* in his anomalous monism.

Davidson (1985a, 1990b) now emphasizes that intentional explanation is *normative* in a way that scientific explanation is not:

> Whatever is studied, the norms of the observer will be involved. But when what is studied is the mental, then the norms of the thing observed also enter. When thought takes thought as subject matter, the observer can only identify what he is studying by finding it rational—that is, in accord with

16. For an attempt to replace various intentional explanations of human behavior with neurophysiological explanations, see Changeux (1986). Changeux's guiding assumption is that "in theory, nothing prevents us from describing human behavior in terms of neuronal activity" (p. 125).

17. See also Davidson (1974b, pp. 230, 239; 1987, pp. 42, 44; 1990b, pp. 22–26). See Davidson (1991, p. 162) on the view that strict laws, unlike intentional explanations, do not employ causal concepts.

18. On the role of *ceteris paribus* clauses in psychological explanation, see Schiffer (1991) and Fodor (1991).

> his own standards of rationality. The astronomer and physicist are under no compulsion to find black holes or quarks to be rational entities. (1990b, p. 25; cf. Davidson 1991, p. 162)

Intentional explanation thus contrasts with scientific explanation on this point: Our giving an intentional explanation of a person's behavior—by reference to that person's beliefs and ends—requires that we regard that person as largely rational from our own standpoint. If we regard the person as too irrational, according to Davidson, we leave no room for that person's having beliefs, desires, and intentions.

Even in "Mental Events" (1970), Davidson stresses the role of normative considerations in the ascription of intentional attitudes. He claims that "the content" of an intentional attitude (for example, a belief) derives from the attitude's place in a pattern involving other intentional attitudes, and that such a holistic consideration blocks massive irrationality. Thus:

> There is no assigning beliefs to a person one by one on the basis of his verbal behaviour, his choices, or other local signs no matter how plain and evident, for we make sense of particular beliefs only as they cohere with other beliefs, with preferences, with intentions, hopes, fears, expectations, and the rest. . . . Crediting people with a large degree of consistency cannot be accounted mere charity: it is unavoidable if we are to be in a position to accuse them meaningfully of error and some degree of irrationality. . . . To the extent that we fail to discover a coherent and plausible pattern in the attitudes and actions of others we simply forego the chance of treating them as [rational] persons. (1970, pp. 221–222)

Davidson regards this holistic normative constraint on intentional explanation as absent from scientific explanation. On this basis, he concludes that intentional explanation is normative in a way that scientific explanation is not. Even if natural science lacks strict laws, as Davidson (1985a) is now prepared to concede, it differs from intentional explanation on the role of holistic normative constraints. (See the Appendix for discussion of Davidson's views on interpretation and charity.)

The holistic normative constraint on intentional explanation (but not on scientific explanation), according to Davidson (1970, p. 222; 1974b, p. 233), accounts for the absence of strict laws in intentional explanation and of strict psychophysical laws linking the mental and the physical. Strict laws connecting reasons and actions would require what Davidson calls "a quantitative calculus that brings all relevent beliefs and desires into the picture" (1974b, p. 233). Davidson denies that the sorts of reasons appropriate to intentional explanation admit of such calculus. Variability in background beliefs, desires, and intentions offers little hope for strict laws bridging reasons and actions. The pertinence of such background intentional states, on Davidson's view, comes from the aforementioned holistic normative constraint on intentional explanation; it contributes to the distinction between intentional and scientific explanation.

We might treat Davidson's two "modes" of explanation—scientific and intentional—with strict ontological equity: Neither mode is ontologically more privileged than the other. This, however, is not Davidson's preferred line. His anomalous monism, while shunning reduction of intentional vocabulary to physical vocabulary (whether through definition or law), implies that *all* events are physical (1970, p. 214; cf. pp. 211–212), and that the mental supervenes on the physical, but not vice versa (1985b). Such subvenient generality credited to the physical domain gives an ontological privilege to the scientific mode of explanation, a privilege not enjoyed by the intentional mode.

Davidson (1970, p. 212) regards as "trouble" an imagined strategy apparently showing every event to be mental. Allowing for such a strategy—apart from merely heuristic purposes—would, as Davidson admits, indicate a failure to capture a widely held notion of the mental: a notion according to which not all events are mental. Still, we might grant that every physical event can be given a coincidental mental description. For example, a certain event of electron emission is "the event that occurred while I thought of fish jumping in Lake Michigan." This suggests a kind of coincidental-description parity for events, but it does not translate into ontological parity. Physical events, according to anomalous monism, still provide the general subvenient basis for mental events.

Davidson holds, as noted, that events are intentional *only as described* (1970, p. 215), but that all events are physical. At the same time, Davidson claims that "physical events are those picked out by descriptions or open sentences that contain only the physical vocabulary essentially" (1970, p. 211). We might take this to suggest the corresponding view that events are physical, too, only as described. Clearly, however, not all events are actually described as physical, just as not all events are actually described as intentional. In fact, some events are described neither in physical nor in intentional terms, but only in topic-neutral terms (for example, as occurring at a certain time); and some, if not most, events are evidently not described at all.[19] Davidson thus cannot plausibly hold that all events are physical because they are all actually described as such, while only some events are intentional because only some are described as such. If Davidson were to hold that events are physical only as actually described, he clearly would have to give up his monistic view that all events are physical.

We cannot profitably clarify Davidson's phrase 'only as described' to mean 'only as describable'. Davidson, however, seemingly takes such a line:

> . . . in my view the mental is not an ontological but a conceptual category. Mental objects and events are at the same time also physical, physiological, biological and chemical objects and events. To say of an event, for example an intentional action, that it is mental, is simply to say that we can describe it in a certain vocabulary—and the mark of that vocabulary is semantic intentionality. (1987, p. 46)[20]

19. On topic-neutral terms, see Smart (1959) and Cornman (1971, chap. 1).

20. Cf. Davidson (1990b, p. 18): "The mental and the physical share *ontologies*, but not, if I am right, classificatory *concepts*."

Given the ambiguity of the modal term 'can', we need to clarify a bit.

The claim cannot plausibly be that events are intentional only as it is *logically* or *causally* possible to describe them as such. With regard to a sufficient condition, such mere possibilities of description clearly do not determine actual intentionally featured events; those mere possibilities apply to many events that are not properly called "intentional." An appeal, moreover, to those mere possibilities as setting a necessary condition on intentional events does no distinctive explanatory work concerning intentional events. Mere logical possibility of intentionalistic description indicates no distinctive feature of the intentional; mere causal possibility of such description has the same defect. We need only consider the various purely physical, nonintentional events that logically or causally could be described (erroneously) in intentional terms—say, with the help of animism.

Perhaps we should consider an *epistemic* modality: Events are intentional only as it is epistemically justifiable for us to describe them as such. This would be a sort of verificationist nonrealism about the intentional, a sort of nonrealism that Davidson does not explicitly endorse for the physical. We thus would still have a questionable asymmetry. Such an appeal to justifiability, moreover, does not have real explanatory value now; for a key issue concerns the conditions under which we can justifiably regard events as intentional, if we actually can at all.

A directly analogous point applies to an alethic construal: Events are intentional only as we can *correctly* describe them as such. We need to know what constitutes the correctness of intentional description, and whether such description is ever actually correct. Short of a questionable ontological asymmetry, then, Davidson's position on the description-dependence of events does little to enlighten.[21]

Davidson's previous remark that "the mental is not an ontological but a conceptual category" fosters the idea of an ontological asymmetry in his view of events. Nowhere does he disown the physical as an ontological category, and call it just a "conceptual" category. In fact, his monistic physicalism rests on the ontological view that all events are physical. Barring that view, physicalism loses its ontological bite.

In contrast with Davidson's seemingly asymmetrical view, ontological equity for the physical and the intentional could hold in either of two ways. First, we could say that even apart from our descriptions, some events are intentional and some physical. This view denies Davidson's thesis that events are intentional "only as described"; it gives equal language-independence to intentional events and physical events. Second, we could say that apart from our descriptions, events are neither intentional nor physical, but neutral between those two categories. This view implies that events are physical as well as intentional only as described. Such a view suggests a Spinozistic neutral identity-theory of the mind-body relation.

21. For further worries on this score, see Johnston (1985, pp. 411, 420–421).

The mind and the body, on a broadly Spinozistic view, are one and the same thing (or set of events) described in different ways: as having mental properties under one description, and as having physical properties under another description. If description-dependence is necessary and sufficient for nonrealism about properties (where a property is description-dependent if and only if it depends for its existence on its being described), the second view entails nonrealism about physical and intentional properties, and the first view entails realism about such properties. If Davidson acknowledged description-dependence for both the physical and the intentional, he would be very close to a Spinozistic neutral identity-theory, but not to monistic physicalism as standardly conceived.

Davidson's seemingly asymmetric view suggests nonrealism about intentional events (that is, events as intentional), but not about physical events—at least if description-dependence is necessary and sufficient for non-realism. As such a concern about realism and nonrealism is undeniably ontological, we may say that Davidson gives an ontological significance to scientific and physical explanation that he does not give to rational and intentional explanation. Physical explanation, on a natural reading of his monistic physicalism, relates us to description-independent subvenient physical events, whereas intentional explanation relates us to description-dependent supervenient intentional events.

If description-independence marks the genuinely ontological, and description-dependence the conceptual, we may return to the previous distinction between ontology and concept. Given that distinction, we may say that physical rather than intentional explanation determines Davidson's ontology for events, whereas intentional explanation (as intentional) delivers only conceptual, nonontological considerations. In short, intentional features as intentional, being description-dependent, are purely conceptual phenomena, lacking a life, in our ontology, among description-independent events.

We may regard Davidson as finding intentional components in our concept of reason-based action, but as ridding such components (as intentional) from our ontology for description-independent events. Holding that all events are physical, Davidson offers a naturalized ontology for action theory. Endorsing the irreducibility of intentional description to physical description, however, Davidson (1987, p. 46) offers a non-naturalistic concept of intentional action. We thus have one-sided, rather than strict, naturalism: naturalism regarding our ontology for action, but not regarding our concept of action.[22]

Intentional explanation, given its lack of ontological footing (as intentional) on Davidson's view, seems to need some special justification. Clearly, Davidson does not favor eliminative physicalism (1985c, pp. 244–245). He does not recommend that we dispense with intentional explanation and mentalistic vocabulary.

How does intentional explanation earn its keep, failing as it does to deal in description-independent events? Davidson does recommend it for its relative

22. Such one-sided naturalism has been proposed also by Bishop (1989, pp. 177–178, 189).

ease of explanation, for enabling explanation without detailed knowledge of complex physical causes of actions (1974b, p. 233). In short, it yields explanation with comparatively little epistemic toil over the actual physical and causal details. This sounds somewhat like the condoning of epistemic laziness and mediocrity, or like settling for cutting corners over careful and thorough explanatory toil. Eliminativists, anyway, will be tempted to object thus. We need not, however, accept such a harsh judgment. Instead, we can appeal, as we shall see, to the instrumental constraints on any suitably well-defined mode of explanation.

B. Physicalism and Explanatory Strategies

A mode of explanation is just a strategy for explanation, for answering certain explanation-seeking questions: typically certain why-questions, how-questions, and what-questions. A well-defined strategy for explanation, like any well-defined strategy, must include certain ends and certain acceptable means, or standards, for achieving those ends. The phenomena selected as needing explanation may or may not be description-dependent; this does not affect the relevance of the aforementioned requirements for a well-defined explanatory strategy.

Whatever explanatory goals and means, or standards, one accepts, one will have to accept a semantically significant vocabulary—a *conceptual apparatus*—for formulating those goals and standards. This conceptual apparatus will also play a crucial role in formulating acceptable explanatory hypotheses. A conceptual apparatus provides a domain of discourse pertinent to an explanatory strategy. It consists of an acceptable (interpreted) vocabulary or at least general criteria for the kind of vocabulary pertinent to an explanatory strategy. Lacking such a conceptual apparatus, an explanatory strategy could proceed with virtually *any* vocabulary, however disparate and disjoint. It could, for example, explain the same phenomena by employing vocabulary from quantum theory, Babylonian theology, Freudian psychology, and voodooism—perhaps even all in one convoluted explanation. Well-defined explanatory strategies seek a kind of explanatory unity that disallows such an "anything goes" approach to explanation.[23]

The general explanatory strategy in the natural sciences—for example, physics, chemistry, and biology—is relatively well-defined, although not algorithmic. It includes, at any given time, a conceptual apparatus and a set of explanatory ends and standards that exclude an "anything goes" approach to explanation. For example, this explanatory strategy excludes natural-scientific explanation of physical phenomena by voodooism and Babylonian theology. (This explains why such publications as *Science* and *Scientific American* are relatively free of voodooism and Babylonian theology.)

23. On unification as a fundamental goal of scientific explanation, see Friedman (1974) and Kitcher (1981, 1989).

An explanatory strategy is individuated by its conceptual apparatus and its explanatory ends and standards. If you make sufficient changes in the conceptual apparatus or the explanatory ends and standards, you thereby change the explanatory strategy. The natural sciences, on this approach to individuation, represent one general explanatory strategy, and intentional explanation another. The intentional vocabulary of the latter, with its talk of beliefs, desires, reasons, and goals, is significantly different from the vocabulary of the natural sciences. The natural sciences will not settle for explanation in such intentional vocabulary; this is part of what makes them *natural* sciences.

Events, as noted earlier, can be described in ways neutral between differing explanatory strategies. Such descriptions are typically rather uninformative, but enable us to speak intelligibly of two explanatory strategies bearing, at least potentially, on the same phenomena—for example, the phenomena described previously in intentional terms as my showing righteous anger toward my daughter. In particular, we can speak topic-neutrally of certain events occurring at a certain time that are explainable—at least in principle—by both natural-scientific and intentional strategies.

Can both a natural-scientific strategy and an intentional strategy, if they are truly independent of each other, fully explain the same phenomena? If, following Davidson (1963, 1991), we take intentional explanation to include a causal component, we must confront an apparent problem. Jaegwon Kim has argued that "two or more complete and independent [causal] explanations of the same event or phenomenon cannot coexist" (1989a, p. 89). His "simple argument for explanatory exclusion for causal explanations" runs as follows:

> Suppose that *C* and *C** are invoked as each giving a complete explanation of *E*. Consider the two questions: (1) Would *E* have occurred if *C* had not occurred? and (2) Would *E* have occurred if *C** had not occurred? If the answer is a "yes" to both questions, this is a classic case of overdetermination, and . . . we can treat this case as one in which either explanation taken alone is incomplete, or else exempt all overdeterminative cases from the requirement of explanatory exclusion. If the answer is a "no" to at least one of the questions, say the first, that must be because if *C* had not occurred, *C** would not have either. And this means that . . . the two explanations are not independent explanations of *E*. (1989a, p. 92)

Kim holds, then, that two complete independent causal explanations of the same thing exclude each other.

Let *E* be some event or set of events described topic-neutrally—for example, "this event occurring right now." By way of a concrete example, we might let *E* be the events described topic-neutrally that were described earlier in intentional terms as my showing righteous anger toward my daughter. Let *C* be a causal intention-based explanation of *E* from an intentional strategy, an explanation in terms of my beliefs, desires, and intentions. Let *C** be a causal and physical explanation of *E* provided by a natural-scientific strategy—say, an explanation in neurophysiological terms that does not appeal to my beliefs, desires, or intentions. Let us suppose also that we have no definitional or nomological reduction between *C*'s explaining *E* and *C**'s explaining *E*. In this respect, we have independent explanations. The issue, in brief, is whether these two explanations, if complete, are copossible.

If we accept both an intentional strategy and a natural-scientific strategy for explaining *E*, we should answer *yes* to Kim's questions (1) and (2). We then have, from the standpoint of the two strategies we accept, a case of causal and explanatory overdetermination. Kim (1989a, p. 91) evidently holds that any explanation that would fail to mention either of the two causes in such a case of overdetermination would fail to give the full causal picture, and so would be an incomplete explanation. Kim suggests by implication, then, that neither the intentional strategy nor the natural-scientific strategy is here complete. Construed thus, Kim's condition for completeness apparently provides a way for us to maintain both an intentional and a natural-scientific explanatory strategy.

The price paid is that neither an intentional nor a natural-scientific strategy will be complete for us. This, however, is a very small price, if it is a price at all. The lack of completeness for each accepted strategy will only be relative to the applicability of a different explanatory strategy accepted by us. Such relative lack of completeness takes nothing away from an individual explanatory strategy considered from its own standpoint. It rather indicates simply that different explanatory strategies are accepted by us, and are applicable to the same phenomena needing explanation. This is no theoretical defect at all for an explanatory strategy. It is simply an indication of the fact that a theorist can use diverse accepted explanatory strategies for the same phenomena (neutrally described). These considerations, furthermore, do not exclude the possibility of one's identifying empirical correlations between events as intentionally described and events as physically described.

Kim's stated concern is this: "Two explanations of one event create a certain epistemic tension, a tension that is dissipated only when we have an account of how they, or the two causes they indicate, are related to each other" (1989a, p. 92). Our two explanatory strategies for *E* relate to each other as follows: They differ by way of conceptual apparatus, wielding irreducibly different vocabularies, and thus are independent of each other. At the same time, they are not complete for us in the sense at issue, as they both are accepted by us and apply to the same phenomena described topic-neutrally. That is, they answer explanation-seeking questions about the same phenomena described topic-neutrally. On my construal of Kim's standards for avoiding epistemic tension, these considerations save us from explanatory exclusion by removing the "epistemic tension."

Kim applies his standards for explanatory exclusion in a curiously different manner. For example:

> The explanatory exclusion principle provides a simple explanation of why the two theories [for example, "vernacular psychology" and "neuroscience"] . . . compete against each other and why their peaceful coexistence is an illusion. For vernacular psychology and neuroscience each claim to provide

> explanations for the same domain of phenomena, and because of the failure of reduction in either domain, the purported explanations must be considered independent. Hence, by the exclusion principle, one of them has to go. (1989a, p. 101)

Kim adds, by way of proposed reconciliation, that the way to save vernacular, or intentional, psychology is to focus on its normative role in evaluating actions, and to stop regarding it as a competitor to neuroscience that generates law-based causal explanations and predictions (1989a, p. 106).

Kim's position here is uncompelling on both points. The argument just quoted is invalid by Kim's own standards. Explanatory independence is not sufficient, but only necessary, for explanatory exclusion. Explanatory completeness, on Kim's account, is also necessary for explanatory exclusion. Kim's argument fully neglects this decisive consideration. Kim, furthermore, has provided no reason whatever to assume that intentional psychology and neuroscience are complete in the relevant sense. Many of us accept intentional psychology and neuroscience as explanatory strategies for the same phenomena, neutrally described. We thus can, and would, plausibly answer yes to Kim's questions (1) and (2) concerning causal overdetermination. We can plausibly deny, then, that intentional psychology and neuroscience are each complete in the relevant sense.

A denial of individual completeness for intentional psychology and neuroscience gains plausibility once we acknowledge the *relativity* of the completeness of an explanation. Neither intentional psychology nor neuroscience is complete, in the relevant sense, if we accept an explanatory perspective, or strategy, relative to which each of those explanatory approaches leaves some explanation-seeking questions unanswered. Intentional psychology raises certain explanation-seeking questions—for example, concerning beliefs, desires, and intentions—that are not accommodated at all by neuroscience; neuroscience does not offer explanations in the language of beliefs, desires, and intentions. If, for example, you seek an explanation of what sort of anger I showed toward my daughter—for example, vindictive, impulsive, or corrective anger—neuroscience will fail to offer a relevant explanation.

Similarly, neuroscience raises certain explanation-seeking questions—for example, concerning neuronal or synaptic functioning and other neurophysiological factors—that are not handled by intentional psychology; intentional psychology does not trade in the language of neuroscience. If, for example, you seek an explanation of the neuronal-synaptic functioning in my brain while I display anger toward my daughter, intentional psychology will not serve your purpose.

As for Kim's proposed reconciliation, we should hesitate to relinquish intentional psychology as a basis for predictions and causal explanations. Many of us have found considerable success in using intentional psychology to predict and to give causal explanations of various phenomena.

Let us consider a specific case involving the following phenomena needing explanation:

(a) At 8:30 A.M. of every Tuesday and Thursday between January 15 and May 1, at least twenty students and I converge on Room 123 of Dumbach Hall of Loyola University of Chicago.
(b) The students carry with them copies of two recent books on cognitive psychology and epistemology, Howard Gardner's *The Mind's New Science* and Stephen Stich's *The Fragmentation of Reason.*
(c) From 8:30 to 9:45 A.M., the students and I utter sentences employing the vocabulary of cognitive psychology and epistemology.
(d) At 9:45 A.M., the students and I depart from Room 123 of Dumbach Hall.

We can describe these phenomena in terms that are more obviously topic-neutral; this would not affect the point at issue.

I am now able to explain and to predict such phenomena as (a) through (d) only by relying on an intentional explanatory strategy. (I suspect the same is true of you too.) In particular, I now must rely on an explanation in terms of the beliefs, desires, and decisions of my students and myself. My students desire to earn a university degree, typically a B.A. degree, and I desire to help in providing the means. My students and I believe that by meeting at the specified time to discuss the philosophical foundations of cognitive psychology, we can contribute to their fulfilling the degree requirements. My students and I have decided (that is, have settled on the plan) that we will contribute to fulfilling the degree requirements by, among other things, meeting at the specified time to discuss cognitive psychology. We have not made any conflicting decisions that override the former decision. As a result of such factors, according to my intentional explanation, phenomena (a) through (d) are realized.

My intentional explanation thus gives causal efficacy to such intentional phenomena as believing, desiring, and deciding. It appeals to such phenomena to explain the *bringing about* of certain events represented by (a) through (d). Without appeal to such phenomena, I would be altogether unable to explain and to predict the events in question. That is a fact partly about me, but it is nonetheless, so far as I can tell, a fact of the matter. In addition, it is doubtful that anyone could now explain or predict the events represented by (a) through (d) solely on the basis of contemporary natural science or neuroscience. Kim's proposal for reconciliation thus would evidently have us relinquish our best available explanation and predictive basis of the events in question. This is a proposal with an obvious explanatory loss and no corresponding benefit.[24]

Suppose that I accept that neuroscience, in addition to intentional psychology, can (at least in principle) explain the events represented by (a) through (d), and that its explanations are altogether nonintentional. In this case, neither neuroscience nor intentional psychology would be complete for me in the rele-

24. For more support for the explanatory value of intentional psychology, see the significantly different approaches of Fodor (1987, chap. 1) and Dennett (1987, chaps. 2, 3). Whereas Fodor is a realist, Dennett (1987, pp. 39, 53, 72; 1991, pp. 460–462) flirts with instrumentalism and verificationism. See also Horgan and Woodward (1985). Searle (1992, pp. 58–63) supports a phenomenological realist approach that is questionable in the light of section 1.7.

vant sense. This consideration, however, takes nothing away from the explanatory value of either strategy. It simply indicates that I accept different explanatory strategies applicable to the same phenomena (neutrally described).

My approach to completeness, as noted earlier, acknowledges a relativity to the strategies accepted (or perhaps used) by an explainer or group of explainers. An eliminativist who rejects intentional explanatory strategies might accept (or use) only a natural-scientific strategy, and no alternative strategy. Such an eliminativist would have a very difficult time explaining many macro-aspects of our daily lives. Even so, the natural-scientific strategy would be complete, at least in principle, for the eliminativist who accepts (uses) no alternative strategy. Kim's own understanding of completeness might not acknowledge such relativity, but in this regard, it is obscure on the exact conditions for completeness.

Kim appeals to "the answer" to his questions (1) and (2). We have, however, no reason to endorse such a singular thing as "the answer" here. Answers about overdetermination will come from different theorists and may vary accordingly. A theoretically useful notion of completeness—one that can help to explain how people actually theorize and should theorize, given their own explanatory ends—must acknowledge such relativity.

How can we sustain relativism about completeness? I referred earlier to *instrumental* constraints on explanation; appeal to such constraints can do much explanatory work now. We can plausibly assume that no single explanatory vocabulary or conceptual apparatus is required of us simply by topic-neutral events needing explanation. In this respect, explanatory vocabularies are optional from the standpoint of the topic-neutral events. In particular, relative to the description or the explanation of events represented by (a) through (d), neither an intentional nor a natural-scientific conceptual apparatus is required of us. Neither an intentional nor a scientific explanatory strategy is mandated by those events themselves, neutrally described.

Kim (1990b, pp. 48–49; 1991, pp. 58–60) worries about the dualism arising from any solution to his exclusion problem implying that intentional explanation and neuroscientific explanation do not share the same explanandum. If we are committed to some phenomena that cannot be explained in terms of physical causes, and other phenomena that can be physically explained, we shall be committed to a dualism of causes and explanations. Such dualism, as Kim suggests, will trouble many philosophers with physicalist inclinations.

Here we do well to recall the distinction between (a) events described topic-neutrally and (b) events described in the vocabulary of an intentional or neuroscientific explanation. My talk of neutrally described events being subject to intentional and neuroscientific explanations is talk of events of one kind: events neutrally described. These are not events described as intentional or as physical. As neutrally described, however, some of these events can be explained intentionally and neuroscientifically, even though they do not then require by themselves either kind of explanation.

When we invoke an intentional and a neuroscientific causal explanation for the same events neutrally described, we thereby acknowledge a dualism of causes and explanations. This dualism is, however, a dualism of items *as described*, not (necessarily) a dualism of items *in themselves*. Commitment to a dualism of items as described should bother nobody committed to using both intentional and neuroscientific causal explanations. The underlying issue of how the pertinent events are *when undescribed* enjoys, in light of section 1.7, no effective answer from us, given the human cognitive predicament.

It will not help now to invoke Kim's explanatory realism, according to which we can evaluate explanations and explanatory strategies by their support from "good reason" or from such "objective criteria as accuracy and truth" (1989a, p. 95). Without denying that there can be coherent objectivist, nonrelativist definitions of truth (on which see Moser 1989, pp. 23–35), we should acknowledge (as did chapters 2 and 4) that epistemic standards defining what in general we may affirm as true, or what in general is supported by good reason, can and do vary among strategies. Such epistemic standards, moreover, are not required of us by the topic-neutral events needing explanation. Alternative sets of epistemic standards can and do coexist with such events.

Realists seeking an objective basis for evaluating explanations are troubled on additional fronts, as section 1.7 shows. We thus have the following question about the explanatory realist's favorite bases: What non-questionbegging reason have we to think that either (a) our cognitive processes such as memory or perception, (b) predictive theoretical success relative to experience, or (c) inference to the best explanation relative to experience provides an accurate indication of the nature of conceiving-independent events?

Realists have not yet delivered the needed non-questionbegging reason. It is doubtful that we shall ever get such a non-questionbegging reason, given the human cognitive predicament noted in section 1.7. It is thus doubtful, as well, that the realist's needed "objective" standard is actually forthcoming. We cannot plausibly assume, then, that an appeal to "good reasons" is suitably objective, or non-questionbegging, for the realist's purpose. Such an appeal seems not to give us a truly strategy-independent, non-questionbegging perspective of the sort needed for a realist, or objectivist, justification of an explanatory strategy.

Davidson, as noted previously, distinguishes scientific and intentional explanation on two points. Scientific explanation allegedly enjoys explanation by strict laws in a way that intentional explanation does not; intentional explanation allegedly is normative in a way that scientific explanation is not. It is highly doubtful, as noted by Hempel (1988) and Suppes (1985), that explanation in the natural sciences actually proceeds via strict laws. Overlooking this matter, however, we cannot plausibly rely on Davidson's two points of distinction to award scientific explanation ontological superiority over intentional explanation, with regard to the acquisition of objective knowledge. Use of a scientific explanatory strategy, however strict and non-normative, is nonetheless constrained by the human cognitive predicament noted earlier. Even if we aspire to explanation via strict laws, we still are without the sort of effective epistemic reasons required to undercut the argument of chapter 1.

We are not left now with an "anything goes" relativism concerning explanatory strategies. We can still acknowledge perspectival semantic and instrumental constraints on explanation, and even evidential constraints that are similarly perspectival. We can still say at times, for example, that one of two explanatory strategies is better, preferable, or even more reliable than the other. Such an evaluative judgment must be understood, however, as depending on certain perspectival standards for betterness, preferability, or reliability—rather than on what Kim and various other realists regard as truly "objective criteria." The relevant perspectival standards can and do vary among explanatory strategies; and we have no effective reason to think that they are required of us by any (neutrally described) events needing explanation. Their being perspectival stems from their being optional, so far as we can tell, apart from certain semantic commitments and explanatory ends some of us have. (On the specific role of such commitments and ends, see section 2.3 on semantic foundationalism and section 4.6 on conceptual instrumentalism.)

Perspectival constraints on explanation ultimately signify, when queried, a theorist's explanatory ends and accepted standards for achieving those ends—both of which, as noted, come with a preferred vocabulary. If you are a thoroughgoing eliminative physicalist who does not share the explanatory ends that give explanatory value to an intentional strategy, I cannot convince you of that strategy's explanatory value. I then have no common ground from which to argue cogently by your lights. Still, I might contend that your explanatory strategies are more restrictive than mine, or that they fail to provide for my broader explanatory ends.

We have no effective basis for thinking an eliminativist strategy to be ontologically more privileged than an intentional strategy, or conversely. Ontological privilege, objectively construed, loses footing after the recognized absence of non-questionbegging reasons for claims to conceiving-independent facts. Given the argument, of chapter 1, we should stop recommending or shunning explanatory strategies on ontological grounds, as if those grounds enjoyed non-questionbegging support. Variable end-dependent reasons are our only wherewithal in the evaluation of explanatory strategies. In this sense, our explanatory strategies and evaluations are ultimately perspectival and instrumental. Where does this leave psychological explanation?

C. Return to Action

My instrumental approach to explanation has obvious implications for attempts to naturalize action theory. Ontological naturalization for the constituents of action is an important project for theorists committed to a natural-scientific explanatory strategy. I aim not to gainsay that strategy, at least not with respect to nonontological effectiveness. The use of that strategy enables us to meet many of our theoretical and practical ends, and even results in our having new ends. These platitudes, however, should not tempt us to attribute ontological privilege to a natural-scientific strategy, as Davidson and various others do. In particular, they should not tempt us to infer that an intentional explanatory strategy is explanatorily or ontologically less privileged simply because it departs from the conceptual apparatus of a natural-scientific strategy.

Many eliminativists seemingly make the simple mistake of assuming that all theorists have, or at least should have, their relatively narrow eliminativist explanatory goals (although talk of goals—and even of assuming—is uncomfortable for unbridled eliminativists). Some of us have broader explanatory goals, and use broader explanatory strategies accordingly.

Given my previous doubts about objectivist ontology, I cannot settle for the asymmetry in Davidson's position, according to which all events are physical and events are intentional "only as described." Given the aforementioned perspectival semantic and instrumental constraints on reasons and explanations, we have to say that, so far as our non-questionbegging reasons go, we cannot find firm support for Davidson's asymmetry. We can plausibly say that some events are physical as described, and some events are intentional as described. Whether they are such *only* as described remains effectively unanswerable from the standpoint of our non-questionbegging reasons, given the human cognitive predicament noted in section 1.7.

Some useful explanatory strategies, I have suggested, do trade in intentional descriptions; other useful strategies do not. Neither sort, however, merits ontological privilege from non-questionbegging reasons. Ontological naturalization may contribute much to a useful explanatory project; but this should not obscure the glaring absence of non-questionbegging reasons for deeming that project ontologically privileged as an avenue to objective knowledge. Naturalism and physicalism must earn their keep in the way any other explanatory hypothesis does: relative to certain variable semantic commitments and explanatory ends and standards. This follows from the semantic foundationalism of section 2.3 and the conceptual instrumentalism of section 4.6. Section 2.3 illustrates in general how a semantic commitment regarding 'adequate explanation' will play a key role in cogent explanation.

Conceptual naturalism seems defective to many of us who wield action-theoretical concepts with some success relative to our conceptual and explanatory ends. Many of us seemingly wield a concept of intentional action that is incurably teleological, resting as it does on some notion of "goal-directed" or "purposive" behavior. The purposiveness comes from the intentionality in intentional action. The notion of intentional action for many of us involves the notion of something's "settling on a plan" of some sort.[25] Such talk of settling involves, for many of us, the notion of something's having as a purpose the execution of a plan, however indefinite. Davidson (1987, pp. 36, 46) and Bishop (1989, p. 40) have noted, in a similar vein, that many of us conceive of intentional actions as "doings" and not mere "happenings," even if doings have an ineliminable causal component. We might, of course, define 'action' otherwise, so as to banish any hint of teleological notions. That, however, would be to change the subject, at least for many of us.

25. On this theme, see Bratman (1987), Mele (1992, chaps. 8, 9), and Mele and Moser (1994).

Many of us see no compelling reason to change the subject, that is, to change our teleological construal of the concept of action. In particular, we see no non-questionbegging reason to make semantic considerations line up with eliminative physicalism. It seems, moreover, that eliminativists themselves need purpose-relative explanatory constraints to recommend, with any cogency, their own explanatory approach to psychological phenomena: Their main *purpose*, as eliminativists, is to promote an explanatory vocabulary free of intentional idiom.

Eliminativists can neither shun nor consistently acknowledge their own explanatory purposes. They are thus in an unfortunate explanatory bind, a bind that prevents them from properly and consistently acknowledging the instrumental constraints crucial to cogent explanation. Eliminativists can, of course, characterize "explanation" in their own terms for their own purposes, as Churchland (1989, chap. 10) does; but this will only betray reliance on purposive considerations, and will not automatically erase the importance of purpose-relative explanatory constraints.[26] Explanatory inquiry, as ordinarily understood, is unavoidably teleological.

We might be accused of harboring teleological obscurity. Notably, however, we have no clear standard for clarity that buttresses such an accusation; hence, two can play this clarity game. Even if we did have a transparent standard, we have no decisive reason to think that all our notions should meet a single standard of clarity. Standards for clarity are slippery tools, since what is not sufficiently clear to one person is often clear *enough* to another. A plausible account of this variability harks back to my observation of varying explanatory standards relative to explanatory strategies: Whether certain talk is "clear enough" will depend on one's explanatory aims. I doubt, then, that a compelling brief for conceptual naturalization of our notion of intentional action can rest just on standards for clarity.

We evidently have no other decisive basis for an attempted naturalization of all concepts of intentional action. Prudence and good judgment recommend that we acknowledge the existence of some non-naturalistic concepts of action, and that we define the term 'action' otherwise if, given certain restrictive explanatory ends, we cannot make do with non-naturalistic concepts. One important lesson has been that we have little reason to expect naturalism, ontological or conceptual, to be supported by a non-questionbegging ontology. Naturalizing action theory is still an option, if but only if it suits our explanatory ends and standards for achieving those ends. However intentional, such explanatory ends make good sense of our complex variable lives as explainers. If modest explanatory relativism ensues, this is a small price to pay for the accompanying explanatory benefits.

It remains to be seen whether in the future we stop thinking of ourselves as explainers—in the interest of an alternative vocabulary, or conceptual apparatus. If we do, we can no longer regard ourselves as answering explanation-

26. For other problems from purposes and pragmatic considerations facing eliminativists, see Putnam (1988, pp. 59–60; 1992, pp. 438–440) and Beakley (1991).

seeking questions, for our using a vocabulary will then have no acknowledged explanatory end. From our current explanatory perspective, this alternative seems remote and perhaps bleak. Whatever its fate, however, we cannot banish it on effective ontological grounds.

Banishing alternative scenarios, at least under that description, rests for its support on one's variable semantic commitments and accepted ends, not (so far as we can tell) on anything more privileged ontologically. Such is the perspectival fate of banishing alternatives. Such also is the modest relativism we as theorizers never escape. These, too, I acknowledge in the face of self-referential worries, are judgments with perspectival support. They nonetheless garner support, however indirect and ad hominem, from the standpoint of a typical realist's own assumptions about supporting reasons—or so I have suggested. Because perspectival, purpose-relative support is what our banishings enjoy anyway, we have no stable cause here for epistemological remorse.

The relevance of all this to psychological explanation is straightforwardly methodological. Warranted explanation need not show allegiance to the vocabulary or the explanatory strategies of eliminative physicalists. Psychologists sometimes feel pressure to employ the vocabulary and the methods of the physical sciences, as a matter of principle—often with the result that they depart from psychological explanation and move toward neuroscience. In acknowledging the importance of perspectival, instrumental constraints on explanation, we can highlight the importance of the distinctive *goals* of psychological explanation—goals that call for a level of explanation different from that of neuroscience. As a result, we can see that psychological explanation faces no threat, as a matter of principle, from standards for explanation set by the physical sciences. The physical sciences have, in the end, no monopoly on explanation of human behavior.

5.4 Whither Philosophy?

At a level of specificity, notions of inquiry and of philosophy are perhaps as many as the theorists wielding a notion of inquiry or philosophy. It would be rash, in any case, to propose any single thing called "the" notion of inquiry or of philosophy.

This book began, in chapter 1, with doubts about realism and idealism, about claims to objective, ontological knowledge characteristic of realism and idealism. It ends now with stress on the relevance of instrumental constraints to explanatory strategies. The latter constraints fit nicely with the semantically based instrumental approach to reasons developed in chapters 2 and 4. Reasons and explanations are perspectival in that they owe their cogency for one to one's semantic commitments, acknowledged ends, and standards for achieving those ends. Such end-dependent cogency offers no conflict with the human cognitive predicament portrayed in chapter 1, and fits well with our ordinary understanding of cogency. One might introduce another (perhaps externalist) notion of cogency, as conceptual relativism allows, but many of us would still raise questions about cogency in the previous, end-dependent sense. Introducing a new notion will not preclude questions formulated with older notions.

Philosophy after objectivity can persist as an explanatory discipline, as a discipline of making sense in perspective—without presumptions of agnostic-resistant objective knowledge. Its explanations, given section 1.7, neither deliver nor purport to deliver non-questionbegging reasons against agnosticism about conceiving-independent truths. Philosophy can offer explanations nonetheless: perspectival explanations depending ultimately for support on a theorist's variable semantic commitments, explanatory ends, and standards for achieving those ends. Even physicalism of some sort can serve, for some theorists, as such a perspectival explanation. We have no effective reason to think, however, that physicalism has a special ontological status, a reliable avenue to conceiving-independent truths.

A theorist will rely on a certain *notion* of justification in arguing for the justification of a favored explanatory principle. This was a central lesson of chapter 2. Typical support for a notion for one is perspectival, being relative to one's conceptual ends and pertinent semantic commitments. Arguing for "support" for a notion will rest on a (variable) notion of "support" relative to which certain considerations can yield "support." This is where an epistemological story comes to an end, where our epistemological spade is turned. Such an end is fitting, as it acknowledges a central role for epistemologists themselves—particularly their ends and standards—in the epistemological and explanatory account they spin.

The immediate lesson is simple but significant: Do not take epistemologists themselves out of their epistemological and explanatory tales. This book's overall lesson is somewhat more general and of general significance: Do not take philosophers and other theorists out of their philosophical, or otherwise theoretical, tales.

Philosophers can make sense—offer explanations—without objectivist pretensions, so long as they acknowledge the perspectival, end-relative nature of their explanatory enterprise and the basis of that enterprise in variable semantic commitments. Explanation itself does not ultimately suffer for being thus perspectival, in the absence of effective reasons for objectivist theses. What suffers, as a result, are only certain misconceptions of explanation and justification in philosophy. We can now do without those misconceptions, and sustain philosophical explanation nonetheless. We can now thrive with philosophy after objectivity, with making good sense in perspective.

Appendix: Charity, Interpretation, and Truth

Various philosophers, including W. V. Quine (1960), Donald Davidson (1983, 1991), and Daniel Dennett (1978, chap. 1; 1987, chap. 10), have endorsed a "principle of charity" implying either that we must *interpret* beliefs as being largely correct or, more strikingly, that one's beliefs must actually *be* largely correct. Given a defensible principle of charity, we could block familiar skeptical worries recommending that we withhold judgment on whether one's beliefs are largely correct. We could then use considerations of charity to show that such skeptical worries are misplaced. What exactly would this antiskeptical argument look like, and is it actually sound? This appendix offers an answer in accord with this book's conditional ontological agnosticism.

1. Twofold Charity

Quine proposes a "maxim of translation" entailing that "assertions startingly false on the face of them are likely to turn on hidden differences of language" (1960, p. 59). He seeks, in this connection, a method of translation specifying how we are to interpret a speaker's logical constants, among other utterances or inscriptions. The rough idea driving Quine's charitable method of translation is that it is useful for translators to translate a speaker's language into their own language in such a way that the speaker's affirmations are largely true relative to the translators' own standards for truth. This pragmatic consideration enables translators to select from the range of empirically adequate alternative translations. Physical facts, according to Quine's thesis of the indeterminacy of translation, do not determine the correctness of either of two conflicting empirically adequate manuals of translation (1981, p. 23; 1990a, pp. 47–48); nevertheless, a principle of charity can assist a choice between such manuals.

Davidson denies that his principle of charity is just a useful device for handling translational indeterminacy. He contends that it not only serves as a requirement on all meaningful interpretation but also entails that our beliefs must actually be largely correct. Davidson's position on the principle of charity is, then, twofold:

> (i) The general policy . . . is to choose truth conditions that do as well as possible in making speakers hold sentences true when (according to the theory [of truth and meaning] and the theory builder's view of the facts) those sentences are true. (1974c, p. 152)
>
> (ii) . . . beliefs are by nature generally true (1983, p. 437); [that is,] it must generally be the case that a sentence is true when a speaker holds it to be. (1975, p. 169)

Claim (i) amounts to the view that we must interpret others to have beliefs largely correct by our own lights, whereas claim (ii) implies that anyone's set of beliefs is actually largely true.

Claim (i) rests on the following considerations offered by Davidson:

> Making sense of the utterances and behaviour of others, even their most aberrant behaviour, requires us to find a great deal of reason and truth in them. To see too much unreason on the part of others is simply to undermine our ability to understand what it is they are so unreasonable about. (1974c, p. 153)

Fallibilism about reasonableness implies that contingent reasonable beliefs can be false, and thus prompts the question whether our finding a great deal of reasonableness in others requires our finding a great deal of truth in them. Even if our understanding others requires our finding their beliefs largely reasonable (at least on the basis of consistency requirements), it evidently is still an open question whether we must also find their beliefs largely correct.

Davidson links understanding and interpreted correctness as follows:

> Since charity is not an option, but a condition of having a workable theory [of meaning], it is meaningless to suggest that we might fall into massive error by endorsing it. Until we have successfully established a systematic correlation of sentences held true with sentences held true, there are no mistakes to make. Charity is forced on us; whether we like it or not, if we want to understand others, we must count them right in most matters. . . . We make maximum sense of the words and thoughts of others when we interpret in a way that optimizes agreement. (1974a, p. 197)

Davidson's point is not that interpretation must eliminate disagreement; it is rather that mistake and meaningful disagreement require considerable agreement: for example, widespread agreement in sentences held true, or in beliefs.

Davidson's position on charity rests on his account of the relation between belief and meaning. "What a sentence means," according to Davidson, "depends partly on the external circumstances that cause it to win some degree of conviction; and partly on the relations . . . that the sentence has to other sentences held true. . . ." (1983, p. 432). Since the latter relations directly involve beliefs, on Davidson's view, meaning depends on belief. In addition, belief depends on meaning, since "the only access to the fine structure and individuation of beliefs is through the sentences speakers and interpreters of speakers use to express and describe beliefs" (1983, p. 432). In short, determinate belief depends on meaningful sentences (see Davidson 1975, p. 170; cf. Moser 1983c).

Davidson infers that to account for the nature of meaning or belief, we must rely on something other than meaning or belief. Following Quine (1960), Davidson uses as his basic explainer "prompted assent": that is, the causal relation between assenting to a sentence and the cause of this assenting (1983, p. 432). Assenting to sentences, on Davidson's view, is just holding them true. Roughly, the principle of charity recommends that when we as interpreters find a speaker assenting regularly to a sentence under conditions we recognize, we regard those conditions as the truth conditions of the speaker's sentence. Davidson proposes that interpretation derives from a Tarski-style rendition of truth for a speaker's language:

> Sentence *S* is true (as English) for speaker *U* at time *t* if and only if *P* (1969, p. 45; cf. 1973, pp. 68–9),

where '*S*' stands for a description of a sentence of English, and '*P*' stands for a sentence giving the conditions under which *S* is true. Indexical and demonstrative components of sentences require the relativity to a speaker and a time.

Our only available method of interpretation, according to Davidson (1983, p. 434), puts a speaker's beliefs in agreement with our standards of logic, our logical truths. "The point of the principle of charity," Davidson claims (1983, p. 433), "is to make the speaker intelligible, since too great deviations from consistency and correctness leave no common ground on which to judge either conformity or difference." Consistency and correctness offer stable ground for identifying beliefs; omitting that ground, according to Davidson, leaves no basis for ascribing beliefs. Davidson thus denies that we can discover a speaker to have largely false beliefs about the world, on the ground that we must interpret "sentences held true (which is not to be distinguished from attributing beliefs) according to the events and objects in the outside world that cause the sentences to be held true" (1983, p. 435).

Davidson seeks support for his twofold principle of charity in the importance of an empirical theory of meaning. He holds that "if a semantic theory claims to apply, however schematically, to a natural language, then it must be empirical in character, and open to test" (1973, p. 73). If we want an empirical theory of meaning, Davidson contends, we need a principle of charity. An empirical semantic theory, on this line of argument, makes the meaning of sentences held true depend on the observable circumstances under which those sentences are uttered. Davidson holds, accordingly: "The causal relations between the world and our beliefs are crucial to meaning not because they supply a special sort of evidence for the speaker who holds the beliefs, but because they are often apparent to others and so form the basis for communication" (1990c, p. 76). Davidson holds, more specifically, that "linguistic communication, the indispensable instrument of fine-grained interpersonal understanding, rests on mutually understood utterances, the contents of which are finally fixed by the patterns and causes of sentences held true" (1990a, p. 326). This is a kind of communitarian causal holism about propositional content.

Davidson claims that "without communication propositional thought is impossible," and that "until a base line has been established by communication with someone else, there is no point in saying a person's thoughts or words have a propositional content" (1991, p. 160). Davidson holds that this "follows at once if we suppose that language is essential to thought, and we agree with Wittgenstein that there cannot be a private language" (1991, p. 157). Davidson maintains that only communication can supply the objective check needed to distinguish between correct and incorrect language use. Interpersonal sharing of verbal reactions to common sensory stimuli, according to Davidson, is crucial to locating the cause of a thought and defining its contents. Two people can observe each other's verbal reactions, and thereby each can correlate the other's reactions to his or her own sensory stimuli with an eye toward identifying a common cause. This commonly identified cause can serve as a basis for objective correctness in belief. Apart from standards set by intersubjectively shared verbal reactions, according to Davidson, talk of objective truth and of determinate belief-contents makes no sense.

We now have the rationale for Davidson's twofold principle of charity before us. Can the principle survive scrutiny?

2. Misplaced Charity?

Let us distinguish between the following:

> (a) We must interpret sentences held true according to the *actual* events and objects in the outside world that cause those sentences to be held true (cf. Davidson 1983, p. 435).

and

> (b) We must interpret sentences held true according to *what we believe to be* the events and objects in the outside world that cause those sentences to be held true.

Thesis (a) entails that we must interpret sentences affirming the existence of external physical objects (for example, chairs, tables, and books) as being about the actual external physical objects that cause those sentences to be believed. This thesis rests on Davidson's assumption that "the causality [actually responsible for the holding of beliefs] plays an indispensable role in determining the content of what we say and believe" (1983, p. 435). Thesis (b) is more modest; its key implication is that we must interpret sentences affirming the existence of external physical objects as being about what we believe to be the objects that cause those sentences to be believed. This thesis presupposes that ascribed content is determined by what we *take* to be causally responsible for a belief, whereas (a) depends on the view that ascribed content is determined by the actual causal basis of a belief.

The key issues now are these: Why must we interpret one's beliefs according to their actual causes or even according to what we believe to be their causes? In addition, why must one's beliefs be largely true in virtue of being about what actually causes them? Until we have answers to these questions, we lack support for Davidson's twofold principle of charity. We can now begin to assess that principle.

Must we interpret a person's beliefs according to their actual causes? The following scenario seems coherent; at least, Davidson has not shown it to be incoherent. Smith's beliefs regarding the external world are actually caused by discrete physical objects (for example, chairs, tables, and books), and we somehow come to know this to be so. Smith himself, however, believes that there are no discrete physical objects, and holds that there actually is, in accord with (Spinozistic) unrestricted neutral monism, only a single nonmental nonphysical thing that at times merely appears to be discrete physical objects. Those fundamental ontological commitments determine the content of virtually all of Smith's beliefs, including all his beliefs about the objects of experience; and we interpret Smith's utterances and inscriptions accordingly. We could, nonetheless, come to know that those fundamental ontological commitments are incorrect (say, on the basis of truths learned from our best experimental science), and, therefore, that Smith's beliefs are largely incorrect. We could grant that Smith's beliefs are largely consistent, but this would not threaten, in any way, our knowledge that his beliefs are largely incorrect. Massive consistency and massive error sit well together. In this case, contrary to Davidson's thesis (a), we do not interpret a person's beliefs according to their actual causes.

What about thesis (b)? We believe (and know), according to the example at hand, that Smith's beliefs regarding the external world are caused by discrete physical objects, but we do not interpret Smith's beliefs according to causation by such physical objects. Instead, we interpret Smith's beliefs as affirming, and thus committing him to, unrestricted neutral monism: the Spinozistic view that there is actually only a single nonmental nonphysical thing that at times merely appears to be discrete physical objects. Our best explanation of Smith's verbal behavior is that he does not share our true beliefs about what actually causes his beliefs. Consequently, we may reasonably interpret his beliefs as differing from what we believe (and, by hypothesis, know) to be their actual causes. Thesis (b), then, suffers the same unhappy fate as (a).

One might reply that my example actually supports (a) and (b). If we know that discrete physical objects cause Smith's beliefs about the external world, we shall interpret his beliefs as actually being about such objects, even if Smith himself claims otherwise. On this reply, what a belief is "actually about" is determined by what actually causes that belief; and since, by hypothesis, discrete physical objects actually cause Smith's beliefs, those beliefs are actually about such objects. Knowing what actually causes Smith's beliefs, we shall interpret those beliefs accordingly, with respect to what they are actually about. We do not have here, then, a problem for theses (a) and (b), for my example has us knowing that Smith's beliefs are actually caused by discrete physical objects.

The anticipated reply assumes that what actually causes a belief determines what that belief is about. If what a belief is about is determined by what its constituents refer to, and if what a belief's constituents refer to is determined by what causes them, then what a belief is about is determined by its cause. This causal approach to what a belief is about will be acceptable so long as we define 'about' and 'refer' in strictly causal terms. If we understand talk of the "meaning" and the "content" of a belief via a strictly causal approach to aboutness and reference, we may say that a belief's meaning, or content, issues from what causes that belief. On this view, meaning is reference, and reference arises just from causal relations between (constituents of) beliefs and their causes.

Davidson cannot plausibly adopt the reply at hand, since his own view of meaning is not strictly causal in the way the reply assumes. Following Grice (1957), Davidson acknowledges a crucial role for intention in meaning and communication, as follows:

> An utterance has certain truth conditions only if the speaker intends it to be interpreted as having those truth conditions. . . . A malapropism or slip of the tongue, if it means anything, means what its promulgator intends it to mean. . . . What matters to successful linguistic communication is the intention of the speaker to be interpreted in a certain way, on the one hand, and the actual interpretation of the speaker's words along the intended lines through the interpreter's recognition of the speaker's intentions, on the other. (1990a, pp. 310–11)

Davidson's view of the role of intention in meaning conflicts with any strictly causal view implying that a belief's meaning depends simply on what causes one to hold that belief. Communication-based *intended* truth-conditions determine meaning, on Davidson's view; a belief's content—what it is "about"—depends specifically on how the pertinent believer intends the belief (or accepted sentence) to be interpreted. The anticipated reply is, then, unavailable to Davidson.

Davidson's account of meaning, in terms of intended truth-conditions, allows for cases where the actual cause of one's belief differs from how one intends the belief to be interpreted. Smith, for instance, intends his beliefs regarding the external world to be interpreted in accord with unrestricted neutral monism; and we, as interpreters, can comply with his intention, even while knowing that discrete physical objects actually cause his beliefs. Smith's intended interpretation, in this case, runs afoul of the actual cause of his beliefs. Once we acknowledge that meaning depends on intended interpretation, as Davidson does, we cannot guarantee agreement between belief-contents and the actual causes of those beliefs or even between belief-contents and what we believe to be the actual causes of those beliefs. The example of Smith makes this clear.

Having allowed intended interpretation to open a gap between belief-contents and their actual causes, we cannot close that gap in all cases of meaningful belief. One might, we have seen, seek refuge in a purely causal account of contents; but this move will depart not only from Davidson's own approach to meaning, but also from our ordinary notion of belief-contents involving what an individual actually understands.

The case of Smith counts against not only Davidson's requirements on interpretation, but also his requirement that one's beliefs must (in virtue of their "nature") be generally true (1983, p. 437; 1975, p. 169). Smith's beliefs would not be generally true in the envisaged situation where discrete objects cause his beliefs but he holds an unrestricted neutral monism that bears on virtually all of his beliefs. We do not need any particular standard for individuating beliefs to make this point; we need only grant that neutral monism figures, directly or indirectly, in most of Smith's beliefs, and (following Davidson) that a theory of truth conditions for a speaker describes "how the speaker intends his utterances to be interpreted" (1990a, p. 312). Smith intends his utterances to be interpreted in a way that runs afoul of what actually causes his beliefs. Consequently, Smith's beliefs are, contrary to Davidson's principle of charity, not generally true. (This result is compatible with Davidson's view (1990a, p. 314) that "it is a mistake to look for . . . any . . . sort of explicit definition or reduction of the concept of truth.")

Even if we, as interpreters, typically ascribe our own (semantic) standards of truth as being satisfied by speakers (including ourselves), we can ask this question: What reason have we to think that those standards always successfully identify the actual causes of one's beliefs? This question is highlighted by Davidson's observation that "we can't get outside our skins to find out what is causing the internal happening of which we are aware," and "introducing intermediate steps or entities into the causal chain, like sensations or observations, serves only to make the epistemological problem more obvious" (1983, p. 429). The actual causes of one's beliefs can be misrepresented by the belief-contents resulting from how one intends one's accepted sentences to be interpreted; and this can hold for most of one's belief-contents. Witness the case of Smith, the unbridled Spinozist.

Davidson has invoked two considerations to block the uncharitable result at hand. First, he appeals to the possibility of an omniscient interpreter to argue that a speaker and an interpreter cannot understand one another on the basis of shared but generally false beliefs. The imagined omniscient interpreter, by hypothesis, knows everything about the world and about what does and would cause a speaker to assent to a sentence. Davidson explains how this possibility bears on fallible speakers and interpreters:

> The omniscient interpreter, using the same method as the fallible interpreter, finds the fallible speaker largely consistent and correct. By his own standards, of course, but since these are objectively correct, the fallible speaker is seen to be largely correct and consistent by objective standards. We may also . . . let the omniscient interpreter turn his attention to the fallible inter-

> preter of the fallible speaker. It turns out that the fallible interpreter can be wrong about some things, but not in general. . . . (1983, p. 435; cf. Davidson 1977, p. 201)

This appeal to an omniscient interpreter does nothing to support Davidson's principle of charity. We now need independent support for Davidson's assumption that the omniscient interpreter would find fallible speakers largely correct; but Davidson has given no such support. So far as Davidson's argument goes, the omniscient interpreter could find fallible speakers largely incorrect. In particular, this interpreter, for all Davidson has shown, could find our beliefs largely incorrect, inasmuch as our presumed causes of our beliefs misrepresent virtually all our beliefs' actual causes.

Davidson's second strategy contends that "global confusion, like universal mistake, is unthinkable, not because imagination boggles, but because too much confusion leaves nothing to be confused about and massive error erodes the background of true belief against which alone failure can be construed" (1970, p. 221). The pertinent claim now is that universal mistake is unthinkable because it removes the background crucial to construing mistake. This claim is arguably true in one respect. One's genuinely thinking that a mistake has occurred arguably requires one's being correct in thinking that *M*: Mistake consists in conditions *C*. One's understanding what mistake is, it is arguable, requires correctness about *M*. If one must be correct about *M*, in one's genuinely thinking that a mistake has occurred, one who thinks that a mistake has occurred cannot be a victim of universal mistake. This line of argument is more promising than Davidson's.

One's beliefs, on whatever topic, cannot be universally, or altogether, false if any genuine belief one has requires a correct (semantic) belief analogous to *M*: a belief about relevant truth-conditions. In that case, any genuine belief that *X* is *F* requires a correct (semantic) belief that being *F* consists in conditions *C*. Semantic beliefs determine truth-conditions, and thus meaning, for one. If one's genuinely understanding what it is for something to be *F* requires such a correct semantic belief, not all one's beliefs can be false, given that belief that *P* requires understanding that *P*, and understanding that *P* requires true semantic beliefs regarding certain truth-conditions that determine meaning. In this case universal mistake is unthinkable.

We cannot conclude now that Davidson's principle of charity is finally substantiated. That principle is not just the thesis that universal mistake is impossible; nor is that principle entailed by the latter thesis. The principle's relevant implication now is that "it must generally be the case that a sentence is true when a speaker holds it to be" (1975, p. 169). Davidson construes this as the view that one's beliefs must be "largely correct" (1991, p. 160). If, however, one intends almost all one's beliefs to be interpreted in accord with unrestricted neutral monism, but those beliefs' being interpreted thus misrepresents the actual causes of one's beliefs (say, discrete physical objects), then one's beliefs could indeed be largely incorrect. This will be the case so long as one's intention to have one's beliefs interpreted in a certain way does not determine, directly or indirectly, what actually causes one's beliefs. This consideration fits, moreover, with the previous view that genuine belief requires true (semantic) belief regarding truth-conditions, and thus that universal mistake is impossible. We have no avenue, then, from the impossibility of universal mistake to Davidson's requirement that one's beliefs must, by "nature," be largely correct. Consequently, Davidson's principle of charity does not compel.

3. Beyond Charity

If our intentions to be interpreted in a certain way determine the content of our beliefs, our beliefs can generally misrepresent their actual causes. Interpreters of our beliefs can, at least in principle, come to know that such widespread misrepresentation occurs, and can interpret our beliefs accordingly. Davidson's twofold principle of charity runs afoul of these considerations. That principle will survive only if (contrary to Davidson's Gricean view of meaning) we eliminate a role for intention in meaning or (contrary to Davidson's non-idealism) we regard intentions as determining what actually causes a belief. Davidson's theory of meaning cannot consistently accommodate either of these options.

Davidson proposes that both causation and intention figure in the determination of meaning. His view bases meaning on how one intends to be interpreted (1990a), but seeks to block massive error in belief while allowing some error. I have argued that we cannot block massive, less-than-universal error once we base meaning on intention. The simplest way to correct Davidson's semantic theory is to make meaning a function not of actual causation, but of the causal relations one intends to be interpreted as endorsing. This revision preserves the Gricean component central to Davidson's account, but jettisons the causal requirements on meaning that lead to Davidson's troubled principle of charity. One can still regard meaning as dependent on observable circumstances, but only on observable circumstances acknowledged by one's interpretive intentions. The latter observable circumstances can, nonetheless, be characterized by a "distal theory" of the stimulus, like Davidson's (1990c), that appeals to shared causes salient for speakers and interpreters.

We still lack compelling support for Davidson's striking thesis that "what stands in the way of global skepticism of the senses is . . . the fact that we must, in the plainest and methodologically most basic cases, take the objects of a belief to be the causes of that belief" (1983, p. 436). We have seen that we need not take the actual causes of one's beliefs to be the objects of one's beliefs (even generally), when intentions fix objects of belief. In addition, we have seen that our own beliefs' objects, when determined by intentions, need not be fixed by the actual causes of our beliefs. Even if universal mistake is impossible, owing to the indispensable role of correct beliefs about truth-conditions, one's beliefs can be generally incorrect. Such is the fate of beliefs whose objects are determined by interpretive intentions rather than actual causes. Davidson's interpretive charity, then, is misplaced, and skepticism about whether our beliefs are largely correct remains a live, if bothersome, option. Such skepticism dies hard, if at all; at least, we need to go beyond considerations of interpretive charity to challenge it. The epistemological lessons of chapter 1, in particular, are not threatened at all by interpretive charity. Davidson has not shown that our beliefs about the external world must be, or even are, largely correct.

References

Almeder, Robert. 1992. *Blind Realism*. Lanham, Md.: Rowman and Littlefield.

Alston, William. 1974. "Semantic Rules." In M. K. Munitz and P. K. Unger, eds., *Semantics and Philosophy*, pp. 17–48. New York: New York University Press.

———. 1985. "Thomas Reid on Epistemic Principles." *History of Philosophy Quarterly* 2, 435–452.

———. 1986. "An Action-Plan Interpretation of Purposive Explanations of Action." In Robert Audi, ed., *Action, Decision, and Intention*, pp. 275–299. Dordrecht: Reidel.

———. 1989a. *Epistemic Justification*. Ithaca, N.Y.: Cornell University Press.

———. 1989b. "A 'Doxastic Practice' Approach to Epistemology." In Marjorie Clay and Keith Lehrer, eds., *Knowledge and Skepticism*, pp. 1–29. Boulder, Colo.: Westview Press.

Annas, Julia, and Jonathan Barnes. 1985. *The Modes of Scepticism*. Cambridge: Cambridge University Press.

Anscombe, G.E.M. 1976. "The Question of Linguistic Idealism." *Acta Philosophica Fennica* 28, 209–225. Reprinted in Anscombe, *From Parmenides to Wittgenstein*, pp. 112–133. Oxford: Basil Blackwell, 1981.

Appiah, Anthony. 1986. *For Truth in Semantics*. Oxford: Basil Blackwell.

Arrington, Robert. 1989. *Rationalism, Realism, and Relativism*. Ithaca, N.Y.: Cornell University Press.

Audi, Robert. 1982. "Believing and Affirming." *Mind* 91, 115–120.

———. 1985. "Rationality and Valuation." In G. Seebass and R. Tuomela, eds., *Social Action*, pp. 243–277. Dordrecht: Reidel. Reprinted in P. K. Moser, ed., *Rationality in Action*, pp. 416–446. Cambridge: Cambridge University Press, 1990. Reference is to this reprint.

Aune, Bruce. 1991. *Knowledge of the External World*. London: Routledge.

Ayer, A. J. 1946. *Language, Truth, and Logic*, 2d ed. London: Victor Gollancz.

———. 1973. *The Central Questions of Philosophy*. London: Weidenfeld and Nicolson.

Baker, Gordon. 1988. *Wittgenstein, Frege, and the Vienna Circle*. Oxford: Basil Blackwell.

Baker, Gordon, and P.M.S. Hacker. 1984. *Language, Sense, and Nonsense*. Oxford: Basil Blackwell.

———. 1985. *Wittgenstein: Rules, Grammar, and Necessity*. Oxford: Basil Blackwell.

———. 1990. "Malcolm on Language and Rules." *Philosophy* 65, 167–179.

Baker, Lynn Rudder. 1987. *Saving Belief: A Critique of Physicalism*. Princeton, N.J.: Princeton University Press.

Barnes, Jonathan. 1990a. *The Toils of Scepticism*. Cambridge: Cambridge University Press.

———. 1990b. "Some Ways of Scepticism." In Stephen Everson, ed., *Epistemology*, pp. 204–224. Cambridge: Cambridge University Press.

Beakley, Brian. 1991. "Cognitive Science and Neuroscientific Reality." *The Quarterly Review of Biology* 66, 317–320.

Bealer, George. 1982. *Quality and Concept*. Oxford: Clarendon Press.

———. 1987. "The Philosophical Limits of Scientific Essentialism." In J. E. Tomberlin, ed., *Philosophical Perspectives*, Vol. 1: *Metaphysics*, pp. 289–365. Atascadero, Calif.: Ridgeview.

Bishop, John. 1989. *Natural Agency*. Cambridge: Cambridge University Press.

Blackburn, Simon. 1980. "Truth, Realism, and the Regulation of Theory." In P. A. French *et al.*, eds., *Midwest Studies in Philosophy*, Vol. 5: *Studies in Epistemology*, pp. 353–371. Minneapolis: University of Minnesota Press.

———. 1984. *Spreading the Word*. Oxford: Clarendon Press.

Blanshard, Brand. 1939. *The Nature of Thought*, Vol. 2. London: Allen and Unwin.

———. 1980. "Reply to Nicholas Rescher." In P. A. Schilpp, ed., *The Philosophy of Brand Blanshard*, pp. 589-600. LaSalle, Ill.: Open Court.

Boden, Margaret. 1972. *Purposive Explanation in Psychology*. Cambridge, Mass.: Harvard University Press.

Boghossian, Paul. 1989. "The Rule-Following Considerations." *Mind* 98, 507–549.

BonJour, Laurence. 1985. *The Structure of Empirical Knowledge*. Cambridge, Mass.: Harvard University Press.

Boyd, Richard. 1988. "How to Be a Moral Realist." In Geoffrey Sayre-McCord, ed., *Essays on Moral Realism*, pp. 181–228. Ithaca, N.Y.: Cornell University Press.

Brand, Myles. 1984. *Intending and Acting*. Cambridge, Mass.: The MIT Press.

Bratman, Michael. 1987. *Intentions, Plans, and Practical Reason*. Cambridge, Mass.: Harvard University Press.

Brentano, Franz. 1924. *Psychology from an Empirical Standpoint*, 2d ed. London: Routledge and Kegan Paul.

Brody, Baruch. 1973. "Why Settle for Anything Less Than Good Old-Fashioned Aristotelian Essentialism?" *Noûs* 7, 351–365.

Budd, Malcolm. 1989. *Wittgenstein's Philosophy of Psychology*. London: Routledge.

Burge, Tyler. 1986a. "Intellectual Norms and Foundations of Mind." *The Journal of Philosophy* 83, 697–720.

———. 1986b. "Individualism and Psychology." *The Philosophical Review* 95, 3–45.

———. 1990. "Wherein Is Language Social?" In C. A. Anderson and Joseph Owens, eds., *Propositional Attitudes*, pp. 113–131. Stanford, Calif.: Center for the Study of Language and Information.

Butchvarov, Panayot. 1979. *Being Qua Being*. Bloomington: Indiana University Press.

Carnap, Rudolf. 1950. *Logical Foundations of Probability*. Chicago: University of Chicago Press.

———. 1952. "Meaning Postulates." *Philosophical Studies* 3, 65–73. Reprinted in Carnap, *Meaning and Necessity*, 2d ed., pp. 222–229. Chicago: University of Chicago Press, 1956. Reference is to this reprint.

———. 1963. "W. V. Quine on Logical Truth." In P. A. Schilpp, ed., *The Philosophy of Rudolf Carnap*, pp. 915–922. LaSalle, Ill.: Open Court.

———. 1966. *Philosophical Foundations of Physics*. New York: Basic Books.

Carroll, Lewis. 1895. "What the Tortoise Said to Achilles." *Mind* n.s. 4, 278–280. Reprinted in Irving Copi and James Gould, eds., *Readings on Logic*, pp. 122–124. New York: Macmillan, 1964.

Carruthers, Peter. 1987. "Conceptual Pragmatism." *Synthese* 73, 205–224.

———. 1992. *Human Knowledge and Human Nature*. Oxford: Oxford University Press.

Carson, Thomas. 1984. *The Status of Morality*. Dordrecht: Reidel.

Cartwright, Nancy. 1983. *How the Laws of Physics Lie*. Oxford: Clarendon Press.

Changeux, J.-P. 1986. *Neuronal Man: The Biology of Mind*. New York: Oxford University Press.

Charlton, William. 1988. *Weakness of Will*. Oxford: Basil Blackwell.

Chisholm, Roderick. 1973. *The Problem of the Criterion*. Milwaukee: Marquette University Press. Reprinted in Chisholm, *The Foundations of Knowing*, pp. 61–75. Minneapolis: University of Minnesota Press, 1982. Reference is to this reprint.

———. 1977. *Theory of Knowledge*, 2d ed. Englewood Cliffs, N.J.: Prentice-Hall.

———. 1989. *Theory of Knowledge*, 3d ed. Englewood Cliffs, N.J.: Prentice-Hall.

Churchland, Paul. 1989. *A Neurocomputational Perspective*. Cambridge, Mass.: The MIT Press.

Coffa, J. Alberto. 1991. *The Semantic Tradition from Kant to Carnap: To the Vienna Station*. Cambridge: Cambridge University Press.

Cohen, L. J. 1951. "Teleological Explanation." *Proceedings of the Aristotelian Society* 51, 255–292.

Cooper, Neil. 1981. *The Diversity of Moral Thinking*. Oxford: Clarendon Press.

Coppock, Paul. 1984. Review of Nathan Salmon's *Reference and Essence*. *The Journal of Philosophy* 81, 261–270.

Cornman, James. 1971. *Materialism and Sensations*. New Haven: Yale University Press.

———. 1980. *Skepticism, Justification, and Explanation*. Dordrecht: Reidel.

Crane, Tim. 1991. "All the Difference in the World." *The Philosophical Quarterly* 41, 1–25.

Crane, Tim, and D. H. Mellor. 1990. "There Is No Question of Physicalism." *Mind* 99, 185–206.

Crystal, David. 1987. *The Cambridge Encyclopedia of Language*. Cambridge: Cambridge University Press.

Davidson, Donald. 1963. "Actions, Reasons, and Causes." In Davidson, *Essays on Actions and Events*, pp. 3–19. Oxford: Clarendon Press, 1980.

———. 1969. "True to the Facts." In Davidson, *Inquiries into Truth and Interpretation*, pp. 37–54. Oxford: Clarendon Press 1984.

———. 1970. "Mental Events." In Davidson, *Essays on Actions and Events*, pp. 207–225. Oxford: Clarendon Press, 1980.

———. 1973. "In Defence of Convention T." In Davidson, *Inquiries into Truth and Interpretation*, pp. 65–75. Oxford: Clarendon Press, 1984.

———. 1974a. "On the Very Idea of a Conceptual Scheme." *Proceedings and Addresses of the American Philosophical Association* 47, 5–20. Reprinted in Davidson, *Inquiries into Truth and Interpretation*, pp. 183–198. Oxford: Clarendon Press, 1984. Reference is to this reprint.

———. 1974b. "Psychology as Philosophy." In Davidson, *Essays on Actions and Events*, pp. 229–239. Oxford: Clarendon Press, 1980.

———. 1974c. "Belief and the Basis of Meaning." In Davidson, *Inquiries into Truth and Interpretation*, pp. 141–154. Oxford: Clarendon Press, 1984.

———. 1975. "Thought and Talk." In Davidson, *Inquiries into Truth and Interpretation*, pp. 155–170. Oxford: Clarendon Press, 1984.

———. 1977. "The Method of Truth in Metaphysics." In Davidson, *Inquiries into Truth and Interpretation*, pp. 199–214. Oxford: Clarendon Press, 1984.

———. 1983. "A Coherence Theory of Truth and Knowledge." In Dieter Henrich, ed., *Kant oder Hegel*, pp. 423–438. Stuttgart: Klett-Cotta.

———. 1985a. "Reply to Patrick Suppes." In Bruce Vermazen and M. B. Hintikka, eds., *Essays on Davidson: Actions and Events*, pp. 247–252. Oxford: Clarendon Press.

———. 1985b. "Reply to Harry Lewis." In Bruce Vermazen and M. B. Hintikka, eds., *Essays on Davidson: Actions and Events*, pp. 242–244. Oxford: Clarendon Press.

———. 1985c. "Reply to J. J. C. Smart." In Bruce Vermazen and M. B. Hintikka, eds., *Essays on Davidson: Actions and Events*, pp. 244–247. Oxford: Clarendon Press.

———. 1987. "Problems in the Explanation of Action." In Philip Pettit, Richard Sylvan, and Jean Norman, eds., *Metaphysics and Morality*, pp. 35–49. Oxford: Basil Blackwell.

———. 1990a. "The Structure and Content of Truth." *The Journal of Philosophy* 87, 279–328.

———. 1990b. "Representation and Interpretation." In K. A. Mohyeldin Said *et al.*, eds., *Modelling the Mind*, pp. 13–26. Oxford: Clarendon Press.

———. 1990c. "Meaning, Truth, and Evidence." In R. B. Barrett and R. F. Gibson, eds., *Perspectives on Quine*, pp. 68–79. Oxford: Basil Blackwell.

———. 1991. "Three Varieties of Knowledge." In A. P. Griffiths, ed., *A. J. Ayer Memorial Essays*, pp. 153–166. Cambridge: Cambridge University Press.

Dennett, Daniel. 1978. *Brainstorms*. Cambridge, Mass.: The MIT Press.

———. 1984. *Elbow Room*. Cambridge, Mass.: The MIT Press.

———. 1987. *The Intentional Stance*. Cambridge, Mass.: The MIT Press.

———. 1990. "The Myth of Original Intentionality." In K. A. Mohyeldin Said *et al.*, eds., *Modelling the Mind*, pp. 43–62. Oxford: Clarendon Press.

———. 1991. *Consciousness Explained*. Boston: Little, Brown.

Devitt, Michael. 1984. *Realism and Truth*. Princeton, N.J.: Princeton University Press.

———. 1991a. "Aberrations of the Realism Debate." *Philosophical Studies* 61, 43–63.

———. 1991b. *Realism and Truth,* 2d ed. Oxford: Basil Blackwell.

Dewey, John. 1938. *Logic: The Theory of Inquiry*. New York: Holt, Rinehart, and Winston.

Dummett, Michael. 1978. "Truth." In Dummett, *Truth and Other Enigmas*. Cambridge, Mass.: Harvard University Press.

———. 1991. *The Logical Basis of Metaphysics*. Cambridge, Mass.: Harvard University Press.

Einstein, Albert. 1949. "Remarks Concerning the Essays Brought Together in This Cooperative Volume." In Paul Schilpp, ed., *Albert Einstein: Philosopher-Scientist*, pp. 665–688. LaSalle, Ill.: Open Court.

Feigl, Herbert. 1950. "De Principiis Non Disputandum . . .?" In Max Black, ed., *Philosophical Analysis*, pp. 113–147. Ithaca, N.Y.: Cornell University Press.

———. 1952. "Validation and Vindication." In Feigl, *Inquiries and Provocations*, pp. 378–392. Dordrecht: Reidel, 1981.

Feldman, Richard. 1985. "Reliability and Justification." *The Monist* 68, 159–173.

Firth, Roderick. 1952. "Ethical Absolutism and the Ideal Observer." *Philosophy and Phenomenological Research* 12, 317–345. Reprinted in Wilfrid Sellars and John Hospers, eds., *Readings in Ethical Theory,* 2d ed., pp. 200–221. Englewood Cliffs, N.J.: Prentice-Hall, 1970.

Fodor, Jerry. 1980. "Methodological Solipsism Considered as a Research Strategy in Cognitive Psychology." *The Behavioral and Brain Sciences* 3, 63–73. Reprinted in Fodor, *Representations*, pp. 225–253. Cambridge, Mass.: The MIT Press, 1981. Reference is to this reprint.

———. 1987. *Psychosemantics*. Cambridge, Mass.: The MIT Press.

———. 1991. "You Can Fool Some of the People All of the Time, Everything Else Being Equal; Hedged Laws and Psychological Explanations." *Mind* 100, 19–34.

Fodor, Jerry, and Ernest Lepore. 1992. *Holism*. Oxford: Basil Blackwell.

Foley, Richard. 1990. "Skepticism and Rationality." In M. D. Roth and G. Ross, eds., *Doubting: Contemporary Perspectives on Skepticism*, pp. 69–81. Dordrecht: Kluwer.

Føllesdal, Dagfinn. 1990. "Indeterminacy and Mental States." In R. B. Barrett and R. F. Gibson, eds., *Perspectives on Quine*, pp. 98–109. Oxford: Basil Blackwell.

Frankena, William. 1983. "Concepts of Rational Action in the History of Ethics." *Social Theory and Practice* 9, 165–197.

Friedman, Michael. 1974. "Explanation and Scientific Understanding." *The Journal of Philosophy* 71, 5–19.

Fumerton, Richard. 1986. "Essential Properties and *De Re* Necessity." In P. A. French *et al.*, eds., *Midwest Studies in Philosophy,* Vol. 11: *Studies in Essentialism*, pp. 281–294. Minneapolis: University of Minnesota Press.

Geertz, Clifford. 1983. *Local Knowledge*. New York: Basic Books.

Gibbard, Allan. 1990. *Wise Choices, Apt Feelings*. Cambridge, Mass.: Harvard University Press.

Goldman, Alan. 1988. *Empirical Knowledge*. Berkeley: University of California Press.

Goldman, Alvin. 1970. *A Theory of Human Action*. Princeton, N.J.: Princeton University Press.

———. 1979. "What Is Justified Belief?" In G. S. Pappas, ed., *Justification and Knowledge*, pp. 1–23. Dordrecht: Reidel.

———. 1980. "The Internalist Conception of Justification." In P. A. French *et al.*, eds., *Midwest Studies in Epistemology,* Vol. 5: *Studies in Epistemology*, pp. 27–52. Minneapolis: University of Minnesota Press.

———. 1986. *Epistemology and Cognition*. Cambridge, Mass.: Harvard University Press.

———. 1988. "Strong and Weak Justification." In James Tomberlin, ed., *Philosophical Perspectives,* Vol. 2: *Epistemology*, pp. 51–69. Atascadero, Calif.: Ridgeview.

———. 1989. "Psychology and Philosophical Analysis." *Proceedings of the Aristotelian Society* 89, 195–209. Reprinted in Goldman, *Liaisons*, pp. 143–153. Cambridge, Mass.: The MIT Press, 1992. Reference is to this reprint.

Goodman, Nelson. 1978. *Ways of Worldmaking*. Indianapolis: Hackett.

Grice, Paul. 1957. "Meaning." *The Philosophical Review* 66, 377–388. Reprinted in Grice, *Studies in the Way of Words*. Cambridge, Mass.: Harvard University Press, 1989. Reference is to this reprint.

———. 1989. *Studies in the Way of Words*. Cambridge, Mass.: Harvard University Press.

Griffin, Nicholas. 1977. *Relative Identity*. Oxford: Clarendon Press.

Grossmann, Reinhardt. 1990. *The Fourth Way: A Theory of Knowledge*. Bloomington: Indiana University Press.

Hacker, P.M.S. 1986. *Insight and Illusion: Themes in the Philosophy of Wittgenstein,* 2d ed. Oxford: Clarendon Press.

———. 1990. *Wittgenstein: Meaning and Mind.* Oxford: Basil Blackwell.

Haller, Rudolf. 1988. "Justification and Praxeological Foundationalism." *Inquiry* 31, 335–345.

Hare, R. M. 1952. *The Language of Morals.* Oxford: Clarendon Press.

———. 1963. *Freedom and Reason.* Oxford: Clarendon Press.

———. 1989. "How to Decide Moral Questions Rationally." In Hare, *Essays in Ethical Theory*, pp. 99–112. Oxford: Clarendon Press.

Heil, John. 1987. "Doubts about Skepticism." *Philosophical Studies* 51, 1–17. Reprinted in M. D. Roth and G. Ross, eds., *Doubting: Contemporary Perspectives on Skepticism*, pp. 147–159. Dordrecht: Kluwer, 1990.

Hellman, Geoffrey, and F. W. Thompson. 1975. "Physicalism: Ontology, Determination, Reduction." *The Journal of Philosophy* 72, 551–564.

Hempel, Carl. 1950. "Problems and Changes in the Empiricist Criterion of Meaning." *Revue Internationale de Philosophie* 11, 41–63. Reprinted in A. J. Ayer, ed., *Logical Positivism*, pp. 108–129. New York: Free Press, 1959.

———. 1951. "The Concept of Cognitive Significance: A Reconsideration." *Proceedings of the American Academy of Arts and Sciences* 80, 61–77.

———. 1952. *Fundamentals of Concept Formation in Empirical Science*, in the *International Encyclopedia of Unified Science*, Vol. 2, pp. 651–745. Chicago: University of Chicago Press.

———. 1988. "Provisos: A Problem Concerning the Inferential Function of Scientific Theories." In Adolf Grünbaum and Wesley Salmon, eds., *The Limitations of Deductivism*, pp. 19–36. Berkeley: University of California Press.

Horgan, Terence. 1982. "Supervenience and Microphysics." *Pacific Philosophical Quarterly* 63, 29–43.

Horgan, Terence, and James Woodward. 1985. "Folk Psychology Is Here to Stay." *The Philosophical Review* 94, 197–226.

Hylton, Peter. 1991. "Translation, Meaning, and Self-Knowledge." *Proceedings of the Aristotelian Society* 91, 269–290.

Irwin, Terence. 1988. *Aristotle's First Principles.* Oxford: Clarendon Press.

James, William. 1896. "The Will to Believe." *New World.* Reprinted in James, *The Will to Believe and Other Essays.* New York: Mackay, 1911.

———. 1907. *Pragmatism.* Cambridge, Mass.: Harvard University Press, 1975.

———. 1909. *The Meaning of Truth.* Cambridge, Mass.: Harvard University Press, 1975.

Johnston, Mark. 1985. "Why Having a Mind Matters." In Ernest Lepore and B. P. McLaughlin, eds., *Actions and Events*, pp. 408–426. Oxford: Basil Blackwell.

Kim, Jaegwon. 1984. "Concepts of Supervenience." *Philosophy and Phenomenological Research* 45, 153–176.

———. 1989a. "Mechanism, Purpose, and Explanatory Exclusion." In James Tomberlin, ed., *Philosophical Perspectives,* Vol. 3: *Philosophy of Mind and Action Theory*, pp. 77–108. Atascadero, Calif.: Ridgeview.

———. 1989b. "The Myth of Nonreductive Materialism." *Proceedings and Addresses of the American Philosophical Association* 63, 31–47.

———. 1990a. "Supervenience as a Philosophical Concept." *Metaphilosophy* 21, 1–27.

———. 1990b. "Explanatory Exclusion and the Problem of Mental Causation." In Enrique Villanueva, ed., *Information, Semantics, and Epistemology*, pp. 36–56. Oxford: Basil Blackwell.

———. 1991. "Dretske on How Reasons Explain Behavior." In Brian McLaughlin, ed., *Dretske and His Critics*, pp. 52–72. Oxford: Basil Blackwell.

Kitcher, Philip. 1981. "Explanatory Unification." *Philosophy of Science* 48, 507–531.

———. 1989. "Explanatory Unification and the Causal Structure of the World." In Philip Kitcher and W. C. Salmon, eds., *Minnesota Studies in the Philosophy of Science,* Vol. 13: *Scientific Explanation*, pp. 410–505. Minneapolis: University of Minnesota Press.

Klein, Peter. 1981. *Certainty: A Refutation of Scepticism.* Minneapolis: University of Minnesota Press.

Kripke, Saul. 1980. *Naming and Necessity*. Cambridge, Mass.: Harvard University Press.

———. 1982. *Wittgenstein on Rules and Private Language*. Cambridge, Mass.: Harvard University Press.

Kuhn, Thomas. 1970a. *The Structure of Scientific Revolutions,* 2d ed. Chicago: University of Chicago Press.

———. 1970b. "Reflections on My Critics." In Imre Lakatos and Alan Musgrave, eds., *Criticism and the Growth of Knowledge*, pp. 321–378. Cambridge: Cambridge University Press.

Kung, Joan. 1977. "Aristotle on Essence and Explanation." *Philosophical Studies* 31, 361–383.

Lakoff, George. 1987. *Women, Fire, and Dangerous Things*. Chicago: University of Chicago Press.

———. 1989. "Some Empirical Results about the Nature of Concepts." *Mind and Language* 4, 103–129.

Laudan, Larry. 1977. *Progress and its Problems*. Berkeley: University of California Press.

Lehrer, Keith. 1974. *Knowledge*. Oxford: Clarendon Press.

———. 1990. *Theory of Knowledge*. Boulder, Colo.: Westview Press.

Levinson, Stephen. 1983. *Pragmatics*. Cambridge: Cambridge University Press.

Lewis, C. I. 1923. "A Pragmatic Conception of the *A Priori*." *The Journal of Philosophy* 20, 169–177. Reprinted in P. K. Moser, ed., *A Priori Knowledge*, pp. 15–25. Oxford: Oxford University Press, 1987.

———. 1926. "The Pragmatic Element in Knowledge." *University of California Publications in Philosophy* 6, 205–227. Reprinted in P. K. Moser and Arnold vander Nat, eds., *Human Knowledge*, pp. 201–211. New York: Oxford University Press, 1987.

———. 1929. *Mind and the World-Order*. New York: Charles Scribner.

Lewis, David. 1983. "New Work for a Theory of Universals." *Australasian Journal of Philosophy* 61, 343–377.

———. 1986. *On the Plurality of Worlds*. Oxford: Basil Blackwell.

Loar, Brian. 1987. "Subjective Intentionality." *Philosophical Topics* 15, 89–124.

———. 1988. "Social Content and Psychological Content." In R. H. Grimm and D. D. Merrill, eds., *Contents of Thought*, pp. 99–110. Tucson: University of Arizona Press. Reprinted in D. M. Rosenthal, ed., *The Nature of Mind*, pp. 568–575. New York: Oxford University Press, 1991.

Lycan, William. 1988. *Judgement and Justification*. Cambridge: Cambridge University Press.

Mackie, J. L. 1973. *Truth, Probability, and Paradox*. Oxford: Clarendon Press.

———. 1976. *Problems from Locke*. Oxford: Clarendon Press.

———. 1977. *Ethics: Inventing Right and Wrong*. London: Penguin Books.

Malcolm, Norman. 1942. "Moore and Ordinary Language." In P. A. Schilpp, ed., *The Philosophy of G. E. Moore*, pp. 345–368. Evanston, Ill.: Northwestern University Press.

———. 1986. *Nothing Is Hidden*. Oxford: Basil Blackwell.

———. 1989. "Wittgenstein on Language and Rules." *Philosophy* 64, 5–28.

Martin, Robert. 1987. *The Meaning of Language*. Cambridge, Mass.: The MIT Press.

McMichael, Alan. 1986. "The Epistemology of Essentialist Claims." In P. A. French *et al.*, eds., *Midwest Studies in Philosophy,* Vol. 11: *Studies in Essentialism*, pp. 33–52. Minneapolis: University of Minnesota Press.

Meerbote, Ralf. 1974. "The Unknowability of Things in Themselves." In L. W. Beck, ed., *Kant's Theory of Knowledge: Selected Papers from the Third International Kant Congress*, pp. 166–174. Dordrecht: Reidel.

Mele, Alfred. 1987. *Irrationality*. New York: Oxford University Press.

———. 1992. *Springs of Action*. New York: Oxford University Press.

Mele, Alfred, and Paul Moser. 1994. "Intentional Action." *Noûs* 28. Forthcoming.

Mellor, D. H. 1977. "Natural Kinds." *British Journal for the Philosophy of Science* 28, 299–312. Reprinted in Mellor, *Matters of Metaphysics*, pp. 123–135. Cambridge: Cambridge University Press, 1991.

Misak, C. J. 1991. *Truth and the End of Inquiry: A Peircean Account of Truth*. Oxford: Clarendon Press.

Moore, G. E. 1899. "The Nature of Judgment." *Mind* n.s. 8, 176–193. Reprinted in Tom Regan, ed., *G. E. Moore: The Early Essays*, pp. 59–80. Philadelphia: Temple University Press, 1986.

———. 1939. "Proof of an External World." *Proceedings of the British Academy* 25, 273–300.

Moser, Paul. 1983a. "Two Notions of Substance in *Metaphysics Z*." *Apeiron: A Journal for Ancient Philosophy and Science* 17, 103–113.

———. 1983b. "William James' Theory of Truth." *Topoi* 2, 217–222.

———. 1983c. "Rationality Without Surprises: Davidson on Rational Belief." *Dialectica* 37, 221–226.

———. 1984. "Types, Tokens, and Propositions." *Philosophy and Phenomenological Research* 44, 361–375.

———. 1985a. *Empirical Justification*. Dordrecht: Reidel.

———. 1985b. "Things in Themselves as Regulative Ideas: What Kant Should Have Said." *Philosophical Inquiry* 7, 21–36.

———. 1988. "Meaning, Justification, and Skepticism." *Philosophical Papers* 17, 77–101.

———. 1989. *Knowledge and Evidence*. Cambridge: Cambridge University Press.

———. 1990a. "A Dilemma for Internal Realism." *Philosophical Studies* 59, 101–106.

———. 1990b. "Some Recent Work in Epistemology." *Philosophical Papers* 19, 75–98.

———. 1990c. "Two Roads to Skepticism." In M. D. Roth and G. Ross, eds., *Doubting: Contemporary Perspectives on Skepticism*, pp. 127–139. Dordrecht: Kluwer.

———. 1990d. "Physicalism and Intentional Attitudes." *Behavior and Philosophy* 19, 33–41.

———. 1990e. "A Dilemma for Sentential Dualism." *Linguistics and Philosophy* 13, 687–698.

———. 1991. "Malcolm on Wittgenstein on Rules." *Philosophy* 66, 101–105.

———. 1992. "Beyond the Private Language Argument." *Metaphilosophy* 23, 77–89.

———. 1993. "Beyond Realism and Idealism." *Philosophia* 23.

———. 1994. "Epistemology: 1900–Present." In John Canfield, ed., *Meaning, Knowl-*

edge, and Value, Vol. 10, Part 2: *Routledge History of Philosophy*. London: Routledge. Forthcoming.

Moser, Paul, and Thomas Carson. 1992. "Rationality, Morality, and 'Why Care?' Questions." Paper presented to an Eastern Division American Philosophical Association Symposium. Abstract in *Proceedings and Addresses of the American Philosophical Association* 66 (1992), 75–77.

Moser, Paul, and Arnold vander Nat. 1988. "The Logical Status of Modal Reductionism." *Logique et Analyse* 31, 69–78.

Munitz, Milton. 1981. *Contemporary Analytic Philosophy*. New York: Macmillan.

Nagel, Ernest. 1961. *The Structure of Science*. New York: Harcourt, Brace, and World.

Nielsen, Kai. 1991. *After the Demise of the Tradition*. Boulder, Colo.: Westview Press.

Noonan, Harold. 1980. *Objects and Identity*. The Hague: Martinus Nijhoff.

Pap, Arthur. 1958. *Semantics and Necessary Truth*. New Haven: Yale University Press.

Papineau, David. 1990. "Why Supervenience?" *Analysis* 50, 66–71.

Peacocke, Christopher. 1988. "The Limits of Intelligibility: A Post-Verificationist Proposal." *The Philosophical Review* 97, 463–496.

Peirce, C. S. 1878. "How to Make Our Ideas Clear." *Popular Science Monthly* 12, 286–301. Reprinted in Justus Buchler, ed., *Philosophical Writings of Peirce*, pp. 23–41. New York: Dover, 1955. Reference is to this reprint.

Phillips, D. Z., and H. O. Mounce. 1969. *Moral Practices*. London: Routledge and Kegan Paul.

Plantinga, Alvin. 1970. "World and Essence." *The Philosophical Review* 79, 461–492. Reprinted in Michael Loux, ed., *Universals and Particulars*, 2d ed., pp. 353–386. Notre Dame, Ind.: University of Notre Dame Press. Reference is to this reprint.

———. 1974. *The Nature of Necessity*. Oxford: Clarendon Press.

Pollock, John. 1967. "Criteria and Our Knowledge of the Material World." *The Philosophical Review* 76, 28-60.

———. 1974. *Knowledge and Justification*. Princeton, N.J.: Princeton University Press.

———. 1984. "Reliability and Justified Belief." *Canadian Journal of Philosophy* 14, 103–114.

———. 1986a. *Contemporary Theories of Knowledge*. Totowa, N.J.: Rowman and Littlefield.

———. 1986b. "A Theory of Moral Reasoning." *Ethics* 96, 506–523.

———. 1987. "Defeasible Reasoning." *Cognitive Science* 11, 481–518.

Post, John. 1987. *The Faces of Existence: An Essay in Nonreductive Metaphysics*. Ithaca, N.Y.: Cornell University Press.

———. 1991. *Metaphysics*. New York: Paragon.

Prichard, H. A. 1912. "Does Moral Philosophy Rest on a Mistake?" *Mind* 21, 21–37. Reprinted in Prichard, *Moral Obligation and Duty and Interest*, pp. 1–17. Oxford: Oxford University Press, 1968. Reference is to this reprint.

Prior, A. N. 1967. "Correspondence Theory of Truth." In Paul Edwards, ed., *The Encyclopedia of Philosophy*, Vol. 2, pp. 223–232. New York: Macmillan.

Putnam, Hilary. 1969. "Logical Positivism and the Philosophy of Mind." In Peter Achinstein and S. F. Barker, eds., *The Legacy of Logical Positivism*, pp. 211–225. Baltimore: The Johns Hopkins University Press.

———. 1975. "The Meaning of 'Meaning'." In Keith Gunderson, ed., *Minnesota Studies in the Philosophy of Science*, Vol. 7: *Language, Mind, and Knowledge*, pp. 131–193. Minneapolis: University of Minnesota Press.

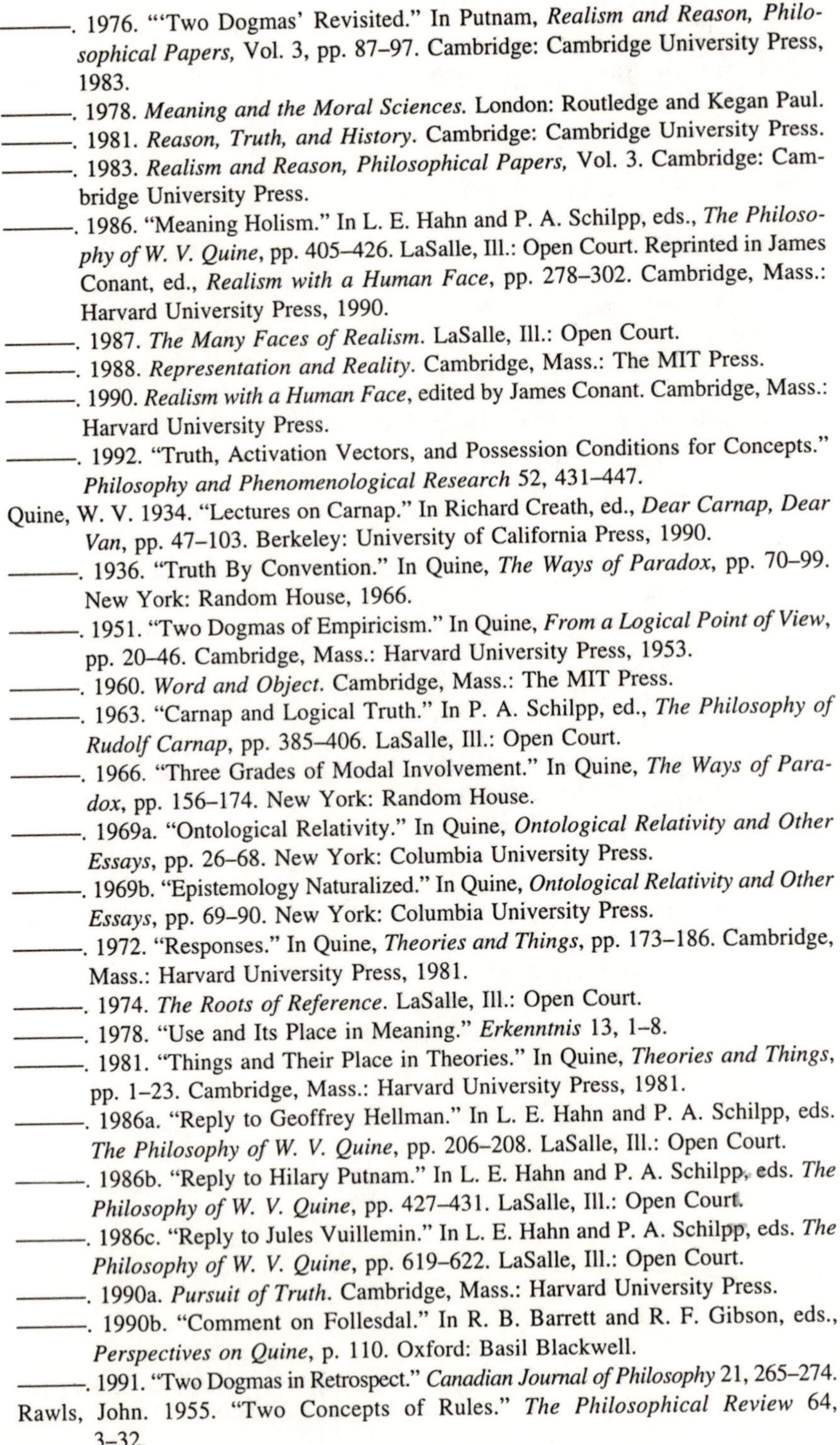

———. 1976. "'Two Dogmas' Revisited." In Putnam, *Realism and Reason, Philosophical Papers,* Vol. 3, pp. 87–97. Cambridge: Cambridge University Press, 1983.

———. 1978. *Meaning and the Moral Sciences.* London: Routledge and Kegan Paul.

———. 1981. *Reason, Truth, and History.* Cambridge: Cambridge University Press.

———. 1983. *Realism and Reason, Philosophical Papers,* Vol. 3. Cambridge: Cambridge University Press.

———. 1986. "Meaning Holism." In L. E. Hahn and P. A. Schilpp, eds., *The Philosophy of W. V. Quine*, pp. 405–426. LaSalle, Ill.: Open Court. Reprinted in James Conant, ed., *Realism with a Human Face*, pp. 278–302. Cambridge, Mass.: Harvard University Press, 1990.

———. 1987. *The Many Faces of Realism.* LaSalle, Ill.: Open Court.

———. 1988. *Representation and Reality.* Cambridge, Mass.: The MIT Press.

———. 1990. *Realism with a Human Face*, edited by James Conant. Cambridge, Mass.: Harvard University Press.

———. 1992. "Truth, Activation Vectors, and Possession Conditions for Concepts." *Philosophy and Phenomenological Research* 52, 431–447.

Quine, W. V. 1934. "Lectures on Carnap." In Richard Creath, ed., *Dear Carnap, Dear Van*, pp. 47–103. Berkeley: University of California Press, 1990.

———. 1936. "Truth By Convention." In Quine, *The Ways of Paradox*, pp. 70–99. New York: Random House, 1966.

———. 1951. "Two Dogmas of Empiricism." In Quine, *From a Logical Point of View*, pp. 20–46. Cambridge, Mass.: Harvard University Press, 1953.

———. 1960. *Word and Object.* Cambridge, Mass.: The MIT Press.

———. 1963. "Carnap and Logical Truth." In P. A. Schilpp, ed., *The Philosophy of Rudolf Carnap*, pp. 385–406. LaSalle, Ill.: Open Court.

———. 1966. "Three Grades of Modal Involvement." In Quine, *The Ways of Paradox*, pp. 156–174. New York: Random House.

———. 1969a. "Ontological Relativity." In Quine, *Ontological Relativity and Other Essays*, pp. 26–68. New York: Columbia University Press.

———. 1969b. "Epistemology Naturalized." In Quine, *Ontological Relativity and Other Essays*, pp. 69–90. New York: Columbia University Press.

———. 1972. "Responses." In Quine, *Theories and Things*, pp. 173–186. Cambridge, Mass.: Harvard University Press, 1981.

———. 1974. *The Roots of Reference*. LaSalle, Ill.: Open Court.

———. 1978. "Use and Its Place in Meaning." *Erkenntnis* 13, 1–8.

———. 1981. "Things and Their Place in Theories." In Quine, *Theories and Things*, pp. 1–23. Cambridge, Mass.: Harvard University Press, 1981.

———. 1986a. "Reply to Geoffrey Hellman." In L. E. Hahn and P. A. Schilpp, eds. *The Philosophy of W. V. Quine*, pp. 206–208. LaSalle, Ill.: Open Court.

———. 1986b. "Reply to Hilary Putnam." In L. E. Hahn and P. A. Schilpp, eds. *The Philosophy of W. V. Quine*, pp. 427–431. LaSalle, Ill.: Open Court.

———. 1986c. "Reply to Jules Vuillemin." In L. E. Hahn and P. A. Schilpp, eds. *The Philosophy of W. V. Quine*, pp. 619–622. LaSalle, Ill.: Open Court.

———. 1990a. *Pursuit of Truth.* Cambridge, Mass.: Harvard University Press.

———. 1990b. "Comment on Follesdal." In R. B. Barrett and R. F. Gibson, eds., *Perspectives on Quine*, p. 110. Oxford: Basil Blackwell.

———. 1991. "Two Dogmas in Retrospect." *Canadian Journal of Philosophy* 21, 265–274.

Rawls, John. 1955. "Two Concepts of Rules." *The Philosophical Review* 64, 3–32.

Rescher, Nicholas. 1973a. *Conceptual Idealism*. Oxford: Basil Blackwell.

———. 1973b. *The Coherence Theory of Truth*. Oxford: Clarendon Press.

———. 1974. "Noumenal Causality." In L. W. Beck, ed., *Kant's Theory of Knowledge: Selected Papers from the Third International Kant Congress*, pp. 175–183. Dordrecht: Reidel.

———. 1977. *Methodological Pragmatism*. Oxford: Basil Blackwell.

———. 1979. *Cognitive Systematization*. Oxford: Basil Blackwell.

———. 1980a. *Scepticism*. Oxford: Basil Blackwell.

———. 1980b. "Blanshard and the Coherence Theory of Truth." In P. A. Schilpp, ed., *The Philosophy of Brand Blanshard*, pp. 574–588. LaSalle, Ill.: Open Court.

———. 1985. *The Strife of Systems*. Pittsburgh: University of Pittsburgh Press.

———. 1988. *Rationality*. Oxford: Clarendon Press.

———. 1991. "Conceptual Idealism Revisited." *The Review of Metaphysics* 44, 495–523.

Robinson, Richard. 1953. *Plato's Earlier Dialectic,* 2d ed. Oxford: Clarendon Press.

———. 1954. *Definition*. Oxford: Clarendon Press.

Rorty, Richard. 1976. "Realism and Reference." *The Monist* 59, 321–340.

———. 1979. *Philosophy and the Mirror of Nature*. Princeton, N.J.: Princeton University Press.

———. 1982. *Consequences of Pragmatism*. Minneapolis: University of Minnesota Press.

———. 1989. *Contingency, Irony, and Solidarity*. Cambridge: Cambridge University Press.

———. 1991. *Objectivity, Relativism, and Truth: Philosophical Papers,* Vol. 1. Cambridge: Cambridge University Press.

Rosch, Eleanor. 1978. "Principles of Categorization." In E. Rosch and B. Lloyd, eds., *Cognition and Categorization*, pp. 27–48. Hillsdale, N.J.: Lawrence Erlbaum Associates.

———. 1983. "Prototype Classification and Logical Classification: The Two Systems." In E. Scholnick, ed., *New Trends in Cognitive Representation*, pp. 73–86. Hillsdale, N.J.: Lawrence Erlbaum Associates.

Rosch, Eleanor, and Carolyn Mervis. 1975. "Family Resemblances: Studies in the Internal Structure of Categories." *Cognitive Psychology* 7, 573–605.

Ross, W. D. 1930. *The Right and the Good*. Oxford: Clarendon Press.

———. 1939. *Foundations of Ethics*. Oxford: Clarendon Press.

Russell, Bertrand. 1912. *The Problems of Philosophy*. Oxford: Oxford University Press.

———. 1927a. *The Analysis of Matter*. London: Kegan Paul, Trench, Trubner and Company.

———. 1927b. *Philosophy*. London: Allen and Unwin.

———. 1940. *An Inquiry into Meaning and Truth*. London: Allen and Unwin.

———. 1959. *My Philosophical Development*. London: Allen and Unwin.

Ryle, Gilbert. 1953. "Ordinary Language." *The Philosophical Review* 62, 167–186. Reprinted in Charles Caton, ed., *Philosophy and Ordinary Language*, pp. 108–127. Urbana: University of Illinois Press, 1963.

Sainsbury, R. M. 1986. "Russell on Acquaintance." In Godfrey Vesey, ed., *Philosophers Ancient and Modern*, pp. 219–244. Cambridge: Cambridge University Press.

Salmon, Nathan. 1981. *Reference and Essence*. Princeton, N.J.: Princeton University Press.

Salmon, Wesley. 1990. *Four Decades of Scientific Explanation*. Minneapolis: University of Minnesota Press.

Schiffer, Stephen. 1987. *Remnants of Meaning*. Cambridge, Mass.: The MIT Press.

———. 1991. "*Ceteris Paribus* Laws." *Mind* 100, 1–17.

Schlick, Moritz. 1930. "Is There a Factual *A Priori*?" In Herbert Feigl and Wilfrid Sellars, eds., *Readings in Philosophical Analysis*, pp. 277–285. New York: Appleton-Century-Crofts, 1949.

Schmitt, Frederick. 1992. *Knowledge and Belief.* London: Routledge.

Searle, John. 1969. *Speech Acts*. Cambridge: Cambridge University Press.

———. 1979. *Expression and Meaning*. Cambridge: Cambridge University Press.

———. 1983. *Intentionality*. Cambridge: Cambridge University Press.

———. 1991. "Response: Meaning, Intentionality, and Speech Acts." In Ernest Lepore and Robert Van Gulick, eds., *John Searle and His Critics*, pp. 81–102. Oxford: Basil Blackwell.

———. 1992. *The Rediscovery of the Mind.* Cambridge, Mass.: The MIT Press.

Sellars, Wilfrid. 1954. "Some Reflections on Language Games." *Philosophy of Science* 21, 204–228. Reprinted in Sellars, *Science, Perception, and Reality*, pp. 321–358. London: Routledge and Kegan Paul, 1963.

———. 1979. *Naturalism and Ontology*. Atascadero, Calif.: Ridgeview.

Shanker, S. G. 1987. *Wittgenstein and the Turning-Point in the Philosophy of Mathematics*. London: Croom Helm.

Shope, Robert. 1983. *The Analysis of Knowing*. Princeton, N.J.: Princeton University Press.

Sidelle, Alan. 1989. *Necessity, Essence, and Individuation*. Ithaca, N.Y.: Cornell University Press.

Sidgwick, Henry. 1907. *The Methods of Ethics,* 7th ed. London: Macmillan.

Smart, J.J.C. 1959. "Sensations and Brain Processes." *The Philosophical Review* 68, 141–156. Reprinted in D. M. Rosenthal, ed., *Materialism and the Mind-Body Problem*, pp. 53–66. Englewood Cliffs, N.J.: Prentice-Hall, 1971.

Soames, Scott. 1989. "Presupposition." In D. Gabbay and F. Guenther, eds., *Handbook of Philosophical Logic,* Vol. 4: *Topics in the Philosophy of Language*, pp. 553–616. Dordrecht: Kluwer.

Sorabji, Richard. 1980. *Necessity, Cause, and Blame: Perspectives on Aristotle's Theory*. Ithaca, N.Y.: Cornell University Press.

Sorensen, Roy. 1991. "'*P*, Therefore, *P*' without Circularity." *The Journal of Philosophy* 88, 245–266.

Sosa, Ernest. 1987. "Serious Philosophy and Freedom of Spirit." *The Journal of Philosophy* 84, 707–726.

———. 1988. "Mind-Body Interaction and Supervenient Causation." In Venant Cauchy, ed., *Philosophy and Culture*, pp. 33–43. Montreal: Editions Montmorency.

———. 1991. *Knowledge in Perspective*. Cambridge: Cambridge University Press.

Stalnaker, Robert. 1972. "Pragmatics." In Gilbert Harman and Donald Davidson, eds., *Semantics of Natural Language*, pp. 380–397. Dordrecht: Reidel. Reprinted in A. P. Martinich, ed., *The Philosophy of Language,* 2d ed., pp. 176–186. New York: Oxford University Press, 1990.

———. 1974. "Pragmatic Presuppositions." In M. K. Munitz and P. K. Unger, eds., *Semantics and Philosophy*, pp. 197–214. New York: New York University Press. Reprinted in Steven Davis, ed., *Pragmatics*, pp. 471–481. New York: Oxford University Press, 1991.

———. 1990. "Narrow Content." In C. A. Anderson and Joseph Owens, eds., *Propositional Attitudes*, pp. 131–145. Stanford, Calif.: Center for the Study of Language and Information.

Stich, Stephen. 1990. *The Fragmentation of Reason*. Cambridge, Mass.: The MIT Press.

Striker, Gisela. 1980. "Sceptical Strategies." In Malcolm Schofield, Myles Burnyeat, and Jonathan Barnes, eds., *Doubt and Dogmatism*, pp. 54–83. Oxford: Clarendon Press.

———. 1990. "The Problem of the Criterion." In Stephen Everson, ed., *Epistemology*, pp. 143–160. Cambridge: Cambridge University Press.

Stroud, Barry. 1984. *The Significance of Philosophical Scepticism*. Oxford: Clarendon Press.

Suppes, Patrick. 1985. "Davidson's Views on Psychology as a Science." In Bruce Vermazen and M. B. Hintikka, eds., *Essays on Davidson*, pp. 189–194. Oxford: Clarendon Press.

Swinburne, R. G. 1975. "Analyticity, Necessity, and Apriority." *Mind* 84, 225–243. Reprinted in P. K. Moser, ed., *A Priori Knowledge*, chap. 9. Oxford: Oxford University Press, 1987.

Swoyer, Chris. 1982. "True For." In J. W. Meiland and M. Krausz, eds., *Relativism: Cognitive and Moral*, pp. 84–108. Notre Dame, Ind.: University of Notre Dame Press.

Taylor, Charles. 1964. *The Explanation of Behaviour*. London: Routledge and Kegan Paul.

Toulmin, Stephen. 1972. *Human Understanding*. Princeton, N.J.: Princeton University Press.

Unger, Peter. 1984. *Philosophical Relativity*. Minneapolis: University of Minnesota Press.

van Fraassen, Bas. 1980. *The Scientific Image*. Oxford: Clarendon Press.

———. 1989. *Laws and Symmetry*. Oxford: Clarendon Press.

von Wright, G. H. 1963. *Norm and Action: A Logical Enquiry*. London: Routledge and Kegan Paul.

———. 1983. *Practical Reason: Philosophical Papers*, Vol. 1. Oxford: Basil Blackwell.

———. 1989. "A Reply to My Critics." In Paul Schilpp and L. E. Hahn, eds., *The Philosophy of Georg Henrik von Wright*, pp. 733–887. LaSalle, Ill.: Open Court.

Waismann, Friedrich. 1939. "What Is Logical Analysis?" In Waismann, *Philosophical Papers*, pp. 81-103, edited by B. F. McGuinness. Dordrecht: Reidel, 1977.

———. 1965. *The Principles of Linguistic Philosophy*. London: Macmillan.

Walker, Ralph. 1989. *The Coherence Theory of Truth*. London: Routledge.

Wallace, John, and H. E. Mason. 1990. "On Some Thought Experiments about Mind and Meaning." In C. A. Anderson and Joseph Owens, eds., *Propositional Attitudes*, pp. 175–199. Stanford, Calif.: Center for the Study of Language and Information.

Walton, Douglas. 1989. *Question-Reply Argumentation*. Westport, Conn.: Greenwood Press.

———. 1991. *Begging the Question*. Westport, Conn.: Greenwood Press.

Warnock, G. J. 1971. *The Object of Morality*. London: Methuen.

Watkins, John. 1984. *Science and Scepticism*. Princeton, N.J.: Princeton University Press.

Watson, Gary. 1977. "Skepticism about Weakness of Will." *The Philosophical Review* 86, 316–339.

Watson, John B. 1924. *Behaviorism*. New York: W. W. Norton.

Weir, Michael. 1984. *Goal-Directed Behaviour*. London: Gordon and Breach.

White, A. R. 1981. "Knowledge, Acquaintance, and Awareness." In P. A. French *et al.*, eds., *Midwest Studies in Philosophy,* Vol. 6: *The Foundations of Analytic Philosophy*, pp. 159–172. Minneapolis: University of Minnesota Press.

White, Nicholas. 1972. "Origins of Aristotle's Essentialism." *The Review of Metaphysics* 26, 57-85.

Wigner, Eugene. 1960. "The Unreasonable Effectiveness of Mathematics in the Natural Sciences." *Communications on Pure and Applied Mathematics* 13, 1–14. Reprinted in T. L. Saaty and F. J. Weyl, eds., *The Spirit and the Uses of the Mathematical Sciences*, pp. 123–140. New York: McGraw-Hill, 1969.

Wittgenstein, Ludwig. 1953. *Philosophical Investigations.* Edited by G.E.M. Anscombe and R. Rhees. Translated by G.E.M. Anscombe. Oxford: Basil Blackwell.

———. 1969. *On Certainty.* Edited by G.E.M. Anscombe and G. H. von Wright. Translated by Denis Paul and G.E.M. Anscombe. Oxford: Basil Blackwell.

———. 1974. *Philosophical Grammar.* Edited by Rush Rhees. Translated by Anthony Kenny. Oxford: Basil Blackwell.

———. 1978. *Remarks on the Foundations of Mathematics,* rev. ed. Edited by G. H. von Wright, Rush Rhees, and G.E.M. Anscombe. Translated by G.E.M. Anscombe. Oxford: Basil Blackwell.

———. 1982. *Last Writings on the Philosophy of Psychology,* Vol. 1. Edited by G. H. von Wright and Heikki Nyman. Translated by C. G. Luckhardt and M. A. Aue. Oxford: Basil Blackwell.

Wolterstorff, Nicholas. 1976. "On the Nature of Universals." In Michael Loux, ed., *Universals and Particulars,* 2d ed., pp. 206–232. Notre Dame, Ind.: University of Notre Dame Press.

———. 1987. "Are Concept-Users World-Makers?" In J. E. Tomberlin, ed., *Philosophical Perspectives,* Vol. 1: *Metaphysics*, pp. 259–260. Atascadero, Calif.: Ridgeview.

———. 1990. "Realism vs. Anti-Realism." In P. K. Moser, ed., *Reality in Focus: Contemporary Readings on Metaphysics*, pp. 50–64. Englewood Cliffs, N.J.: Prentice-Hall.

Woods, John, and Douglas Walton. 1982. "Question-Begging and Cumulativeness in Dialectical Games." *Noûs* 16, 585–605.

Wright, Crispin. 1987. *Realism, Meaning, and Truth.* Oxford: Basil Blackwell.

Wright, Larry. 1968. "The Case against Teleological Reductionism." *The British Journal for the Philosophy of Science* 19, 211–223. Reprinted in Frank George and Les Johnson, eds., *Purposive Behaviour and Teleological Explanations*, pp. 110–122. London: Gordon and Breach, 1985.

———. 1972. "Explanation and Teleology." *Philosophy of Science* 39, 204–218. Reprinted in Frank George and Les Johnson, eds., *Purposive Behaviour and Teleological Explanations*, pp. 123–140. London: Gordon and Breach, 1985.

———. 1976. *Teleological Explanations*. Berkeley: University of California Press.

Zemach, E. M. 1989. "Wittgenstein on Meaning." *Grazer Philosophische Studien* 33/34, 415–435.

———. 1992. *The Reality of Meaning and the Meaning of 'Reality'*. Hanover, N.H.: Brown University Press.

Ziff, Paul. 1960. *Semantic Analysis*. Ithaca, N.Y.: Cornell University Press.

Index